"...the book you are holding is something I have wished for practically every day for years! I've wished for it because I believed you and lots of other people would find it truly helpful....And here it is. Well printed... well bound...well planned...and yours for a price so small that you can afford to keep one upstairs and one down....A lot of good wishes ...went into its making. I hope that as you use it they come out again in the form of the help you need!"

from the Introduction by Elizabeth Woody

The Pocket Cook Book

ELIZABETH WOODY

Editorial Consultant

(Formerly Director of Foods, *McCall's* Magazine
Consulting Food Editor, *Holiday* Magazine
Consulting Food Editor, *Collier's* Magazine)

*A Complete Cookery Book for Everybody
from Kitchen Beginners to Chefs
1300 recipes tested under the direction of*
Gertrude Lynn and **Peg Heffernan**
Home Economics Consultants

PUBLISHED BY **POCKET BOOKS** NEW YORK

THE POCKET COOK BOOK

POCKET BOOK edition published October, 1942
59th printing......................October, 1976

This book contains many new and original recipes by the authors. It also includes selected recipes which previously appeared in *McCall's Magazine* and are reprinted with the consent of McCall Corporation, the proprietor of the copyright therein.

This original POCKET BOOK edition is printed from brand-new plates made from newly set, clear, easy-to-read type.
POCKET BOOK editions are published by
POCKET BOOKS,
a division of Simon & Schuster, Inc.,
A GULF+WESTERN COMPANY
630 Fifth Avenue,
New York, N.Y. 10020.
Trademarks registered in the United States and other countries.

CONTENTS

ABOUT THIS BOOK AND WHY I THINK YOU'LL LIKE IT

In my younger and more innocent days I believed that you would get almost anything if only you wished for it hard enough. Now I find myself on the point of swinging back to that naive conviction, for the book you are holding is something I have wished for practically every day for years! I've wished for it because I believed you and lots of other people would find it truly helpful.

You see, as a food editor, I received many letters from readers—men and women—telling me what they needed and asking me where and how to get it. In the years B.P.C.B. (Before THE POCKET COOK BOOK), one question always left me up a tree: *"Where can I get a complete and completely reliable cook book for a very little money?"*

Complete? That means it should offer a *wide assortment of tried and tested recipes*. It should be *conveniently indexed* and *cross-referenced* for easy consultation. It should be up-to-the-minute in advice on such practical matters as *money-saving tricks*, the use of *leftovers*, and the foundation facts of *good nutrition*. It should include tables of *standard measurements* and handy *definitions* of any terms it uses which might possibly be puzzling.

Many a cook book already published measures up to all these requirements. But, to the best of my knowledge, none other has offered such completeness at a *nominal cost*. When the publisher of POCKET BOOKS told me that he planned to add a cook book to his already famous collection of how-do-they-do-it-for-the-money volumes, I leaped at the chance to write it.

And here it is. Well printed . . . well bound . . . well planned (I hope!) . . . and yours for a price so small that you can afford to keep one upstairs and one down. You may even send it to a friend as you would a greeting card! A lot of good wishes for you went into its making. I hope that as you use it they come out again in the form of the help you need!

—ELIZABETH WOODY

The Pocket
Cook Book

1. COOKERY TERMS AND DEFINITIONS

Bake...............To cook by dry heat, usually in an oven.

Baste...............To ladle water, drippings or other liquid over food while baking or roasting.

Batter...............A semi-liquid mixture of flour, liquid, etc., thin enough to be poured.

Beat...............To mix smooth and light with a brisk, even, rotary motion.

Blanch...............To submerge in boiling water for a short time and then plunge into cold water.

Blend...............To combine gently until even and smooth.

Boil...............To cook in liquid at boiling temperature.

Boiling Point...The temperature reached when a mixture maintains a full bubbling motion on its surface.

Braise...............To brown meat or vegetables in a small amount of fat or salad oil; then to cover and cook slowly in the juices or in a small amount of added liquid.

Bread...............To cover with fine bread or cracker crumbs before cooking.

Brew...............To cook in hot liquid until flavor is extracted.

Broil...............To cook by direct heat.

Chop...............To cut into small, even pieces.

Coats Spoon....When a mixture forms a thin even film on the spoon.

Coddle...............To cook slowly and gently in a liquid just below the boiling point.

Combine.........To mix enough to mingle ingredients.

Cook...............To prepare, using heat.

Cream...............To make soft, smooth and creamy.

Cube...............To cut in even-sided pieces.

Cut in...............To distribute a solid mixture in small pieces evenly through a dry mixture, using a cutting motion.

1

Dice................To cut into cubes.

Dissolve...........To combine in solution a dry and a liquid substance.

Dot................To scatter small pieces over the surface.

Dough.............A stiffened mixture of flour, liquid, etc., thick enough to be kneaded or rolled.

Dredge............To coat with a dry substance.

Dust................To sprinkle or coat lightly with a dry substance.

Evaporate.......To heat until dry and concentrated.

Flour..............To cover with a thin film of flour.

Fold................To combine, using a motion beginning vertically down through the mixture, continuing across the bottom of the bowl and ending with an upward and over motion.

Fry................To cook in fat or salad oil until brown and tender.

Garnish...........To decorate.

Grate..............To cut into fine pieces by rubbing against a grater.

Grill................See "Broil."

Grind..............To reduce to small pieces or powder.

Infuse.............To steep without boiling.

Julienne..........To cut food in match-like strips.

Knead.............To roll and press firmly with the heel of the hand.

Marinate.........To mix with an oil and acid mixture and chill.

Mash...............To make soft by beating or pressing.

Mask...............To cover completely, as with mayonnaise.

Melt................To heat until liquid.

Mince.............To cut or chop very fine.

Mix................To combine ingredients until evenly distributed.

Mush...............A soft, thick mixture.

Pan-broil.........To cook, uncovered, in hot skillet (ungreased or greased) pouring off fat as it accumulates.

Parboil...........Partially to cook in boiling water.

Pare................To cut off outer covering.

Paste..............A fine, smooth mixture.

Peel.................To strip off outer covering.

Plank.............To cook and serve on a heavy wooden board made for the purpose.

Purée.............To make a smooth, semi-liquid mixture by rubbing through a sieve.

Roast.............To cook, uncovered, in the oven without added moisture.

Sauté.............To cook in a small amount of fat or salad oil until brown and tender.

Scald.............To bring to a temperature just below the boiling point.

Score.............To cut narrow grooves or gashes.

Shred.............To cut or tear in thin strips or pieces.

Sift................To put through a fine sieve.

Simmer...........To cook in a liquid just below the boiling point.

Skewer...........To pierce with, or string on, pointed thin pieces of wood or metal.

Soften.............To mash until smooth and creamy.

Steam.............To cook, covered, over boiling water.

Steep.............To extract flavor by soaking in hot liquid.

Sterilize...........To free from living micro-organisms, as by the use of boiling water.

Stir................To blend ingredients, using circular motion.

Stock.............A liquid in which food has been cooked.

Stuff.............To pack a mixture into a cavity.

Toast.............To brown by dry heat.

Truss.............To fasten closely or tightly.

Unmold...........To loosen and remove from a container.

Whip.............To incorporate air into a mixture by beating with a brisk, even, rotary motion.

TABLE OF ABBREVIATIONS

Diameter	diam.	Pound	lb.
Minute(s)	min.	Quart(s)	qt.
Ounce(s)	oz.	Tablespoon(s)	tbs.
Package	pkg.	Teaspoon(s)	tsp.
Pint(s)	pt.		

2. TABLE OF STANDARD MEASUREMENTS

Dash or few grains ....less than ⅛ teaspoon
 3 teaspoons .... 1 tablespoon
 2 tablespoons ....⅛ cup
 4 tablespoons ....¼ cup
 5 tablespoons + 1 teaspoon ....⅓ cup
 8 tablespoons ....½ cup
10 tablespoons + 2 teaspoons ....⅔ cup
12 tablespoons ....¾ cup
16 tablespoons .... 1 cup
 2 cups .... 1 pint
 4 cups or 2 pints .... 1 quart
 4 quarts .... 1 gallon

All measurements are level and based on standard measuring spoons, cups, etc.

3. HINTS FOR EASY MEASURING

Measuring cups need less washing if you measure dry ingredients before measuring liquids.

Flour packs down as it stands, so be sure to sift it (with the exception of whole-wheat or rye flour) just before you measure it. To save spilling, sift the flour onto a square of paper, then spoon it lightly into the measuring cup. Don't joggle the cup as you level it off with your knife or spatula —it will just pack the flour down again if you do!

Solid fats are sticky and hard to measure in quantities of less than a cupful. Outwit them by using what the experts call the water displacement method. Suppose your recipe calls for ⅔ cup fat. Then simply fill your measuring cup ⅓ full of cold water, add the fat piece by piece until the water is just at the one cup mark. Pour off the water and there's your fat neatly and accurately measured.

Sugar sometimes gets lumpy, in which case you must sift before you measure. By the way, do you know that white sugars should be measured with a light touch, like flour, while brown sugar should be packed down tightly in the cup?

Sirup and molasses are inclined to cling to the measuring spoon or cup. They will flow more easily if you rinse the spoon or cup in cold water or grease it lightly.

For accuracy, measure half spoonfuls by dividing the levelled-off spoonful lengthwise with a thin, sharp knife.

4. SAFE SUBSTITUTIONS

WHEN I think of the care that went into the testing and perfecting of the recipes in this book, I'm tempted to urge you always to use them just as they are given. Of course, if you're the ultra-rare genius who knows by inspiration exactly what subtle shifts may be made without upsetting the apple cart I wouldn't think of lecturing you. Which is just as well, because you wouldn't listen for a minute!

However, some substitutions are safe for everybody. There aren't many, but those there are should be borne in mind for convenience and economy.

Instead of . . .	*. . . you may use*
1 cup fresh sweet milk	½ cup evaporated milk plus ½ cup water or . . .
	¼ cup non-fat dry milk

	(skim milk powder) plus 1 cup water and 2 tsp. melted fat or salad oil or . . .
	1 cup non-fat milk (skim milk) plus 2 tsp. melted fat or salad oil.
1 cup sour milk	1 cup fresh sweet milk plus 1⅓ tbs. vinegar or . . .
	1 cup fresh sweet milk plus 1½ tbs. lemon juice.
1 square (1 oz.) unsweetened chocolate (for baking)	3 tbs. cocoa plus 1 tbs. shortening.
1 tbs. flour (for thickening)	½ tbs. cornstarch.

5. HOW TO FOLLOW A RECIPE

1. Read the recipe carefully and thoughtfully.

2. Check your supplies to be sure you have all the ingredients called for.

3. Refer to the Glossary of Cookery Terms and Definitions on p. 1 if anything in the wording of the recipe puzzles you.

4. Assemble all your ingredients.

5. Assemble all your measuring and working equipment.

6. Do all possible preparation in advance (such as greasing pans).

7. If necessary, preheat the oven to the desired temperature.

8. Measure the ingredients accurately.

9. Follow the recipe method exactly.

10. Do not stop while combining ingredients or completing a process.

11. It is possible in most instances to double the quantity of a recipe's yield by doubling the amount of each ingredient. However, the size pan stipulated in the original recipe must be used so that oven temperatures and times may remain unchanged.

12. It is possible in some instances to halve the quantity of a recipe's yield by halving the amount of each ingredient. However, this should be attempted only with recipes in which the ingredients can be easily divided. (See Table of Standard Measurements on p. 4 for help in dividing ingredient measures.) Avoid halving recipes which are leavened. Pans of approximately half the measurements stipulated in the original recipe should be used so that oven temperatures and times may remain virtually unchanged.

6. HINTS FOR SUCCESSFUL CAKE BAKING

MANY a woman has won an enviable reputation as a "born" cook because of her ability to bake fluffy, delicious cakes. Although whole books have been written on the art of baking, there are only a few essentials to remember. Whether you're a new cook or an old hand at baking, you can profit by these suggestions. If you're a novice you'll soon be confident by following these tips and even if you have been baking for years, I'll wager that you'll find some brand new helps to take the gamble out of your results. By knowing these rules and using the carefully tested recipes in this book, you'll be certain every time of a cake to serve proudly.

BEFORE MIXING

1. *Use the exact ingredients specified in the recipe.* The recipes in this book have been carefully tested and perfected. Substitutions (other than the Safe Substitutions listed on p. 6) can endanger the success of your cake.

2. *Allow all ingredients to come to room temperature.* If the ingredients are at room temperature, your cake will be higher and fluffier.

3. *Be sure you have the size and type pan called for in the recipe.* If you use too large a pan, your cake will not bake properly nor rise to the top and brown well. If you use too small a pan, your cake will rise and run over the sides and will not brown evenly.

4. *Be sure the bottom of the pan is smooth and level and the sides are not warped or bent.* If the bottom of the pan is roughened, your cake may stick when you try to remove it from the pan. If the pan is warped or bent, your cake will not rise and brown evenly. The finished cake will be misshapen and difficult to remove from the pan.

5. *Use a light coating of fat to grease the bottom and sides of the pan when the recipe stipulates greasing the pan.* If the pan is not greased, your cake will stick. If the pan is too heavily greased, the cake crust will be too thick. For the majority of cakes, it is not necessary to line the pan with greased paper. However, for heavily fruity cake, line the pan with greased paper to permit easier removal of the cake from the pan.

6. *Do not grease the pans for sponge or angel cake mixtures.* These cakes are leavened by the air beaten into the egg whites. The batter needs to cling to, and be supported by, the sides of the pan. Greasing the sides may keep the cake from rising properly.

7. *Check to make sure the oven racks are in the proper position for baking.* When baking a sheet of loaf cake, place one rack in the center of the oven. When baking cake layers, use two racks, placing each at an equal distance from the top (or bottom) and the center of the oven. If the racks are not in the correct position, your cake may not rise fully or brown properly.

8. *Check to make sure the oven racks are level.* If the racks are not level, your cake may rise unevenly.

9. *Preheat the oven to the desired temperature.* If you do not have a regulated oven, use a portable thermometer. Place the thermometer in the oven on a rack and adjust the heat until the desired temperature is maintained. If the temperature is not correct, your cake will not bake properly.

DURING MIXING

1. *Cream together the shortening and the sugar until they are light and fluffy.* If the creaming is not thorough, your cake will not be light, fluffy and of a fine, even texture.

2. *Add the dry and liquid ingredients alternately to the creamed mixture.* Add about one-fourth the dry ingredients to the creamed mixture; stir them in gently; beat until smooth. Then add one-third the liquid ingredients; stir gently; beat until smooth. Repeat, alternating the ingredients. If the ingredients are not properly combined, your cake may not be tender nor evenly textured.

3. *Spread the batter evenly as you pour it into the pan.* If the batter is not spread evenly, the top of your cake may be uneven.

DURING BAKING

1. *Place the cake in the correct position on the oven rack.* When baking a sheet or loaf cake, place it in the center position on the rack. When baking cake layers, place each layer on a separate rack so that one layer is not directly above the other layer. If the cake or the layers are not in the correct position, they may not rise or brown evenly.

2. *Do not open the oven door until after one-fourth of the baking time has elapsed.* If the oven door is opened too soon after baking is begun, your cake may not rise properly.

3. *Do not open the oven door too frequently.* If the oven door must be opened to check the oven temperature, open it only at one-fourth intervals of the baking time. If the oven door is opened unnecessarily often, your cake may not rise and brown properly.

4. *Test the cake for doneness before removing it from the oven*. The surface of the cake should spring back when pressed lightly with a finger. The cake should be browned and the sides should have shrunk slightly from the sides of the pan. A wire cake tester inserted in the center of the cake should come out dry. If your cake is baked too long, it may be tough and dry. If your cake is not baked long enough, it may fall upon removal from the oven. Also, the crust may be sticky and not well browned.

AFTER BAKING

1. *Cool the cake away from drafts*. If your cake is placed in a draft, it may fall.

2. *Frost the cake as soon as it is cool*. If your cake is allowed to stand after it is cool, the crust may become dry.

3. *Frost the cake carefully*. Brush away any crumbs on the crust in order that the frosting may spread evenly. When frosting the outside of the cake, swirl the frosting smoothly on the sides, spreading from the top down towards the bottom. Pile the remaining frosting on the top of the cake and spread it out toward the edges. In frosting a layer cake, frost the top of one layer, then add the second layer. Next frost the sides of the cake and then the top.

4. *Store the cake in a ventilated, covered container*. If your cake is not properly stored, it may either dry out or become soggily moist.

7.   GOOD NUTRITION SIMPLIFIED

I REALIZE this is a cook book and not a treatise on the science of nutrition. But with good nutrition and our nation's need for it so much in the limelight nowadays, I can't resist sharing with you these four easy reference charts that reduce the whole story to its simplest terms.

The first is a practical translation of the "diet yardstick" released by the government at the President's National Nutrition Conference in Washington. It tells just *what* you must be sure to serve every day. The second and third are primers of the *why's* that underlie the yardstick, while the fourth is a chart of the calorie values of everyday foods.

A MENU CHECK-UP CHART
For Good Nutrition Eat These Every Day

Food	Average Adult (moderately active)	Average Child (10-12 years)
Milk	1 pint	1 quart
Meat or Fish	1 or more servings of a wide variety Liver once a week	Same as adult
Eggs	1 egg Dried peas or beans may be substituted 3 times a week	Same as adult
Vegetables	1 leafy green or yellow and 1 other (Serve one raw) 1 potato	Same as adult
Fruits	½ cup citrus or 1 cup tomato juice plus other fruits (raw, cooked or canned)	¾ cup citrus or 1½ cups tomato juice plus other fruits (raw, cooked or canned)
Bread and Cereals	3 servings whole grain or "enriched" bread or cereal	Same as adult
Butter or vitamin fortified margarine	2 tablespoons	2-3 tablespoons

To round out the diet, to add interest and satisfy appetites, include sugar, additional fats, etc. To supplement sunshine, extra sources of vitamin D (fish liver oils, vitamin D milk, etc.) are needed.

A VITAMIN PRIMER
All These Vitamins Are Necessary for Growth, Good Health and Long Life

Vitamin	Use in Body	Best Sources
A	For normal vision	Leafy greens Yellow vegetables and fruits Egg Liver Milk
B₁ (Thiamin)	For good appetite, good digestion and steady nerves	"Enriched" and whole grain bread and cereal Dried peas and beans Peanuts Pork and liver
C (Ascorbic acid)	For healthy teeth, gums, bones and blood vessels	Citrus fruits Tomato juice Leafy greens Potato
D	For normal development of teeth and bones	Salmon, sardines, mackerel and fish liver oils Vitamin D milk Egg yolk
G (Riboflavin)	For healthy skin and eyes	Liver and kidney Lean beef Leafy greens Milk
Niacin (Nicotinic acid)	For healthy skin	"Enriched" and whole grain bread and cereal Liver, lean meats

Mineral	Use	Best Sources
Iron	For healthy red blood cells	Dried fruits Liver, lean meats Dried peas or beans Whole grain cereals Green vegetables Molasses Eggs
Calcium	For strong bones and teeth	Cheese Milk Leafy greens
Phosphorus	For development of healthy bones and teeth	Cereals Cheese Eggs Milk Meat Fish Dried peas or beans

A menu adequate in these three minerals will be adequate in the other minerals.

A HANDY CALORIE CHART
Cereals and Breads

Food	Measure	Calories
Bran	1 cup	100
Bread, rye	1⅓ slices 3½" x 4" x ½"	100
Bread, white	1 slice 3" x 3½" x ½"	50
Bread, whole-wheat, 100%	1 slice 3" x 3¾" x ½"	100
Bread, whole-wheat, 50%	1 slice 3¾" x 3¼" x ½"	100
Bread crumbs, dried	1 cup	400
Bread crumbs, soft	1 cup	150
Corn flakes	¾ cup	100
Corn meal, uncooked	½ cup	252
Corn meal, cooked	⅔ cup	100

Cereals and Breads (Cont'd.)

Food	Measure	Calories
Cornstarch	1 tablespoon	34
Cracker crumbs	1 tablespoon	29
Crackers, graham	1 cracker 2½″ x 2¾″ x ¼″	40
Crackers, saltines	1 cracker 2″ square	17
Crackers, soda	1 cracker 2¾″ x 2½″	25
Farina, uncooked	½ cup	307
Farina, cooked	¾ cup	100
Flour, white, sifted	1 tablespoon	25
Flour, white, sifted	1 cup	395
Macaroni, uncooked	½ cup of 1″ pieces	200
Macaroni, cooked	¾ cup	100
Oats, rolled, uncooked	½ cup	200
Oats, rolled, cooked	½-¾ cup	100
Rice, uncooked	½ cup	348
Rice, steamed	¾ cup	100
Tapioca, uncooked	1 tablespoon	50
Wheat, puffed	1 cup	50
Wheat, shredded	1 biscuit	100

Dairy Products and Eggs

Food	Measure	Calories
Butter	1 tablespoon	100
Buttermilk	1 cup	84
Cheese, American	1⅛″ cube	100
Cheese, cottage, skim	5 tablespoons	100
Cheese, Roquefort	Piece 1½″ x 1¼″ x ⅞″	100
Cheese, soft cream	2 tablespoons	100
Cream (40% fat)	1 tablespoon plain or 1¾ tablespoons whipped	60
Cream (18.5% fat)	1 tablespoon	30
Egg, whole	1	70
Egg white	1	14
Egg yolk	1	56
Milk, whole	1 cup	170
Milk, condensed, sweetened	1 tablespoon	66
Milk, evaporated	4½ tablespoons	100
Milk, skim	1⅛ cups	100
Milk, top (10 oz.)	¼ cup	100

Fats

Food	Measure	Calories
Cod liver oil	1 tablespoon	100
Cottonseed oil	1 tablespoon	100
Halibut liver oil	10 capsules—10 drops in each	18
Lard	1 tablespoon (scant)	100
Margarine	1 tablespoon	100
Mayonnaise	1 tablespoon	100
Salad oil	1 tablespoon	100
Salad dressing, boiled	¼ cup	100
Shortening	1 tablespoon	100
Shortening	½ cup	801

Fruits

Food	Measure	Calories
Apple	1 medium	80
Apricots, canned	3-4 halves plus 2 tablespoons sirup	100
Apricots, dried	9 halves	100
Avocado	1 medium	618
Banana	1 medium	100
Blackberries	1 cup	100
Blueberries	1 cup	100
Cantaloupe	1 5″ in diameter	100
Cherries	20 ⅞″ in diameter	100
Cranberries	2 cups	100
Fig, dried	1 large	80
Grape juice	⅔ cup	100
Grapefruit	½ medium	100
Grapefruit juice	1 cup	100
Grapes, blue	1 large bunch	100
Grapes, red	25-30	100
Lemon	1 large	33
Lemon juice	¼ cup	20
Orange	1 large	100
Orange juice	¾ cup	100
Peach	1 medium	50

Fruits (Cont'd.)

Food	Measure	Calories
Peaches, canned	2 large halves plus 3 tablespoons sirup	200
Pear	1 medium	50
Pears, canned	3 halves plus 3 tablespoons sirup	100
Pineapple, canned	1 slice plus 3 tablespoons sirup or ¼ cup crushed	100
Pineapple juice	⅔ cup	100
Plum	1 1¾" in diameter	100
Prunes, dried	4 medium	100
Raisins	¼ cup seeded or 2 tablespoons seedless	100
Raspberries	1⅛ cups	100
Rhubarb	1 cup diced	20
Strawberries	1⅓ cups	100
Watermelon	¾" slice 6" diameter	100

Meats, Poultry and Fish

Food	Measure	Calories
Bacon, cooked	4-5 small slices	100
Beef, corned, boiled (with fat)	Slice 4½" x 1½" x 1¼"	100
Beef, dried	4 thin slices 4" x 5"	100
Beef, ground, broiled	Cake 2½" diameter, ⅞" thick	100
Beef, rib, lean, roasted	Slice 5" x 2½" x ¾"	100
Beef, round, lean, pot roasted	Slice 4¾" x 3½" x ⅛"	100
Beef, sirloin, steak	Slice ¾" x 1½" x ¾"	100
Bologna sausage	Slice 2⅛" diameter, ¼" thick	50
Chicken, canned, boned	1 cup	384
Chicken, roasted	1 slice 4" x 2½" x ¼"	100
Clams	12 or ⅔ cup	100
Crab meat, canned	¾ cup	100
Frankfurter	1	100
Halibut steak, cooked	Piece 3" x 1¼" x 1"	100
Ham, boiled	Slice 4¾" x 4" x ⅛"	100

Meats, Poultry and Fish (Cont'd.)

Food	Measure	Calories
Lamb chops, broiled	Lean meat of one chop 2" x 1½" x ¾"	100
Lamb, leg, roasted	Slice 3½" x 4½" x ⅛"	100
Lobster, canned	¾ cup	100
Mackerel, Spanish, fresh (entrails, head and tail removed)	1 11" long	413
Oysters	6-15 or ⅔ cup solid	100
Pork chop, broiled	Lean meat of one chop	200
Pork sausage, cooked	1 3" long, ¾" diameter	60
Salmon, canned	½ cup (scant)	100
Sardines, canned	1 3" long	25
Scallops	¾ cup	100
Shrimp, canned without oil	20 or ⅔ cup	100
Sweetbreads	1 pair, medium size	400
Turkey, cooked	1 slice 4" x 2½" x ¼"	100
Veal kidney	1 4¾" long	250
Veal leg, roasted	Slice 2" x 2¾" x ⅛"	100
Veal liver, pan-broiled	Slice 3½" x 2½" x ⅜"	100

Nuts

Food	Measure	Calories
Almond nut meats	12-15	100
Brazil nut meats	2	100
Peanut butter	1 tablespoon (scant)	100
Peanut meats	20-24	100
Pecan nut meats	12	100
Walnut meats	8-16 meats or 1¼ tablespoons chopped	100

Sweets

Food	Measure	Calories
Corn sirup	1 tablespoon	75
Cranberry sauce	¼ cup (scant)	100
Honey, liquid	1 tablespoon	75

Sweets (Cont'd.)

Food	Measure	Calories
Ice cream, commercial vanilla	½ cup	200
Jelly (fruit)	1 tablespoon	57
Maple sirup	1 tablespoon	66
Marshmallows	5 1¼″ in diameter	100
Molasses	1 tablespoon	66
Sugar, brown	1 tablespoon	33
Sugar, brown	1 cup	625
Sugar, granulated	1 tablespoon (scant)	50
Sugar, granulated	1 cup	840

Vegetables

Food	Measure	Calories
Asparagus	20 large stalks	100
Asparagus, canned	15 large stalks	100
Beans, green	2⅓ cups diced	100
Beans, lima	½ cup	100
Beans, lima, dried	1 cup	546
Beans, navy, dried	1 cup	684
Beet greens, cooked	1½ cups	100
Beets	4 2″ in diameter or 1⅓ cups sliced	100
Broccoli, cooked	2⅓ cups	100
Brussels sprouts	12 1½″ diameter	100
Cabbage	3½ cups chopped or 4-5 cups shredded	100
Carrots	1⅔ cups diced or 4-5 whole 3-4″ long	100
Cauliflower	1 small head 4½″ in diameter	100
Celery	4 cups diced	100
Chard, cooked	1⅓ cups	100
Corn, fresh, on cob	1 ear 6″ long	50
Corn, whole kernel, canned	⅓ cup	100
Cucumber	1 10″ long	50
Eggplant	6 slices 4″ diameter ½″ thick	100

Vegetables (Cont'd.)

Food	Measure	Calories
Kale, cooked	2⅓ cups	100
Lettuce	1 large head	50
Okra	5-6 pods	20
Onions	3-4 medium	100
Parsnip	1 7″ long, 2″ diameter at top	100
Peas, dried, split	1 cup	675
Peas, green	¾ cup	100
Pepper, green	1 3½″ long	20
Potato, sweet	1 medium	200
Potato, white	1 medium	100
Pumpkin, cooked	1 cup	70
Radishes	36	100
Sauerkraut	2½ cups	100
Spinach, cooked	2½ cups	100
Squash, Hubbard, cooked	1 cup	100
Tomato juice	1 cup (scant)	50
Tomatoes	2-3 medium	100
Tomatoes, canned	1 cup	50
Turnip greens, cooked	1⅔ cups	100
Turnips	2 cups cubed	100

Miscellaneous

Food	Measure	Calories
Chocolate, unsweetened	1 square (1 oz.)	173
Citron, dried	Piece 1¼″ x 1″ x 1″	100
Cocoa powder	1 tablespoon	40
Coconut, shredded	3 tablespoons	100
Dates, pitted	¼ cup	152
Gelatin, flavored	1 package	362
Gelatin, unflavored	1 envelope (1 tablespoon)	37
Ginger ale	1 cup	72
White sauce, medium	¼ cup	100
Yeast, compressed	1 cake	18

HOW TO SAVE VITAMINS AND MINERALS

BUYING the right foods for a healthful diet is an important part of living these days. But no less important is knowing how to handle those foods after we get them home. Many a vitamin disappears into thin air somewhere between the market and the table and many a valuable mineral detours down the sink or into an unappreciative garbage can.

Wrong methods of handling foods waste money. Even worse, they deprive you and the members of your family of the elements you need to build strong bodies and steady nerves.

There are many ways in which vitamins may be lost in preparation. Heat destroys some of them. The oxygen in the air actually "burns up" others. Water dissolves still others, which means that they are among the missing when food is cooked in too much water or for too long a time. Soda and other alkaline substances cut down on vitamin value while acids tend to preserve it.

General guides in cooking vegetables

To save vitamins, cook vegetables at high temperatures for short periods of time rather than at low temperatures for longer periods. Be on your guard against overcooking. And don't stir in air unnecessarily during cooking or heating. Use the smallest possible amount of water (except in the case of some strong-flavored vegetables listed later). Use any cooking water that is left over to make soups, gravies, sauces, etc. And remember that this rule applies as well to the liquid in which canned or glassed vegetables are packed.

And speaking of canned or glassed vegetables—do you heat them in the scientifically approved way? If you don't, you're a vitamin and mineral spendthrift. First empty the liquid from the can into a large skillet or saucepan. Boil it, uncovered, over high heat until half the liquid is evaporated. Add the vegetables, heat quickly, season and serve.

Other practical pointers

. . . Pressure cookers are wonderful vitamin savers. If

you're lucky enough to have one, use it regularly. The sauce-pan-sized ones are ideal for vegetables and stews.

. . . Fruits and vegetables lose vitamins as they travel from the field to you. It's important to get the freshest ones you can.

. . . Because they are processed soon after they are gathered and because they are protected from the vitamin-destroying oxygen in air, vacuum-canned (or glassed) and quick-frozen foods are often far richer in vitamins than so-called "fresh" produce which may have been several days in transit.

. . . Baked white potatoes supply an appreciable amount of vitamin C. Baking in the skin shuts out air, vitamin C's arch enemy.

. . . Fresh or commercially-canned (or glassed) peas are a valuable source of vitamins B_1 and C. Since B_1 is destroyed by alkaline substances, it is wrong to add soda to fresh peas to preserve their green color.

. . . The green, outer leaves of lettuce are far richer in vitamin A than the white inner leaves. Don't strip them off and throw them away. They make a health-protecting, money-saving salad when they're shredded.

. . . To save vitamins, cut or shred vegetables and fruits just before cooking or serving; do not let them stand exposed to air any longer than is absolutely necessary. Avoid soaking. Cook mild-flavored vegetables, tightly covered, in a small amount of boiling, salted water; cook strong-flavored varieties (for example, cauliflower, turnips, onions, whole cabbage), uncovered, in larger amounts of boiling, salted water.

. . . Cook vegetables whole, or cut into large pieces whenever possible; smaller pieces lose more vitamins and minerals to the cooking water and the air. Never mash or sieve vegetables while they are hot if it can be avoided; the heat increases the oxidation of vitamin C.

. . . Best of all, eat vegetables and fruits raw as often as you can.

. . . And remember that liver is a prize package of minerals and of all the vitamins, especially iron and vitamin A. Serve it at least once every week.

8. LEFTOVERS

SOMEBODY has said the mark of a good explorer is that he never has any dangerous adventures. He plans so wisely they don't happen! Similarly, it's the mark of a super-cook and a fine idea to avoid having leftovers. Now that we know more about nutrition, we realize that food value is highest when foods are freshly cooked or prepared. A second cooking, or even a moderately-long exposure to air, cuts down vitamin value.

But it would take an archangel cooking for a family of cherubs to avoid leftovers entirely. So what to do? Certainly, they should not be wasted! And, to forget food value for the moment and talk about flavor, it's a well-known fact that good things often taste better in their second incarnation than they did in their first.

One trick is to use leftovers in salads. No second cooking, you see. And salads are perfect for combining a dib of this and a dab of that. Salads aren't the whole story, though, by any means. Here is a listing, grouped by types of foods, of recipes in this book especially suited to helping you solve the puzzle of leftovers, and the pages where you'll find them.

9. PENNY STRETCHERS

No CONSCIENTIOUS cook book could face the public these days without blushing if it failed to offer good ideas (and lots of them) for making food-buying pennies stretch further than ever they stretched before. Emphatically, no blush need mantle *The Pocket Cook Book*. The recipes in its pages are predominantly penny stretchers. (A few, of course, are admittedly lavish. There *are* times when penny stretching is something best put off until tomorrow!)

For those dark moments when the kitchen cash box is almost empty and inspiration for appetizing economy dishes seems to have fled forever, here is a handy check list of penny-stretching, *Pocket Cook Book* recipes.

Finally and for good measure, here are some general hints for making one penny do the work of two:

Plan, Plan, PLAN! Short-range planning and hand-to-mouth buying are always costly. Plan meals by the week and you're sure to save money.

Buy in larger quantities. There's no economy, of course, in buying more of a food than your family wants nor in laying in a stock that may spoil before the last of it is used. But it does stretch pennies to buy in the largest amounts practicable.

Eat more of what you pay for. Cook beet tops, cauliflower leaves and stems, tough stalks of celery, outside leaves of lettuce and serve them as extra vegetables. Ask the butcher to give you the trimmings with the meat; make soup with the bones.

Save bacon drippings and use them for such cookery purposes as frying eggs, "buttering" the crumbs for a vegetable casserole topping, greasing the pans for corn muffins, etc.

Make sensible substitutions. Use evaporated milk, which has the same nutritive value as fresh, in some of your cooking. Buy sliced peaches, instead of matched halves, for pies and compotes. Try the vitamin-fortified margarines for at least some of the uses to which you put butter.

Be sure nothing wholesome or edible ever sees the inside of your garbage pail. (For hints on using leftovers, see p. 23.)

10. PRESSURE COOKERY

THE POPULARITY of pressure saucepans, which cook foods rapidly in live steam, has encouraged manufacturers to such a degree that there are now more than a dozen different models on the market! It is important for the prospective buyer, therefore, to know something about the principles of pressure saucepan cookery, and what features to look for, before deciding which pressure saucepan to buy.

What Is Pressure Saucepan Cookery? In ordinary top-stove cooking, the boiling point of water, 212°F., is the highest temperature that can be reached. In a pressure saucepan, the pressure of live steam raises the temperature above the boiling point and drives the heat through the food at a much faster rate than is possible with ordinary cooking methods, thus cutting the total cooking time by more than half. For example:

Pressure	Temperature Inside Saucepan
5 lbs.	228°F.
10 lbs.	240°F.
15 lbs.	250°F.

Which Pressure Saucepan Shall I Buy? Take plenty of time before making a decision. If possible, watch a demonstration of several types. Read advertisements carefully and don't skip over the technical descriptions of safety features and general construction. Limit your choice to pressure saucepans made by reliable manufacturers of national reputation.

Pressure saucepans range in size from 1½ quarts to 4 quarts. Some have a pressure range of 5, 10 and 15 pounds, others operate only at 15 pounds. Some are equipped with an inset pan or a divider which makes it possible to cook two or three foods at once, provided that these foods all require the same pressure for the same length of time.

Meal preparation is simplified if two pressure saucepans are used. In this case it is best to buy two different sizes and possibly two different types. For *home-canning*, a pressure canner of 16-quart capacity is more practical than a pressure saucepan, although some of the larger saucepans are recommended for this purpose by their manufacturers.

General Rules for Pressure Saucepan Cookery: Before you use a pressure saucepan for the first time, study the instruction book with great care. Follow directions to the letter. They have been worked out in the manufacturer's laboratories to insure safety in operation and the best possible results. It is to your advantage to heed them.

1. Prepare foods as directed in the recipe you are using. Place with recommended amount of water in the pressure saucepan, using a trivet if so indicated.

2. Never fill the saucepan more than ⅔ full, or food will clog the steam outlet and prevent proper operation.

3. Adjust cover in accordance with instructions.

4. Place saucepan over high heat, with the steam vent open, until a steady flow of steam comes through.

5. Close steam vent.

6. Bring pressure up to desired degree. Lower heat. Maintain correct pressure by regulating heat under saucepan.

7. Time the cooking period carefully. A kitchen timer which can be set for the exact number of minutes is a great help.

8. When cooking period is over, remove saucepan from heat and reduce the pressure quickly or slowly as directed in the recipe.

9. *Never try to remove the cover until the pressure gauge registers zero.* Some manufacturers have increased the safety of their pressure saucepans by making it impossible to remove the cover until all pressure has receded.

What About Food Values? Pressure cooking conserves the vitamin content of foods because air and light are excluded during the cooking period. The small amount of water needed in cooking conserves those minerals which are soluble. If any cooking water is left, it can be used in soups, sauces or gravies. Less-choice cuts of meat are made tender in a minimum amount of time. The starch grains in cereals burst open and become well cooked and digestible after a few minutes in the pressure saucepan.

CARE, CLEANING AND STORAGE

1. Handle indicator weight or control carefully. Dropping it may put it out of commission. Never immerse in water. Use a pipe cleaner when the steam vent needs cleaning.

2. If the saucepan is equipped with a pressure gauge, have it checked occasionally for accuracy.

3. Wash the saucepan in hot soapy water. If necessary scour the inside and the rack with steel wool or a metal sponge. Scald and dry thoroughly.

4. Never pour cold water inside a dry, overheated saucepan, for the sudden temperature change may warp or crack the metal.

5. Polish the outside of the saucepan with a suitable cleanser.

6. Set the saucepan in the sun occasionally.

7. Store saucepan with cover off, to prevent accumulation of stale odors.

COOK BOOKS

You may wish to increase your store of pressure-sauce-pan recipes. If so, either of these books will be helpful:

Cooking Under Pressure by Marian Tracy. Viking Press, 1949.

Pressure Cooking by Ida Bailey Allen. Garden City Publishing Co., 1947.

11. QUICK-FROZEN FOODS

QUICK-FROZEN foods are labor-savers and time-savers. (Most of the arduous work of cleaning and preparation has been done.) Quick-frozen foods are economical. (All possible waste has been eliminated and you pay only for usable food.) Quick-frozen foods are healthful. (They are picked at peak of goodness and frozen before that goodness has a chance to deteriorate.) And quick-frozen foods lend variety to your menus at all seasons of the year.

What Foods Are Quick-Frozen? The list of commercially quick-frozen foods is a long one. It includes many varieties of fruits and vegetables, meats, poultry, fish, shellfish, dairy products, shortenings, baked goods, doughs, prepared dishes for reheating, salads, soups, whip toppings, ice cream and other desserts.

Only a few foods have resisted quick-freezing: salad greens, cucumbers, radishes and tomatoes. Other vegetables which keep well at ordinary temperatures, such as turnips and parsnips, are not commercially frozen.

Buying Quick-Frozen Foods: It is up to the homemaker to buy only those quick-frozen foods which are packed by reliable companies. These organizations maintain high standards of quality in their nationally-known brands. They institute careful dealer-check-ups and do everything possible to assure the satisfaction of the products they offer.

How to Store Quick-Frozen Foods: There are many types of zero storage cabinets for home use. They range in size from units of about 4 cubic foot capacity for small kitchens, to farm freezers of 20 to 25 cubic foot capacity. For suburban homes there are upright cabinets with a 6 to 8 cubic foot capacity, or top-lifting units which offer this same storage space. Many refrigerators are equipped with a generous zero storage area. Blueprints for new housing projects often contain plans for locker storage in the basements of apartment buildings.

In some localities, department stores maintain a service whereby frozen food may be ordered in quantity and delivered in refrigerated trucks to homes with zero storage equipment.

Arrangement of Storage Cabinets: For maximum convenience, the homemaker should follow a definite plan in storing frozen foods.

The shelves in the upright-type of cabinet make it easier to arrange foods and get at them. Top-opening units present a more difficult problem. Some are equipped with a basket where a week's supply may be kept for easy access. Large meat cuts and poultry for immediate use may be stored directly under the basket. All other food which is not to be used for two weeks or more may be stored at the bottom.

Certain articles which must be stored over a fairly long period should be placed in the coldest section of the cabinet. These include meats, fat fish, cooked foods, baked goods, ice cream, fruit pies and fruits in sirup.

Two things make it easier to manage a zero storage cabinet efficiently: a running inventory, for purposes of re-stocking when supplies of certain foods run low, and a complete sorting of the contents every two weeks or so, to assure rotation of items.

The Refrigerator as a Partner: The automatic refrigerator is a necessary partner to the zero storage cabinet. It is needed for certain vegetables that do not take kindly to freezing, dairy products such as milk and eggs, left-over foods that must be used promptly, and the day's supply of all other perishables.

The refrigerator also provides the best temperature for slow defrosting of quick-frozen foods, the method which is generally conceded to give best results.

The Locker Plant: If a locker plant is located near your home you are fortunate indeed, for with these facilities and a zero storage cabinet in your kitchen, you will find it an easy matter to have a well-stocked larder the year around.

Locker plants offer some or all of the following services:

1. Slaughtering.
2. Aging, cutting, packing and freezing of meat.
3. Plucking, dressing, packing and freezing of poultry.
4. Lard rendering.
5. Sausage making.
6. Smoking (ham, bacon, etc.).
7. Sale of packing materials.
8. Storage locker rentals.

Most locker plants do not prepare and pack fruits and vegetables, because the majority of their customers would rather do this work at home in order to avoid the service charge. Some plants do offer kitchen facilities which their customers may use for preparing and packing their own garden produce.

Sometimes the locker operator may be able to supply you with food you have not been able to produce yourself, or help you to sell any surplus you may have. Often he can direct you to the best sources of home-grown produce.

Freezing Your Own: For those who have their own vegetable gardens and orchards, or who live near enough to farming country to buy produce at its best, quick-freezing is a joy. It is easy work and cool work, too. With the exception of apples, fruit is packed without cooking. Meat, poultry, fish and sea-food are frozen when raw, and vegetables require only a brief scalding in water or steam by way of preparation.

Of course food will be no better after freezing than it was before, so only top quality materials should go into the freezer. Garden-fresh fruits and vegetables at the peak of ripeness—high quality meats and poultry—ocean-fresh fish and shellfish—these are the foods to be frozen.

Poor quality packing materials can ruin your work. All wrappings must be both moisture proof and vapor proof, and containers must be properly sealed. Department stores, locker plants and mail order houses sell packing materials. Remember when ordering that it is true economy to buy the best. You will need containers for fruits and vegetables. Rectangular folding cartons with heat-sealable bags are the most efficient space savers in storage cabinets. Wrapping materials for meats, poultry and fish include moisture-vapor-proof cellophane (MSAT 83 or 87); pliofilm of the frozen-food type; aluminum foil (.001 gauge) and specially coated paper. Sometimes stockinette is used over wrapped packages of irregular shape, to hold the paper snugly in place.

To seal the bags inside cartons, fold over twice and apply a warm (not hot) iron. Sealing tape is used on other packages.

Label each package carefully, describing the product inside. Be sure to include the date it was packed and frozen.

Packages should go into the freezer immediately. If there must be a slight delay, keep them in the refrigerator.

Don't overcrowd the freezer and don't pile packages one on top of another. Place them flat against the freezing coils on the sides and bottom of the freezing compartment. As soon as they are frozen, transfer them to the storage compartment. Follow manufacturer's directions as to the amount of food which can be frozen at one time.

In addition to the manufacturer's direction booklet, you may wish to purchase one of the following comprehensive books on the best foods to freeze and how to freeze them:

Zero Storage in Your Home by Boyden Sparks. Doubleday Doran, 1944.

Home Freezing for Everyone by Lura Jim Alkire and Stanley Schuler. M. Barrows & Co., 1949.

Making the Most of Your Food Freezer by Marie Armstrong Essipoff. Rinehart & Company, 1951.

Important Note: All recipes in this book are based on level measurements and standard measuring equipment. (See Table of Standard Measurements, p. 4.)

12. APPETIZERS

Tomato Juice Cocktail

Chill tomato juice; season as desired with any of the following seasonings—salt, celery, onion or garlic salt, pepper, cayenne, lemon juice, onion juice, Worcestershire sauce, tabasco, etc.

Tomato Juice Frappé

Season tomato juice as desired. Pour into freezing tray of automatic refrigerator with cold control set at point recommended by manufacturer for freezing ice cream. Freeze to mush, stirring once. Beat with fork before serving. Serve immediately.

Tomato and Sauerkraut Juice Cocktail   Serves 4

   1 cup tomato juice   4 lemon slices
   1 cup sauerkraut juice

Chill tomato and sauerkraut juices; combine. Garnish with lemon.

Spiced Apricot Cocktail   Serves 4

    ½ cup water   1 12-oz. can (1½ cups)
    6 whole cloves   apricot nectar
    1" stick cinnamon   1 tbs. lemon juice

Combine water and spices; simmer 3 minutes. Cool; strain.
Add nectar and lemon juice; chill.

Cranberry Frost   Serves 4

    1 pt. cranberry juice   1 egg white
    1 tbs. lemon juice   Nutmeg

Chill cranberry juice; combine with lemon juice. Beat egg
white stiff. Add cranberry mixture; beat until frothy. Pour
into glasses. Sprinkle with nutmeg.

Minted Fruit Juice   Serves 4

    1 cup orange juice   Few drops peppermint
    1 cup pineapple juice   extract

Combine orange and pineapple juices; chill. Add peppermint extract.

Tropic Tang Cocktail   Serves 4

    1 cup grapefruit juice   1 cup cranberry juice

Combine grapefruit and cranberry juices; chill.

Washington Apple Foam   Serves 4

    1 pt. apple juice   1 tsp. lemon juice
    1 egg white   Cinnamon
    1 tbs. sugar   Sugar

Chill apple juice. Beat egg white stiff; add sugar, beating
constantly. Add apple and lemon juices. Pour into glasses.
Mix a little cinnamon and sugar; sprinkle on fruit juice
mixture.

Grape Juice Frappé   Serves 4

    1 pt. grape juice   1 tbs. lemon juice

Combine grape and lemon juices. Pour into freezing tray of automatic refrigerator with cold control set at point recommended by manufacturer for freezing ice cream. Freeze to mush, stirring once. Beat with fork before serving. Serve immediately.

Banana Fruit Cup
Serves 4

¾ cup orange juice
½ cup grapefruit juice

3 bananas

Chill orange and grapefruit juices; combine. Peel bananas; slice. Place in individual serving dishes; add fruit juices.

Ginger Pear Appetizer
Serves 4

4 pears
1 cup orange juice
2 tbs. lemon juice

2 tbs. powdered sugar
2 tbs. minced preserved ginger

Pare pears; core; slice. Arrange in individual serving dishes. Combine orange and lemon juices, sugar and ginger; pour over pears. Chill.

Iced Cranberry Fruit Cup
Serves 6-8

1 No. 2½ can (3½ cups) fruit cocktail

Cranberry Sherbet (pp. 201-2)

Chill fruit cocktail; place in individual serving dishes. Top with sherbet.

Loganberry Cup

Combine membrane-free grapefruit and orange sections; place in individual serving dishes. Fill with loganberry juice. Chill.

Watermelon Cup
Serves 4

3 cups watermelon balls
½ cup orange juice

¼ cup grape juice
Mint sprigs

Combine watermelon balls, orange and grape juices; chill. Garnish with mint.

Cocktail Bouquet

Combine peeled seedless grapes and melon balls; sprinkle with orange juice and powdered sugar. Chill. Cut centers from small lace paper doilies, fit doilies around edges of sherbet glasses. Fill with grape and melon ball mixture; garnish with maraschino cherries and mint sprigs.

Minted Strawberries

Wash large strawberries; hull. Combine a little orange juice and chopped mint; pour over berries. Sprinkle with powdered sugar; chill.

Frosty Fruit Cup   Serves 4-6

2 bananas
2 cups halved, seeded red grapes

½ cup pineapple juice
Raspberry Sherbet (p. 202)

Peel bananas; dice. Combine with grapes. Add pineapple juice. Place in individual serving dishes; top with sherbet.

Ginger Ale Melon Frappé   Serves 4

1 pt. ginger ale
Few grains salt

2 cups melon balls

Pour ginger ale into freezing tray of automatic refrigerator with cold control set at point recommended by manufacturer for freezing ice cream; freeze to mush, stirring once. Sprinkle salt on melon balls; fold into ginger ale.

Pineapple Grape Freeze   Serves 6

¼ cup powdered sugar
1 No. 2 can (2½ cups) pineapple juice

1 egg white
1½ cups halved, seeded red grapes

Dissolve sugar in pineapple juice. Beat egg white stiff; fold in. Pour into freezing tray of automatic refrigerator with cold control set at point recommended by manufacturer for freezing ice cream. Freeze to mush; fold in grapes. Serve immediately.

Anchovy Canapés   Serves 8

4 large anchovies   8 toast rounds
1 pkg. (3 oz.) cream cheese   Sieved hard-cooked egg yolk
2 tbs. chopped pimiento

Mash anchovies; blend with cream cheese and pimiento.
Spread on toast. Garnish with border of egg yolk.

Cheese Anchovy Canapés

Mash soft American cheese; season with Worcestershire
sauce and tabasco. Spread on toast rounds or crackers;
garnish each with rolled anchovy.

Cheese Canapés   Serves 4

¼ cup mashed American   ⅛ tsp. chili powder
  cheese   Chopped nut meats
1 tbs. cream   Crackers

Mash cheese; blend in cream. Add chili powder; mix well.
Sprinkle nut meats on crackers. Force cheese mixture
through pastry tube on crackers.

Salmon and Egg Canapés

Blend hard-cooked egg yolks, flaked salmon and mayonnaise or salad dressing to smooth paste. Toast sliced bread
squares on one side; spread salmon mixture on untoasted
side. Garnish with finely chopped parsley and hard-cooked
egg white.

Tangy Liverwurst Canapés

Mash liverwurst; blend to smooth paste with mayonnaise or
salad dressing. Season with prepared mustard; add minced
crisp bacon. Spread on whole-wheat toast triangles or
rounds. Garnish with pickle slices.

Zesty Roquefort Chips

Mash Roquefort-style cheese; mix to smooth paste with
cream cheese. Season with ketchup. Spread on potato chips.
Garnish with stuffed olive slices.

Anchovy Cheese Pinwheels

Using 1 cup biscuit mix, make biscuit dough according to directions on package. Roll out ⅛″ thick in oblong on lightly floured board. Spread lightly with anchovy paste. Sprinkle with grated American cheese. Roll up jelly-roll fashion. Slice ¼″ thick. Place on baking sheet. Bake in hot oven (400°F.) 15 min. Serve with fruit or vegetable cocktails, soup or salad.

Hot Tuna Canapés

Mix flaked tuna with mayonnaise or salad dressing; add chopped stuffed olives. Season with Worcestershire sauce. Spread on toast strips; sprinkle with grated American cheese. Place under broiler unit or burner until cheese is melted. Serve hot.

Devilled Cheese Rolls   Makes 12

1 pkg. (3-oz.) cream cheese   1 tbs. chopped pickle
1 tbs. ketchup   12 slices tongue
1 tbs. chopped stuffed
  olives

Mash cream cheese; blend in ketchup. Add olive and pickle. Spread on tongue slices. Roll up; fasten with picks. Chill.

Cheese Beef Sticks

Cut American cheese in sticks 2″ x ⅜″. Wrap each stick in dried beef square. Place 3″ below broiler unit or tip of flame; broil until cheese is slightly melted. Serve with picks.

Cornucopias

Mash cream cheese; season with minced onion and drained sweet pickle relish. Spread on thin slices boiled ham or dried beef. Roll cornucopia fashion; chill.

Cheese Rolls

Blend cottage cheese and milk to smooth paste. Season with

grated onion, salt and pepper. Form into small balls. Roll in chopped parsley. Chill. Serve with picks.

Limburger Cheese Tidbits

Mash Limburger cheese; blend to smooth paste with cream cheese. Add chopped dill pickle. Spread on thin slices pumpernickel bread.

Anchovy Pecans

Toast pecan nut meat halves in moderate oven (350°F.) 5 min.; spread bottoms with thin layer anchovy paste. Press each 2 halves together. Serve immediately.

Pickle Pick-Ups

Wrap sweet pickles in ½ slices bacon; fasten each with pick. Place under broiler unit or burner until bacon is brown and crisp, turning to brown on all sides.

Corned Beef Pickle Skewers

Chill canned corned beef; cut in 1″ cubes. Skewer each cube with tiny sweet gherkin on pick.

Garlic Olives

Rub small bowl with cut garlic clove. Put ripe olives in bowl; cover with salad oil. Let stand about 30 min.; drain off oil.

Stuffed Celery

Wash celery; trim leaves. Cut large stalks in 2″ lengths. Fill with one of following mixtures pressed through pastry tube or spread with knife.

Roquefort Filling: Mash Roquefort-style cheese; blend to smooth paste with cream cheese and a little milk. Season with grated onion and tabasco.

Devilled Ham Filling: Blend devilled ham, cream cheese

and mayonnaise or salad dressing to smooth paste. Season with prepared mustard and horse-radish.

Mixed Shellfish Cocktail

Use any combination of cooked or canned crab meat, lobster or shrimp. Flake crab meat or lobster; chill. Line individual cocktail glasses with crisp lettuce; fill with fish combination. Place spoonful Red Cocktail Sauce (p. 331) in center of each.

Crab, Lobster or Shrimp Cocktail

Flake cooked or canned crab meat or lobster. Chill crab meat, lobster or cooked or canned shrimp. Line individual cocktail glasses with crisp lettuce; fill with crab meat, lobster or shrimp. Place spoonful Red Cocktail Sauce (p. 331) in center of each. Serve with lemon wedges.

Oysters or Clams on Half Shell

Allow 4-6 medium or large oysters or hard-shelled clams per person. Scrub shells; rinse in cold water. Insert blade of thin knife between edges of shells, cutting through muscle of oysters; pry open. Arrange oysters or clams on half shell in dishes of crushed ice; place individual glass of Red Cocktail Sauce (p. 331) in center of each. Serve with lemon wedges.

Crab Meat Diablo   Serves 4

    2 cups tomato juice   1 tsp. prepared horse-radish
    1½ cups cooked or canned   1 tsp. Worcestershire sauce
        crab meat   1 tsp. lemon juice
    Few drops Tabasco

Pour tomato juice into freezing tray of automatic refrigerator with cold control set at point recommended by manufacturer for freezing ice cream. Freeze to mush, stirring once. Mix crab meat, tabasco, horse-radish, Worcestershire sauce and lemon juice; chill. Place tomato juice in bottom of cocktail glasses. Top with crab meat mixture.

Tuna Tomato Appetizers   Serves 4

4 small tomatoes
¼ cup flaked tuna
3 tbs. mayonnaise or salad dressing

2 tbs. chopped cucumber
1 tsp. sweet pickle relish
Paprika

Peel tomatoes; quarter, but do not cut through to bottom. Place on individual salad plates, force open. In center of each, place 1 tbs. tuna. Mix mayonnaise or salad dressing, cucumber and relish; place spoonful in each tomato. Sprinkle with paprika.

13. BEVERAGES

How To Make Coffee

Drip Method: Scald coffee maker with boiling water. For each serving, measure 2 tbs. drip grind coffee into coffee compartment. Measure 1 cup cold water for each serving; bring to boiling point. Pour into upper part of coffee maker; cover. Place on asbestos pad over low heat or in warm place. When water has dripped through to bottom, remove coffee compartment. Stir coffee brew; cover. Serve immediately.

Vacuum Method: For each serving, measure 1 cup cold or freshly boiling water. Pour into lower bowl of coffee maker; place over heat; bring to boiling point. Adjust filter on upper bowl; measure 2 tbs. drip grind coffee for each serving into upper bowl. When water comes to boiling point, fit upper bowl in position on lower bowl, twisting slightly to make air-tight seal. Reduce heat; allow all but small quantity of water to rise into upper bowl. Stir mixture in upper bowl; remove from heat. Allow brew to return to lower bowl; remove upper bowl. Serve immediately.

Percolator Method: For each serving, measure 1 cup cold

water into coffee maker. Place coffee basket in coffee maker. Measure 2 tbs. percolator grind coffee for each serving into coffee basket. Cover; place over heat. Allow water to percolate; reduce heat. Percolate slowly 8-10 min. Remove coffee basket; cover. Serve immediately.

Old-Fashioned Method: For each serving, measure 2 tbs. all-purpose grind coffee into coffee maker. For each serving, measure 1 cup freshly boiling water into coffee maker; stir well. Cover tightly; let stand on asbestos pad over low heat or in warm place 8-10 min. Strain brew immediately; pour into heated serving pot. Serve immediately.

How To Make Extra Strength Coffee

Follow any one of the above recipes for making coffee, using 3 tbs. ground coffee for each serving.

How To Make Iced Coffee

Method I: Follow any one of the above recipes for making coffee; pour into enamel, glass, china or earthenware container. Cover tightly; cool. If desired, chill. Serve in tall glasses with ice. Allow ¾-1 cup cooled coffee brew for each serving.

Method II: Make Extra Strength Coffee (see above). Fill tall glasses with ice; pour hot coffee brew over ice. Allow ½-⅔ cup hot coffee brew for each serving.

Café Au Lait

Follow recipe for Extra Strength Coffee (see above). Measure. Heat equal quantity milk. Pour hot coffee and milk simultaneously into serving cups. If desired, garnish with whipped cream.

Mochalate With Nutmeg   Serves 4

1 square (1 oz.) unsweetened chocolate	1½ cups freshly made hot coffee brew
3 tbs. sugar	¼ cup whipping cream
1½ cups milk	Nutmeg
Few grains salt	

Chop chocolate; add sugar and ½ cup milk. Cook over hot water, stirring occasionally, until chocolate is melted. Add salt and remaining milk; cook 10 min. Beat with rotary beater until frothy. Add coffee slowly, beating constantly. Pour into pitcher. Whip cream; use as garnish. Serve with nutmeg.

Coffee Delight

2 cups Iced Coffee (p. 46)	5 tbs. Sugar Sirup (p. 51)
½ cup whipping cream	1 pt. ginger ale

Mix coffee and sirup. Fill 4 tall glasses ¼ full of crushed ice. Whip cream; into each glass put ¼ cup cream, ½ cup coffee mixture and ½ cup ginger ale. Stir slightly.

How To Make Tea

Scald tea pot with boiling water. For each serving, measure 1 tsp. tea into pot; add 1 additional tsp. tea. For each serving, measure 1 cup freshly boiling water into tea pot. Let stand 3-5 min.; strain. Serve immediately.

How To Make Iced Tea

Method I: Follow recipe for making tea (see above); pour into enamel, glass, china or earthenware container. Cover tightly; cool. If desired, chill. Pour tea infusion over ice in tall glasses. Allow ¾-1 cup cooled tea for each serving.

Method II: Follow recipe for making tea, using 2 tsp. tea for each serving. Pour hot tea infusion over ice in tall glasses. Allow ½-⅔ cup hot tea for each serving.

Saigon Tea   Serves 4

3 tbs. tea	12 allspice berries
4 cups freshly boiling water	1 2" stick cinnamon
12 whole cloves	Lemon wedges

Put tea into heated pot; add water. Add cloves, allspice and cinnamon; let stand 5 min. Pour through strainer over ice in tall glasses. Garnish with lemon.

Celebration Tea Punch
Serves 25

1 pt. pitted sweet cherries
2 qt. freshly boiling water
3 tbs. tea
½ cup chopped fresh mint leaves

1 qt. Lemon Ice (p. 199)
Sugar
Orange slices
Lemon slices

Pour water over tea; cover. Let stand 5 min.; strain. Sweeten slightly with sugar. Add cherries and mint. Cover; chill several hours. Pour over ice in punch bowl; add lemon ice. Garnish with orange and lemon.

Cocoa
Serves 4

2 tbs. cocoa
2 tbs. sugar
Few grains salt

1 cup water
3 cups milk

Mix cocoa, sugar and salt; add water. Bring to boiling point over low heat; boil 2 min., stirring constantly. Add milk; heat.

Spiced Cocoa
Serves 4-6

¼ cup cocoa
¼ cup sugar
Few grains salt
⅛ tsp. cinnamon
2 cups water

1 13½-oz. can evaporated milk
½ tsp. vanilla extract
Whipped cream

Mix cocoa, sugar, salt and cinnamon; add water. Bring to boiling point; boil 3 min. Add milk; heat. Beat with rotary beater until frothy; add vanilla extract. Garnish with cream.

Hot Chocolate
Serves 4-6

1½ squares (1½ oz.) unsweetened chocolate
¾ cup water

2½ tbs. sugar
Few grains salt
2¼ cups milk

Combine chocolate and water; cook, stirring constantly, until chocolate is melted. Add sugar and salt; bring to boiling point. Boil 4 min., stirring constantly. Place over boiling water; gradually add milk, stirring constantly. Heat. Just before serving, beat with rotary beater until frothy.

Chocolate Chip Bracer
Serves 4

4 cups hot milk

1 cup finely chopped semi-sweet chocolate

Pour milk over chocolate; stir well. Beat with rotary beater until chocolate is dissolved.

Choc-O-Spice Shake
Serves 4

4 cups milk
4 egg yolks
½ cup malt-cocoa
Nutmeg

¼ cup whipping cream
Finely chopped semi-sweet chocolate

Chill milk. Beat egg yolks; add milk. Add malt-cocoa; beat with rotary beater until dissolved. Flavor with nutmeg. Pour into tall glasses. Whip cream; use as garnish. Sprinkle with chocolate.

How To Make Malt-Cocoa

Hot Malt-Cocoa: For each serving, measure 1-2 tbs. malt-cocoa; add 2 tbs. milk; blend to smooth paste. Add ½-⅔ cup hot milk; stir until dissolved.

Cold Malt-Cocoa: For each serving, measure 1 cup milk; add 2-3 tbs. malt-cocoa. Shake well or beat with rotary beater until well blended.

How To Make Malted Milk

Hot Malted Milk: For each serving, measure 2-3 tbs. malted milk; add ¾ cup hot water or milk. Stir until dissolved.

Cold Malted Milk: For each serving, measure 1 cup water or milk; add 2-3 tbs. malted milk. Beat with rotary beater until well blended.

Eggnog
Serves 4

4 egg yolks	1 tsp. vanilla extract
3 tbs. sugar	4 egg whites
4 cups milk	Nutmeg

Beat egg yolks; add sugar. Add milk and vanilla extract. Beat egg whites stiff; fold in. Pour into tall glasses; sprinkle with nutmeg.

Spiced Orange Milk
Serves 4

1½ cups orange juice	3 egg yolks
1 tbs. sugar	3 egg whites
1½ cups evaporated milk	Nutmeg
1 cup water	

Combine juice, sugar, milk and water. Beat egg yolks; add milk mixture. Beat egg whites stiff; fold in. Serve in tall glasses with ice; sprinkle with nutmeg.

Orange Julep
Serves 8

4 cups orange juice	Charged water
1 cup lime juice	Mint sprigs
1 cup powdered sugar	Orange slices
½ cup chopped fresh mint	

Combine orange and lime juices, sugar and chopped mint; chill 1 hour. Strain. Pour over ice in tall glasses; fill with charged water; stir slightly. Garnish with mint and orange.

Pink Lemonade
Serves 4

⅔ cup lemon juice	Sugar Sirup (p. 51)
1½ cups cold water	Maraschino cherries
⅓ cup maraschino cherry sirup	Lemon slices

Combine lemon juice, water and cherry sirup. Sweeten with sugar sirup. Serve in tall glasses with ice. Garnish with cherries and lemon.

Grapefruit Fizz
Serves 8

1 No. 2 can (2½ cups)
grapefruit juice
1½ cups loganberry juice

1 pt. charged water
Sugar Sirup (p. 51)

Chill grapefruit and loganberry juices and charged water.
Combine; sweeten with sirup. Serve in tall glasses with ice.

Grape Ginger Ale
Serves 4

1 cup grape juice
1 pt. ginger ale
⅓ cup orange juice

¼ cup lemon juice
Sugar Sirup (p. 51)
Orange slices

Chill grape juice and ginger ale; combine grape, orange and
lemon juices. Sweeten with sirup. Combine with ginger ale.
Serve in tall glasses with ice. Garnish with orange.

Mulled Cider Punch
Serves 25

6 qt. cider
2 tsp. whole cloves

½ tsp. nutmeg
¾ cup sugar

Combine cider, cloves, nutmeg and sugar; bring to boiling
point. Boil 5 min.; strain. Serve hot.

Pot O'Gold Punch
Serves 12

3 cups pineapple juice
2 cups orange juice

3 cups ginger ale
Orange slices

Chill pineapple and orange juices and ginger ale. Combine;
pour over ice in punch bowl. Garnish with orange.

Sugar Sirup

Combine equal quantities sugar and water; bring to boil.
Boil 5 min. Store in covered jar in refrigerator. Use to
sweeten cold drinks.

Cherry Ice Cubes

Place 1 maraschino cherry in each section of grids of freezing tray of automatic refrigerator; fill with water. Freeze with cold control set at point recommended by manufacturer for freezing ice cubes.

14.   BREADS AND DOUGHNUTS

Baking Powder Biscuits   Makes 14

2 cups flour	¼ cup shortening
3 tsp. baking powder	¾-1 cup milk
½ tsp. salt	Melted butter or margarine

Sift together flour, baking powder and salt; cut in shortening with 2 knives or pastry blender. Add enough milk to make soft dough. Roll out ½″ thick on lightly floured board; cut with round cutter 2″ in diameter. Place on baking sheet; brush with butter or margarine. Bake in very hot oven (450°F.) 15 min. Serve hot.

Apricot Folds: Follow recipe for Baking Powder Biscuits, rolling dough ¼″ thick. Cut with round cutter 3½″ in diameter. On ½ of each round place 2 tsp. chopped cooked dried apricots. Sprinkle with brown sugar; dot with butter or margarine. Fold over; press edges together with tines of fork. Place on baking sheet. Bake in very hot oven (450°F.) 15 min. Serve hot.

Bacon Breakfast Wheels: Follow recipe for Baking Powder Biscuits, rolling dough into oblong ¼″ thick. Cream ¼ cup butter or margarine; add ½ cup chopped crisp bacon; spread on dough. Roll up jelly-roll fashion; cut in 1″ slices. Place in greased muffin pans; bake in hot oven (425°F.) 15 min. Serve hot.

Butter Flakes: Follow recipe for Baking Powder Biscuits,

wrapping dough in waxed paper; chill. Divide into 4 pieces; roll out each piece ⅛" thick in oblong 6½" x 3". Brush with melted butter or margarine; sprinkle with cinnamon and sugar. Place together in layers. Roll up jelly-roll fashion; cut in 1½" slices. Place in greased muffin pans; bake in very hot oven (475°F.) 12 min. Serve hot.

Cheese Biscuits: Follow recipe for Baking Powder Biscuits, cutting in with shortening ½ cup grated American cheese. Serve hot.

Chocolate Coconut Tea Ring: Follow recipe for Baking Powder Biscuits, rolling dough into oblong 10" x 6½" x ¼". Chop ½ 7-oz. bar semi-sweet chocolate; sprinkle on dough with 1⅓ cups shredded moist-pack coconut, 2 tbs. sugar and ¼ tsp. cinnamon. Roll up jelly-roll fashion. Moisten edge; seal. Place in circle on greased baking sheet. Cut gashes 1" apart; turn cut side up. Bake in moderately hot oven (375°F.) 40 min. Cover with Confectioners' Sugar Glaze (p. 100). Serve hot.

Griddle Biscuits: Follow recipe for Baking Powder Biscuits, baking on greased griddle over low heat 15 min., turning to brown. Serve hot.

Love Letters: Follow recipe for Baking Powder Biscuits, rolling dough ¼" thick. Cut in 2½" squares; spread with melted butter or margarine. Place 1 tsp. currant jelly on each; fold corners toward center. Place on baking sheet. Bake in hot oven (425°F.) 15 min. Serve hot.

Quick Maple Buns: Follow recipe for Baking Powder Biscuits, placing in each section of greased small muffin pans 2 tsp. broken walnut meats, 2 tsp. maple sirup and ¼ tsp. melted butter or margarine; fill ⅔ full with dough. Bake in hot oven (400°F.) 20 min. Serve hot.

Tea Triangles: Follow recipe for Baking Powder Biscuits, rolling dough ¼" thick. Cut in 2½" squares. Mix ⅓ cup each peanut butter and orange marmalade; put spoonful on each square. Fold over to make triangles; press edges together with tines of fork. Place on baking sheet. Bake in hot oven (400°F.) 15 min. Spread with Confectioners' Sugar Glaze (p. 100). Serve hot.

Individual Shortcake Biscuits   Makes 4

1½ cups flour
2¼ tsp. baking powder
2 tbs. sugar
Few grains salt

¼ cup shortening
⅓-½ cup milk
Melted butter or margarine

Sift together flour, baking powder, sugar and salt. Cut in shortening with 2 knives or pastry blender. Add enough milk to make soft dough. Roll out ½" thick on lightly floured board. Cut with round cutter 3½" in diameter. Place on baking sheet; brush with butter or margarine. Bake in very hot oven (450°F.) 15 min. Serve hot.

Scotch Scones   Makes 12

2 cups flour
2 tbs. sugar
3 tsp. baking powder
½ tsp. salt

¼ cup shortening
1 egg yolk
⅓ cup light cream
1 egg white

Sift together flour, 1 tbs. sugar, baking powder and salt. Cut in shortening with 2 knives or pastry blender. Beat egg yolk; add cream; add to dry ingredients. Roll out ½" thick on lightly floured board. Cut in 2" triangles; place on baking sheet. Beat egg white slightly; brush on triangles; sprinkle with remaining sugar. Bake in very hot oven (450°F.) 15 min. Serve hot.

Plain Muffins   Makes 12

2 cups flour
2 tbs. sugar
3 tsp. baking powder
½ tsp. salt

1 egg
1 cup milk
¼ cup melted shortening
     or salad oil

Sift together flour, sugar, baking powder and salt. Beat egg; add milk and shortening or salad oil. Add to dry ingredients, stirring just enough to moisten. Fill greased muffin pans ⅔ full. Bake in hot oven (400°F.) 25 min. Serve hot.

Corn Meal Muffins: Follow recipe for Plain Muffins, substituting 1 cup yellow corn meal for 1 cup flour.

Date Cheese Muffins: Follow recipe for Plain Muffins, adding ¼ cup each grated American cheese and finely chopped pitted dates to batter.

Fig Muffins: Follow recipe for Plain Muffins, adding ¾ cup finely chopped dried figs to batter.

Harlequin Muffins: Follow recipe for Plain Muffins, adding mixture of 1 tbs. each milk, cocoa, sugar and ½ tsp. cinnamon to ½ of batter and filling greased muffin pans with ½ light and ½ dark batters.

Rich Muffins   Makes 12

¼ cup shortening	3 tsp. baking powder
⅓ cup sugar	1 tsp. salt
2 eggs	⅔ cup milk
2 cups flour	

Cream together shortening and sugar. Beat eggs; add. Sift together flour, baking powder and salt; add alternately with milk to creamed mixture. Fill greased muffin pans ⅔ full. Bake in hot oven (400°F.) 25 min. Serve hot.

Apricot Tea Muffins: Follow recipe for Rich Muffins, placing in each section of greased muffin pans 1 cooked dried apricot, cut side up, 1 tsp. brown sugar and ½ tsp. melted butter or margarine before filling with batter.

Berry Muffins: Follow recipe for Rich Muffins, carefully folding 1 cup hulled, sliced strawberries or 1 cup blueberries into batter.

Oatmeal Muffins: Follow recipe for Rich Muffins, substituting 1 cup rolled oats for 1 cup flour and adding ½ cup seedless raisins to batter.

Orange Marmalade Muffins: Follow recipe for Rich Muffins, filling greased muffin pans ⅓ full. Place 1 tsp. orange marmalade in each section; add remaining batter.

Bran Muffins   Makes 12

1¼ cups bran	¾ cup flour
1 cup milk	2 tbs. sugar
1 egg	3 tsp. baking powder
3 tbs. melted shortening or salad oil	½ tsp. salt

Combine bran and milk; let stand 5 min. Beat egg; add with shortening or salad oil. Sift together flour, sugar, baking powder and salt; combine with bran mixture. Fill greased muffin pans ⅔ full. Bake in hot oven (400°F.) 25 min. Serve hot.

Bran Fruit Muffins: Follow recipe for Bran Muffins, adding ½ cup seedless raisins, chopped pitted dates or figs to batter.

Honey Pecan Bran Muffins: Follow recipe for Bran Muffins, placing in each section of greased muffin pans 1 tsp. liquid honey and 4 pecan nut meats.

Buttermilk Sally Lunn Muffins   Makes 18

2 cups flour	2 eggs
½ cup sugar	1 cup buttermilk
1 tsp. cream of tartar	¼ cup melted shortening or salad oil
¾ tsp. baking soda	
½ tsp. salt	

Sift together flour, sugar, cream of tartar, soda and salt. Beat eggs; add milk and shortening or salad oil. Add to dry ingredients, stirring just enough to moisten. Fill small greased muffin pans ⅔ full. Bake in hot oven (400°F.) 25 min. Serve hot.

Doughnut Muffins   Makes 24

1½ tbs. shortening	½ tsp. nutmeg
½ cup sugar	½ cup milk
1 egg	Melted butter or margarine
2 cups flour	Confectioners' sugar
2 tsp. baking powder	Mixed sugar and cinnamon
½ tsp. salt	

Cream together shortening and sugar. Add egg; beat well.
Sift together flour, baking powder, salt and nutmeg; add
alternately with milk to creamed mixture. Fill greased small
muffin pans ⅔ full. Bake in hot oven (400°F.) 20-25 min.
Dip in melted butter or margarine. Roll ½ in confectioners'
sugar and ½ in cinnamon mixture. Serve hot.

Sweet Potato Muffins
Makes 15

1½ cups flour
1 tbs. sugar
5 tsp. baking powder
½ tsp. salt
2 eggs

1 cup milk
1 cup sieved cooked or
  canned sweet potatoes
½ cup melted shortening

Sift together flour, sugar, baking powder and salt. Beat
eggs; add milk. Add potatoes; beat smooth. Combine with
dry ingredients; add shortening. Fill greased muffin pans ⅔
full. Bake in hot oven (400°F.) 30 min. Serve hot.

Blueberry Sally Lunn

½ cup melted shortening
½ cup sugar
2 eggs
1¾ cups flour
3 tsp. baking powder
½ tsp. salt

1 cup milk
⅔ cup blueberries
¼ cup firmly packed brown
  sugar
½ tsp. cinnamon

Cream together shortening and sugar. Beat eggs; add. Sift
together flour, baking powder and salt; add alternately with
milk to creamed mixture. Carefully fold in blueberries. Pour
into greased pan 8″ x 8″ x 2″. Mix brown sugar and cinnamon; sprinkle on batter. Bake in moderate oven (350°F.)
50 min. Serve hot.

Golden Waffles
Serves 4

2 cups flour
3 tsp. baking powder
¼ tsp. salt
2 tbs. sugar
2 egg yolks

1¼ cups milk
6 tbs. melted shortening or
  salad oil
2 egg whites

Sift together flour, baking powder, salt and sugar. Beat egg yolks; add milk. Combine with dry ingredients, mixing smooth. Add shortening or salad oil. Beat egg whites stiff; fold in. Bake according to manufacturer's directions for operating waffle iron. Serve hot.

Cheese Waffles: Follow recipe for Golden Waffles, adding ½ cup grated American cheese to batter.

Coconut Waffles: Follow recipe for Golden Waffles, adding ½ cup shredded coconut to batter.

Molasses Waffles: Follow recipe for Golden Waffles, substituting ⅓ cup molasses for 2 tbs. sugar.

Griddle Cakes   Serves 4

2 cups flour	2 eggs
2 tbs. sugar	1¼ cups milk
¾ tsp. salt	¼ cup melted shortening or
3 tsp. baking powder	salad oil

Sift together flour, sugar, salt and baking powder. Beat eggs; add milk. Combine with dry ingredients, mixing smooth. Add shortening or salad oil. Drop by spoonfuls on hot griddle, spreading thin. Bake, turning to brown on both sides. Serve hot.

Corn Griddle Cakes   Serves 4

1½ cups flour	1 cup milk
3½ tsp. baking powder	1 cup cooked or canned
3 tbs. sugar	whole kernel corn
¾ tsp. salt	3 tbs. melted shortening or
1 egg	salad oil

Sift together flour, baking powder, sugar and salt. Beat egg; add milk. Combine with dry ingredients, mixing smooth. Add corn and shortening or salad oil. Drop by spoonfuls on hot griddle, spreading thin. Bake, turning to brown on both sides. Serve hot.

Corn Bread

1 cup corn meal
1 cup flour
3 tsp. baking powder
½ tsp. salt

1 egg
1 cup milk
¼ cup melted shortening or salad oil

Sift together corn meal, flour, baking powder and salt. Beat egg; add milk and shortening or salad oil. Add to dry ingredients, stirring just enough to moisten. Pour into greased pan 8″ x 8″ x 2″. Bake in hot oven (400°F.) 30 min.

Cheese Corn Bread

1 cup flour
1 tbs. sugar
1½ tsp. salt
2 tsp. baking powder
1 egg

2½ cups cooked or canned whole kernel corn
½ cup grated American cheese
¼ cup melted shortening or salad oil

Sift together flour, sugar, salt and baking powder. Beat egg; add corn and cheese. Add shortening or salad oil. Combine with dry ingredients. Pour into greased pan 8″ x 8″ x 2″; bake in hot oven (400°F.) 35 min. Serve hot.

Kernel Spoon Bread

Serves 4-6

½ cup flour
¾ cup yellow corn meal
2 tsp. baking powder
2½ tbs. sugar
¾ tsp. salt
1 egg

1 cup canned cream-style corn
¾ cup milk
¼ cup melted shortening or salad oil

Sift together flour, corn meal, baking powder, sugar and salt. Beat egg; combine with corn, milk and shortening or salad oil. Combine with dry ingredients. Fill greased mold ⅔ full; cover tightly. Steam 1 hour. Serve hot.

Popovers   Makes 6

1 cup flour	1 tsp. melted butter or
¼ tsp. salt	margarine
⅞ cup milk	2 eggs

Sift together flour and salt; gradually add milk. Add butter
or margarine. Beat eggs well; add. Beat batter 2 min. with
rotary beater. Fill hot greased popover pans or custard cups
⅔ full. Bake in very hot oven (450°F.) 15 min.; reduce to
moderate (350°F.); bake 20 min. Serve hot.

Orange Coffee Cake

1 egg	2 cups flour
½ cup milk	½ cup melted shortening
½ cup sugar	½ cup orange juice
½ tsp. salt	3 tsp. baking powder
2 tbs. grated orange rind	Nut Topping (see below)

Beat egg; add milk, sugar, salt and orange rind. Add ½ cup
flour and shortening. Add orange juice. Sift together remaining flour and baking powder; add. Pour into greased
pan 10″ in diam.; sprinkle with topping. Bake in moderately
hot oven (375°F.) 20-30 min.

Nut Topping

2 tbs. butter or margarine	½ cup finely chopped nut
½ cup firmly packed brown	meats or coconut
sugar	1 tsp. cinnamon
	1 tsp. nutmeg

Cream butter or margarine; add sugar, creaming well. Add
nut meats or coconut, cinnamon and nutmeg.

Quick Coffee Cake   Serves 4-6

1 loaf unsliced bread	½ cup firmly packed brown
Melted butter or margarine	sugar
¾ cup flour	Cinnamon
	¼ tsp. salt

Remove crusts from bread; cut loaf in ½ lengthwise. Brush tops and sides with butter or margarine. Combine flour, sugar, ¼ tsp. cinnamon and salt. Add ⅓ cup butter or margarine; mix until crumbly. Sprinkle crumbs on bread slices. Sprinkle generously with cinnamon. Bake in hot oven (400°F.) 15 min. Serve hot.

Fruit Nut Bread

½ cup dried apricots	¼ tsp. salt
1 large orange	½ cup chopped nut meats
½ cup seeded raisins	1 egg
2 cups flour	2 tbs. melted shortening or
2 tsp. baking powder	salad oil
1 tsp. baking soda	1 tsp. vanilla extract
1 cup sugar	

Cover apricots with cold water; let stand ½ hour; drain. Squeeze juice from orange, reserving peel; add enough boiling water to juice to make 1 cup. Using medium blade, put apricots, orange peel and raisins through food chopper. Sift together flour, baking powder, soda, sugar and salt. Add fruit mixture and nut meats. Add orange juice. Beat egg; add with melted shortening or salad oil and vanilla extract. Pour into greased loaf pan 8½" x 4½" x 2½". Bake in moderate oven (350°F.) 50 min. Remove from pan; cool on wire rack.

Prune Bread

½ lb. dried prunes	1 egg
¾ cup boiling water	2 tbs. melted shortening or
1¾ cups flour	salad oil
¾ cup sugar	1 tsp. baking soda
½ tsp. salt	

Soak prunes in cold water 2 hours; drain. Pit prunes; chop. Add boiling water; let stand 5 min. Sift together flour, sugar, soda and salt. Add prune mixture. Beat egg; add. Add shortening or salad oil. Pour into greased loaf pan 8½" x 4½" x 2½". Bake in moderate oven (325°F.) 1 hour. Remove from pan; cool on wire rack.

Steamed Brown Bread

Serves 6-8

1 cup flour
1 cup whole-wheat flour
1 cup yellow corn meal
½ cup sugar
1½ tsp. salt

1 tsp. baking soda
½ cup molasses
1½ cups sour milk
2 tbs. melted shortening or salad oil

Mix flour, whole-wheat flour, corn meal, sugar, salt and soda. Add molasses and sour milk; mix well. Add shortening or salad oil; pour into greased mold, filling ⅔ full; cover tightly. Steam 3 hours. Serve hot.

Spiced Sugar Doughnuts

Makes 24

3 tbs. shortening
1¾ cups sugar
2 eggs
4½ cups flour
4 tsp. baking powder

1 tsp. salt
1 tsp. nutmeg
1 cup milk
2 tbs. cinnamon

Cream together shortening and 1 cup sugar. Beat eggs; add. Sift together flour, baking powder, salt and nutmeg. Add alternately with milk to creamed mixture. Roll out ½″ thick on lightly floured board. Cut with doughnut cutter. Fry in deep fat or salad oil heated to 375°F. 3 min. or until brown, turning once. Drain on absorbent paper. Mix remaining sugar and cinnamon. Shake warm doughnuts with cinnamon mixture in paper bag.

Doughnut Links: Follow recipe for Spiced Sugar Doughnuts, substituting ¾ tsp. cinnamon for 1 tsp. nutmeg. Divide dough in ½; to ½ add 1 square (1 oz.) unsweetened chocolate melted over hot water with 2 tbs. milk. Roll out both doughs ½″ thick on lightly floured board. Cut with doughnut cutter. Cut through chocolate doughnuts; link around plain doughnuts; seal. Fry in deep fat or salad oil heated to 375°F. 3 min. or until brown, turning once. Drain on absorbent paper. Makes 12 pairs.

Cinnamon Toast

Slice bread thin; remove crusts. Toast bread slices; cut in strips or triangles. To each ¼ cup sugar or firmly packed brown sugar, add ½ tsp. cinnamon. Spread toast with softened butter or margarine; sprinkle with sugar mixture. Place under broiler unit or burner until sugar melts. Serve hot.

French Toast   Serves 4

1 egg   4 bread slices
⅔ cup milk   Butter or margarine
Few grains salt

Beat eggs; add milk and salt. Dip bread slices in egg mixture. Brown in butter or margarine, turning once. Serve hot. If desired, serve with maple sirup, honey or jam.

Croustades

Cut bread in slices 2″ thick; remove crusts. Hollow out centers, leaving ¼″ wall around edge and bottom. Brush top and sides with melted butter or margarine; place on baking sheet. Bake in moderate oven (350°F.) 10-15 min. or until brown. Serve hot filled with creamed meat, fish or vegetable mixture.

Melba Toast

Slice stale bread ⅛″ thick; remove crusts. Cut bread slices in 1″-1½″ strips. Place on baking sheet. Bake in slow oven (300°F.) 20-25 min., or until evenly browned and crisp, turning several times.

Croutons

Cube stale bread; brown on all sides in butter or margarine. Use as garnish on soup.

Basic White Bread

Makes 2 1-lb. loaves

1 cup milk
2 tbs. sugar
2 tsp. salt
1 tbs. shortening or salad
   oil

1 cup water
1 cake compressed yeast
2 tbs. lukewarm water
6 cups flour (about)

Scald milk; add sugar, salt and shortening or salad oil; stir until dissolved. Add 1 cup water; cool to lukewarm. Dissolve yeast in lukewarm water; add to first mixture. Gradually add flour, mixing to smooth stiff dough. Knead on lightly floured board until smooth and satiny. Shape into ball; place in greased bowl. Cover; let rise in warm place until double in bulk. Knead; divide in ½. Shape each ½ into ball; cover; let stand 10-15 min. Mold each ½ into loaf; place in greased loaf pans 8½″ x 4½″ x 2½″. Cover; let rise in warm place until double in bulk. Bake in hot oven (400°F.) 40-45 min. Remove from pan; cool on wire rack.

Pan Rolls: Follow recipe for Basic White Bread, shaping dough into 1½″ balls after first rising. Place close together in 2 greased pans 8″ x 8″ x 2″. Cover; let rise in warm place until double in bulk. Bake in very hot oven (450°F.) 20-25 min. Serve hot.

Whole-Wheat Bread

Makes 2 1-lb. loaves

1 cup milk
3 tbs. liquid honey
2½ tsp. salt
2 tbs. shortening or salad
   oil

1 cake compressed yeast
1 cup lukewarm water
5 cups whole-wheat flour

Scald milk; add honey, salt and shortening or salad oil; stir until dissolved. Cool to lukewarm. Dissolve .yeast in lukewarm water; add to first mixture. Gradually add flour, mixing to smooth stiff dough. Knead on lightly floured board until smooth and satiny. Shape into ball; place in greased bowl. Cover; let rise in warm place until double in bulk. Knead; divide in ½. Shape each ½ into ball; cover; let stand 10-15 min. Mold each ½ into loaf; place in greased loaf pans 8½″ x 4½″ x 2½″. Cover; let rise in warm place until double in bulk. Bake in moderately hot oven (375°F.) 1 hour. Remove from pans; cool on wire rack.

Rolled Oats Bread

Makes 2 loaves

2 cups rolled oats
2 tsp. salt
⅓ cup molasses
1 tbs. shortening or salad oil

2 cups boiling water
1 cake compressed yeast
¼ cup lukewarm water
4½ cups flour (about)

Mix oats, salt, molasses and shortening or salad oil; add boiling water. Cool to lukewarm. Dissolve yeast in lukewarm water; add to first mixture. Gradually add flour, mixing to smooth stiff dough. Knead on lightly floured board until smooth and satiny. Shape into ball; place in greased bowl. Cover; let rise in warm place until double in bulk. Knead; divide in ½. Shape each ½ into ball. Cover; let stand 10 min. Mold each ½ into loaf; place in greased loaf pans 8½″ x 4½″ x 2½″. Cover; let rise in warm place until double in bulk. Bake in moderately hot oven (375°F.) 50-60 min. Remove from pans; cool on wire rack.

Sugarplum Loaf

¾ cup milk
½ cup shortening
½ cup sugar
2 eggs
1 cake compressed yeast
2 tbs. lukewarm water
5 cups flour
1 tsp. salt

½ cup seedless raisins
½ cup chopped walnut meats
½ cup chopped citron
½ cup chopped candied cherries
Confectioners' Sugar Glaze (p. 100)

Scald milk; cool to lukewarm. Cream together shortening and sugar. Beat eggs; add. Dissolve yeast in lukewarm water. Add with milk to creamed mixture. Add 1 cup flour; mix well. Cover; let rise in warm place until double in bulk. Add salt, raisins, nut meats, citron and cherries. Gradually add remaining flour; knead on lightly floured board until thoroughly mixed. Place in greased round pan 8″ in diam.

and 3″ high. Cover; let rise in warm place until double in
bulk. Bake in moderate oven (350°F.) 1 hour 15 min. Remove from pan; cool on wire rack. Spread with glaze.

Refrigerator Rolls   Makes 2½ dozen

1 cup milk	2 cakes compressed yeast
¼ cup sugar	¼ cup lukewarm water
1½ tsp. salt	2 eggs
⅓ cup shortening or salad oil	5 cups sifted flour (about)

Scald milk; add sugar, salt and shortening or salad oil; stir
until dissolved. Cool to lukewarm. Dissolve yeast in lukewarm water; add to first mixture. Beat eggs; add. Gradually add flour, mixing to smooth soft dough. Knead on lightly
floured board until smooth and satiny. Shape into ball;
place in greased bowl. Cover; let rise in warm place until
double in bulk. Knead lightly on lightly floured board. Shape
into ball; place in greased bowl. Cover; set in refrigerator
until needed. Remove from refrigerator; let rise in warm
place until double in bulk. Shape according to directions
given in one of the following variations. Cover; let rise in
warm place until double in bulk. Bake in hot oven (425°F.)
15-20 min.

Bowknots: Roll out dough on lightly floured board into
rope-like strips 6″ long and ½″ in diam. Tie each strip
in knot. Place on greased baking sheet. Finish as above.

Butter Flake Rolls: Roll out dough into very thin oblong on
lightly floured board; brush with melted butter or margarine. Cut in strips 1″ wide; place each 6 strips together
in layers. Cut in pieces 1½″ in length. Place, cut ends up,
in greased muffin pan. Finish as above.

Cloverleaf Rolls: Form dough in small balls. Place 3 balls in
each section of greased muffin pans; brush with melted
butter or margarine. Finish as above.

Parker House Rolls: Roll dough ¼″ thick on lightly floured
board; cut with round cutter 2″ in diam. Make crease
through center of each round. Brush with melted butter

or margarine; fold over, pressing down lightly. Place on greased baking sheet. Finish as above.

Caraway Horns   Makes 16

½ cup milk	¾ tsp. salt
3 tbs. shortening	3 cups flour (about)
3 tbs. sugar	Melted butter or margarine
1 egg	Caraway seeds
½ cake compressed yeast	Coarse salt
2 tbs. lukewarm water	

Scald milk; cool to lukewarm. Cream together shortening and sugar. Beat egg; add. Dissolve yeast in lukewarm water; add with salt and milk to creamed mixture. Gradually add flour, mixing to smooth stiff dough. Knead on lightly floured board until smooth and satiny. Shape into ball; place in greased bowl. Cover; let rise in warm place until double in bulk. Knead; divide in ½. Shape each ½ into ball. Cover; let stand 10 min. Roll each ½ out into circle ¼" thick on lightly floured board; cut in 8 wedge-shaped pieces. Roll up each piece, starting with wide end; bend into half circle. Place on greased baking sheet. Brush with butter or margarine; sprinkle with caraway seeds and coarse salt. Cover; let rise in warm place until double in bulk. Bake in hot oven (425°F.) 10 min.

Currant Wheat Sticks   Makes 12

½ cup milk	¾ cup dried currants
2 tbs. molasses	1 cake compressed yeast
2 tbs. shortening or salad oil	½ cup lukewarm water
	2½ cups whole-wheat flour
1 tsp. salt	¾ cup flour (about)

Scald milk; add molasses, shortening or salad oil, salt and currants. Cool to lukewarm. Dissolve yeast in lukewarm water; add to first mixture. Gradually add whole-wheat flour; mix smooth. Gradually add flour, mixing to smooth dough. Knead on lightly floured board until smooth and satiny. Shape into ball; place in greased bowl. Cover; let rise in warm place until double in bulk. Knead; shape dough into 5″ strips. Place in greased bread stick pans. Cover; let rise in warm place until double in bulk. Bake in hot oven (425°F.) 15 min.

Old-Fashioned Foldovers   Makes 15

1 cup scalded milk
½ tbs. sugar
½ tsp. salt
1 tbs. shortening or salad oil

1 cake compressed yeast
1 tbs. lukewarm water
2¾ cups flour (about)
Strawberry or raspberry jam

Scald milk; add sugar, salt and shortening or salad oil; stir until dissolved. Cool to lukewarm. Dissolve yeast in lukewarm water; add to first mixture. Gradually add flour, mixing to smooth stiff dough. Knead on lightly floured board until smooth and satiny. Shape into ball. Place in greased bowl. Cover; let rise in warm place until double in bulk. Knead. Cover; let stand 10 minutes. Roll out ¼″ thick on lightly floured board; cut in 3″ squares. Place spoonful of jam on each square; moisten edges with water. Fold over to form triangle; press edges together with tines of fork. Cover; let rise in warm place until double in bulk. Fry in deep fat or salad oil heated to 375°F. 3 min. or until lightly browned.

Basic Sweet Dough

⅓ cup milk
¼ cup sugar
1 tsp. salt
3 tbs. shortening or salad oil

1 cake compressed yeast
2 tbs. lukewarm water
1 egg
2⅓ cups flour (about)

Scald milk; add sugar, salt and shortening or salad oil; stir until dissolved. Cool to lukewarm. Dissolve yeast in lukewarm water; add to first mixture. Beat egg; add. Gradually add flour, mixing to smooth soft dough. Knead on lightly floured board until smooth and satiny. Shape into ball; place in greased bowl. Cover; let rise in warm place until double in bulk. Shape; let rise and bake according to directions given in one of the following variations.

Mystery Fold Rings: Combine ½ cup sieved cooked dried prunes, 3 tbs. liquid honey, 1 tsp. grated orange rind and 1 tbs. orange juice. After first rising, roll Basic Sweet Dough into oblong 20″ x 9″ x ⅛″. Spread with prune mixture; roll up jelly-roll fashion. Moisten edge with water; seal. Flatten roll by pressing lightly with rolling pin. Then pressing more firmly, make deep groove lengthwise through center of roll. Cut through center of groove; put strips on greased baking sheet, placing cut edges up. Twist strips around each other; form into ring. Cover; let rise in warm place until double in bulk. Bake in moderately hot oven (375°F.) 30 min. Cool on wire rack.

Cinnamon Snails: After first rising, divide Basic Sweet Dough into 4 pieces. Roll out each piece into oblong 12″ x 3″, on lightly floured board. Spread with melted butter or margarine; sprinkle with sugar and cinnamon. Roll each up jelly-roll fashion; halve crosswise. Stretch each piece lengthwise; twist; form in coil on greased baking sheet. Cover; let rise in warm place until double in bulk. Beat 1 egg white slightly; add 1 tsp. water. Brush over tops of coils; sprinkle with sugar. Bake in hot oven (400°F.) 15 min. Makes 8.

Brazil Nut Bread: Combine ½ cup each chopped pitted dates and toasted Brazil nut meats, 1 tsp. each grated lemon rind and juice. After first rising, knead Basic Sweet Dough on lightly floured board, adding date mixture. Place in greased 8″ tube pan; cover; let rise in warm place until double in bulk. Bake in moderate oven (350°F.) 50-60 min. Remove from pan; cool on wire rack. Combine ½ cup sugar, ¼ cup water and 1 tbs. corn sirup; boil 2 min. Pour over bread; sprinkle with sliced toasted Brazil nut meats.

Pineapple Braid: After first rising, divide Basic Sweet Dough in 3 pieces; roll out each piece into oblong 12″ x 4″ on lightly floured board. Spread with melted butter or margarine and ¾ cup very well-drained crushed pineapple; sprinkle with brown sugar and cinnamon. Fold each piece lengthwise; moisten edge with water; seal. Place strips on greased baking sheet; braid. Cover; let rise in warm place until double in bulk. Bake in moderately hot oven (375°F.) 25-30 min. Cool on wire rack. Spread with Confectioners' Sugar Glaze (p. 100).

Jelly Doughnuts: After first rising, roll out Basic Sweet Dough 1/3″ thick on lightly floured board; cut with doughnut cutter 3″ in diameter. Place on greased baking sheet; cover; let rise until double in bulk. Fry in deep fat or salad oil heated to 375°F., 4 min. Drain on absorbent paper. Spread tops with jelly; sprinkle with confectioners' sugar. Makes 10.

Coffee Braids: Mix 1 cup ground almond nut meats, 1/4 cup sugar and 1/2 tsp. cinnamon. After first rising, divide Basic Sweet Dough in 3 pieces. Roll out each piece into oblong 14″ x 4″ on lightly floured board. Sprinkle with almond mixture. Fold lengthwise; twist. Place on greased baking sheet; braid. Cover; let rise in warm place until double in bulk. Bake in moderate oven (350°F.) 50 min. Frost with Confectioners' Sugar Glaze (p. 100); sprinkle with chopped toasted almond nut meats.

Orange Pocket Book Rolls: After first rising, roll out Basic Sweet Dough on lightly floured board. Cut with round cutter 3½″ in diameter. Place membrane-free orange section on each round; sprinkle with brown sugar and cinnamon; fold over, pressing down lightly. Cover; let rise in warm place until double in bulk. Bake in hot oven (400°F.) 20 min. Spread with Confectioners' Sugar Glaze (p. 100). Makes 10.

15. CAKES, FROSTINGS, AND FILLINGS

Two Egg Cake Layers — I

Makes 18

½ cup shortening
1 cup sugar
2 eggs
2 cups cake flour

3 tsp. baking powder
½ tsp. salt
⅔ cup milk
1 tsp. vanilla extract

Cream together shortening and sugar. Add eggs, 1 at a time, beating after each. Sift together flour, baking powder and salt; add alternately with milk to creamed mixture. Add vanilla extract. Pour into 2 greased 8″ layer pans. Bake in moderately hot oven (375°F.) 25 min. Cool 5 min. Remove layers from pans; cool on wire rack.

Cup Cakes: Follow recipe for Two Egg Cake Layers I, pouring batter into greased medium cup cake pans; fill ⅔ full. Bake in hot oven (400°F.) 20-25 min. Cool 5 min. Remove from pans; cool on wire rack.

Apricot Cream Cake

Prepare Two Egg Cake Layers I. Prepare Apricot Cream Filling (p. 101); spread between layers. Sprinkle with confectioners' sugar.

Orange Walnut Cake

Prepare Two Egg Cake Layers I. Prepare Seven Minute Orange Frosting (p. 95). To ⅓ frosting add ¼ cup chopped walnut meats and ¼ cup chopped candied orange peel; spread between layers. Spread remaining frosting on top and sides of cake. Garnish with whole walnut meats and strips of candied orange peel.

Orange Banana Cake

Prepare Two Egg Cake Layers I (p. 71). Prepare Banana Filling (p. 102); spread between layers. Prepare Lemon Orange Confectioners' Sugar Frosting (p. 98); spread on top and sides of cake.

Banana Grape Cake

Prepare Two Egg Cake Layers I (see p. 71). Mash 1 cup grape jelly; spread ½ on 1 layer. Peel and slice 1 banana; sprinkle with lemon juice. Arrange slices on jelly. Cover with second layer; spread with remaining jelly. Sprinkle with shredded coconut.

Two Egg Cake Layers — II

⅔ cup shortening	4½ tsp. baking powder
1¼ cups sugar	¾ tsp. salt
2 eggs	1 cup milk
3 cups cake flour	1 tsp. vanilla extract

Cream together shortening and sugar. Add eggs, 1 at a time, beating after each. Sift together flour, baking powder and salt; add alternately with milk to creamed mixture. Add vanilla extract. Pour into 2 greased 9″ layer pans. Bake in moderately hot oven (375°F.) 25 min. Cool 5 min. Remove layers from pans; cool on wire rack.

Chocolate Dessert Cake

Prepare Two Egg Cake Layers II. Prepare Creamy Milk Chocolate Topping (p. 102); spread between layers and on top of cake.

Lemon Date Cake

Prepare Two Egg Cake Layers II. Prepare Lemon Date Filling (p. 101); spread between layers. Prepare Boiled Frosting I (p. 94); spread on top and sides of cake. Sprinkle with shredded coconut.

Three Egg Cake Layers

¾ cup shortening	4½ tsp. baking powder
1½ cups sugar	¾ tsp. salt
3 eggs	1 cup milk
3 cups cake flour	1½ tsp. vanilla extract

Cream together shortening and sugar. Add eggs, 1 at a time, beating after each. Sift together flour, baking powder and salt; add alternately with milk to creamed mixture. Add vanilla extract. Pour into 2 greased 9″ layer pans. Bake in moderately hot oven (375° F.) 25 min. Cool 5 min. Remove layers from pans; cool on wire rack.

Chocolate Frosted Cake

Prepare Three Egg Cake Layers (see above). Prepare Never-Fail Chocolate Frosting (p. 97); spread between layers and on top and sides of cake.

Lemon Coconut Cake

Prepare Three Egg Cake Layers. Prepare Stratford Filling (p. 101); spread ½ between layers (using remaining ½ as tart filling). Prepare Boiled Frosting I (p. 94); spread on top and sides of cake. Sprinkle with shredded coconut.

Velvet Cake Layers

1 cup shortening	2 tsp. baking powder
2 cups sugar	½ tsp. salt
4 eggs	1 cup milk
3 cups cake flour	1 tsp. vanilla extract

Cream together shortening and sugar. Add eggs, 1 at a time, beating after each. Sift together flour, baking powder and salt. Add alternately with milk to creamed mixture. Add vanilla extract. Pour into 2 greased 9″ layer pans. Bake in moderately hot oven (375°F.) 35 min. Cool 5 min. Remove layers from pans; cool on wire rack.

Chocolate Orange Cake

Prepare Velvet Cake Layers (see above). Prepare Orange

Filling (p. 101); spread between layers. Prepare Chocolate
Walnut Confectioners' Sugar Frosting (p. 97); spread on
top and sides of cake.

Lord Baltimore Cake

Prepare Velvet Cake Layers (see above). Prepare Lord Baltimore Frosting (p. 95); spread between layers and on top
and sides of cake.

Daisy Chain Birthday Cake

Prepare Velvet Cake Layers (above). Prepare Decorative
Frosting (p. 99), adding ½ tsp. almond extract. Tint green
with vegetable coloring. Tint ⅓ cup darker green. Spread
lighter frosting between layers and on top and sides of cake.
Arrange sugar-coated Jordan almonds on cake in daisy
petal design. Using pastry tube and small plain tip, make
stems of darker green frosting to connect daisies. Using
small leaf tip, make leaves along stem. Place yellow candle
holder and candle in center of each daisy.

Christmas Star Cake

Prepare Velvet Cake Layers (see p. 73). Prepare Decorative
Frosting (p. 99). Combine ⅓ cup each chopped walnut
meats, candied pineapple and candied cherries; add 1½
tsp. sherry flavoring. Let stand 5 min. Combine with ⅓ cup
frosting; spread between layers. Tint ¼ cup frosting green
with vegetable coloring. Add 1½ tsp. sherry flavoring to
remaining frosting; spread on top and sides of cake. Using
pastry tube and small plain tip, make star design on cake
with green frosting.

Inexpensive White Cake Layers

⅓ cup shortening	¼ tsp. salt
¾ cup sugar	½ cup milk
1½ cups cake flour	¾ tsp. almond extract
2 tsp. baking powder	3 egg whites

Cream together shortening and sugar. Sift together flour, baking powder and salt. Add alternately with milk to creamed mixture. Add almond extract. Beat egg whites stiff; fold in. Pour into 2 greased 8″ layer pans. Bake in moderately hot oven (375°F.) 25 min. Cool 5 min. Remove layers from pans; cool on wire rack.

Family Favorite Cake

Prepare Inexpensive White Cake Layers (see above). Prepare Caramel Frosting (see p. 96); spread between layers and on top of cake.

Caramel Divinity Cake

Prepare Inexpensive White Cake Layers (see above). Prepare Caramel Frosting (see p. 96); spread between layers and on top of cake.

Fluffy White Layers

¾ cup shortening	½ tsp. salt
1½ cups sugar	1 cup milk
3 cups cake flour	1 tsp. almond extract
4 tsp. baking powder	5 egg whites

Cream together shortening and sugar. Sift together flour, baking powder and salt; add alternately with milk to creamed mixture. Add almond extract. Beat egg whites stiff; fold in. Pour into 2 greased 8″ x 8″ x 2″ layer pans or 2 greased 9″ layer pans. Bake in moderately hot oven (375°F.) 30 min. Cool 5 min. Remove layers from pans; cool on wire rack.

Luscious Chocolate Maple Cake

Prepare Fluffy White Layers (see above). Prepare Chocolate Cream Filling (p. 99); spread between layers. Prepare Maple Boiled Frosting (pp. 94-95); spread on top and sides of cake. Using tip of spatula, make swirls in frosting on top of cake. Melt 1½ squares (1½ oz.) unsweetened chocolate; drip from tip of spoon on cake following swirls of frosting.

Lady Baltimore Cake

Prepare Fluffy White Layers (see p. 75). Prepare Lady Baltimore Frosting (p. 95); spread between layers and on top and sides of cake.

Golden Glory Cake

Prepare Fluffy White Layers (see p. 99). Prepare Apricot Almond Filling (p. 101); spread between layers. Prepare Boiled Frosting I (p. 94); spread on top and sides of cake. Sprinkle with coconut; garnish with border of finely chopped dried apricots.

Jiffy Cake Layers

2⅔ cups flour	¾ cup shortening
4½ tsp. baking powder	1 cup milk
½ tsp. salt	1 tsp. vanilla extract
1½ cups sugar	3 eggs

Mix together flour, baking powder, salt and sugar; sift. Measure ¾ cup dry ingredients; blend with shortening. Add ¾ cup milk alternately with remaining dry ingredients to shortening mixture; mix smooth. Add remaining milk and vanilla extract. Add eggs; beat well. Pour into 3 greased 8″ layer pans. Bake in moderately hot oven (375°F.) 30 min. Cool 5 min. Remove layers from pans; cool on wire rack.

Busy Day Cake

Prepare Jiffy Cake Layers (see above). Prepare Orange Confectioners' Sugar Frosting (p. 98); spread between layers and on top of cake.

Quick Coconut Currant Cake

Prepare Jiffy Layers (see above). Mash 1 cup currant jelly; spread between and on top layers. Sprinkle with shredded coconut.

Quick Layer Cake

2 cups cake flour	1/3 cup softened shortening
3 tsp. baking powder	2 eggs
1 cup sugar	3/4 cup milk
Few grains salt	1 tsp. vanilla extract

Sift together flour, baking powder, sugar and salt 3 times. Cut in shortening with 2 knives or pastry blender until mixture resembles corn meal. Beat eggs until thick and lemon colored; add milk and vanilla extract. Add to first mixture gradually; stir well. Pour into 2 greased 8" layer pans. Bake in moderately hot oven (375°F.) 25 min. Cool 5 min. Remove layers from pans; cool on wire rack.

Raisin Spice Cup Cakes: Follow recipe for Quick Layer Cake, sifting 2 tsp. cinnamon, 1/2 tsp. nutmeg and 1/4 tsp. cloves with dry ingredients. Mix 2/3 cup seedless raisins with 2 tbs. flour mixture; fold into batter. Pour into greased medium cup cake pans; fill 2/3 full. Bake in hot oven (400°F.) 20-25 min. Makes 18.

Cocoa Layer Cake: Follow recipe for Quick Layer Cake, sifting 1/2 cup cocoa with dry ingredients and increasing milk to 1 cup.

Maple Nut Layer Cake: Follow recipe for Quick Layer Cake, adding 1 cup chopped walnut meats to batter.

Maple Cocoa Cake

Prepare Cocoa Layer Cake (see above). Prepare Maple Boiled Frosting (pp. 94-95); spread between layers and on top and sides of cake.

Square Loaf Cake

1/2 cup shortening	2 tsp. baking powder
1 cup sugar	1/2 tsp. salt
2 eggs	1/2 cup milk
1 3/4 cups cake flour	1 tsp. vanilla extract

Cream together shortening and sugar. Add eggs, 1 at a

time, beating after each. Sift together flour, baking powder and salt; add alternately with milk to creamed mixture. Add vanilla extract. Pour into greased pan 8" x 8" x 2". Bake in moderate oven (350°F.) 50 min. Cool 5 min. Remove cake from pan; cool on wire rack.

Orange Square Loaf Cake

Prepare Square Loaf Cake (see above). Prepare Seven Minute Orange Frosting (p. 96); spread on top and sides of cake.

Brown Sugar Loaf Cake

⅓ cup shortening	3 tsp. baking powder
¾ cup firmly packed brown sugar	¼ tsp. salt
	⅔ cup milk
2 eggs	1 tsp. vanilla extract
1¾ cups flour	

Cream together shortening and sugar. Add eggs, 1 at a time, beating after each. Sift together flour, baking powder and salt; add alternately with milk to creamed mixture. Add vanilla extract. Pour into greased pan 8" x 8" x 2". Bake in moderate oven (350°F.) 45 min. Cool 5 min. Remove cake from pan; cool on wire rack.

Brown and White Loaf Cake

Prepare Brown Sugar Loaf Cake (see above). Prepare Seven Minute Frosting (pp. 95-96); spread on top and sides of cake.

Wedding Bell Cake

1½ cups shortening	2½ tsp. baking powder
2⅓ cups powdered sugar	1¾ cups milk
7 egg yolks	1½ tsp. vanilla extract
4½ cups cake flour	Ornamental Frosting (p. 99)
¾ tsp. salt	

Cream together shortening and sugar. Beat egg yolks until thick and lemon-colored; add. Sift together flour, salt and baking powder 3 times; add alternately with milk to creamed mixture. Add vanilla extract. Pour into 2 greased 12″ layer pans. Bake in moderately hot oven (375°F.) 35-40 min. Cool 10 min. Remove layers from pans; cool on wire rack. Using paper pattern, cut each layer in bell shape. Fill, frost and decorate. To decorate, use rose tip of pastry tube making fancy edge. If desired, write names or initials and date in center of cake using plain tip.

Pecan Pound Cake

1 cup shortening
1½ cups sugar
2 tbs. milk
5 eggs
2 cups flour
½ tsp. mace
1 tsp. salt
¾ cup broken pecan nut meats
2 tsp. lemon juice
1 tsp. grated lemon rind

Cream together shortening and sugar; add milk. Mix well. Add eggs, 1 at a time, beating after each. Sift together flour, mace and salt; add to creamed mixture. Toast nut meats; add ½ cup to batter. Add lemon juice and rind. Pour into greased 9″ tube pan; sprinkle with remaining nut meats. Bake in moderate oven (325°F.) 1 hour 25 min. Cool 5 min. Remove cake from pan; cool on wire rack.

Gold Cake

2½ cups cake flour
4 tsp. baking powder
½ tsp. salt
⅔ cup shortening
1¼ cups sugar
7 egg yolks
⅔ cup milk
1½ tsp. vanilla extract

Sift together flour, baking powder and salt 3 times. Cream together shortening and sugar. Beat egg yolks until thick and lemon-colored; add to creamed mixture; beat well. Add flour mixture alternately with milk; add vanilla extract. Pour into greased tube pan 9″ in diameter. Bake in moderate oven (350°F.) 1-1¼ hours. Cool 10 min. Remove cake from pan; cool on wire rack.

Marble Cake

1 cup shortening	1 tsp. vanilla extract
2 cups sugar	2 squares (2 oz.)
4 eggs	unsweetened chocolate
3 cups flour	3 tbs. boiling water
4 tsp. baking powder	⅛ tsp. baking soda
¾ tsp. salt	¼ tsp. almond extract
1 cup milk	

Cream together shortening and sugar. Add eggs, 1 at a time, beating after each. Sift together flour, baking powder, and salt. Add alternately with milk to creamed mixture. Add vanilla extract. Melt chocolate over hot water; add water and soda. Divide batter in ½; to ½ add chocolate mixture and almond extract. Place batters by alternate spoonfuls in greased 9″ tube pan. Bake in moderate oven (350°F.) 1¼ hours. Cool 10 min. Remove cake from pan; cool on wire rack.

Frosted Marble Cake

Prepare Marble Cake. Prepare Confectioners' Sugar Frosting II (p. 98); spread on top and sides of cake. Garnish with semi-sweet chocolate drops.

Goldenrod Cake

Prepare Gold Batter; prepare White Batter (see below). Place batters by alternate spoonfuls in greased 9″ tube pan. Bake in moderate oven (350°F.) 50-60 min. Cool 5 min. Remove cake from pan; cool on wire rack. Prepare Confectioners' Sugar Frosting I (p. 97); divide in ½. Tint ½ yellow with vegetable coloring. Spread ½ cake with white frosting; ½ with yellow frosting.

Gold Batter

½ cup shortening	2 tsp. baking powder
¾ cup sugar	¼ tsp. salt
3 egg yolks	½ cup milk
1¾ cups flour	1 tsp. vanilla extract

Cream together shortening and sugar. Add egg yolks; beat well. Stir together flour, baking powder and salt. Add alternately with milk to creamed mixture. Add vanilla extract.

White Batter

3 egg whites	1¾ cups flour
¾ cup sugar	2 tsp. baking powder
½ cup shortening	¼ tsp. salt
½ cup milk	½ tsp. almond extract

Beat egg whites stiff. Gradually add ¼ cup sugar, beating constantly. Cream together shortening and remaining sugar. Sift together flour, baking powder and salt. Add alternately with milk to creamed mixture. Fold in egg white mixture and almond extract.

Magic Meringue Cake

¼ cup shortening	¼ tsp. salt
½ cup sugar	⅓ cup milk
2 egg yolks	¼ tsp. vanilla extract
1 tsp. baking powder	Shredded coconut
¾ cup flour	

Cream together shortening and sugar. Add egg yolks; beat well. Sift together flour, baking powder and salt; add alternately with milk to creamed mixture. Add vanilla extract. Pour into greased pan 8″ x 10″ x 2″. Sprinkle with coconut; spread with Meringue Mixture (see below). Bake in moderate oven (325°F.) 40 min. Cool; cut in squares.

Meringue Mixture

2 egg whites	¼ cup currant jelly
2 tbs. sugar	

Beat egg white stiff; add sugar gradually, beating constantly. Mash jelly; fold into egg white mixture.

Standard Chocolate Layers

½ cup shortening	1¾ cups flour
1¼ cups sugar	1 tsp. baking soda
2 eggs	Few grains salt
4 squares (4 oz.)	1 cup milk
unsweetened chocolate	1 tsp. vanilla extract

Cream together shortening and sugar. Add eggs, 1 at a time, beating after each. Melt chocolate over hot water; add. Sift together flour, soda and salt. Add alternately with milk to creamed mixture. Add vanilla extract. Pour into 2 greased 8″ layer pans. Bake in moderately hot oven (375°F.) 30 min. Cool 5 min. Remove layers from pans; cool on wire rack.

Chocolate Maple Cake

Prepare Standard Chocolate Layers. Prepare Maple Confectioners' Sugar Frosting (p. 98); spread between layers and on top of cake. Decorate with halved walnut meats.

Almond Chocolate Cake

Prepare Standard Chocolate Layers (p. 82). Prepare Boiled Frosting I (p. 94); to ⅓ add ½ cup chopped chocolate-covered almonds. Spread between layers. Spread remaining frosting on top and sides of cake. Decorate with chocolate-covered almonds.

Sour Milk Chocolate Layers

½ cup shortening	¾ tsp. baking soda
1 cup sugar	¼ tsp. salt
2 eggs	3 tsp. baking powder
3 squares (3 oz.)	1¼ cups sour milk
unsweetened chocolate	1 tsp. vanilla extract
2 cups cake flour	

Cream together shortening and sugar. Add eggs, 1 at a time, beating after each. Melt chocolate over hot water; add. Sift together flour, soda, salt and baking powder; add alternately with milk to creamed mixture. Add vanilla extract.

Pour into 2 greased 9″ layer pans. Bake in moderately hot oven (375°F.) 25 min. Cool 5 min. Remove layers from pans; cool on wire rack.

Chocolate Butterscotch Cake

Prepare Sour Milk Chocolate Layers (see above). Prepare Brown Sugar Boiled Frosting (p. 95); spread between layers and on top and sides of cake.

Chocolate Cream Cake

Prepare Sour Milk Chocolate Layers (see above). Prepare Cream Filling (p. 100); spread between layers. Prepare Boiled Frosting I (p. 94); spread on top and sides of cake.

Brown Sugar Fudge Layers

¾ cup shortening	3 egg yolks
1¾ cups firmly packed brown sugar	2¼ cups flour
	1½ tsp. baking soda
1 egg	¼ tsp. salt
4 squares (4 oz.) unsweetened chocolate	1½ cups milk
	1½ tsp. vanilla extract

Cream together shortening and sugar. Add egg; beat well. Add egg yolks, 1 at a time, beating after each. Melt chocolate over hot water; add. Sift together flour, baking soda and salt; add alternately with milk to creamed mixture. Add vanilla extract. Pour into 2 greased 9″ layer pans. Bake in moderate oven (350°F.) 40 min. Cool 5 min. Remove layers from pans; cool on wire rack.

Black and White Cake

Prepare Brown Sugar Fudge Layers. Prepare Boiled Frosting II (p. 95); spread between layers and on top and sides of cake.

Witch's Web

Prepare Brown Sugar Fudge Layers. Prepare Boiled Frosting II (p. 95), substituting ½ tsp. grated orange rind for 1 tsp. vanilla extract. Tint orange with vegetable coloring. Spread between layers and on top and sides of cake. Melt ½ square (½ oz.) unsweetened chocolate over hot water. Carefully drip chocolate from tip of spoon on cake in spiral design. Mark circumference at edge of cake in eighths; draw point of knife lightly from marks to center. When frosting is partially set, if desired, place witch candle or figure in center.

Milk Chocolate Layers

½ cup shortening	¼ tsp. baking soda
1¼ cups sugar	2½ tsp. baking powder
2 eggs	1 tsp. salt
2 squares (2 oz.) unsweetened chocolate	1 cup milk
2 cups flour	1 tsp. vanilla extract

Cream together shortening and sugar. Add eggs, 1 at a time, beating after each. Melt chocolate over hot water; add. Sift together flour, soda, baking powder and salt; add alternately with milk to creamed mixture. Add vanilla extract. Pour into two greased 9″ layer pans. Bake in moder- (350°F.) 30 min. Cool 5 min. Remove layers from pans; from pans; cool on wire rack.

Charleston Chocolate Cake

Prepare Milk Chocolate Layers (see above). Prepare Creamy Fudge Frosting (p. 97); spread between layers and on top of cake. Garnish with pecan nut meats.

Almond Milk Chocolate Cake

Prepare Milk Chocolate Layers (see above). Prepare Almond Confectioners' Sugar Frosting (p. 98); spread between layers and on top and sides of cake. Garnish with almond nut meats.

Devil's Food Layers

¾ cup shortening	2⅓ cups flour
2 cups sugar	3½ tsp. baking powder
4 eggs	½ tsp. salt
4 squares (4 oz.) unsweetened chocolate	1 cup milk
	1 tsp. vanilla extract

Cream together shortening and sugar. Add eggs, 1 at a time, beating after each. Melt chocolate over hot water; add. Sift together flour, baking powder and salt. Add alternately with milk to creamed mixture. Add vanilla extract. Pour into 2 greased 9″ layer pans. Bake in moderate oven 350°F.) 30 min. Cool 5 min. Remove layers from pans; cool on wire rack.

Cotton Blossom Cake

Prepare Devil's Food Layers. Prepare Creamy Fudge Frosting (p. 97); spread between layers and on top of cake. Decorate with cut marshmallow flowers, making centers of chocolate frosting.

Chocolate Mocha Cake

Prepare Devil's Food Layers. Prepare Mocha Confectioners' Sugar Frosting (p. 98); spread between layers and on top and sides of cake. Sprinkle with ⅓ cup chopped pecan nut meats.

Spicy Chocolate Layers

½ cup shortening	2 tsp. baking powder
1 cup sugar	½ tsp. salt
2 eggs	½ tsp. cinnamon
2 squares (2 oz.) unsweetened chocolate	¼ tsp. nutmeg
1¾ cups cake flour	¾ cup milk

Cream together shortening and sugar. Beat eggs; add. Melt chocolate over hot water; add. Sift together flour, baking powder, salt, cinnamon and nutmeg; add alternately with

milk to creamed mixture. Pour into 2 greased 8″ layer
pans. Bake in moderately hot oven (375°F.) 25 min. Cool
5 min. Remove layers from pans; cool on wire rack.

Spicy Chocolate Walnut Cake

Prepare Spicy Chocolate Layers (see above). Prepare Chocolate Confectioners' Sugar Frosting (p. 98); spread between
layers and on top and sides of cake. Garnish with halved
walnut meats.

Black-Eyed Susan Cake

Prepare Spicy Chocolate Layers (see above). Prepare Banana Filling (p. 102); spread between layers. Prepare Maple
Confectioners' Sugar Frosting (p. 98); spread on top and
sides of cake. Decorate with flowers made with salted almonds for petals and chopped semi-sweet chocolate for
centers.

Spice Loaf Cake

½ cup shortening	1 tsp. baking soda
1 cup sugar	1 tsp. cinnamon
2 eggs	½ tsp. cloves
1¾ cups flour	1 tsp. nutmeg
¼ tsp. salt	⅔ cup milk

Cream together shortening and sugar. Add eggs, 1 at a time,
beating after each. Sift together flour, salt, soda, cinnamon,
cloves and nutmeg; add alternately with milk to creamed
mixture. Pour into greased pan 8″ x 8″ x 2″. Bake in
moderate oven (325°F.) 1 hour. Cool 5 min. Remove cake
from pan; cool on wire rack.

Frosted Spice Loaf

Prepare Spice Loaf Cake (see above). Prepare Confectioners' Sugar Frosting I (p. 97); spread on top and sides of
cake.

Quick Maple Spice Cake

1 egg
½ cup sour milk
¼ cup maple sirup
¼ cup melted shortening
  or salad oil
½ cup sugar
1½ cups flour
½ tsp. baking soda
¾ tsp. cinnamon
¼ tsp. cloves
½ tsp. salt
½ cup chopped walnut
  meats

Beat egg; add milk, maple sirup and shortening or salad oil. Sift together sugar, flour, soda, cinnamon, cloves and salt; add first mixture. Mix well. Pour into greased pan 11" x 8" x 1"; sprinkle with nut meats. Bake in moderate oven (325°F.) 35 min. Cool 5 min.; cut in squares.

Economy Lemon Allspice Cake

¼ cup shortening
1 cup sugar
1 egg
6 tbs. evaporated milk
6 tbs. water
2 cups cake flour
2 tsp. baking powder
¼ tsp. salt
1 tsp. lemon extract
3 tbs. sugar
½ tsp. allspice
1 tsp. grated lemon rind
½ cup broken walnut
  meats

Cream together shortening and 1 cup sugar. Beat egg; add. Combine milk and water. Sift together flour, baking powder and salt; add alternately with milk to creamed mixture. Add lemon extract. Pour into greased pan 8" x 8" x 2". Mix 3 tbs. sugar, allspice, rind and nut meats. Sprinkle on batter. Bake in moderate oven (350°F.) 50 min. Cool 5 min.; cut in squares.

Spicy Diamonds

½ cup shortening
1 cup sugar
3 egg yolks
2 cups cake flour
3 tsp. baking powder
1 tsp. cinnamon
½ tsp. nutmeg
¾ cup milk
Confectioners' Sugar
  Frosting I (p. 97)
Walnut meat halves

Cream together shortening and sugar. Beat egg yolks; add. Sift together flour, baking powder, cinnamon and nutmeg 3 times. Add alternately with milk to creamed mixture. Pour into greased pan 8″ x 8″ x 2″. Bake in moderate oven (350°F.) 45 min. Cool 5 min. Remove cake from pan; cool on wire rack. Frost. Cut in diamonds; top each with nut meat.

Choco-Spice Layers

¾ cup shortening	¾ tsp. salt
1½ cups sugar	4½ tsp. baking powder
3 eggs	2 tsp. cinnamon
1 square (1 oz.)	½ tsp. nutmeg
unsweetened chocolate	¼ tsp. ginger
1¼ cups milk	1½ tsp. vanilla extract
3 cups cake flour	

Cream together shortening and sugar. Add eggs, 1 at a time, beating after each. Melt chocolate in ¼ cup milk; add. Sift together flour, salt, baking powder, cinnamon, nutmeg and ginger; add alternately with remaining milk to creamed mixture. Add vanilla extract. Pour into 2 greased 9″ layer pans. Bake in moderately hot oven (375°F.) 25 min. Cool 5 min. Remove layers from pans; cool on wire rack.

Dixie Chocolate Cake

Prepare Choco-Spice Layers. Prepare Fudge Frosting (pp. 96-97); spread between layers and on top of cake.

Molasses Cake

¾ cup shortening	1 tsp. cinnamon
⅔ cup sugar	½ tsp. nutmeg
3 eggs	½ tsp. cloves
¾ cup dark molasses	¾ tsp. salt
2¾ cups flour	1 cup milk
1 tsp. baking soda	

Cream together shortening and sugar. Add eggs, 1 at a time, beating after each. Add molasses. Sift together flour, soda, cinnamon, nutmeg, cloves and salt; add alternately with milk to creamed mixture. Pour into 9″ greased springform pan. Bake in moderate oven (350°F.) 1¼ hours. Cool 5 min.; remove cake from pan. Cool on wire rack.

Sponge Cake

1 cup cake flour	6 egg yolks
1 cup sugar	2 tbs. water
6 egg whites	1 tsp. grated lemon rind
¼ tsp. salt	4 tsp. lemon juice
½ tsp. cream of tartar	

Sift together 3 times flour and ½ cup sugar. Beat egg whites until foamy; add salt and cream of tartar. Beat whites until stiff, but not dry. Gradually add ½ cup sugar, beating constantly. Mix egg yolks, water, lemon rind; beat until foamy. Add lemon juice slowly. Sift ¼ cup flour over egg yolk mixture; fold in lightly. Continue until all is used. Pour egg yolk mixture over egg white mixture; fold in. Pour into 9″ ungreased tube pan. Bake in moderate oven (325°F.) 1-1¼ hours. Invert pan on wire rack 1 hour, or until cold. Remove cake from pan.

Boston Cream Pie

Prepare Sponge Cake (above). Prepare Cream Filling (p. 100). Cut sponge cake in half crosswise; spread filling between halves. Sprinkle with confectioners' sugar.

Hot Milk Sponge Cake

1 cup cake flour	1 cup sugar
1 tsp. baking powder	2 tsp. lemon juice
Few grains salt	6 tbs. milk
3 eggs	1 tsp. butter or margarine

Sift together 3 times flour, baking powder and salt. Beat eggs until light and foamy. Gradually add sugar, beating constantly. Add lemon juice. Fold in flour mixture. Combine milk and butter or margarine; heat. Quickly add to egg mixture; stir until smooth. Pour into 9″ ungreased tube pan. Bake in moderate oven (350°F.) 45 minutes. Invert pan on wire rack 1 hour, or until cold. Remove cake from pan.

Orange Sponge Cake

1 cup cake flour	1 cup sugar
1 tsp. baking powder	7 tbs. orange juice
Few grains salt	1 tsp. grated orange rind
3 eggs	1 tsp. butter or margarine

Sift together 3 times flour, baking powder and salt. Beat eggs until light and foamy. Add sugar gradually, beating constantly. Fold in flour mixture. Combine orange juice, orange rind and butter or margarine; heat. Add to egg mixture; stir until smooth. Pour into lightly greased pan 11" x 7" x 1½". Bake in moderate oven (325°F.) 1 hour. Invert pan on wire rack 1 hour, or until cold. Remove cake from pan.

Jelly Roll   Serves 8

¾ cup cake flour	3 egg yolks
1 tsp. baking powder	2 tbs. cold water
¼ tsp. salt	½ tsp. lemon extract
3 egg whites	Confectioners' sugar
¾ cup sugar	¾ cup jelly

Sift together 3 times flour, baking powder and salt. Beat egg whites stiff, but not dry; gradually fold in ½ cup sugar. Mix egg yolks and water; beat until foamy. Add ¼ cup sugar, beating until thick and lemon-colored. Add lemon extract. Fold egg yolk mixture into egg white mixture. Fold in flour mixture. Line pan 9" x 14" x 1" with greased waxed paper; pour in batter. Bake in moderate oven (350°F.) 25 min. Turn out on towel dusted with confectioners' sugar. Remove paper; trim crisp edges. Mash jelly; spread on cake. Roll up lengthwise; wrap in towel. Cool; remove towel. Sprinkle with confectioners' sugar.

Chocolate Sponge Roll
Serves 8

6 tbs. cake flour
6 tbs. cocoa
½ tsp. baking powder
¼ tsp. salt
4 egg whites

¾ cup sugar
4 egg yolks
1 tsp. vanilla extract
Confectioners' sugar
½ cup whipping cream

Sift together 3 times flour, cocoa, baking powder and salt. Beat egg whites stiff but not dry; gradually fold in sugar. Beat egg yolks until thick and lemon-colored; add vanilla extract. Fold egg yolks into egg white mixture. Fold in flour mixture. Line pan 9" x 14" x 1" with greased waxed paper; pour in batter. Bake in hot oven (400°F.) 12 min. Turn out on towel dusted with confectioners' sugar. Remove paper; trim crisp edges. Roll up lengthwise; wrap in towel. Cool slightly. Whip cream stiff. If desired, flavor and sweeten. Unroll cake, spread with cream; roll up. Sprinkle with confectioners' sugar.

Angel Food

1 cup cake flour
1⅓ cups sugar
1¼ cups (10-12) egg whites

¼ tsp. salt
1¼ tsp. cream of tartar
1 tsp. vanilla extract

Sift together 3 times flour and ⅓ cup sugar. Beat egg whites until foamy; add salt and cream of tartar; beat until stiff, but not dry. Sift sugar 3 times; sprinkle 2 tbs. over egg white mixture; fold in. Continue until sugar is used. Add vanilla extract. Sift ¼ cup flour over mixture; fold in lightly. Continue until flour is used. Pour into 9" ungreased tube pan. Bake in moderate oven (325°F.) 1 hour 15 min. Invert pan on wire rack 1 hour, or until cold. Remove cake from pan.

Toasted Almond Angel Food: Follow recipe for Angel Food, substituting 1½ tsp. almond extract for 1 tsp. vanilla extract. Pour ½ batter into 10" ungreased tube pan; add ¼ cup finely chopped toasted almond nut meats. Add remaining batter; sprinkle with ¼ cup finely chopped toasted almond nut meats. Bake in moderate oven (325°F.) 1 hour 15 min. Invert pan on wire rack 1 hour, or until cold. Remove cake from pan.

Frugal Fruit Cake

3 cups sugar
1½ tsp. cinnamon
¾ tsp. cloves
3 cups water
1½ lbs. seeded raisins
3 tbs. shortening
4½ cups flour
1½ tsp. baking soda
1½ tsp. baking powder
¾ tsp. salt
¾ cup chopped citron
⅓ cup chopped candied orange peel

Combine sugar, cinnamon, cloves, water, raisins and shortening. Bring to boil; boil 5 min. Cool. Sift together flour, soda, baking powder and salt; add to first mixture. Add citron and orange peel; mix well. Line 9″ tube pan with greased waxed paper; pour in batter. Bake in slow oven (300°F.) 2 hours. Let stand until cold; remove cake from pan. Wrap in waxed paper. Store in covered container.

Applesauce Cake

½ cup shortening
1 cup sugar
1 egg
2 cups flour
1 tsp. baking soda
½ tsp. salt
½ tsp. cloves
1 tsp. cinnamon
1 cup strained thick applesauce
⅔ cup chopped raisins
⅔ cup chopped walnut meats

Cream together shortening and sugar. Add egg; beat well. Sift together flour, soda, salt, cloves and cinnamon. Add alternately with applesauce to creamed mixture. Add raisins and nut meats. Pour into 9″ greased tube pan. Bake in moderate oven (350°F.) 1 hour. Let stand until cold. Remove cake from pan.

Christmas Gift Fruit Cake

2/3 cup shortening
2/3 cup sugar
1 cup canned strained
  cranberry sauce
2½ cups flour
1 tsp. baking soda
½ tsp. salt
1 tsp. nutmeg
1 tsp. cloves

1 tsp. allspice
1¼ tsp. cinnamon
3 tsp. baking powder
2/3 cup milk
1¼ cups seedless raisins
1¼ cups currants
1¼ cups chopped pitted
  dates
2/3 cup chopped citron

Cream together shortening and sugar. Mash cranberry sauce; add. Sift together flour, soda, salt, nutmeg, cloves, allspice, cinnamon and baking powder. Add alternately with milk to creamed mixture. Add raisins, currants, dates and citron. Pour into greased oven-proof container 10" in diam. Bake in slow oven (300°F.) 2½ hours. Let stand until cold; remove cake from container. Wrap in waxed paper. Cover; store.

White Fruit Cake

1 cup shortening
2/3 cup sugar
1 egg
3 egg yolks
1 tbs. grated orange rind
2 tbs. orange juice
1 cup sultana raisins

½ cup chopped citron
½ cup chopped candied
  pineapple
2½ cups flour
1 tsp. baking powder
½ tsp. salt

Cream together shortening and sugar; add egg; beat well. Add egg yolks, 1 at a time, beating after each. Add orange rind and juice. Dredge fruit with ½ cup flour. Sift together remaining flour, baking powder and salt; add to creamed mixture. Add fruit. Pour into greased spring-form pan 7½" in diam. Bake in slow oven (300°F.) 1½-2 hours. Cool 5 min. Remove cake from pan; cool on wire rack.

Dark Fruit Cake

½ cup shortening	¾ cup currants
1 cup firmly packed brown sugar	1 cup chopped citron
3 egg yolks	2 cups seeded raisins
¼ cup molasses	½ cup chopped candied orange peel
3 egg whites	½ cup chopped candied cherries
2 cups flour	
2 tsp. allspice	½ cup chopped candied pineapple
2 tsp. cinnamon	
¼ tsp. nutmeg	¼ cup grape juice
½ tsp. mace	1/16 tsp. baking soda
½ tsp. cloves	1 tbs. hot water

Cream together shortening and sugar. Beat egg yolks; add with molasses. Beat egg whites stiff; fold in. Sift together flour, allspice, cinnamon, nutmeg, mace and cloves. Add to creamed mixture, reserving ½ cup. Dredge currants, citron, raisins, orange peel, cherries and pineapple with remaining flour mixture; add to creamed mixture. Add grape juice. Dissolve soda in hot water; add. Line greased loaf pan 10" x 5" x 3¼" with greased heavy paper; pour in batter. Bake in slow oven (300°F.) 2½ hours. Makes 3¼ lb. loaf.

Boiled Frosting — I

1 cup sugar	2 egg whites
⅓ cup water	¾ tsp. vanilla extract
1 tsp. vinegar	

Boil together sugar, water and vinegar to 238°F. (or until sirup spins long thread when dropped from tip of spoon). Beat egg whites stiff; gradually add sirup, beating constantly, until frosting holds shape. Add vanilla extract. Makes enough to fill and frost 2 8" cake layers.

Chocolate Boiled Frosting: Follow recipe for Boiled Frosting I, adding 1½ squares (1½ oz.) melted unsweetened chocolate.

Maple Boiled Frosting: Follow recipe for Boiled Frosting I, substituting ½ tsp. maple flavoring for ¾ tsp. vanilla extract.

Boiled Frosting — II

1½ cups sugar	3 egg whites
½ cup water	Few grains salt
1½ tsp. vinegar	1 tsp. vanilla extract

Boil together sugar, water and vinegar to 238°F. (or until sirup spins long thread when dropped from tip of spoon). Beat egg whites stiff; gradually add sirup, beating constantly, until frosting holds shape. Add salt and vanilla extract. Makes enough to fill and frost 2 9″ cake layers.

Lady Baltimore Frosting: Prepare Boiled Frosting II. Fold in ¼ cup chopped dried figs, ½ cup chopped pitted dates and ½ cup chopped seedless raisins.

Lord Baltimore Frosting: Prepare Boiled Frosting II. Fold in ½ cup toasted coconut, ½ cup chopped candied cherries and ¼ cup chopped pecan nut meats.

Brown Sugar Boiled Frosting

1½ cups firmly packed brown sugar	2 egg whites
	Few grains salt
⅓ cup water	1 tsp. vanilla extract

Boil together sugar and water to 240°F. (or when small quantity dropped into cold water forms semi-firm ball). Beat egg whites stiff; gradually add sirup, beating constantly, until frosting holds shape. Add salt and vanilla extract. Makes enough to fill and frost 2 8″ cake layers.

Seven Minute Frosting

2 egg whites	¼ tsp. cream of tartar
1½ cups sugar	⅓ cup water
Few grains salt	1 tsp. vanilla extract

Combine egg whites, sugar, salt, cream of tartar and water;

place over boiling water. Beat with rotary beater about 7 min., or until frosting holds shape. Add vanilla extract. Makes enough to fill and frost 2 8″ cake layers.

Seven Minute Orange Frosting

2 egg whites
1 cup sugar
3 tbs. orange juice
½ tsp. cream of tartar

Few grains salt
8 marshmallows
½ tsp. grated orange rind

Combine egg whites, sugar, orange juice, cream of tartar and salt; place over boiling water. Beat with rotary beater about 7 min., or until frosting holds shape. Quarter marshmallows; fold into frosting until partially dissolved. Add orange rind. Makes enough to fill and frost 2 8″ cake layers.

Caramel Frosting

1 lb. (2¼ cups) firmly
  packed brown sugar
1 cup milk

⅓ cup butter or margarine
Few grains salt
1 tsp. vanilla extract

Combine sugar, milk, butter or margarine and salt. Bring to boiling point. Boil, stirring constantly, to 234°F. (or when small quantity dropped into cold water forms soft ball). Remove from heat; cool to lukewarm (110°F.). Add vanilla extract. Beat until creamy and of right consistency for spreading. Makes enough to fill and frost 3 9″ cake layers or frost 1 9″ tube cake.

Fudge Frosting

2 squares (2 oz.)
  unsweetened chocolate
1 cup milk
2 cups sugar

Few grains salt
2 tbs. light corn sirup
2 tbs. butter or margarine
1 tsp. vanilla extract

Combine chocolate and milk; cook over low heat, stirring constantly, until smooth. Add sugar, salt and corn sirup; cook, stirring constantly, until sugar dissolves and mixture boils. Boil, without stirring, to 232°F. (or when small quantity dropped into cold water forms soft ball). Remove from heat; add butter or margarine and vanilla extract. Cool to lukewarm (110°F.); beat until spreading consistency. Place over hot water to keep soft while spreading. Makes enough to fill and frost 2 9″ cake layers.

Creamy Fudge Frosting

4½ squares (4½ oz.) unsweetened chocolate
¼ cup hot water
2¼ cups confectioners' sugar
4 egg yolks
4 tbs. butter or margarine
1 tsp. vanilla extract

Melt chocolate over hot water; remove from heat. Add water and sugar. Add egg yolks, 1 at a time, beating after each. Add butter or margarine, 1 tbs. at a time. Add vanilla extract. Makes enough to fill and frost 2 9″ cake layers.

Never-Fail Chocolate Frosting

4 squares (4 oz.) unsweetened chocolate
1 tbs. water
1 13-oz. can (1⅓ cups)
sweetened condensed milk
½ tsp. vanilla extract
½ tsp. almond extract

Melt chocolate over hot water; add milk; cook 5 min., stirring constantly, until thickened. Add water, vanilla and almond extracts. Makes enough to fill and frost 2 9″ cake layers.

Confectioners' Sugar Frosting — I

¼ cup butter or margarine
2 cups confectioners' sugar
3 tbs. milk (about)
Few grains salt
¾ tsp. vanilla extract

Cream butter or margarine. Sift sugar; gradually add, creaming constantly. Add enough milk to make mixture right consistency for spreading. Add salt and vanilla extract. Makes enough to fill and frost 2 8″ cake layers or 12 medium cup cakes.

Almond Confectioners' Sugar Frosting: Follow recipe for Confectioners' Sugar Frosting I, substituting ½ tsp. almond extract for ¾ tsp. vanilla extract.

Chocolate Walnut Confectioners' Sugar Frosting: Follow recipe for Confectioners' Sugar Frosting I, adding 1 square (1 oz.) melted unsweetened chocolate and ¼ cup chopped walnut meats.

Lemon Orange Confectioners' Sugar Frosting: Follow recipe for Confectioners' Sugar Frosting I, substituting 3 tbs. orange juice for 3 tbs. milk and adding ½ tsp. grated lemon rind.

Maple Confectioners' Sugar Frosting: Follow recipe for Confectioners' Sugar Frosting I, substituting ½ tsp. maple flavoring for ¾ tsp. vanilla extract.

Confectioners' Sugar Frosting — II

5 tbs. butter or margarine	6 tbs. milk (about)
1 lb. (3½ cups) confectioners' sugar	Few grains salt
	1 tsp. vanilla extract

Cream butter or margarine. Sift sugar; gradually add, creaming constantly. Add enough milk to make mixture right consistency for spreading. Add salt and vanilla extract. Makes enough to fill and frost 2 9″ cake layers.

Chocolate Confectioners' Sugar Frosting: Follow recipe for Confectioners' Sugar Frosting II, adding 2 squares (2 oz.) melted unsweetened chocolate.

Mocha Confectioners' Sugar Frosting: Follow recipe for Confectioners' Sugar Frosting II, sifting 2 tbs. cocoa with sugar and substituting 3 tbs. freshly made coffee for 3 tbs. milk.

Orange Confectioners' Sugar Frosting: Follow recipe for Confectioners' Sugar Frosting II, substituting 6 tbs. orange juice for 6 tbs. milk and adding 1 tsp. grated orange rind.

Chocolate Cream Filling

1½ squares (1½ oz.)
    unsweetened chocolate
1¼ cups milk
½ cup sugar
3 tbs. flour

¼ tsp. salt
1 egg yolk
1 tbs. butter or margarine
½ tsp. vanilla extract

Add chocolate to milk; heat over hot water until chocolate is melted. Beat with rotary beater until blended. Mix sugar, flour and salt; gradually add chocolate mixture. Cook over hot water, stirring constantly, until thick. Beat egg yolk slightly; pour chocolate mixture over egg yolk. Cook over hot water 2 min. Add butter or margarine. Cool; add vanilla extract. Makes enough to fill 2 9″ cake layers.

Decorative Frosting

1 lb. (3½ cups)
    confectioners' sugar
½ tsp. cream of tartar

3 egg whites
1 tsp. vanilla extract

Sift together sugar and cream of tartar; add egg whites and vanilla extract. Beat with rotary beater until frosting holds shape. Cover with damp cloth until ready to use. Makes 2½ cups. To decorate cakes, press frosting through pastry tube, using fancy tips.

Ornamental Frosting

5⅔ cups confectioners'
    sugar
¾ tsp. cream of tartar

5 egg whites
1¾ tsp. vanilla extract

Sift together confectioners' sugar and cream of tartar. Add egg whites and vanilla extract. Beat until frosting holds shape. Cover with damp cloth until ready to use. Makes 4½ cups. To decorate cakes, press frosting through pastry tube, using fancy tips.

Confectioners' Sugar Glaze

1 cup confectioners' sugar
2 tbs. water
¼ tsp. vanilla extract

Blend together sugar and water. Add vanilla extract. Spread on warm cake or bread. Makes ⅓ cup.

Cream Custard Filling

⅓ cup sugar
3 tbs. flour
⅛ tsp. salt
1 cup milk

2 egg yolks
½ cup whipping cream
1 tsp. vanilla extract

Mix sugar, flour and salt. Scald milk; gradually add. Cook over hot water, stirring constantly, until thick. Cover; cook 10 min. Beat egg yolks; add hot milk mixture. Cook over hot water 2 min. Chill. Whip cream; fold into custard with vanilla extract. Makes enough to fill 3 8" cake layers.

Cream Filling

⅓ cup sugar
3 tbs. flour
Few grains salt

1 cup milk
1 egg
1 tsp. vanilla extract

Mix sugar, flour and salt. Scald milk; add. Cook over hot water, stirring constantly, 15 min. Beat egg; pour hot mixture over egg. Cook over hot water 3 min. Cool; add vanilla extract. Makes enough to fill 2 9" cake layers.

Apricot Cream Filling

1 tbs. flour
¼ cup sugar
Few grains salt
½ cup milk

1 egg
⅔ cup sieved cooked dried apricots
½ tsp. lemon juice

Mix flour, sugar and salt; add milk gradually. Cook over hot water, stirring constantly, until thick. Beat egg; add. Cook 3 min. Add apricots and lemon juice. Cool. Makes enough to fill 2 8" cake layers.

Apricot Almond Filling

1½ cups dried apricots
½ cup water
¾ cup sugar
2 tbs. butter or margarine

½ cup chopped toasted
almond nut meats
1 tsp. almond extract

Boil together apricots, water and sugar 5 min. Press through sieve. Add butter or margarine, almond extract and nut meats. Makes enough to fill 2 9″ cake layers.

Orange Filling

⅓ cup sugar
¼ cup flour
¼ tsp. salt
½ cup water

1 egg yolk
½ cup orange juice
1 tbs. lemon juice
1 tsp. grated orange rind

Mix sugar, flour and salt; add water. Beat egg yolk; add. Add orange and lemon juices. Cook over hot water, stirring constantly, until thick. Cover; cook 5 min. Add orange rind; cool. Makes enough to fill 2 9″ cake layers.

Lemon Date Filling

¼ cup sugar
3 tbs. flour
½ tsp. salt
½ cup water
2 tbs. lemon juice

½ tsp. grated lemon rind
1 tbs. butter or margarine
⅓ cup chopped walnut
meats
1 cup chopped pitted dates

Mix sugar, flour and salt; add water. Cook over hot water, stirring constantly, until thick. Add lemon juice and rind, butter or margarine, nut meats and dates. Cool; makes enough to fill 2 9″ cake layers.

Stratford Filling

Makes 2 cups

3 eggs
1 cup sugar
¼ cup lemon juice

2 tbs. melted butter or
margarine
1 tsp. vanilla extract

Beat eggs; add sugar, lemon juice and butter or margarine.

Cook over hot water, stirring constantly, until thick. Cool; add vanilla extract. Chill. (Will keep several days in refrigerator.) Use to fill cake layers or small tart shells.

Banana Filling

3 tbs. flour	½ cup mashed bananas
3 tbs. sugar	3 tbs. melted butter or
½ cup milk	margarine
2 tsp. lemon juice	Few grains salt

Mix flour and sugar; add milk. Cook over hot water, stirring constantly, until thick. Mix lemon juice and banana; add milk mixture. Cool; add butter or margarine and salt. Makes enough to fill 2 8″ cake layers.

Creamy Milk Chocolate Topping

¼ lb. sweet milk chocolate	1 cup whipping cream
1 egg	½ tsp. vanilla extract

Melt chocolate over hot water; add egg. Beat until blended. Cool slightly. Whip cream stiff; fold in with vanilla extract. Makes enough to fill and top 2 9″ cake layers or top 8″ x 8″ x 2″ loaf cake.

Strawberry Topping

To Boiled Frosting I (p. 94) add ½ cup drained sliced strawberries. Makes enough to top Angel Food (p. 91) or Sponge Cake (p. 89).

Cream Cheese Topping

1 cup cream cheese	Few grains salt
1 tsp. grated orange rind	3 tbs. orange juice
2 tsp. confectioners' sugar	

Mash cream cheese; add orange rind, sugar and salt. Slowly add orange juice, creaming constantly. Whip until light and fluffy. Makes enough to top gingerbread 8″ x 8″ x 2″.

Jelly Cream Topping

1 cup jelly   1 cup whipping cream

Mash jelly. Beat cream stiff; fold in jelly. Makes enough to
fill and top 2 8″ cake layers.

16. CANDIES AND CONFECTIONS

Vanilla Fudge   Makes 1⅛ lbs.

2 cups sugar   ¼ cup light corn sirup
⅔ cup heavy cream   ¼ tsp. salt
1 cup milk   1 tsp. vanilla extract

Combine sugar, cream, milk, corn sirup and salt. Cook slowly, stirring constantly, until mixture boils. Boil slowly, stirring occasionally, to 234°F. (or when small quantity dropped
into cold water forms soft ball). Remove from heat. Cool
to lukewarm (110°F.). Add vanilla extract; beat until mixture thickens and loses gloss. Pour into greased pan 8″ x 8″
x 2″. Cool; cut in squares. Makes 1⅛ lbs.

Cherry Almond Fudge: Follow recipe for Vanilla Fudge,
substituting 1 tsp. almond extract for 1 tsp. vanilla extract.
Just before pouring, add ½ cup halved candied cherries.
While fudge is still warm, top with additional halved candied cherries. Cool; cut in diamonds.

Chocolate Marbled Fudge: Follow recipe for Vanilla Fudge,
pausing after pouring half. Sprinkle with ½ cup chopped
semi-sweet chocolate; cover with remaining fudge; top with
additional chopped chocolate. Cool; cut in bars.

Toasted Ambrosia Fudge: Follow recipe for Vanilla Fudge.
Immediately after pouring, sprinkle over fudge ½ cup

toasted coconut and 1 tsp. grated orange rind. Press down lightly with back of spoon. Cool; cut in triangles.

Chocolate Fudge   Makes 1¼ lbs.

1 cup sugar
1 cup firmly packed brown sugar
¾ cup milk
2 tbs. light corn sirup

2 squares (2 oz.) unsweetened chocolate
3 tbs. butter or margarine
1 tsp. vanilla extract

Combine sugars, milk and corn sirup. Chop chocolate; add. Cook slowly, stirring constantly, until mixture boils. Boil slowly, stirring occasionally, to 236°F. (or when small quantity dropped into cold water forms soft ball). Remove from heat; add butter or margarine without stirring. Cool to lukewarm (110°F.). Add vanilla extract; beat until fairly thick. Pour into greased pan 8″ x 8″ x 2″. Cool; cut in squares.

Date and Walnut Fudge: Follow recipe for Chocolate Fudge. Just before pouring into pan, add ⅓ cup chopped pitted dates and ⅓ cup chopped walnut meats. Immediately after pouring, mark in diamonds; press half walnut meat on each. Cool; cut in diamonds.

Almond Pistachio Fudge: Follow recipe for Chocolate Fudge, substituting ½ tsp. almond extract for ½ tsp. vanilla extract. Just before pouring, add ⅔ cup halved pistachio nut meats. Top with additional nut meats. Cool; cut in bars.

Peanut Marshmallow Fudge: Follow recipe for Chocolate Fudge, adding ⅓ cup peanut butter with butter or margarine. Cut 10 marshmallows in small pieces. Just before pouring, add marshmallows. Cool; cut in triangles.

Brown Sugar Fudge   Makes 1¼ lbs.

3 cups firmly packed light brown sugar
1½ tbs. butter or margarine

1 cup light cream or evaporated milk
1½ tsp. vanilla extract

Combine sugar and cream or evaporated milk. Cook slowly, stirring constantly, until mixture boils. Boil slowly, stirring occasionally, to 236°F. (or when small quantity dropped into cold water forms soft ball). Remove from heat; add butter or margarine without stirring. Cool to lukewarm (110°F.). Add vanilla extract; beat until mixture holds shape and has creamy consistency. Pour into greased pan 8" x 8" x 2". Cool; cut in squares.

Toasted Marshmallow Fudge: Follow recipe for Brown Sugar Fudge. Immediately after pouring, mark fudge in diamonds; press marshmallow into center of each. Cool. Place under broiler unit or burner to toast marshmallows slightly. Cool; cut in diamonds.

Brazil Nut Fudge: Follow recipe for Brown Sugar Fudge. Just before pouring, add ½ cup coarsely chopped Brazil nut meats. Mark fudge in bars. Top with additional chopped Brazil nut meats. Cool; cut in bars.

Pineapple Cherry Fudge: Follow recipe for Brown Sugar Fudge. Immediately after pouring, mark fudge in triangles. Place triangular piece of candied pineapple and ½ candied cherry on each. Press down lightly. Cool; cut in triangles.

Coconut Fudge Drops: Follow recipe for Brown Sugar Fudge, adding 1 cup shredded coconut just before beating. Quickly drop by tablespoons on waxed paper.

Raisin Fudge Squares: Follow recipe for Brown Sugar Fudge. Just before pouring, add 1 cup seedless raisins.

Divinity Fudge   Makes 1¼ lbs.

2⅓ cups sugar	¼ tsp. salt
⅔ cup light corn sirup	2 egg whites
½ cup water	½ tsp. vanilla extract

Combine sugar, corn sirup, water and salt. Cook slowly, stirring constantly, until mixture boils. Cook slowly, without stirring, to 265°F. (or when small quantity dropped into cold water forms very hard ball), washing away crystals which form on sides of pan with moist cloth wrapped around tines of fork. Beat egg whites stiff. Gradually pour hot sirup on egg whites, beating constantly, until mixture holds shape. Add vanilla extract. Pour into greased pan 8″ x 8″ x 2″. Cut into squares.

Orange Divinity Fudge: Follow recipe for Divinity Fudge, adding 3 tbs. coarsely grated orange rind with vanilla extract.

Coconut Divinity Fudge: Follow recipe for Divinity Fudge, adding 1 cup moist-pack shredded coconut with vanilla extract. Drop by teaspoons on waxed paper.

Fondant
Makes 1 lb.

2 cups sugar	2 tbs. light corn sirup
1¼ cups water	1 tsp. vanilla extract

Combine sugar, water and corn sirup. Cook slowly, stirring constantly, until sugar is dissolved. Cook slowly, without stirring, to 238°F. (or when small quantity dropped into cold water forms soft ball). Wash away crystals which form on sides of pan with moist cloth wrapped around tines of fork. Remove from heat; pour immediately on cold wet platter. Cool to lukewarm (110°F.). Beat until white and creamy. Add vanilla extract. Knead until smooth and free from lumps. Before using, store in covered jar in refrigerator 2-3 days to ripen.

Chocolate Fondant: Measure 1 cup ripened Fondant. Melt 2 squares (2 oz.) unsweetened chocolate; knead gradually into fondant with ½ tsp. vanilla extract.

Coffee Fondant: Prepare Fondant, substituting 1¼ cups freshly made strong coffee for 1¼ cups water.

Brown Sugar Fondant: Prepare Fondant, substituting 1 cup firmly packed brown sugar for 1 cup sugar and omitting corn sirup.

Melted Fondant Candies

Place 1 cup ripened Fondant over hot water, keeping water below boiling point. Allow to melt, stirring only enough to blend. Add coloring and flavoring (see below). If fondant is too thin to form patties, allow to stand over hot water 5-10 min. until thickened. If fondant is too thick to drop from spoon, add few drops hot water gradually, stirring only enough to blend. Drop by teaspoons or tablespoons on waxed paper or lightly greased surface or into greased small muffin pans or molds. Chill until firm; loosen from paper or surface immediately or invert molds on folded towel, tapping gently to remove patties.

Peppermint Fondant Patties: To melted Fondant, add few drops oil of peppermint or peppermint extract, stirring only enough to blend.

Wintergreen Fondant Patties: To melted Fondant, add few drops oil of wintergreen or wintergreen extract and enough red vegetable coloring to tint pink, stirring only enough to blend.

Spearmint Fondant Patties: To melted Fondant, add few drops oil of spearmint and enough vegetable coloring to tint light green, stirring only enough to blend.

Fruit and Nut Fondant Loaves: Into ripened Fondant, knead any of the following combinations, kneading only enough to blend. Form into loaf; wrap in waxed paper. Chill until firm; slice. Or, pack into loaf pan; chill until firm. Unmold; slice.
1. Chopped candied cherries, candied pineapple and pistachio nut meats or coconut.
2. Chopped pitted dates and walnut meats.
3. Chopped dried apricots, raisins and Brazil nut meats.
4. Chopped dried figs and almond nut meats.

Fondant Center Balls: Form ripened Fondant into balls about ¾" in diam. Roll in chopped coconut, ground nut meats, cocoa or finely chopped semi-sweet chocolate.

Cherry or Nut Balls: Form ripened Fondant into balls about ½" in diam. Press each between two candied cherry halves, two walnut meats or pecan halves.

Neapolitan Fondant: Divide ripened Fondant into three equal parts. Into ⅓ knead chopped walnut meats and few drops maple flavoring. Into ⅓ knead chopped candied cherries and enough red vegetable coloring to tint fondant pink. Into ⅓ knead chopped shredded coconut and few drops almond extract. Pack maple flavored fondant in layer in small loaf pan; top with layer of pink fondant; top with layer of almond flavored fondant. Press firmly together. Chill until firm. Unmold; slice.

Clove or Cinnamon Fondant Patties: To melted Fondant, add few drops oil of clove or cinnamon or clove or cinnamon extract and enough vegetable coloring to color red, stirring only enough to blend. Drop by tablespoons on waxed paper or greased surface. Let stand until firm.

Lemon Fondant Patties: To melted Fondant, add few drops oil of lemon or lemon extract, and enough vegetable coloring to tint yellow, stirring only enough to blend. Drop by tablespoons on waxed paper or greased surface. Let stand until firm.

Coconut Fondant Kisses: To melted Fondant, add enough vegetable coloring to tint pink, yellow or green as desired. Add ⅓ cup shredded coconut, stirring only enough to blend. Drop by tablespoons on waxed paper or greased surface. Let stand until firm.

Nut Fondant Kisses: To melted Fondant, add ⅓ cup chopped walnut, pecan, almond or Brazil nut meats, stirring only enough to blend. Drop by tablespoons on waxed paper or greased surface. Let stand until firm.

Fruited Fondant Kisses: To melted Fondant, add ⅓ cup mixed chopped candied pineapple and cherries and few drops almond extract, stirring only enough to blend. Drop by tablespoons on waxed paper or greased surface. Let stand until firm.

Velvet Uncooked Fondant

Makes ¾ lb.

1 egg white
2 cups sifted confectioners' sugar

1/16 tsp. cream of tartar
2 tsp. butter or margarine
½ tsp. vanilla extract

Combine egg white, confectioners' sugar and cream of tartar. Mix thoroughly. Add butter or margarine and vanilla extract. Mix until smooth and creamy.

Chocolate Uncooked Fondant: Follow recipe for Velvet Uncooked Fondant, adding 2 squares (2 oz.) melted unsweetened chocolate with few drops of water to fondant. Blend thoroughly.

Chocolate Mint Pinwheels: Follow recipe for Velvet Uncooked Fondant, substituting few drops oil of peppermint or peppermint extract for ½ tsp. vanilla extract and adding enough red vegetable coloring to tint pink. Prepare recipe for Chocolate Uncooked Fondant. Roll each between 2 pieces waxed paper into oblong same size 1/16″ thick. Place pink fondant on chocolate fondant. Roll up jelly-roll fashion. Chill until firm. Slice ⅛″ thick.

Chocolate Almond Diamonds: Follow recipe for Velvet Uncooked Fondant, substituting ½ tsp. almond extract for ½ tsp. vanilla extract. Add enough vegetable coloring to tint green. Prepare double recipe for Chocolate Uncooked Fondant. Press chocolate fondant between 2 pieces waxed paper into 2 oblongs same size ⅛″ thick; repeat shaping green-tinted fondant into 1 oblong same size. Place green-tinted fondant between 2 chocolate layers; press together. Cut in diamond shaped pieces.

Maple Walnut Creams: Follow recipe for Velvet Uncooked Fondant, substituting ½ tsp. maple flavoring for ½ tsp. vanilla extract. Shape into balls ¾″ in diam.; press each between 2 walnut meat halves.

Lucky Horseshoes: Follow recipe for Velvet Uncooked Fondant, substituting few drops oil of wintergreen or wintergreen extract for ½ tsp. vanilla extract. Add enough vegetable coloring to tint green. Form into rolls 3″ in length. Roll in green-tinted sugar. Bend to form horseshoes. Chill until firm. Dip ends in melted unsweetened chocolate.

Marzipan: Blanch almond nut meats (p. 115). Using fine knife, put through food chopper. Measure; mix thoroughly with equal amount Velvet Uncooked Fondant. Add few drops almond extract. Shape into balls. If desired, roll in cocoa or grated semi-sweet chocolate.

Oriental Gems   Makes 1 lb.

2 envelopes (2 tbs.) unflavored gelatin	Few grains salt
½ cup cold water	Vegetable coloring
¾ cup boiling water	Flavoring
2 cups sugar	Powdered sugar

Soften gelatin in cold water. Combine boiling water, sugar and salt; stir until sugar is dissolved. Bring to boiling point. Add gelatin; stir until dissolved. Boil slowly 15 min. Remove from heat; tint and flavor as desired. Pour into pan 8″ x 8″ x 2″ which has been rinsed in cold water. Let stand at least 12 hours or until firm. (Do not chill in refrigerator.) Using wet knife, loosen candy from edges of pan; invert on board which has been sprinkled with sifted powdered sugar. Tap lightly to remove from pan. Cut in squares. Roll in powdered sugar.

Christmas Gems: Follow recipe for Oriental Gems, tinting green and flavoring mixture with few drops oil of peppermint. Follow recipe for Oriental Gems, tinting red and flavoring mixture with few drops of cinnamon.

Can't-Fail Caramels   Makes 1¼ lbs.

2 cups sugar	1 cup heavy cream
1 cup firmly packed brown sugar	1 cup milk
1 cup light corn sirup	1 cup butter or margarine
	4 tsp. vanilla extract

Combine sugars, corn sirup, cream, milk and butter or margarine. Cook slowly, stirring constantly, to 248°F. (or when small quantity dropped into cold water forms firm ball). Remove from heat; add vanilla extract. Pour into greased pan 8″ x 8″ x 2″. Cool. When firm, turn out on board; cut in squares. Wrap each square in waxed paper.

Chocolate Nut Caramels   Makes 2½ lbs.

1 cup sugar
1 cup firmly packed brown
   sugar
1 cup light corn sirup
1 cup sweetened condensed
   milk
½ cup light cream or
   evaporated milk

1 cup milk
6 squares (6 oz.)
   unsweetened chocolate
2 tbs. butter or margarine
2 tsp. vanilla extract
⅛ tsp. salt
1½ cups chopped walnut
   meats

Combine sugars, corn sirup, condensed milk, cream or
evaporated milk and milk; cook slowly, stirring constantly,
until sugars dissolve. Melt chocolate over hot water; add
with butter or margarine. Cook slowly, stirring constantly,
to 246°F. (or when small quantity dropped into cold water
forms firm ball). Remove from heat; add vanilla extract,
salt and nut meats. Pour into greased pan 8″ x 8″ x 2″.
Cool. When firm, turn out on board; cut in squares. Wrap
each square in waxed paper.

Butterscotch   Makes ¾ lb.

1 cup sugar
¼ cup firmly packed brown
   sugar
½ cup butter or margarine

1 tbs. vinegar
2 tbs. boiling water
Few grains salt

Combine sugars, butter or margarine, vinegar, water and
salt. Cook slowly, stirring constantly, until mixture boils.
Boil slowly, stirring frequently toward end of cooking, to
290°F. (or when small quantity dropped into cold water
separates into heavy threads). Pour into greased pan 8″ x 8″
x 2″. Cool; break into small pieces.

Crunchies

½ cup dark corn sirup
1 tbs. vinegar
⅛ tsp. salt

¼ cup molasses
2 tbs. butter or margarine
4 cups puffed cereal

Mix corn sirup, vinegar, salt and molasses; cook slowly,
stirring occasionally, to 240°F. (or when small quantity

dropped into cold water forms semi-firm ball). Add butter or margarine. Quickly stir in cereal. Pack firmly into greased pan 8″ x 8″ x 2″; cool. Cut in 2″ squares.

Molasses Taffy   Makes 1 lb.

¾ cup sugar
1½ cups light molasses

1½ tbs. butter or
   margarine
2 tsp. vinegar

Combine sugar, molasses, butter or margarine and vinegar. Cook slowly, stirring constantly, until mixture boils. Boil slowly, stirring constantly toward end of cooking, to 260°F. (or when small quantity dropped into cold water forms very hard ball). Remove from heat. Pour into greased pan; cool enough to handle. Grease hands. Form mixture into ball; pull until light yellow in color. Stretch in long rope. Cut in small pieces; wrap each piece in waxed paper.

Molasses Peppermint Taffy: Follow recipe for Molasses Taffy, adding few drops oil of peppermint to cooked mixture after removing from heat.

New Orleans Pralines   Makes 1¼ lbs.

2 cups firmly packed brown
   sugar
¼ cup water

2 cups pecan nut meats
⅓ cup butter or margarine

Combine sugar, water and butter or margarine. Cook slowly, stirring constantly, until mixture boils. Add nut meats. Boil slowly, stirring constantly, to 246°F. (or when small quantity dropped into cold water forms firm ball). Remove from heat. Drop by tablespoons on waxed paper, making patties 3″-4″ in diameter.

Butter Crunch   Makes 1 lb.

½ lb. milk chocolate
1 cup butter or margarine
1½ cups sugar

1 cup chopped walnut
   meats

Chop chocolate. Melt butter or margarine in large skillet.

Add sugar. Cook over medium heat, stirring constantly, until blended. (The butter or margarine may separate out during cooking, but after about 8 min. mixture will be smooth.) Add nut meats; pour into greased pan 8" x 8" x 2". Sprinkle immediately with chocolate; allow chocolate to melt slightly. Spread smoothly over surface. Cool. Break into small pieces.

Peanut Brittle   Makes 1½ lbs.

    1 qt. peanuts in shell   2 cups light molasses
    ½ tsp. salt   ⅔ cup sugar
    3 tbs. butter or margarine

Shell peanuts; remove skins. Separate in halves; sprinkle with salt. Melt butter or margarine; add molasses and sugar. Cook slowly to 290°F. (or when small quantity dropped into cold water separates into heavy threads). Remove from heat; add peanut meats. Pour into large greased pan, spreading as thin as possible. Cool; break into small pieces.

Molasses Popcorn Balls   Makes 8

    ⅓ cup light molasses   ¼ tsp. salt
    ¾ cup sugar   1½ tbs. butter or
    ¼ cup water   margarine
    ¼ tsp. vinegar   6 cups popped corn

Combine molasses, sugar, water, vinegar and salt; cook slowly, without stirring, to 270°F. (or when small quantity dropped into cold water separates into heavy threads). Remove from heat; add butter or margarine, stirring only enough to mix; pour over popped corn, stirring constantly. Shape lightly and quickly into balls.

Molasses Mint Popcorn Balls: Follow recipe for Molasses Popcorn Balls, adding ¼ tsp. peppermint extract with butter or margarine.

Taffy Apples

    6 large red apples   ¾ cup water
    2 cups sugar   Red vegetable coloring
    ½ cup light corn sirup   Few drops oil of cinnamon

Wash apples; dry thoroughly. Insert wooden skewer into stem end of each. Combine sugar, corn sirup and water in deep saucepan. Cook slowly, stirring constantly, until sugar is dissolved. Add enough coloring to color deep red. Cook slowly, without stirring, to 300°F. (or when small quantity dropped into cold water becomes brittle). Remove from heat; add oil of cinnamon, stirring only enough to mix. Place over boiling water. Dip apples, 1 at a time, in sirup, twirling as apple is removed. Placed on waxed paper; cool.

Orange Sugared Walnuts   Makes ¾ lb.

  1½ cups sugar   ½ tsp. grated orange rind
  ¼ cup water   2 cups walnut meats
  3 tbs. orange juice

Combine sugar, water and orange juice. Cool slowly, stirring until mixture boils. Boil slowly, without stirring, to 240°F. (or when small quantity dropped into cold water forms semi-firm ball). Remove from heat; add orange rind and nut meats. Stir until sirup begins to look cloudy. Drop by teaspoons on waxed paper. (Any nut meats may be substituted for walnut meats.)

Date Nut Roll   Makes 50

  2 cups sugar   1½ cups chopped pitted
  1 cup milk   dates
  2 tbs. butter or margarine   1 cup chopped nut meats

Combine sugar, milk and butter or margarine. Cook slowly, stirring constantly, until mixture boils. Boil slowly to 240°F. (or when small quantity dropped into cold water forms semi-firm ball). Remove from heat. Add dates and nut meats; stir until mixture thickens. Form into 2 rolls, 1½" in diam. Wrap in damp cloth; chill until firm. Slice ¼" thick.

Walnut Clusters   Makes 12

  4 oz. sweet cooking   ¾ cup broken walnut
    chocolate   meats

Chop chocolate; melt over hot water (120°F.), stirring constantly. Stir in walnut meats. Drop by tablespoons on waxed paper. Chill.

Crystallized Fruit Peels

Select oranges, grapefruit or lemons of bright color, thick peel, and without blemishes. Wash carefully; break oil cells by rubbing lightly on fine grater. Cut peel in small fancy shapes or in strips about ¼" wide. Measure peel; add 3 times as much cold water. Bring to boiling point; boil 10 min.; drain. Repeat process until peel is tender and as much bitter flavor is removed as desired. Cool peel; weigh. For each 1 lb. peel, add 2 cups sugar, ⅓ cup water. Bring to boiling point; boil slowly until sirup is absorbed. Remove immediately from heat. Put peel and some sugar into paper bag. Shake well. Pour from bag; separate pieces.

Stuffed Fruits

Use prunes, figs or dates. Steam dried prunes or figs over hot water 15 min., or until tender; dry thoroughly. Slit fruits on one side. Remove pits from prunes and dates; remove stems from figs. Stuff fruits with plain or salted walnut or pecan meat halves, Brazil nut meats, almond nut meats, peanut butter, mixed cream cheese and chopped nut meats, Fondant (p. 106), marshmallows, candied grapefruit, orange or lemon peel, cherries, pineapple, citron or ginger. Store in covered container. If desired, roll in powdered or granulated sugar.

Blanched Nut Meats

Shell almonds, pistachio nuts or nuts with thick skins. Place 2 cups or less at a time in bowl; cover with boiling water. Let stand 5 min.; drain. Plunge into cold water; rub off skins. Place nut meats in moderate oven (350°F.) until dry.

Toasted Nut Meats

Blanch nut meats if necessary; spread out in shallow pan.

If desired, sprinkle with salt. Bake in moderate oven (350°F.) 15-20 min., turning occasionally.

Salted Nut Meats

Blanch nut meats if necessary. Heat ½ cup fat or salad oil in skillet; add 1 cup nut meats at a time. Cook over low heat, stirring constantly, until browned. Drain on absorbent paper; sprinkle with salt.

17. CANNING, PICKLING, JELLY-MAKING AND PRESERVING

Canning Pointers

Checking jars and closures: Examine glass jars and closures before using to make sure there are no cracks, chips or dents and that zinc-lined closures have no loose linings. If necessary, tighten loose wire clamps on jars. Buy new rubber rings. Buy new self-sealing lids. (Do not re-use rubber rings or self-sealing lids.)

Preparing jars and closures: Wash jars and closures in soapy water; rinse in hot water. Sterilize jars by placing in pan of warm water with cloth or rack in bottom to prevent bumping. Bring to boil; boil 15-20 min. Or heat jars by placing in pan of warm water; keep hot until ready to fill. Dip rubber rings in boiling water before placing on jars. Dip self-sealing closures in boiling water before placing on jars.

Filling jars: Remove 1 jar at a time from water. If rubber ring is used, place wet ring on sealing rim of jar. Quickly fill jars. Using knife blade, work out any air bubbles formed in jar. When each is filled, wipe rubber ring and edge of jar to remove any particles of food.

Cooling and testing jars: Cool jars away from drafts. When cold, invert rubber-ring jars; observe for leakage. If seal is not complete, open jars, reheat contents and completely reprocess. When cold, test self-sealing jars, tapping with spoon. A clear ringing sound denotes seal is complete. If sound is dull, seal is not complete. Reprocess for long enough to complete seal.

Labeling jars: Wipe jars clean; label with name, date and lot number (if more than 1 lot is canned on that day).

Checking jars: Keep jars at room temperature 10 days. Observe carefully; if one jar shows any signs of spoilage, carefully examine all jars from same lot. Do not use jars which show any sign of spoilage.

Storing Jars: Store jars in cool, dark, dry place.

Directions For Closing Jars

To adjust closures before processing: For glass jar with porcelain-lined metal screw cap, place rubber ring on sealing rim of jar. Screw cap tight; turn back ¼".
For glass jar with glass disk cover, place rubber ring on sealing rim of jar. Place glass disk cover on rubber ring; snap top clamp in place, leaving side clamp up.
For glass jar with self-sealing lid, place lid on jar. Tightly fasten screw band or clamp in place.

To complete seal after processing: Immediately after removing glass jar with porcelain-lined metal screw cap from canner, screw cap tight.
Immediately after removing glass jar with glass disk cover from canner, snap side clamp down in place.
For glass jar with self-sealing lid no tightening is necessary, unless screw band has become loosened during processing. Hold lid firmly in place; screw band tight. Let jar stand overnight; remove screw band or clamp.

Directions For Using Steam Pressure Canner

All meats and non-acid vegetables should be processed in steam pressure canner. Follow manufacturer's directions for use and care of canner. Each time canner is used, add enough hot water to reach level just below rack. Place filled jars on rack leaving enough space between to allow for circulation of steam. Adjust cover; fasten securely. Leave petcock open until steam escapes in steady stream 4-7 min. (depending on size of canner and altitude). Close petcock; allow pressure to rise until desired point is registered. Start counting processing time as soon as the desired pressure point registers. Maintain constant pressure by regulating heat. When processing is completed, remove canner from heat. Cool slowly until zero point is registered. (Do not apply cold, wet cloths.) Gradually open petcock. Open canner, lifting cover carefully so that steam will not come in contact with face or hands. Let jars stand 3-4 min. Remove jars, 1 at a time. Complete seal. (See Directions for Closing Jars, p. 117.)

Directions For Using Boiling Water Bath

To process fruits and acid vegetables in boiling water bath, use water bath canner or kettle or wash boiler which is large enough to hold several jars and at least 3″ higher than jars. The kettle or boiler should be equipped with a tightly fitting cover. Place rack in canner so that jars are ½″ above bottom. Fill with boiling water. Jars should be hot when placed in canner; heat in hot water if necessary. Place jars on rack leaving enough space to allow for circulation of water. Add boiling water to cover tops of jars by 1″-2″. Bring water to boil. As soon as water boils vigorously, cover; start counting processing time immediately. Maintain constant boiling by regulating heat. If necessary, add boiling water to keep jars covered 1″-2″. When processing is completed, open canner, lifting cover carefully so that steam will not come in contact with face or hands. Remove jars, 1 at a time. Complete seal. (See Directions for Closing Jars, p. 117.)

Processing At High Altitudes

Steam pressure canner: For recipes in this book, increase

pressure for altitude above 2000', adding 1 lb. pressure for each additional 2000'.

Boiling water bath: For recipes in this book, increase processing time for altitudes above 1000', allowing 20% longer processing time for each additional 1000'.

Whole Kernel Corn

Use tender, freshly gathered sweet corn. Husk corn; cut from cob deeply enough to remove most of kernels but not hulls. Do not scrape. Measure kernels; for each quart corn add 1 teaspoon salt. Add boiling water to cover; bring to boil. Pack hot corn loosely into hot jars to within 1½" of top; add vegetable liquor to within 1" of top. Adjust covers. (See Directions for Closing Jars, p. 117.) Using steam pressure canner at 240°F., or 10 lbs. pressure, process pint jars 60 min., or quart jars 70 min.; complete seal. (See Directions for Closing Jars.)

Beets

Use uniform, young, tender, freshly gathered beets. Remove tops leaving at least 1" of stems. Do not remove roots. Wash beets; add enough boiling water to cover. Let stand 15 min. Remove skins, stems and roots. Pack beets in hot jars to within 1" of top. Add 1 tsp. salt for each quart; add hot water to within ½" of top. Adjust covers. (See Directions for Closing Jars, p. 117.) Using steam pressure canner at 240°F., or 10 lbs. pressure, process pint jars 30 min. or quart jars 35 min.; complete seal. (See Directions for Closing Jars.)

Carrots

Use uniform, young, tender, freshly gathered carrots. Remove tops; wash carrots; scrape; rinse. Add enough boiling water to cover; let stand 15 min. Pack hot carrots into hot jars to within 1" of top; add 1 tsp. salt for each quart. Add hot vegetable water to within ½" of top. Adjust covers. (See Directions for Closing Jars, p. 117.) Using steam pressure canner at 240°F., or 10 lbs. pressure, process pint jars 30 min. or quart jars 35 min.; complete seal. (See Directions for Closing Jars.)

Green Beans

Use freshly gathered green beans. Wash beans; remove ends. Cut in uniform lengths. Add boiling water to cover; simmer 5 min. or until beans are soft enough to bend without breaking. Pack hot beans loosely into hot jars to within 1″ of top; add 1 tsp. salt for each quart. Add vegetable liquor to within ½″ of top. Adjust covers. (See Directions for Closing Jars, p. 117.) Using steam pressure canner at 240°F., or 10 lbs. pressure, process pint jars 30 min. or quart jars 35 min.; complete seal. (See Directions for Closing Jars.)

Green Lima Beans

Use young, tender, freshly gathered lima beans. Shell beans; wash. Add boiling water to cover; bring to boil. Pack hot beans loosely into hot jars to within 1½″ of top. Add 1 tsp. salt for each quart; add vegetable liquor to within 1″ of top. Adjust covers. (See Directions for Closing Jars, p. 104.) Using steam pressure canner, at 240°F., or 10 lbs. pressure, process pint jars 50 min. or quart jars 55 min.; complete seal. (See Directions for Closing Jars.)

Green Peas

Use tender, freshly gathered peas. Shell peas; wash. Add hot water to cover; simmer 5 min. Pack hot peas loosely into hot pint jars to within 1½″ of top; add ½ tsp. salt for each pint; add vegetable liquor to within 1″ of top. Adjust covers. (See Directions for Closing Jars, p. 117.) Using steam pressure canner at 240°F., or 10 lbs. pressure, process pint jars 45 min.; complete seal. (See Directions for Closing Jars.)

Tomatoes

Use firm, ripe, freshly gathered tomatoes. Wash tomatoes; cover with boiling water; let stand about 1 min. Plunge into cold water, core, remove skins and any imperfect parts.

Quarter tomatoes; bring to boil. Pack closely into hot jars to within 1″ of top; add 1 tsp. salt for each quart. Add vegetable liquor or boiling water, if necessary, to within ½″ of top. Adjust covers. (See Directions for Closing Jars, p. 117.) Using boiling water bath, process pint or quart jars 5 min.; complete seal. (See Directions for Closing Jars.)

Tomato Juice

Use firm, ripe, freshly gathered tomatoes. Wash tomatoes; core. Remove any imperfect parts. Cut tomatoes in small pieces. Cover; simmer until soft. Quickly put through fine sieve, preferably cone-shaped; measure; add ½-1 tsp. salt for each quart. Bring to boiling point; pour into hot, sterilized jars filling to top; seal. (See Directions for Closing Jars, p. 117.)

Apples

Use firm, ripe, freshly gathered apples. Using 2 qt. water, 1 tbs. each salt and vinegar, make solution. Core apples; pare. Quarter, immediately putting into solution to prevent discoloration. Remove apples; add Light Sirup (p. 123) to cover. Boil 5 min. until tender but not soft. Pack hot apples into hot jars to within 1″ of top; add boiling sirup to within ½″ of top. Adjust covers. (See Directions for Closing Jars, p. 117.) Using boiling water bath, process pint or quart jars 15 min.; complete seal. (See Directions for Closing Jars.)

Apricots or Peaches

Use firm, ripe, freshly gathered apricots or peaches. Cover apricots or peaches with boiling water; let stand about 1 min. Plunge into cold water. Remove skins and any imperfect parts. Halve fruit, remove pits. One cracked pit may be used for every qt. of sirup; strain out before using. Add Light or Medium Sirup (p. 123) to cover. Simmer 4-8 min. or until fruit is tender but not soft. Pack hot fruit, cut side down, in overlapping layers into hot jars to within 1″ of top; add hot sirup to within ½″ of top. Adjust covers. (See

Directions for Closing Jars, p. 117.) Use boiling water bath, process pint or quart jars 15 min.; complete seal. (See Directions for Closing Jars.)

Berries

Use firm, ripe, freshly gathered blueberries, blackberries, huckleberries, dewberries, loganberries or raspberries. Carefully wash berries; remove caps and stems, discarding imperfect berries. Pack berries into hot jars to within 1" of top; add hot Medium Sirup (p. 123) to within ½" of top. Adjust covers. (See Directions for Closing Jars, p. 117.) Using boiling water bath, process pint and quart jars 20 min.; complete seal. (See Directions for Closing Jars.)

Cherries

Use firm, ripe, freshly gathered cherries. Wash cherries; remove stems. Prick cherries several times, reserving juice. Pack cherries and juice into hot jars to within 1" of top. To sour red cherries add hot Heavy Sirup (p. 123) or to sweet cherries add Medium Sirup (p. 123) to within ½" of top. Adjust covers. (See Directions for Closing Jars, p. 117.) Using boiling water bath, process pint or quart jars 25 min.; complete seal. (See Directions for Closing Jars.) If desired, pit cherries; add Medium Sirup (p. 123) to cover; boil 5 min. Pack hot cherries into hot jars to within 1" of top; add boiling sirup to within ½" of top. Adjust covers. (See Directions for Closing Jars.) Using boiling water bath, process pint or quart jars 5 min.; complete seal. (See Directions for Closing Jars.)

Pears

Use firm, ripe, freshly gathered pears. Using 2 qt. water, 1 tbs. each salt and vinegar, make solution. Core pears; pare. Halve, immediately putting into solution to prevent discoloration. Remove pears; add Medium Sirup (below) to cover. Boil 4-8 min., or until pears are tender but not soft. Pack hot pears into hot jars to within 1" of top; add boiling sirup to within ½" of top. Adjust covers. (See Directions for

Closing Jars, p. 117.) Using boiling water bath, process pint or quart jars 20 min.; complete seal. (See Directions for Closing Jars.)

Plums

Use firm, ripe, freshly gathered plums. Wash plums; prick skins several times. Pack plums into hot jars to within 1″ of top; add hot Medium Sirup (below) to within ½″ of top. Adjust covers. (See Directions for Closing Jars, p. 117.) Using boiling water bath, process pint or quart jars 20 min.; complete seal. (See Directions for Closing Jars.)

Light Sirup

Makes 4¼ cups

1¼ cups sugar	4 cups water

Boil together sugar and water 5 min.; skim. Allow ¾-1 cup sirup for each pt. of packed fruit.

Medium Sirup

Makes 3¾ cups

2¼ cups sugar	3 cups water

Boil together sugar and water 5 min.; skim. Allow ¾-1 cup sirup for each pt. of packed fruit.

Heavy Sirup

Makes 3⅔ cups

3½ cups sugar	2 cups water

Boil together sugar and water 5 min.; skim. Allow ¾-1 cup sirup for each pt. of packed fruit.

Bread and Butter Pickles

6 onions	6 cups sugar
6 qt. sliced cucumbers	⅓ cup mustard seed
1 cup salt	1½ tbs. celery seed
1½ qt. vinegar	¼ tsp. cayenne

Slice onions; combine with cucumbers and salt; let stand 3 hours. Drain. Combine vinegar, sugar, mustard and celery seed and cayenne. Bring to boil; boil 5 min. Add cucumbers and onions. Heat to simmering point. Pack into 8 hot, sterilized pint jars, filling to top; fasten covers at once.

Mustard Pickles

1 qt. green beans	2 tbs. turmeric
1 qt. green tomatoes	1 tbs. prepared mustard
3 green peppers	1 tbs. celery seed
1 small head cauliflower	1 tsp. whole cloves
1 qt. sliced cucumbers	⅓ cup dry mustard
1 qt. small white pearl onions	½ tbs. allspice
Salt	Vinegar
¾ cup firmly packed brown sugar	¼ cup flour
	Water

Wash beans, tomatoes, peppers and cauliflower. Halve beans. Core tomatoes; remove any imperfect parts; quarter. Cut peppers in eighths; remove stems and seeds. Separate cauliflower into small flowerets. Combine beans, tomatoes, peppers, cauliflower, cucumbers and onions; sprinkle with salt. Let stand overnight. Drain; add sugar, turmeric, prepared mustard, celery seed, cloves, dry mustard, allspice and enough vinegar to cover. Bring to boil; boil 15 min. Mix flour to smooth paste with a little water; add. Boil 5 min. or until vegetables are tender but not soft. Pack into 6 hot, sterilized pint jars, filling to top; fasten covers at once.

Piccalilli

2 qt. green tomatoes	2 cups vinegar
2 cups gherkins	¼ cup sugar
2 green peppers	1 tbs. peppercorns
¾ cup chopped onion	1 tbs. mustard seed
¼ cup salt	12 whole cloves

Wash tomatoes, gherkins and green peppers. Core tomatoes; remove any imperfect parts; chop. Chop gherkins. Halve peppers; remove stem and seeds. Chop peppers. Mix tomatoes, gherkins, peppers and onion with salt; let stand overnight. Drain, pressing out all superfluous liquid. Combine vinegar, sugar, peppercorns, mustard seed and cloves; heat.

Add vegetables; bring to boiling point. Pack into 4 hot, sterilized pint jars, filling to top; fasten covers at once.

Watermelon Sweet Pickle

8 lbs. watermelon rind
Salt
4 lbs. sugar

1 qt. vinegar
½ cup pickling spice

Use thick watermelon rind. Pare; remove any red portion. Cut in 1" cubes. Using ¼ cup salt to 1 qt. water, make solution. Add enough to cover melon rind; let stand overnight. Drain; cover with boiling water; boil until rind is tender but not soft. Combine sugar, vinegar and pickling spice; boil 5 min. Drain rind; add to sugar mixture. Boil until rind is transparent; let stand overnight. Bring to boiling point; pack in 8 hot, sterilized pint jars, filling to top; fasten covers at once.

Cinnamon Apple Jelly

5 lbs. tart ripe apples
3 cups hot water
10 drops oil of cinnamon

1 tsp. red liquid vegetable coloring
1 3-oz. pkg. powdered pectin
7 cups sugar

Wash apples; remove blossom and stem ends. (Do not pare or core.) Cut in small pieces; add water. Bring to boiling point; cover. Simmer 15 min. Mash; simmer 5 min. Place in jelly bag; squeeze out juice. (There should be 6 cups.) Pour juice into large saucepan; place over high heat. Add cinnamon, coloring and pectin; mix well. Bring to boil, stirring constantly. Add sugar, stirring; bring to full rolling boil. Boil ½ min. Remove from heat; skim. Quickly pour into 12 hot, sterilized ⅓-pint jelly glasses; paraffin at once. Cool; cover.

Blackberry Jelly

2 qt. ripe blackberries
4 cups sugar

1 3-oz. pkg. powdered pectin

Wash berries; remove caps and stems. Thoroughly crush berries. Place in jelly bag; squeeze out juice. (There should be 3 cups.) Pour juice into large saucepan; place over high heat. Add pectin; mix well. Bring to boil, stirring constantly. Add sugar, stirring. Bring to full rolling boil. Boil ½ min. Remove from heat; skim. Quickly pour into 7 hot, sterilized ⅓-pint jelly glasses; paraffin at once. Cool; cover.

Blackberry and Red Cherry Jelly

2 lbs. ripe sour red cherries	5 cups sugar
¼ cup hot water	2 cups light corn sirup
1½ qt. ripe blackberries	1 cup liquid pectin

Wash cherries; remove stems. Crush cherries; add water. Bring to boiling point; cover. Simmer 10 min. Wash berries; remove caps and stems. Crush or, using fine blade, put berries through food chopper. Place berries and cherries in jelly bag; squeeze out juice. (There should be 4 cups.) Place juice, sugar and corn sirup in large saucepan over high heat; mix well. Bring to boil; add pectin, stirring constantly. Bring to full rolling boil; boil hard ½ min. Remove from heat; skim. Quickly pour into 11 hot, sterilized ⅓-pint jelly glasses; paraffin at once. Cool; cover.

Red Cherry Jelly

2½ lbs. ripe sour red cherries	1 3-oz. pkg. powdered pectin
½ cup hot water	4 cups sugar

Wash cherries; remove stems. Crush cherries; add water. Bring to boiling point; cover. Simmer 10 min. Place in jelly bag; squeeze out juice. (There should be 3 cups.) Pour juice into large saucepan; place over high heat. Add pectin; mix well. Bring to boil, stirring constantly. Add sugar, stirring; bring to full rolling boil. Boil ½ min. Remove from heat; skim. Quickly pour into 8 hot, sterilized ⅓-pint jelly glasses; paraffin at once. Cool; cover.

Currant Jelly

3 qt. ripe red currants   1 3-oz. pkg. powdered pectin
1½ cups hot water   6½ cups sugar

Wash currants; remove stems. Crush currants; add water. Bring to boiling point; simmer 10 min. Place in jelly bag; squeeze out juice. (There should be 6 cups.) Pour juice into large saucepan; place over high heat. Add pectin; mix well. Bring to boil, stirring constantly. Add sugar, stirring; bring to full rolling boil. Boil ½ min. Remove from heat; skim. Quickly pour into 12 sterilized ⅓-pint jelly glasses; paraffin at once. Cool; cover.

Grape Jelly

5 lbs. ripe Concord grapes   7½ cups sugar
½ cup hot water   ½ cup liquid pectin

Wash grapes; remove stems. Crush grapes; add water. Bring to boiling point; cover. Simmer 5 min. Place in jelly bag; squeeze out juice. (There should be 4 cups.) Place juice and sugar in large saucepan over high heat; mix well. Bring to boil; add pectin, stirring constantly. Bring to full rolling boil; boil hard ½ min. Remove from heat; skim. Quickly pour into 11 hot, sterilized ⅓-pint jelly glasses; paraffin at once. Cool; cover.

Honey Jelly

2½ cups liquid honey   ¾ cup water
½ cup liquid pectin

Place honey and water in large saucepan over high heat; mix well. Bring to boil. Add pectin, stirring constantly. Bring to full rolling boil. Remove from heat; skim. Quickly pour into 5 hot, sterilized ⅓-pint jelly glasses; paraffin at once. Cool; cover.

Marjoram and Lemon Jelly

1 cup boiling water   3 cups sugar
2 tbs. marjoram   ½ cup liquid pectin
⅓ cup lemon juice

Pour water over marjoram. Cover; let stand 15 min. Strain through fine-mesh cheesecloth. Measure marjoram infusion; add water to make 1 cup. Strain lemon juice through fine-mesh cheesecloth. Place infusion, lemon juice and sugar in large saucepan over high heat. Bring to boil; add pectin, stirring constantly. Bring to full rolling boil; boil hard ½ min. Remove from heat; skim. Quickly pour into 4 hot, sterilized ⅓-pint jelly glasses; paraffin at once. Cool; cover.

Peach and Plum Jelly

2 lbs. ripe peaches	1 3-oz. pkg. powdered pectin
1 lb. ripe red plums	4 cups sugar
¾ cup hot water	

Wash fruit. Crush; add water. Bring to boiling point; cover. Simmer 10 min. Place in jelly bag; squeeze out juice. (There should be 3 cups.) Pour juice into large saucepan; place over high heat. Add pectin; mix well. Bring to boil, stirring constantly. Add sugar, stirring; bring to full rolling boil. Boil ½ min. Remove from heat; skim. Quickly pour into 8 hot, sterilized ⅓-pint jelly glasses; paraffin at once. Cool; cover.

Thyme and Grape Jelly

½ cup boiling water	1½ cups grape juice
1 tbs. thyme	½ cup liquid pectin
3 cups sugar	

Pour water over thyme. Cover; let stand 15 min. Strain through fine-mesh cheesecloth. Measure thyme infusion; add water to make ½ cup. Place infusion, sugar and grape juice in large saucepan over high heat; mix well. Bring to boil; add pectin, stirring constantly. Bring to full rolling boil; boil hard ½ min. Remove from heat; skim. Quickly pour into 5 hot, sterilized ⅓-pint jelly glasses; paraffin at once. Cool; cover.

Apricot or Peach Jam

Use firm, ripe, freshly gathered apricots or peaches. Cover apricots or peaches with boiling water; let stand about 1 min. Plunge into cold water. Remove skins and any imperfect parts. Halve fruit; remove pits. Weigh fruit; weigh ¾ amount sugar to fruit. For each lb. apricots; add 2 tbs. lemon juice to sugar. Crush fruit; alternate layers fruit and sugar in saucepan, ending with sugar. Cover; let stand 3-4 hours. Bring to boil, stirring constantly; boil slowly, stirring occasionally, until thick. Pour into hot, sterilized pint jars, filling to top; fasten covers at once.

Berry Jam

Use firm, ripe, freshly gathered strawberries, raspberries or blackberries; wash. Remove hulls or caps and stems. Weigh berries; weigh equal amount sugar to fruit. Crush berries; bring to boil. Add sugar; boil slowly, stirring occasionally until thick. Pour into hot, sterilized pint jars, filling to top; fasten covers at once.

Concord Conserve

2½ qt. ripe Concord grapes
1 cup hot water
4 cups sugar
1 cup orange pulp
2 cups drained crushed pineapple
2 cups seedless raisins
1½ cups broken walnut meats

Wash grapes; separate pulp and skins. Place pulp in saucepan; simmer 10 min. Press through sieve. Add water to skins; bring to boiling point. Simmer 15 min. Combine pulp, skins, sugar, orange pulp, pineapple and raisins; bring to boil. Boil slowly, stirring occasionally, 45 min. or until thick. Add walnut meats. Pour into 3 hot, sterilized pint jars, filling to top; fasten covers at once.

Orange Walnut Marmalade

1 grapefruit
3 oranges
6 cups water
6 cups sugar
1 cup coarsely chopped walnut meats

Wash fruit; cut in eighths. Remove seeds and pulp. Cut peel in thin strips; add pulp, water and sugar. Let stand overnight. Boil slowly, stirring occasionally, about 1½ hours or until thick and peel is tender. Add walnut meats. Pour into 2 hot, sterilized pint jars, filling to top; fasten covers at once.

Peach Chutney

1 large onion	⅔ cup chopped crystallized
½ lb. seedless raisins	ginger
1 small garlic clove	2 tbs. mustard seed
4 lbs. ripe peaches	1 tbs. salt
2 tbs. chili powder	1 qt. vinegar
	1¼ lbs. brown sugar

Using medium blade, put onion, raisins, garlic through food chopper. Peel peaches; cut in small pieces. Add to first mixture with remaining ingredients. Bring to boiling point; boil slowly, stirring occasionally, 1 hour, or until thick and rich brown in color. Pour into 3 hot, sterilized pint jars, filling to top; fasten covers at once.

Pear Chips

8 lbs. ripe pears	¼ lb. preserved ginger
4 lbs. sugar	4 lemons

Wash pears; remove stems. Core pears; pare. Cut in small pieces. Add sugar and ginger; let stand overnight. Cut lemon in small pieces; remove seeds. Add lemon to pear mixture. Bring to boiling point; boil slowly, stirring occasionally, 3 hours or until thick. Pour into 6 hot, sterilized pint jars, filling to top; fasten covers at once.

Plum Conserve

3 pt. ripe purple plums	3 cups seeded raisins
2 lemons	1 cup chopped walnut
2 oranges	meats
4½ cups sugar	

Wash plums; remove pits. Cut pulp in small pieces. Grate rind from lemons and oranges; squeeze juice. Combine plum pulp, lemon and orange juice and rind, sugar and raisins. Bring to boil; boil slowly, stirring occasionally, until thick. Add walnut meats. Pour into 3 hot, sterilized pint jars, filling to top; fasten covers at once.

Apple Butter

Use firm, ripe, freshly gathered apples. Core apples; pare; slice. Measure apples; add equal amount cider. Simmer apples until soft. Press through sieve; measure sieved fruit. Add ½ as much sugar and few grains salt. Bring to boil. Boil, stirring frequently, until thick and no rim of liquid separates out when butter is dropped on cold surface. Pour into hot, sterilized jars, filling to top; fasten covers at once. If desired, add stick cinnamon and whole cloves tied in cheesecloth to butter while cooking. Remove before pouring into jars.

Apricot or Peach Butter

Use firm, ripe, freshly gathered apricots or peaches. Cover apricots or peaches with boiling water; let stand about 1 min. Plunge into cold water. Remove skins and any imperfect parts. Halve fruit; remove pits. Crush fruit; simmer until soft. Press through sieve; measure sieved fruit. Add ½ as much sugar and few grains salt. Bring to boil. Boil, stirring frequently, until thick and no rim of liquid separates out when butter is dropped on cold surface. Pour into hot, sterilized pint jars, filling to top; fasten covers at once. If desired, add stick cinnamon and whole cloves tied in cheesecloth to butter while cooking. Remove before pouring into jars.

18. CEREALS, MACARONI, NOODLES, SPAGHETTI AND RICE

Quick-Cooking Oats

Serves 4-6

To 3 cups rapidly boiling salted water, gradually add 1½ cups quick-cooking oats. Cook 2½ min., or longer if desired, stirring constantly.

Rolled Oats

Serves 4-6

To 3 cups rapidly boiling salted water, gradually add 1½ cups rolled oats. Cook 5 min., or longer if desired, stirring constantly.

Wheat Cereal

Serves 4-6

To 3 cups rapidly boiling salted water, gradually add ½ cup wheat cereal, stirring constantly until thickened. Cook slowly 15 min.

Quick-Cooking Wheat Cereal

Serves 4-6

To 2½-3 cups rapidly boiling salted water, gradually add ½ cup quick-cooking wheat cereal, stirring constantly until thickened. Cook slowly 5 min.

Cereal Cooked in Milk

To cook cereal in milk, add cereal to scalded milk, substituting milk for water specified in recipe and cooking, covered, over hot water until thickened and done.

To Serve Cooked or Ready-To-Serve Cereal

1. Top with sugar, brown sugar, maple sirup, corn sirup, molasses or honey; serve with milk, top milk or cream.

2. If desired, sprinkle cereal with cinnamon or nutmeg. Top with chopped dried apricots, prunes or figs, pitted dates, raisins or nut meats; serve with milk, top milk or cream.
3. Top with fruit; serve with milk, top milk or cream.
4. Combine equal quantities 2 or more ready-to-serve cereals; serve as suggested above.

Cereal Cooked With Fruit

Follow recipe for cooking cereal, adding ¼ cup chopped dried apricots, prunes or figs, pitted dates, raisins or nut meats a few minutes before cooking is completed.

Yellow Corn Meal Mush   Serves 4-6

Combine ½ cup yellow corn meal and ½ cup water; to 2½ cups rapidly boiling salted water, gradually add corn meal mixture. Cook, stirring constantly, 5 min., or until thickened. Place over boiling water; cover. Cook 30 min., stirring occasionally.

White Corn Meal Mush   Serves 4-6

To 3 cups hot salted water, gradually add ½ cup white corn meal. Cook, stirring constantly, until thick and boiling. Place over boiling water; cover. Cook 30 min., stirring occasionally.

Sautéed Mush   Serves 4-6

Prepare white or yellow Corn Meal Mush (above); pour into greased mold. Cover; chill until firm. Cut slices ½" thick; coat with flour or corn meal. Sauté in fat or salad oil, turning to brown on both sides. If desired, serve with maple sirup, corn sirup, molasses or honey.

Polenta   Serves 4-6

1 cup yellow corn meal	Grated Parmesan-style
4 cups water	cheese
1 tsp. salt	Meat and Tomato Sauce
	(p. 291)

Combine corn meal and 1 cup cold water. Bring remaining water to boil. Gradually add corn meal mixture and salt. Cook, stirring constantly, 5 min., or until thickened. Place over hot water; cover. Cook 30 min. Add ½ cup cheese; pour into greased baking dish. Sprinkle with cheese. Bake in moderate oven (350°F.) until brown. Serve with sauce.

Ham Scrapple   Serves 4-6

⅔ cup quick-cooking wheat cereal
3 cups boiling water
1 cup minced cooked or canned ham
¾ tsp. salt
Few grains pepper
1½ tsp. sage
Flour
Fat or salad oil

Gradually add cereal to water, stirring constantly until thickened. Cook slowly 5 min. Add ham, salt, pepper and sage. Pour into greased mold. Cover; chill until firm. Cut slices ½" thick; coat with flour. Sauté in fat or salad oil, turning to brown on both sides. If desired, serve with maple sirup, corn sirup, molasses or honey.

Giblet Scrapple Squares   Serves 6

Turkey giblets
½ cup white corn meal
1½ cups boiling water
1¼ tsp. salt
1 tsp. sage
1½ cups cooked or canned whole kernel corn
1 tsp. sugar
3 tbs. fat or salad oil
Flour

Cook giblets according to directions (pp. 275-76); mince. Gradually add corn meal to water; cook, stirring constantly, until thick and boiling. Place over boiling water; cover. Cook 30 min., stirring occasionally. Add salt and sage. Chop corn; add sugar. Combine giblets, corn meal mush and corn. Pour into greased mold. Cover; chill until firm. Cut slices ½" thick; coat with flour. Sauté in fat or salad oil, turning to brown on both sides.

Boiled Rice   Serves 4

1 cup rice
3 tsp. salt
2 qt. boiling water

Wash rice in cold running water until water is clear; drain. Add salt to water; gradually add rice. Boil 20-25 min., or until tender, lifting several times with fork to prevent sticking. Rinse with hot water; drain. To keep hot, place in colander; cover with towel. Place over hot water.

Rice Cooked in Milk
Serves 4

1 cup rice
1½ cups milk

1 tsp. salt

Wash rice in cold running water until water is clear; drain. Combine rice, milk and salt; cover. Cook over boiling water about 1 hour or until rice is tender and milk absorbed. If desired, water may be substituted for milk.

Creamy Rice Croquettes
Serves 4

1 cup cooked rice
½ cup Thick White Sauce
 (p. 326)
½ cup chopped dried
 apricots
¼ cup sugar

¼ tsp. cinnamon
Few grains salt
2 egg whites
1 tsp. water
Dry crumbs

Combine rice, sauce, apricots, sugar, cinnamon and salt. Beat 1 egg white stiff; fold in. Chill until firm. Shape into croquettes. Beat remaining egg white slightly; add water. Dip croquettes in egg white mixture; roll in crumbs. Fry in shallow fat or salad oil heated to 375°F. 3 min. or until brown. Drain on absorbent paper. If desired, roll in confectioners' sugar.

Boiled Macaroni or Spaghetti
Serves 4-6

1 tbs. salt
4 qt. boiling water

1 9-oz. pkg. macaroni or
 spaghetti

Add salt to water; gradually add macaroni or spaghetti. Boil 9 min., stirring occasionally. Drain.

Baked Macaroni and Cheese
Serves 4-6

1 9-oz. pkg. macaroni
½ lb. American cheese

Salt and pepper
Milk

Cook macaroni according to directions for Boiled Macaroni (see above). Cube cheese. Alternate layers macaroni and cheese in greased baking dish, sprinkling with salt and pepper. Add enough milk to come to within ½" of top of macaroni. Bake in moderate oven (350°F.) 40 min.

Macaroni American
Serves 4-6

1 9-oz. pkg. macaroni
1 No. 2 can (or 2½ cups cooked) tomatoes
1 tsp. sugar
½ tsp. Worcestershire sauce

1 tsp. salt
Few grains pepper
1 bay leaf
½ lb. American cheese

Cook macaroni according to directions for Boiled Macaroni (p. 135). Combine tomatoes, sugar, Worcestershire sauce, salt, pepper and bay leaf; heat. Cube cheese. Alternate layers macaroni, tomatoes and cheese in greased baking dish. Cover; bake in moderate oven (350°F.) 15 min.

Chicken Cassolettes

Melt butter or margarine; season with Worcestershire sauce. Add ½" bread cubes; brown. Heat cooked or canned macaroni and cheese. Add chopped, cooked left-over chicken and chicken livers. Place in individual casseroles; top with bread cubes. Bake in moderate oven (350°F.) 15 min.

Spaghetti With Sauce
Serves 4-6

Prepare Meat and Tomato Sauce (p. 328), Creole Sauce (p. 328) or Quick Tomato Sauce (p. 329). Cook spaghetti, according to directions for Boiled Spaghetti (p. 135). Combine spaghetti and sauce; sprinkle generously with grated Parmesan-style cheese.

Quick Spaghetti Casserole

Combine cooked or canned spaghetti and diced cooked frankfurters. Place in greased baking dish; top with soft bread crumbs; dot with butter or margarine. Bake in moderate oven (325°F.) 20 min.

Boiled Noodles   Serves 4

1 tbs. salt
4 qt. boiling water

1 6-oz. pkg. noodles

Add salt to water; gradually add noodles. Boil 9 min., stirring occasionally. Drain.

Noodle Cheese Ring   Serves 4-6

1 6-oz. pkg. noodles
3 eggs
1 cup milk

1½ cups grated American
   cheese
1 tsp. salt
Few grains pepper

Break noodles in 1" pieces. Cook according to directions for Boiled Noodles (p. 137). Beat eggs. Scald milk; add. Add cheese, salt and pepper. Add noodles. Pour into greased ring mold 8½" in diameter. Bake in moderate oven (325°F.) 1 hour 10 min. or until inserted knife comes out clean. Unmold; if desired, serve creamed meat, fish or vegetable mixture in center.

Noodles Creole   Serves 4-6

¼ cup chopped onion
¼ cup chopped green
   pepper
2 tbs. chopped ripe olives
⅔ cup chopped
   mushrooms

3 tbs. fat or salad oil
2 cups cooked or canned
   tomatoes
1½ tbs. flour
Salt and pepper
1 6-oz. pkg. noodles

Combine onion, green pepper, olives, mushrooms and tomatoes; cook in fat or salad oil 10 min. Blend in flour; cook, stirring constantly, until thickened. Cook 5 min. Season with salt and pepper. Cook noodles according to directions for Boiled Noodles (p. 137). Serve tomato mixture on noodles.

19. CHEESE

Cheese Fondue   Serves 4-6

1 cup milk	½ tsp. salt
3 egg yolks	1¼ cups grated American
1 tbs. butter or margarine	cheese
1 cup bread cubes	3 egg whites

Scald milk over hot water. Beat egg yolks; add milk. Add butter or margarine, bread and salt. Cook over hot water, stirring constantly, until thickened. Add cheese; cool. Beat egg whites stiff, but not dry; fold in. Pour into greased baking dish. Bake in moderate oven (350°F.) 55 min. (If desired, pour mixture into individual baking dishes; bake in moderate oven [350°F.] 30 min.) Serve immediately.

Cheese Casserole   Serves 4-6

6 bread slices	1 cup milk
½ lb. thinly sliced	½ tsp. salt
American cheese	Few grains pepper
2 eggs	Butter or margarine

Place 2 bread slices in greased baking dish; top with ½ cheese. Repeat; top with remaining bread. Beat eggs; add milk, salt and pepper; pour into baking dish. Dot with butter or margarine. Bake in moderate oven (325°F.) 30 min.

Cheese Soufflé   Serves 4-6

3 tbs. butter or margarine	Dash tabasco
3 tbs. flour	¾ cup milk
½ tsp. salt	1½ cups grated American
Few grains pepper	cheese
¼ tsp. Worcestershire	4 egg yolks
sauce	4 egg whites

Melt butter or margarine; blend in flour, salt, pepper, Worcestershire sauce and tabasco. Gradually add milk. Cook over hot water, stirring constantly, until thick. Add cheese. Beat egg yolks; add. Cool. Beat egg whites stiff, but not dry; fold in. Pour into greased baking dish. Bake in moderate oven (325°F.) 1 hour. Serve immediately.

Tomato Cheese Soufflé   Serves 4-6

3 tbs. butter or margarine	1 cup grated American
3 tbs. flour	cheese
½ tsp. salt	3 egg yolks
Few grains cayenne	3 egg whites
1 cup tomato juice	

Melt butter or margarine; blend in flour, salt and cayenne. Gradually add tomato juice. Cook over hot water, stirring constantly, until thick. Add cheese. Beat egg yolks; add. Cool. Beat egg whites stiff, but not dry; fold in. Pour into greased baking dish. Bake in moderate oven (325°F.) 50 min. (If desired, pour mixture into individual baking dishes; bake in moderate oven [325°F.] 30 min.) Serve immediately.

Welsh Rarebit   Serves 4

2 tbs. butter or margarine	¼ tsp. Worcestershire
2 tsp. flour	sauce
¼ tsp. salt	1 cup milk
Few grains cayenne	1 lb. Cheddar cheese
1 tsp. dry mustard	1 egg
	4 slices toast

Melt butter or margarine; blend in flour, salt, cayenne, mustard and Worcestershire sauce. Gradually add milk; cook over hot water, stirring constantly, until thick. Grate cheese; add. Stir constantly until cheese is melted. Beat egg slightly; add; cook 2 min. Serve on toast.

Cheese Puffs   Makes 36

½ lb. American cheese	36 salted crackers
2 egg whites	

Grate cheese. Beat egg whites stiff; fold in cheese. Mound on crackers. Place 3″ below broiler unit or tip of flame; broil until puffed and brown. Serve hot. Serve with soup or salad.

Cheddar Pennies   Makes 48

½ cup shortening
3 tbs. sugar
1 egg
1½ cups grated Cheddar
    cheese
1¾ cups flour

1 tsp. baking powder
½ tsp. salt
Few grains cayenne
2 tbs. milk
Paprika

Cream together shortening and sugar. Beat egg; add. Add cheese. Sift together flour, baking powder, salt and cayenne; add alternately with milk. Mix well; chill until firm. Roll out ⅛″ thick on lightly floured board; cut with round cutter 1½″ in diam.; sprinkle with paprika. Bake in moderately hot oven (375°F.) 15 min. Serve with soup or salad.

Cheesettes

Cut fresh bread in 1-1½″ cubes. Beat 1 egg; add 1 tbs. melted butter or margarine. Dip cubes in egg mixture; roll in grated Parmesan-style cheese. Place on greased baking sheet. Bake in moderately hot oven (375°F.) 15 min. Serve hot. Serve with soup or salad.

Refrigerator Cheese Chips   Makes 50

1½ cups flour
½ tsp. salt
¼ tsp. paprika
Few grains cayenne
½ cup shortening

¾ cup grated American
    cheese
Milk
Caraway, celery or poppy
    seeds
Cold water

Sift together flour, salt, paprika and cayenne. Cut in shortening with 2 knives or pastry blender. Add cheese. Add enough water to hold ingredients together. Shape into roll 1½″ in diam. Wrap in waxed paper. Chill until firm. Slice thin; place on greased baking sheet. Brush tops with milk; sprinkle with seeds. Bake in hot oven (400°F.) 10 min. Serve hot. Serve with soup or salad. (Dough will keep several days in refrigerator.)

Cheese Croutons   Makes 50

¼ lb. American cheese	½ cup flour
¼ cup shortening	Few grains cayenne

Grate cheese; combine with shortening. Blend in flour and cayenne. Chill until firm. Pinch off bits of dough; roll into tiny balls about size of peas. Bake in very hot oven (450°F.) 5 min. Serve with soup.

Superlative Cheese Cake

Crust:

1 6-oz. pkg. zwieback	1 tsp. cinnamon
¼ cup melted butter or margarine	½ tsp. allspice
	½ tsp. ginger
¼ cup sugar	½ tsp. cloves

Roll zwieback into fine crumbs; blend with butter or margarine. Mix together sugar, cinnamon, allspice, ginger and cloves. Combine with zwieback mixture. Reserve ½ cup crumb mixture for topping; press remainder firmly on bottom and sides of 9″ spring-form pan.

Filling:

1 lb. cream cheese	1 tbs. lemon juice
¾ cup powdered sugar	1 tsp. grated lemon rind
2 tbs. flour	½ cup whipping cream
¼ tsp. salt	½ cup milk
4 egg yolks	4 egg whites

Mash cheese; beat until light and fluffy. Sift together sugar, flour and salt; mix with cheese. Beat egg yolks until thick and lemon colored; add with lemon juice and rind. Add milk and cream slowly; mix thoroughly. Beat egg whites stiff, but not dry; fold in. Pour into crumb-lined 9″ spring-form pan; sprinkle with remaining crumb mixture. Bake in moderate oven (350°F.) 1½ hours. Cool.

20. COOKIES

Vanilla Wafers

Makes 75

½ cup shortening
1 cup sugar
3 eggs
2 tbs. milk
1½ tsp. vanilla extract

2¾ cups flour
2 tsp. baking powder
1 tsp. salt
Shredded coconut or
  chopped walnut meats

Cream together shortening and sugar. Beat 2 eggs; add. Add milk and vanilla extract. Sift together flour, baking powder and salt; add. Mix well. Wrap in waxed paper; chill until firm. Roll out ⅛″ thick on lightly floured board; cut with fancy cookie cutter 2″ in diam. Beat 1 egg; brush on cookies. Sprinkle with coconut or nut meats. Place on greased baking sheet; bake in hot oven (400°F.) 8 min. (If desired, omit nut meats or coconut and frost cookies with Orange Confectioners' Sugar Frosting, p. 98.)

Chocolate Sticks

Makes 75

½ cup shortening
1 cup sugar
3 squares (3 oz.)
  unsweetened chocolate
2 eggs

1 tsp. vanilla extract
2¼ cups flour
½ tsp. salt
¾ tsp. baking soda

Cream together shortening and sugar. Melt chocolate over hot water; add. Beat eggs; add. Add vanilla extract. Sift together flour, soda and salt; add. Mix well. Wrap in waxed paper; chill until firm. Roll out ⅛″ thick on lightly floured board; cut in 1″ x 3″ strips. Place on greased baking sheet; bake in moderately hot oven (375°F.) 10 min.

Pinwheel Cookies

Makes 80

Follow recipes for Vanilla Wafers and Chocolate Sticks (see p. 142), rolling out vanilla and chocolate dough in oblongs 8″ x 15″ x ⅛″ on waxed paper. Place chocolate dough on vanilla dough; trim edges. Roll up jelly-roll fashion. Wrap in waxed paper; chill until firm. Slice ¼″ thick. Place on greased baking sheet; bake in moderately hot oven (375°F.) 12 min.

Filled Cookies

Makes 25

⅔ cup shortening
½ cup sugar
1 egg

3 tbs. milk
¼ tsp. vanilla extract
2 cups flour

Cream together shortening and sugar. Add egg, milk and vanilla extract. Add flour; mix well. Chill until firm. Roll out ⅛″ thick on lightly floured board; cut with round cutter 2½″ in diameter. Put teaspoon Raisin Filling or Honey Fruit Filling in center of ½ the rounds; cover with remaining rounds. Press edges together with tines of fork. Place on greased baking sheet; bake in moderately hot oven (375°F.) 10 min.

Raisin Filling:

½ cup chopped seedless raisins
¼ cup firmly packed brown sugar
1 tbs. flour

Few grains salt
1 tbs. lemon juice
2 tbs. water
¼ cup chopped walnut meats

Combine raisins, sugar, flour, salt, lemon juice and water; cook over low heat, stirring constantly, until thick. Add nut meats. Cool.

Honey Fruit Filling:

½ cup chopped pitted dates
½ cup chopped seedless raisins
3 tbs. lemon juice

1 tbs. liquid honey
1½ tbs. butter or margarine
¼ cup chopped walnut meats

Combine dates, raisins, lemon juice, honey, butter or margarine and nut meats; heat. Cool.

Rich Golden Cookies   Makes 45

1¼ cups shortening	½ tsp. almond extract
1½ cups sugar	3¼ cups flour
3 eggs	¼ cup grated orange rind

Cream together shortening and 1 cup sugar. Add eggs, 1 at a time, beating after each. Add almond extract. Add flour; mix well. Using rose tip, press dough through pastry tube on greased baking sheet, making cookies 2″ in diam. Mix rind and remaining sugar; sprinkle on cookies. Bake in hot oven (400°F.) 13 min.

Budapest Beauties: Follow recipe for Rich Golden Cookies, placing dough by teaspoons on greased baking sheet and pressing down tops slightly. After baking, spread with Chocolate Confectioners' Sugar Frosting (p. 98) or Orange Confectioners' Sugar Frosting (p. 98).

Sprits   Makes 35

½ cup shortening	½ tsp. almond extract
¼ cup sugar	1¼ cups flour
1 egg	½ tsp. baking powder
½ tsp. vanilla extract	

Cream together shortening and sugar. Beat egg; add. Add vanilla and almond extracts. Sift together flour and baking powder; add. Mix well. Put through cookie press, making cookies 2″ in diam., on greased baking sheet. Or, wrap in waxed paper; chill until firm. Roll out ¼″ thick on lightly floured board; cut with round cutter 2″ in diam. Bake in hot oven (400°F.) 8 min.

Chocolate Sprits: Follow recipe for Sprits, adding 1½ squares (1½ oz.) melted unsweetened chocolate and 2 tsp. milk to creamed mixture.

Fancy Cookies   Makes 40

1 cup shortening	3½ cups flour
1 cup sugar	½ tsp. baking powder
2 eggs	½ tsp. salt
1¼ tsp. vanilla extract	

Cream together shortening and sugar. Add eggs, 1 at a time, beating after each. Add vanilla extract. Sift together flour, baking powder and salt; add. Mix well. Wrap in waxed paper; chill until firm. Roll out small amount of dough at a time ¼" thick on lightly floured board. Cut with fancy-shaped cutter about 2" in diam. Place on greased baking sheet; bake in moderate oven (350°F.) 15 min.

Holly Wreath Cookies: Follow recipe for Fancy Cookies, cutting dough with doughnut cutter 3" in diam. After baking, brush with egg white. Decorate with holly wreath of sliced green gumdrops and bits of candied cherries. Bake in moderate oven (350°F.) 5 min. to set garnish.

Holly Leaf Cookies: Follow recipe for Fancy Cookies, cutting dough in holly leaf shape using cardboard pattern. Immediately after baking, brush cookies with egg white; sprinkle with sugar tinted green with vegetable coloring.

Crisp Chocolate Spice Cookies: Follow recipe for Fancy Cookies, adding 1 square (1 oz.) melted unsweetened chocolate to creamed mixture and sifting with dry ingredients 2 tsp. cinnamon and ½ tsp. nutmeg. Cut dough in 2" squares.

Chocolate Holly Spray Cookies: Follow recipe for Crisp Chocolate Spice Cookies. After baking, immediately brush with egg white. Decorate with holly spray of sliced citron and bits of candied cherries. Bake in moderate oven (350°F.) 5 min. to set garnish.

Quick Ginger Cookies   Makes 36

¼ cup milk	¼ cup melted shortening
1 pkg. gingerbread mix	or salad oil

Add milk and shortening or salad oil to gingerbread mix.

Mix well. Chill until firm. Roll out ¼″ thick on lightly floured board. Cut with round cutter 2″ in diam. Place on greased baking sheet. Bake in moderate oven (350°F.) 12 min.

Quick-Change Cookies   Makes 40

½ cup shortening
½ cup sugar
1 egg
¾ tsp. vanilla extract

1¼ cups flour
1½ tsp. baking powder
¼ tsp. salt

Cream together shortening and sugar. Beat egg; add. Add vanilla extract. Sift together flour, baking powder and salt; add. Mix well. Chill until firm. Roll out ⅛″ thick on lightly floured board; cut with round cutter 2″ in diam. Place on greased baking sheet; bake in moderate oven (350°F.) 10 min.

Tropicovals: Follow recipe for Quick-Change Cookies, omitting vanilla extract and sifting with dry ingredients ½ tsp. cinnamon, ¼ tsp. nutmeg and ⅛ tsp. cloves.

Dresden Delights: Follow recipe for Quick-Change Cookies, substituting ¼ tsp. almond extract for ¾ tsp. vanilla extract.

Autumn Leaves: Follow recipe for Quick-Change Cookies, adding 1 square (1 oz.) unsweetened melted chocolate to creamed mixture.

Orange Crescents: Follow recipe for Quick-Change Cookies, rolling out dough ¼″ thick and cutting with crescent-shaped cutter. Before baking, sprinkle with mixture of 1 tbs. sugar and ½ tsp. grated orange rind.

Coconut Jumbles: Follow recipe for Quick-Change Cookies, rolling out dough ¼″ thick and cutting with fluted round cutter 2″ in diam. Before baking, sprinkle with plain or colored shredded coconut.

Nibbles: Follow recipe for Quick-Change Cookies, cutting

dough in fancy shapes and sprinkling with chopped nut meats.

Marmalade Triangles: Follow recipe for Quick-Change Cookies, cutting dough in 2″ squares; spread squares with marmalade. Fold over; press edges together with tines of fork.

Horns of Plenty: Follow recipe for Quick-Change Cookies, cutting dough in 2″ squares. Spread with mixture of ½ cup chopped seedless raisins, ½ cup chopped candied lemon peel and 2 tbs. lemon juice. Fold cornucopia-fashion.

Oases: Follow recipe for Quick-Change Cookies, cutting dough with round cutter 2½″ in diam. Spread ½ with mixture of ½ cup chopped pitted dates, ⅔ cup peanut butter, 2 tbs. corn sirup and 2 tbs. water. Cut center from remaining rounds; place on filling; press edges together with tines of fork.

Diamond Sweetmeats: Follow recipe for Quick-Change Cookies, cutting dough with diamond-shaped cutter. Spread ½ with mixture of ½ cup chopped walnut meats, 6 tbs. liquid honey and 1 tsp. lemon juice. Top with remaining diamonds; press edges together with tines of fork.

Chocolate Gingerbread Men   Makes 24

½ cup shortening	⅔ cup sugar
½ cup molasses	1 tsp. baking powder
2 squares (2 oz.)	½ tsp. baking soda
unsweetened chocolate	1 tsp. ginger
Confectioners' Sugar	¼ tsp. salt
Frosting I (p. 97)	¼ cup milk
2½ cups flour	

Combine shortening, molasses and chocolate; heat over hot water, stirring occasionally, until blended. Cool. Sift together flour, sugar, baking powder, soda, ginger and salt; add first mixture. Add milk; mix well. Chill until firm. Roll out ⅛″ thick on lightly floured board; cut in shape of gingerbread men about 6″ in length. Bake in moderately hot oven (375°F.) 6 min. Cool; decorate with frosting.

Chocolate Crispies   Makes 48

⅓ cup shortening	1½ cups flour
1 cup sugar	¼ tsp. baking soda
2 eggs	½ tsp. salt
2 squares (2 oz.) unsweetened chocolate	½ cup chopped walnut meats
½ tsp. vanilla extract	

Cream together shortening and sugar. Beat eggs; add. Melt chocolate over hot water; add. Add vanilla extract. Sift together flour, soda and salt; add. Add nut meats; mix well. Form in 2 rolls 2″ in diam.; wrap in waxed paper. Chill until firm; slice ⅛″ thick. Place on greased baking sheet; bake in moderately hot oven (375°F.) 8 min. (For variety, chill dough in cookie forms of clubs, hearts, spades or diamonds.)

Crisp Maple Refrigerator Cookies   Makes 60

1 cup shortening	1 tsp. maple flavoring
⅔ cup firmly packed brown sugar	3 cups flour
	1½ tsp. baking powder
1 egg	½ tsp. salt

Cream together shortening and sugar. Add egg; beat well. Add flavoring. Sift together flour, baking powder and salt; add. Mix well. Shape into 2 rolls 2″ in diam.; wrap in waxed paper. Chill until firm; slice ⅛″ thick. Place on greased baking sheet; bake in hot oven (400°F.) 8 min.

Marble Cookies   Makes 36

½ cup shortening	1 square (1 oz.) unsweetened chocolate
⅔ cup sugar	5 tsp. milk
1 tsp. vanilla extract	
1¼ cups flour	

Cream together shortening and sugar; add vanilla extract.

Add flour; mix well. Divide dough in ½. Add milk to ½ of dough, mix well. Melt chocolate over hot water; add to remaining dough; mix well. Roll vanilla dough into oblong ⅛″ thick on lightly floured board; roll chocolate dough same size. Place chocolate dough on vanilla dough; roll up jelly-roll fashion. Fold in ½ lengthwise; press together. Shape into 2 rolls 2″ in diam.; wrap in waxed paper. Chill until firm; slice ¼″ thick. Place on greased baking sheet; bake in moderate oven (350°F.) 12 min.

Quick Peanut Cookies   Makes 36

½ cup shortening	1 tsp. baking powder
½ cup firmly packed brown sugar	¾ tsp. salt
	2 tbs. milk
1 egg	½ cup chopped peanut meats
1½ tsp. vanilla extract	
2 cups flour	

Cream together shortening and ½ cup sugar. Beat egg; add. Add vanilla extract. Sift together flour, baking powder and salt; add. Mix well. Shape into 2 rolls 2″ in diam.; wrap in waxed paper. Chill until firm; slice ⅛″ thick. Place on greased baking sheet. Brush with milk; sprinkle with nut meats. Bake in hot oven (400°F.) 8 min.

Sugar Cookies   Makes 60

1 cup shortening	1½ tsp. baking powder
½ cup sugar	¾ tsp. salt
1 egg	Milk
1 tsp. lemon extract	Sugar
2¼ cups flour	

Cream together shortening and ½ cup sugar. Beat egg; add. Add lemon extract. Sift together flour, baking powder and salt; add. Mix well. Shape into 2 rolls 2″ in diam.; wrap in waxed paper. Chill until firm; slice ⅛″ thick. Place on greased baking sheet; brush with milk; sprinkle with sugar. Bake in hot oven (400°F.) 6 min.

Brownies

½ cup shortening
1 cup sugar
2 eggs
½ cup flour
2 squares (2 oz.) unsweetened chocolate

Few grains salt
1 cup chopped walnut meats
½ tsp. vanilla extract

Cream together shortening and sugar. Beat eggs; add. Melt chocolate over hot water; add. Beat thoroughly. Mix flour, salt and nut meats; add. Add vanilla extract; mix well. Spread in greased pan 8" x 8" x 2". Bake in moderate oven (350°F.) 30 min. Cool; cut in squares.

Bran Brownies

1 cup shortening
1 cup sugar
2 eggs
2 squares (2 oz.) unsweetened chocolate

½ cup bran
⅓ cup flour
½ tsp. salt
1 cup broken walnut meats
1 tsp. vanilla extract

Cream together shortening and sugar. Beat eggs; add. Melt chocolate over hot water; add. Beat thoroughly. Mix together bran, flour, salt, nut meats; add. Add vanilla extract; mix well. Spread in greased pan 8" x 8" x 2". Bake in moderate oven (350°F.) 45 min. Cool; cut in squares.

Brownie Bars: Follow recipe for Bran Brownies, reserving ½ cup walnut meats and sprinkling on batter in pan. Cut in bars.

Brownie Cup Cakes: Follow recipe for Bran Brownies, putting batter into small greased cup cake pans. Frost with Confectioners' Sugar Frosting I (p. 97). Makes about 12.

Butterscotch Corn Flake Bars

2 eggs
1 cup firmly packed brown sugar
½ tsp. grated orange rind
¾ cup corn flakes

¾ cup flour
1 tsp. baking powder
⅛ tsp. salt
1 cup walnut meats

Beat eggs; add sugar. Cook over hot water, stirring constantly, 15 min. Add rind; cool. Add corn flakes. Sift together flour, baking powder and salt; add. Add nut meats; mix well. Spread in greased pan 8" x 8" x 2". Bake in moderate oven (350°F.) 20 min. Cool; cut in bars.

Date Bars

1 egg
½ cup sugar
½ cup melted shortening or salad oil
1 cup chopped pitted dates
¼ cup chopped walnut meats
½ cup flour
½ tsp. baking powder
¼ tsp. salt
Powdered sugar

Beat egg; add sugar; mix well. Add shortening or salad oil. Add dates and nut meats. Sift together flour, baking powder and salt; add. Mix well. Spread in greased pan 8" x 8" x 2". Bake in moderate oven (325°F.) 30 min. Cool; cut in bars. Roll in powdered sugar.

Date Marguerites

2 egg whites
½ cup sugar
½ cup coarse graham cracker crumbs
1 tsp. baking powder
¼ tsp. salt
1 cup chopped pitted dates
½ cup chopped walnut meats
½ tsp. vanilla extract

Beat egg whites stiff; add sugar gradually, beating constantly. Mix crumbs, baking powder and salt; fold into egg white mixture with dates, nut meats and vanilla extract. Spread in greased pan 8" x 8" x 2". Bake in moderate oven (350°F.) 35 min. Cool; cut in squares.

Oatmeal Bars

½ cup shortening
¾ cup firmly packed brown sugar
1 cup flour
½ tsp. baking powder
Few grains salt
¾ cup milk
1 cup rolled oats
¾ cup chopped seedless raisins
Confectioners' Sugar Frosting I (p. 97)

Cream together shortening and sugar. Sift together flour, baking powder and salt; add alternately with milk to creamed mixture. Add oats and raisins; mix well. Spread in greased pan 8" x 8" x 2". Bake in moderate oven (350°F.) 45 min. Cool; cut in bars. Frost.

Wheat Flake Bars

½ cup shortening
1 cup firmly packed brown sugar
2 eggs
2 tsp. vanilla extract
1½ cups flour
2 tsp. baking powder

½ tsp. salt
1 cup chopped pitted dates
1 cup chopped walnut meats
3 cups wheat flakes
Confectioners' sugar

Cream together shortening and sugar. Beat eggs; add. Add vanilla extract. Sift together flour, baking powder and salt; add. Add dates, nut meats and wheat flakes; mix well. Spread in greased pan 8" x 8" x 2". Bake in hot oven (400°F.) 18 min. Cool; cut in bars. Roll in confectioners' sugar.

Wheat Flake Diamonds: Follow recipe for Wheat Flake Bars, cutting in diamond-shaped pieces. Frost with Chocolate Confectioners' Sugar Frosting (p. 98).

Wheat Flake Peaks: Follow recipe for Wheat Flake Bars, substituting 1 cup moist-pack shredded coconut for 1 cup chopped pitted dates. Drop by teaspoons on greased baking sheet; bake in hot oven (400°F.) 10 min. Makes 36.

Chocolate Coconut Cookies   Makes 40

½ cup shortening
½ cup sugar
½ cup firmly packed brown sugar
1 egg
1½ cups flour

½ tsp. baking soda
¼ tsp. salt
1 7-oz. bar semi-sweet chocolate
½ cup moist-pack shredded coconut

Cream together shortening and sugars. Beat egg; add. Sift

together flour, soda and salt; add. Chop chocolate; add with coconut. Mix well. Drop by teaspoons on greased baking sheet; bake in moderately hot oven (375°F.) 10 min.

Coconut Macaroons   Makes 24

½ cup sweetened   2 cups shredded coconut
  condensed milk   1 tsp. almond extract

Combine milk and coconut. Add almond extract. Drop by teaspoons on greased baking sheet. Bake in moderate oven (350°F.) 10 min. Immediately remove from sheet.

Molasses Drop Cookies   Makes 42

½ cup shortening   ½ cup sour milk
½ cup sugar   2½ cups flour
½ cup molasses   1½ tsp. cinnamon
1 egg   ½ tsp. ginger
1 tsp. baking soda   ¼ tsp. cloves
½ cup chopped seedless   ½ tsp. salt
  raisins

Cream together shortening and sugar; add molasses. Beat egg; add. Dissolve soda in milk. Sift together flour, cinnamon, ginger, cloves and salt; add alternately with milk mixture to creamed mixture. Add raisins; mix well. Drop by teaspoons on greased baking sheet; bake in moderate oven (350°F.) 12 min.

Nuggets   Makes 40

⅔ cup shortening   1 tsp. cinnamon
1 cup firmly packed brown ½ tsp. salt
  sugar   ¾ cup broken walnut
2 eggs   meats
1½ cups flour   ¾ cup chopped seedless
2 tsp. baking powder   raisins or pitted dates

Cream together shortening and sugar. Beat eggs; add. Sift together flour, baking powder, cinnamon and salt; add. Add nut meats and raisins or dates. Drop by teaspoons on greased baking sheet; bake in moderately hot oven (375°F.) 15 min.

Oatmeal Cookies   Makes 30

½ cup shortening	1 tsp. baking powder
⅔ cup sugar	1 tsp. cinnamon
2 eggs	½ tsp. nutmeg
¼ cup milk	½ tsp. salt
1 cup flour	1 cup rolled oats

Cream together shortening and sugar. Beat eggs; add with milk. Sift together flour, baking powder, cinnamon, nutmeg and salt; mix with oats. Add; mix well. Drop by teaspoons on greased baking sheet. Bake in moderate oven (350°F.) 20 min.

Sugarplum Cookies: Follow recipe for Oatmeal Cookies, adding 1 cup chopped walnut meats and 1 cup seedless raisins to batter.

Chocolate Oatmeal Cookies: Follow recipe for Oatmeal Cookies, adding 2 squares (2 oz.) melted unsweetened chocolate and 2 tbs. milk to creamed mixture.

Tropical Cookies: Follow recipe for Oatmeal Cookies, adding 1 cup chopped pitted dates and ½ cup moist-pack shredded coconut to batter.

English Rolled Wafers   Makes 40

½ cup molasses	⅔ cup sugar
½ cup butter or margarine	1 tsp. ginger
1 cup flour	¼ tsp. salt

Heat molasses to boiling point; add butter or margarine. Stir until melted. Sift together twice flour, sugar, ginger and salt. Add to molasses mixture gradually; mix well. Drop by ½ teaspoons 2½" apart on greased baking sheet. Bake in moderate oven (350°F.) 12 min. Cool slightly; turn over. Roll, glossy side out, over handle of wooden spoon. (If cookies become too crisp to roll, heat a few minutes in oven.)

Marguerites   Makes 12

1 egg white
3 tbs. sugar
¼ tsp. almond extract
Few grains salt

3 tbs. chopped walnut
meats
12 salted crackers

Beat egg white stiff, but not dry; add sugar, beating constantly. Add almond extract, salt and nut meats. Mound by teaspoons on crackers. Place on ungreased baking sheet; bake in slow oven (300°F.) 15 min.

21. DESSERTS

Baked Apples   Serves 4

Select 4 firm, uniform, large baking apples; wash; core. Pare ⅓ way down from top; place apples in baking dish. Fill cavity of each apple with 2 tbs. sugar, few grains cinnamon and 1 tsp. butter or margarine. Add ½ cup hot water; cover. Bake in moderate oven (350°F.) 50 min., or until tender. Remove apples; boil sirup until thick; pour over apples. Serve hot or cold with thin cream.

Jack Horner Apples   Serves 4

4 red baking apples
⅓ cup crushed corn flakes
2 tbs. chopped walnut
meats

¼ cup chopped pitted
dates
½ cup firmly packed brown
sugar
½ cup hot water

Wash apples; core. Pare ⅓ way down from top. Combine corn flakes, nut meats and dates; fill apples. Place in baking dish; sprinkle with sugar. Add water; cover. Bake in moderate oven (350°F.) 50 min.

Breakfast Apples   Serves 4

⅔ cup sugar	1 stick cinnamon
½ cup water	½ lemon peel
2 whole cloves	6 medium cooking apples

Combine sugar, water, cloves, cinnamon and lemon peel; bring to boiling point. Pare apples; core. Cut in eighths; add to sirup. Cook slowly 5-8 min., or until apples are almost tender. Remove from heat; cool in sirup. Remove spices and peel.

Apple Delight   Serves 4

6 cups cubed peeled apples	½ cup water
1 tbs. coarsely grated orange rind	½ cup powdered sugar
	Whipped cream

Combine apple, rind and water; simmer about 20 min., or until tender. Place in individual serving dishes. Sprinkle with sugar; top with cream.

Apricot Cream   Serves 4-6

¼ cup butter or margarine	½ cup sieved cooked dried apricots
1 cup confectioners' sugar	1 cup whipping cream
1 tsp. vanilla extract	12 lady fingers

Cream butter or margarine and sugar. Add vanilla extract; add apricots. Whip cream; fold in. Split lady fingers; line sherbet glasses. Top with apricot mixture.

Apricot Whip   Serves 4

1 cup sieved cooked dried apricots	Few grains salt
⅓ cup sugar	2 egg whites
1 tsp. lemon juice	Custard Sauce (p. 322)

Combine apricots, sugar, lemon juice and salt. Beat egg whites stiff; fold into apricot mixture. Chill; serve with sauce.

Baked Bananas
Serves 4

4 firm bananas
2 tsp. sugar

Few grains salt
2 tbs. butter or margarine

Peel bananas. Place in shallow greased baking dish. Sprinkle with sugar and salt; dot with butter or margarine. Bake in moderately hot oven (375°F.) 15 min. Serve immediately.

Brazilian Bananas
Serves 4

¼ cup confectioners' sugar
1 tbs. cocoa
4 bananas

Chopped Brazil nut meats
Whipped cream

Sift together sugar and cocoa. Peel bananas; roll in sugar mixture. Chill. Sprinkle with nut meats; top with cream.

Blueberries Columbia
Serves 4

1 pt. blueberries
½ cup whipping cream
1 banana

1 tbs. powdered sugar
Few grains nutmeg

Wash blueberries; place in individual serving dishes. Whip cream slightly. Peel banana; press through fine sieve. Add banana purée, sugar and nutmeg to cream. Pour over blueberries.

Broiled Honeyed Grapefruit

Halve grapefruit; remove seeds. Core; loosen sections. Spread with liquid honey; sprinkle with cinnamon and mace. Dot with butter or margarine. Brown under broiler unit or burner. Serve immediately.

Baked Grapefruit
Serves 4

2 cups crushed corn flakes
½ cup firmly packed brown sugar
½ tsp. cinnamon

¼ cup melted butter or margarine
2 grapefruit

Combine corn flakes, sugar, cinnamon and butter or margarine. Halve grapefruit; remove seeds. Core; loosen sections. Fill and top with corn flake mixture. Bake in hot oven (400°F.) 10-15 min. Serve immediately.

Peach Dessert Bowl
Serves 4-6

1 No. 2½ can (3½ cups)
   peach halves
Almond extract

Thinly-sliced Brazil nut
   meats

Chill peach halves; drain, reserving sirup. Flavor sirup to taste with almond extract. Arrange peach halves in serving dish; cover with sirup. Mound nut meats in center.

Spiced Peach Cup
Serves 4-6

1 No. 2½ can (3½ cups)
   peach halves
½ cup water

2″ stick cinnamon
6 whole cloves
Few grains ginger

Drain peach halves, reserving sirup. Add water, cinnamon, cloves and ginger to sirup. Simmer 15-20 min.; strain. Pour hot sirup over peach halves. Chill.

Prune Russe
Serves 4

1 lb. prunes
2 tbs. sugar
1 tbs. lemon juice

½ cup whipping cream
12 lady fingers

Wash prunes; cover with water. Cook slowly about 45 min., or until soft. Drain; cool. Remove pits. Reserve 6 whole prunes. Press remaining prunes through fine sieve. Add sugar and lemon juice. Place in serving dish; chill. Whip cream; spread on prune mixture. Arrange lady fingers around edge of bowl. Garnish with prunes.

Peaches Parisiennes
Serves 4

½ cup whipping cream
1 tbs. brandy flavoring
Few grains salt

3 tbs. powdered sugar
Few grains mace
8 peaches

Whip cream slightly; add flavoring, salt, 1 tbs. sugar and mace. Whip until cream is thickened. Peel peaches; slice. Add remaining sugar; mix well. Arrange in individual serving dishes; top with cream mixture.

Baked Honey Pears   Serves 4

4 pears
½ cup liquid honey

4 tsp. minced candied or
  preserved ginger
½ cup hot water

Halve pears; core; place in baking dish. Add honey; sprinkle with ginger. Add water; cover. Bake in moderate oven (350°F.) 45 min. or until tender.

Pineapple Ambrosia   Serves 4

1 No. 2 can (2½ cups)
  pineapple cuts

Sherry flavoring
½ cup shredded coconut

Chill pineapple cuts; drain off most of sirup. Flavor pineapple to taste with sherry flavoring; place in serving dish. Sprinkle with coconut.

Rhubarb Compote   Serves 4

1½ lbs. rhubarb
1 cup sugar
2" stick cinnamon

1 orange
Mint sprigs

Wash rhubarb; do not peel. Cut in 4" pieces; combine with sugar. Place in baking dish. Break cinnamon in small pieces; add. Cover; bake in moderate oven (350°F.) 40 min., or until tender, stirring after 20 min. Chill. Arrange in individual serving dishes. Peel orange; slice; use as garnish with mint.

Spiced Apricots and Cherries   Serves 4-6

1 No. 2 can (2½ cups)
  apricot halves
1 stick cinnamon

1 No. 2 can (2½ cups)
  pitted sour red cherries
6 whole cloves

Drain apricot halves and cherries, reserving sirup; combine

fruits. Add cinnamon and cloves to sirup; boil 5 min. Cool; strain. Pour over fruit; chill.

Cherry Grapefruit Cup

Combine equal quantities black cherries and membrane-free grapefruit sections. Chill.

Pineapple Zip
Serves 4

2 cups diced pineapple
½ cup orange juice
2 tbs. maraschino sirup

¼ cup powdered sugar
Few grains cinnamon

Combine pineapple, juice, maraschino sirup, sugar and cinnamon. Chill.

Canton Fruit Cup

Combine diced pineapple, membrane-free orange sections and sliced bananas. Add a little minced preserved ginger. Chill.

Strawberry Pineapple Cup
Serves 4

1 cup halved strawberries
1 cup diced pineapple

Mint sprigs
2 tbs. powdered sugar

Combine strawberries and pineapple. Crush mint leaves with sugar; add to fruit. Chill. Garnish with mint.

Strawberry Orange Cup
Serves 4

2 cups strawberries
¼ cup powdered sugar

½ cup orange juice
2 tsp. grated orange rind

Wash strawberries; hull. Sprinkle with sugar. Add orange juice and rind; chill.

Minted Fruit Mélange
Serves 4

1 cup cubed pears
1 cup cubed pineapple
Sugar

1 cup membrane-free
  orange sections
Chopped fondant mints

Combine pears, pineapple and orange sections; sprinkle with sugar and mints. Chill.

Spring Fruit Cup   Serves 4

½ cup whipping cream
½ cup diced cooked or
  canned apricots
½ cup halved pitted grapes

½ cup diced membrane-
  free orange sections
½ cup diced pineapple
2 tbs. powdered sugar

Whip cream; fold in apricots, orange sections, grapes, pineapple and sugar. Chill.

Baked Cantaloupe   Serves 4

2 cantaloupes
3 cups sliced peaches
½ cup sugar

Few grains mace
Mint sprigs

Halve cantaloupes; remove seeds. Combine peaches, sugar and mace. Fill cantaloupes with peaches, arranging slices in radiating pattern on top. Bake in hot oven (425°F.) 15 min. Garnish with mint. Serve at once.

Watermelon Hawaii

Cut watermelon in balls. Mix a little grenadine with pineapple juice; pour over watermelon. Chill. Garnish with mint.

Honey Fruit Bowls

Arrange overlapping membrane-free orange sections in individual serving dishes. Arrange melon balls in ring around orange sections. Arrange pitted halved red grapes and mint leaves in center. Serve with mixed liquid honey and lemon juice.

Honeyed Fruit Compote   Serves 4-6

1½ lbs. rhubarb
⅓ cup liquid honey
⅓ cup sugar

1 No. 2 can (2½ cups)
  pear halves

Wash rhubarb; do not peel. Cut in 2″ pieces; place in shallow baking dish. Mix honey and sugar; pour over rhubarb. Cover; bake in moderate oven (350°F.) 40 min. or until tender, stirring after 20 min. Chill. Arrange in serving dish. Drain pears; place on rhubarb.

Rhubarb Strawberry Compote   Serves 4-6

2 lbs. rhubarb	Sugar
2 tbs. water	1 pt. strawberries

Wash rhubarb; do not peel. Cut in 1″ pieces. Place in baking dish; add water and sugar. Cover; bake in moderate oven (350°F.) 30 min. Wash strawberries; hull. Add; bake 10 min. Chill.

Soft Custard   Serves 4

2 tbs. sugar	2 egg yolks
1 tsp. flour	1½ cups milk
Few grains salt	½ tsp. vanilla extract

Mix sugar, flour and salt. Beat yolks slightly; add milk. Add to sugar mixture. Cook over hot water, stirring constantly, until mixture thickens and coats spoon. Add vanilla extract. Chill.

California Custard   Serves 4

¼ cup sugar	1 cup evaporated milk
2 tbs. cornstarch	½ tsp. almond extract
Few grains salt	2 oranges
1 egg	8 pitted cooked prunes
1 cup water	Shredded coconut

Mix sugar, cornstarch and salt. Beat egg; add with water and milk. Cook over hot water, stirring constantly, until thick. Cool. Add almond extract. Pour into serving dish. Separate oranges into membrane-free sections; use as garnish with prunes and coconut.

Fresh Fruit Floating Island   Serves 4

¼ cup sugar
2 tsp. cornstarch
¼ tsp. salt
2 cups milk
3 egg yolks
½ tsp. vanilla extract
⅛ tsp. almond extract

Few grains nutmeg
2 cups well-drained pitted cherries, sliced peaches, plums, pears or blueberries
Meringue Crown (below)

Mix sugar, cornstarch and salt; gradually add milk. Cook over hot water, stirring constantly, until slightly thickened. Beat egg yolks; add hot milk mixture. Cook over hot water, stirring constantly, until mixture thickens and coats spoon. Cool. Add vanilla and almond extracts and nutmeg. Pour into shallow serving dish; add 1 cup fruit. Chill. Top with meringue crown. Fill crown with remaining fruit.

Meringue Crown

3 egg whites
6 tbs. sugar

Few grains salt

Beat egg whites stiff, but not dry. Gradually add sugar and salt, beating constantly. Pile meringue in ring on greased 9″ pie plate. Place in shallow pan of warm water. Bake in moderate oven (325°F.) 20 min. Cool.

Strawberry Puff   Serves 4-6

2 tbs. sugar
1 tbs. cornstarch
Few grains salt
2 eggs
1 cup milk

1 cup whipping cream
½ tsp. vanilla extract
¼ tsp. almond extract
12 lady fingers
Preserved strawberries

Mix sugar, cornstarch and salt. Beat eggs; add with milk. Cook over hot water, stirring constantly, until mixture thickens and coats spoon. Chill. Whip cream; fold in. Add vanilla and almond extracts. Split lady fingers; halve. Arrange in sherbet glasses; top with cream mixture. Garnish with strawberries.

Individual Baked Custards   Serves 4

3 cups milk	Few grains salt
3 eggs	1 tsp. vanilla extract
3 tbs. sugar	Nutmeg

Scald milk. Beat eggs; add sugar, salt and vanilla extract. Gradually add milk. Pour into individual custard cups; sprinkle with nutmeg. Place in pan of hot water; bake in moderate oven (350°F.) 30 min. or until inserted knife comes out clean. Cool. If desired, serve with Spiced Pineapple Sauce (p. 324).

Zabaglione   Serves 4

6 egg yolks	3 tbs. sherry flavoring
3 tbs. sugar	3 tbs. water
Few grains salt	

Beat egg yolks slightly; add sugar, salt, sherry flavoring and water. Place over hot water; beat with rotary beater about 3 min. or until thick. (Do not let water boil.) Serve immediately.

Large Baked Custard   Serves 4-6

4 cups milk	Few grains salt
6 eggs	1 tsp. vanilla extract
¼ cup sugar	Nutmeg

Scald milk. Beat eggs; add sugar, salt and vanilla extract. Gradually add milk. Pour into baking dish; sprinkle with nutmeg. Place in pan of hot water; bake in moderate oven (350°F.) 1 hour or until inserted knife comes out clean. Cool.

Bread Pudding   Serves 4-6

1 qt. milk	⅓ cup sugar
2 cups bread cubes	½ tsp. salt
¼ cup butter or margarine	1 tsp. vanilla extract
2 eggs	Few grains nutmeg

Scald milk; add bread cubes and butter or margarine. Beat

eggs; add sugar and salt. Add milk mixture and vanilla extract. Pour into baking dish; sprinkle with nutmeg. Place in pan of hot water. Bake in moderate oven (350°F.) 1 hour 15 min., or until inserted knife comes out clean. (If desired, 1 cup raisins may be added to mixture before baking.)

Tropical Bread Pudding

Prepare Bread Pudding, sustituting 2 cups whole-wheat bread cubes for 2 cups bread cubes and adding 1 cup chopped pitted dates. Before baking, sprinkle generously with shredded coconut.

Whole-Wheat Raisin Bread Pudding

Prepare Bread Pudding, substituting 2 cups whole-wheat raisin bread cubes for 2 cups bread cubes and omitting 1 cup raisins.

Lemon Sponge Pudding
Serves 4

½ cup sugar
2 tbs. flour
½ tsp. salt
2 egg yolks

1 cup milk
2 tbs. lemon juice
2 tsp. grated lemon rind
2 egg whites

Mix sugar, flour and salt. Beat egg yolks slightly; add with milk. Add lemon juice and rind. Beat egg whites stiff; fold in. Pour into greased baking dish. Place in pan of hot water; bake in moderate oven (350°F.) 45 min. Chill.

Indian Pudding
Serves 4

4 cups milk
½ cup yellow corn meal
2 tbs. melted butter or margarine
½ cup molasses

1 tsp. salt
1 tsp. cinnamon
¼ tsp. ginger
2 eggs
Hard Sauce (p. 321)

Scald milk. Pour slowly on corn meal, stirring constantly. Cook over hot water 20 min. Combine butter or margarine, molasses, salt, cinnamon and ginger. Beat eggs well; add with molasses mixture to corn meal. Pour into greased baking dish. Place in pan of hot water. Bake in moderate oven (350°F.) 1 hour. Serve hot with sauce. Instead of Hard Sauce, if desired, use plain or whipped cream, or vanilla ice cream.

Baked Squash Pudding

Serves 4

1¼ cups cooked Hubbard squash
⅓ cup firmly packed light brown sugar
¼ cup molasses
½ tsp. salt
¼ tsp. cinnamon
2 eggs
¾ cup top milk

If squash is very moist, cook slowly to evaporate some liquid. Strain squash. Combine with sugar, molasses, salt and cinnamon. Beat eggs; add with milk. Pour into greased baking dish. Bake in moderate oven (325°F.) 1 hour 30 min.

Cereal Pudding

Serves 4

½ cup quick-cooking wheat cereal
¼ cup sugar
¼ tsp. salt
3 cups milk
1 tsp. vanilla extract
Hot Fudge Sauce (p. 320)

Mix cereal, sugar and salt. Scald milk; gradually add cereal mixture. Cook over low heat, stirring constantly, until thick. Cover. Cook over hot water 10 min. Add vanilla extract. Pour into greased individual molds; chill until firm. Unmold. Serve with sauce.

Baked Rice Pudding

Serves 4

½ cup rice
4 cups milk
½ tsp. nutmeg
¼ cup sugar
½ tsp. salt

Wash rice thoroughly in running water; drain. Combine with milk, nutmeg, sugar and salt. Pour into greased baking dish. Bake in slow oven (300°F.) 2 hours 30 min. or until rice is tender, stirring several times during first hour. (If desired, ½ cup raisins may be added to mixture before baking.)

Creamy Rice   Serves 4

¾ cup rice   ¼ tsp. almond extract
3 cups milk   Spiced Cherry Sauce
6 tbs. sugar   (pp. 323-24)
¾ tsp. vanilla extract

Wash rice thoroughly in running water; drain. Combine with milk and sugar; cover; cook over hot water about 1 hour or until tender. Add vanilla and almond extracts. Serve hot with sauce.

Walnut Prune Pudding   Serves 4

½ cup rice   ½ cup chopped pitted
3 cups milk   cooked prunes
⅓ cup sugar   2 tsp. grated lemon rind
¾ tsp. salt   2 egg yolks
¼ tsp. nutmeg   2 egg whites
¼ cup chopped walnut   6 tbs. sugar
    meats

Wash rice thoroughly in cold running water; drain. Combine with milk; cover; cook over hot water about 1 hour, or until tender. Add ⅓ cup sugar, salt, nutmeg, prunes, nut meats and lemon rind. Beat egg yolks; add rice mixture. Pour into baking dish. Beat egg whites stiff; gradually add 6 tbs. sugar, beating constantly. Swirl on rice mixture. Bake in moderate oven (325°F.) 20 min.

Cream Tapioca Pudding   Serves 4

3 tbs. quick-cooking   1 egg yolk
    tapioca   ½ tsp. vanilla extract
¼ cup sugar   1 egg white
Few grains salt   Cream
2 cups milk

Mix tapioca, sugar and salt. Add milk. Beat egg yolk; add. Cook over boiling water, stirring constantly, 10 min., or until slightly thickened. Add vanilla extract. Beat egg white stiff; fold in. Serve with plain or whipped cream.

Spiced Apricot Tapioca Pudding   Serves 4

3 tbs. quick-cooking tapioca
¼ cup sugar
¼ tsp. salt
¼ tsp. cinnamon
¼ tsp. nutmeg

1 No. 2 can (2½ cups) apricot halves
2 egg yolks
2 egg whites
6 tbs. sugar

Mix tapioca, ¼ cup sugar, salt, cinnamon and nutmeg. Drain apricots, reserving sirup. Add water to sirup to make 2 cups; add to tapioca mixture. Beat egg yolks; add. Cook over boiling water, stirring constantly, 10 min., or until slightly thickened. Reserve 8 apricot halves; chop remaining halves; add to tapioca mixture. Pour into baking dish. Beat egg whites stiff; gradually add 6 tbs. sugar, beating constantly. Swirl around edge of pudding; place apricot halves in center. Bake in moderate oven (325°F.) 20 min.

Strawberry Tapioca Pudding   Serves 4

2½ tbs. quick-cooking tapioca
½ cup sugar
Few grains salt

1 cup water
1¾ cups sliced strawberries
2 tbs. lemon juice
½ cup whipping cream

Mix tapioca, sugar and salt; add water. Bring to boiling point, stirring constantly; remove from heat. Cool, stirring occasionally. Fold in strawberries and lemon juice. Whip cream slightly stiff; fold in.

Tutti-Frutti Tapioca   Serves 4

3 tbs. quick-cooking tapioca
⅓ cup firmly packed brown sugar
Few grains salt
2 cups milk
1 egg

⅓ cup chopped raisins
⅓ cup chopped pitted dates
⅓ cup chopped walnut meats
½ tsp. vanilla extract

Mix tapioca, sugar and salt. Add milk. Beat egg; add. Cook

over boiling water, stirring constantly, 10 min., or until slightly thickened. Add raisins, dates and nut meats; cool. Add vanilla extract; chill. If desired, garnish with whipped cream, dates and nut meats.

Vanilla Cornstarch Pudding   Serves 4

2 tbs. cornstarch
3 tbs. sugar
¼ tsp. salt

2 cups milk
¾ tsp. vanilla extract

Mix cornstarch, sugar and salt. Add ¼ cup milk, stir until dissolved. Scald remaining milk; add to sugar mixture. Cook over hot water, stirring constantly, until thick. Cover; cook 10 min. Add vanilla extract; pour into individual serving dishes. Chill. If desired, serve with Quick Chocolate Cinnamon Sauce (p. 320).

Chocolate Cornstarch Pudding   Serves 4

2 squares (2 oz.)
    unsweetened chocolate
2 cups evaporated milk
1⅓ cups water
2 tbs. cornstarch

½ cup sugar
½ tsp. salt
2 eggs
1 tsp. vanilla extract

Melt chocolate over hot water. Combine evaporated milk and 1 cup water. Add to chocolate; heat. Mix cornstarch, sugar and salt with remaining water. Add; cook over hot water, stirring constantly, until thick. Cover; cook 20 min. Beat eggs; add hot mixture. Add vanilla extract; pour into individual serving dishes. Chill. If desired, serve with cream.

Butterscotch Cornstarch Pudding   Serves 4

2 tbs. cornstarch
¾ cup firmly packed brown
    sugar
¼ tsp. salt

2 cups milk
2 tbs. butter or margarine
1 tsp. vanilla extract

Mix cornstarch, sugar and salt; add ¼ cup milk. Stir until

dissolved. Scald remaining milk; add butter or margarine. Add to sugar mixture; cook over hot water, stirring constantly, until thick. Cover; cook 10 min. Add vanilla extract; pour into individual serving dishes. Chill. If desired, serve with cream.

Tangerine Coconut Pudding
Serves 4

1 pkg. prepared vanilla pudding
½ cup toasted shredded coconut
2 cups milk
⅔ cup cubed tangerine sections
1 tsp. grated tangerine rind

Prepare pudding according to directions on package, using 2 cups milk. Cool slightly. Add coconut, tangerine sections and rind. Pour into individual serving dishes. Chill.

Chocolate Peppermint Chiffon
Serves 4

1 pkg. prepared chocolate pudding
2 cups milk
Few drops peppermint extract
2 egg whites

Prepare pudding according to directions on pkg., using 2 cups milk; cool. Add peppermint extract. Beat egg whites stiff; fold in. Pour into individual serving dishes. Chill.

Cottage Pudding
Serves 6

¼ cup shortening
¾ cup sugar
2 eggs
2¼ cups flour
¼ tsp. salt
3 tsp. baking powder
¾ cup milk
½ tsp. lemon extract
Lemon Sauce (p. 322)

Cream together shortening and sugar. Add eggs, 1 at a time, beating well after each. Sift together flour, salt and baking powder; add alternately with milk to first mixture. Add lemon extract. Pour into greased pan 8" x 8" x 2". Bake in moderately hot oven (375°F.) 40 min. Serve hot with sauce. Instead of Lemon Sauce, if desired, use Hot Fudge Sauce (p. 320), Butterscotch Sauce (p. 320), Winter

Fruit Sauce (p. 322) or Hot Spiced Blueberry Sauce (p. 323).

Chocolate Chip Pudding: Follow recipe for Cottage Pudding, omitting lemon extract and adding to batter ½ cup chopped semi-sweet chocolate.

Apple Betty   Serves 4

3 cups soft bread crumbs	¾ cup firmly packed brown sugar
3 tbs. melted butter or margarine	¼ tsp. nutmeg
3 large tart apples	½ tsp. cinnamon
1½ tbs. lemon juice	⅔ cup hot water
½ tsp. grated lemon rind	Hard Sauce (p. 321)

Toast crumbs; mix with butter or margarine. Place ⅓ crumbs in greased baking dish. Pare apples; core; slice thin. Arrange ½ apples on crumbs. Sprinkle with ½ juice and rind, sugar, nutmeg and cinnamon. Repeat, ending with crumbs. Add water. Bake in moderate oven (350°F.) 45 min. or until apples are tender. Serve hot with sauce.

Cheddar Betty: Prepare Apple Betty; cool slightly. Whip ½ cup whipping cream stiff; place spoonfuls on pudding. Sprinkle with ½ cup grated Cheddar cheese. Garnish with thin wedges of unpeeled red apple.

Apple and Cranberry Betty   Serves 4

4 cups soft bread crumbs	¾ tsp. nutmeg
3 large tart apples	3 tbs. butter or margarine
1 cup firmly packed brown sugar	2 cups cranberries
	Lemon Sauce (p. 322)

Toast crumbs. Pare apples; core; slice thin. Place ½ apples in greased baking dish; sprinkle with ½ sugar and nutmeg. Dot with ½ butter or margarine. Add ½ bread crumbs and cranberries. Repeat, ending with crumbs. Dot with butter or margarine. Bake in moderate oven (350°F.) 1 hour. Serve hot with sauce.

Apple Wheat Betty   Serves 4

4 wheat-shred biscuits   2 tbs. butter or margarine
4 apples   1 tbs. lemon juice
1 cup firmly packed brown   ½ cup water
   sugar   Orange Tang Custard Sauce
1 tsp. cinnamon   (p. 322)

Crush wheat-shred biscuits. Pare apples; core; slice. Combine sugar and cinnamon. Place alternate layers cereal and apples in baking dish, sprinkling with sugar mixture. Dot with butter or margarine. Mix juice and water; add. Cover; bake in moderate oven (350°F.) 50 min. Serve hot with sauce.

Blueberry Flake Pudding   Serves 4

1¼ cups crushed corn   2 tbs. melted butter or
   flakes   margarine
¼ tsp. cinnamon   Cream or Custard Sauce
¼ cup sugar   (p. 322)
2 cups blueberries

Combine crumbs, cinnamon, sugar and butter or margarine. Place 1 cup berries in bottom of baking dish; cover with ½ crumb mixture. Repeat. Bake in moderate oven (350°F.) 20 min. Serve hot with cream or sauce.

Apple Cobbler   Serves 4

3 large tart apples   1½ tsp. baking powder
⅔ cup sugar   Few grains salt
1 tsp. cinnamon   2 tbs. shortening
¼ tsp. nutmeg   ⅓ cup milk
2 tbs. butter or margarine   Hard Sauce (p. 321)
1 cup flour

Core apples; pare; slice thin. Combine sugar, cinnamon and nutmeg. Place apples in greased pan 8″ x 8″ x 2″; sprinkle with sugar mixture. Dot with butter or margarine. Sift together flour, baking powder and salt; cut in shortening with 2 knives or pastry blender. Add milk to make soft dough. Roll out on lightly floured board to 8″ x 8″; place on apples. Score dough in squares. Bake in hot oven (400°F.) 35 min. Serve hot with sauce.

Pineapple Betty   Serves 4

1 No. 2 can (2½ cups) crushed pineapple
2½ cups corn flakes
½ cup firmly packed brown sugar
¼ tsp. nutmeg
1 tsp. lemon juice
½ tsp. grated lemon rind
3 tbs. melted butter or margarine
Sherry Fluff Sauce (p. 321)

Drain pineapple; place in baking dish. Combine corn flakes, sugar, nutmeg, lemon juice and rind and butter or margarine. Sprinkle over pineapple. Bake in hot oven (400°F.) 20 min. Serve hot with sauce.

Red Cherry Betty   Serves 4

1 No. 2 can (2½ cups) pitted sour red cherries
3 cups corn flakes
1 tbs. butter or margarine
⅔ cup firmly packed brown sugar
1 tsp. cinnamon
½ tsp. nutmeg

Drain cherries, reserving sirup. Mix corn flakes, sugar, cinnamon and nutmeg. Place alternate layers corn flake mixture and cherries in baking dish. Dot with butter or margarine; add ¼ cup cherry sirup. Bake in moderately hot oven (375°F.) 20 min.

Blushing Betty   Serves 4-6

2 lbs. rhubarb
1⅓ cups sugar
⅓ cup seedless raisins
2 tbs. shortening
1 egg
1 cup flour
1½ tsp. baking powder
¼ tsp. salt
⅓ cup milk
½ tsp. vanilla extract

Wash rhubarb; do not peel. Cut in 1″ pieces; mix with 1 cup sugar. Place in greased baking dish; add raisins.

Cream shortening and ⅓ cup sugar. Add egg; beat well. Sift together flour, baking powder and salt. Add alternately with milk to creamed mixture; add vanilla extract. Spread over fruit. Bake in moderate oven (350°F.) 1 hour. Serve hot.

Plum Crumb Pudding   Serves 4

2 cups graham cracker crumbs	¼ cup melted butter or margarine
⅓ cup sugar	3 tbs. water
1 tsp. cinnamon	2 cups sliced pitted plums
½ tsp. nutmeg	Vanilla or butter pecan ice cream

Combine crumbs, sugar, cinnamon, nutmeg, butter or margarine and water. Place alternate layers crumb mixture and plums in individual baking dishes, ending with plums. Bake in moderate oven (350°F.) 25 min. Serve hot with ice cream.

Cherry Cobbler   Serves 4

⅔ cup sugar	1½ tsp. baking powder
2 tbs. flour	Few grains salt
1 No. 2 can (2½ cups) pitted sour red cherries	3 tbs. shortening
1 cup flour	⅓ cup milk

Mix sugar, 2 tbs. flour and cherries; place in greased pan 8″ x 8″ x 2″. Sift together 1 cup flour, baking powder and salt. Cut in shortening with 2 knives or pastry blender. Add milk to make soft dough. Roll out on lightly floured board to 8″ x 8″; place on cherries. Score dough in squares. Bake in hot oven (400°F.) 30 min. Serve hot.

Apricot Roly-Poly   Serves 4

Make baking powder biscuit dough, using 1½ cups biscuit mix. Roll out ⅛″ thick on lightly floured board; cut in pieces 4″ x 4½″. On each piece place 2 well-drained cooked or canned apricot halves; dot with butter or margarine.

Roll up. Bake in very hot oven (450°F.) 15-20 min. Serve hot with Orange Sauce (p. 323).

Berry Jumble   Serves 4

1 qt. strawberries	1 tsp. baking powder
1/4 cup water	Few grains salt
1 1/3 cups sugar	2 tbs. shortening
1 cup flour	1/3 cup milk

Wash strawberries; hull; halve. Add water and 1 cup sugar. Place in large saucepan. Heat to boiling point. Sift together flour, remaining sugar, baking powder and salt. Cut in shortening with 2 knives or pastry blender. Add milk; mix well. Drop by tablespoons on strawberry mixture. Cover tightly; cook slowly 20 min. without removing cover. Serve hot.

Cheese Apple Cake

Follow recipe for Baking Powder Biscuits (p. 52), rolling 1/2" thick. Pat into greased pan 9" x 9" x 1 1/2". Sprinkle generously with grated American cheese. Top with overlapping peeled apple slices. Sprinkle with brown sugar and cinnamon. Dot with butter or margarine. Bake in hot oven (400°F.) 35 min. Serve hot with cream.

Apple Bandana Dumplings   Serves 4

4 cooking apples	1/4 cup sugar
Pastry II (p. 229)	Butter or margarine
1 cup grated American cheese	2 tbs. brown sugar
1/4 cup mincemeat	2 tbs. cream

Pare apples; core. Divide pastry in fourths; roll out each 1/8" thick on lightly floured board into square. Sprinkle with cheese. Place apple in center of each square; fill with mincemeat. Sprinkle with sugar; dot with butter or margarine. Fold 2 opposite corners of pastry over apple; tie remaining corners bandana fashion on top of apple. Place greased waxed paper under pastry "ears." Combine brown sugar and cream; brush on pastry, except "ears." Bake in hot oven (400°F.) 55 min.; brush "ears" with cream mixture; bake 5 min.

Old-Fashioned Strawberry Shortcake   Serves 4

Prepare Individual Shortcake Biscuits (p. 54). While hot, split; spread with butter or margarine. Wash 1 pt. strawberries; hull. Crush; add enough sugar to sweeten. Place strawberries between and on top biscuit halves. If desired, serve with plain or whipped cream.

Peach Shortcake Georgia   Serves 4

2 cups flour	Ice water
½ tsp. salt	Sliced peaches
1 tsp. baking powder	Plain cream
⅔ cup shortening	

Sift together flour, salt and baking powder. Cut in shortening with 2 knives or pastry blender. Add enough water to hold ingredients together; chill. Divide into thirds; roll out each ⅛″ thick on lightly floured board in 8″ circle. Place each in 8″ layer pan; bake in hot oven (425°F.) 15 min., or until brown. Arrange peaches between pastry circles and on top. Serve immediately with cream.

Devil's Food Peach Shortcake   Serves 8-10

Prepare Standard Chocolate Layers (p. 72); cool. Whip 1 cup whipping cream; add 2 tbs. sugar and 1 tsp. vanilla extract. Spread ½ cream mixture on bottom layer. Cover with sliced peaches; top with second layer. Swirl remaining cream on cake. Garnish top with sliced peaches.

Raspberry Shortcake Dessert   Serves 8-10

Prepare Hot Milk Sponge Cake (pp. 89-90); cool. Cut in half crosswise. Spread whipped cream and raspberries between and on top cake.

Blackberry Pineapple Treat   Serves 4

    1" thick sponge cake layer   2 egg whites
    4 slices pineapple   6 tbs. sugar
    1 cup blackberries

Cut sponge cake in 4 rounds size of pineapple slices. Top
each with pineapple slice and blackberries. Beat egg whites
stiff; gradually add sugar, beating constantly. Spread meringue over fruits. Bake in moderate oven (325°F.) 20 min.

Gingerbread

    ½ cup shortening   ½ tsp. cinnamon
    ¼ cup sugar   ½ tsp. cloves
    1 egg   1 tsp. ginger
    ½ cup dark molasses   ½ tsp. salt
    1¾ cups flour   ½ cup milk
    1 tsp. baking soda

Cream together shortening and sugar. Add egg; beat well.
Add molasses. Sift together flour, baking soda, cinnamon,
cloves, ginger and salt; add alternately with milk to
creamed mixture. Pour into greased pan 8" x 8" x 2".
Bake in moderate oven (350°F.) 45 min. Cut in squares.
If desired, serve with Hard Sauce (p. 321) or Cream Cheese
Topping (p. 102).

Orange Gingerbread Dessert   Serves 4-6

    1 pkg. gingerbread mix   ½ cup sugar
    ¾ cup seedless raisins   ½ cup orange juice

Prepare gingerbread according to directions on pkg.; add
raisins. Pour into greased pan 8" x 8" x 2". Bake in moderate oven (350°F.) 50 min. Blend sugar and orange juice;
pour over hot gingerbread. Serve immediately.

Chocolate Mallow Gingerbread   Serves 4-6

Prepare Gingerbread (above). Split in 2 layers. Fill and top
with quartered marshmallows and chopped semi-sweet

chocolate. Heat in moderate oven (350°F.) until marsh-mallows are slightly melted.

Apricot Gingerbread Cake   Serves 4-6

2 tbs. melted butter or
  margarine
½ cup firmly packed
  brown sugar

Cooked dried apricots
1 pkg. gingerbread mix
Cream

Blend together butter or margarine and sugar. Spread in greased pan 11" x 7" x 1½". Arrange apricots, cut side up, on sugar mixture. Prepare gingerbread mix according to directions on pkg.; pour over apricots. Bake in moderate oven (350°F.) 35-40 min.

Plum Pudding   Serves 8

¼ cup shortening
½ cup sugar
3 eggs
½ cup molasses
2½ cups flour
½ tsp. baking powder
1½ tsp. cinnamon
½ tsp. cloves
½ tsp. allspice
1 tsp. salt

¼ lb. finely ground suet
1 cup seeded raisins
1 cup chopped citron
1 cup chopped pitted dates
½ cup chopped candied
  orange peel
½ cup chopped dried figs
1 cup cider
Hard Sauce (p. 321)

Cream together shortening and sugar; add eggs, 1 at a time, beating after each. Add molasses. Sift together flour, baking powder, cinnamon, cloves, allspice and salt. Add to creamed mixture, reserving 1 cup; mix well. Dredge suet, raisins, citron, dates, orange peel and figs with remaining flour mixture. Combine with first mixture; add cider. Mix well. Fill 1½-2 quart greased pudding mold ¾ full. Cover tightly. Steam 2 hours 15 min., or until done. Unmold. Serve with sauce.

Economy Plum Pudding   Serves 8

1 9-oz. pkg. dry mincemeat
½ cup water
¼ cup strong freshly made
   coffee brew
2 tbs. shortening
½ cup firmly packed brown
   sugar
2 eggs
1½ cups soft bread crumbs

1 tsp. baking powder
1 tsp. cinnamon
¼ tsp. cloves
¼ tsp. nutmeg
1 cup seeded raisins
Candied cherries
Citron
Hard Sauce (p. 321)

Break mincemeat into pieces; add water. Cook slowly, stirring constantly, until all lumps are thoroughly broken up. Bring to boiling point; boil 3 min., or until liquid is evaporated. Add coffee; cool. Cream together shortening and sugar. Beat eggs slightly; add to creamed mixture. Add crumbs, baking powder, cinnamon, cloves, nutmeg and raisins. Fold in mincemeat. Fill greased pudding mold ¾ full; cover tightly. Steam 1 hour 30 min. Unmold; garnish with cherries and citron. Serve hot with sauce.

Suet Pudding   Serves 8

1 cup ground suet
1 cup molasses
1 cup milk
3 cups flour
2 tsp. baking powder
1 tsp. salt
1 tsp. cinnamon

½ tsp. nutmeg
¼ tsp. cloves
1 cup seedless raisins
½ cup chopped walnut
   meats
Lemon Sauce (p. 322)

Combine suet, molasses and milk. Sift together flour, baking powder, salt, cinnamon, nutmeg and cloves; add to first mixture. Add raisins and nut meats. Fill greased pudding mold ¾ full; cover tightly. Steam 3-3 hours 30 min. Unmold. Serve hot with sauce.

Steamed Carrot Pudding
Serves 8

½ cup shortening
1 cup sugar
1½ cups grated raw carrot
1 cup grated raw potato
1 cup flour
1 tsp. baking soda

1 tsp. salt
1 tsp. cinnamon
½ tsp. cloves
1 cup seedless raisins
⅓ cup chopped citron
Custard Sauce (p. 322)

Cream together shortening and sugar. Add carrot and potato. Sift together flour, soda, salt, cinnamon and cloves; add with raisins and citron. Fill greased pudding mold ¾ full; cover tightly. Steam 2 hours 30 min. Unmold. Serve hot with sauce.

Date and Nut Pudding
Serves 8

1 egg
¾ cup molasses
1 tsp. baking soda
½ cup water
1½ cups flour
½ tsp. salt
½ tsp. cinnamon
⅛ tsp. cloves

⅛ tsp. nutmeg
¾ cup chopped pitted dates
¼ cup chopped walnut meats
2 tbs. melted shortening or salad oil
Satiny Dessert Sauce (pp. 321-22)

Beat egg; add molasses. Dissolve soda in water; add to egg mixture. Sift together 1¼ cups flour, salt, cinnamon, cloves and nutmeg; add. Dredge dates and nut meats with remaining flour; add. Add fat or salad oil. Fill greased pudding mold ¾ full; cover tightly. Steam 1 hour 30 min. Unmold. Serve hot with sauce.

Marbled Date Pudding
Serves 8

1 tbs. shortening
¾ cup sugar
1 egg
1½ cups flour
1½ tsp. baking powder
½ tsp. salt
½ cup milk

1 tsp. vanilla extract
1 square (1 oz.) unsweetened chocolate
⅓ cup chopped pitted dates
Whole pitted dates
Hard Sauce (p. 321)

Cream together shortening and sugar; add egg. Beat well. Sift together flour, baking powder and salt; add alternately to creamed mixture with milk. Add vanilla extract. Melt chocolate over hot water; add with chopped dates to ½ batter. Fill greased pudding mold ¾ full with alternate spoonfuls of batters; cover tightly. Steam 1 hour 30 min. Unmold. Stuff whole dates with sauce; garnish pudding. Serve hot with remaining sauce.

Quick Chocolate Steamed Pudding Serves 8

Prepare 1 pkg. devil's food mix according to directions on package. Fill greased pudding mold ¾ full; cover tightly. Steam 1 hour 30 min. Unmold. Serve hot with whipped cream or Sunshine Sauce (p. 321).

Cranberry Lemon Molds Serves 4-6

    1 pkg. lemon gelatin   ½ cup canned cranberry
    2 cups water   sauce
                                ¼ cup whipping cream

Dissolve gelatin in 2 cups water according to directions on package; chill until sirupy. Press cranberry sauce through fine sieve. Whip cream. Fold cranberry sauce and cream into ½ gelatin. Pour clear gelatin into individual molds which have been rinsed in cold water; chill until firm. Add remaining gelatin. Chill until firm. Unmold.

Fruit Fluff Serves 4-6

    1 pkg. orange gelatin   1 cup sliced strawberries
    1 cup water   1 cup sliced bananas
    1 cup orange juice

Dissolve gelatin in 1 cup water according to directions on package. Add orange juice; chill until sirupy. Beat with rotary beater until fluffy. Fold in berries and bananas. Pile in individual serving dishes. Chill until firm. If desired, garnish with whipped cream.

Orange Bavarian Cream   Serves 4-6

1 pkg. orange gelatin
2 cups water

1 cup membrane-free
  orange sections
1 cup whipping cream

Dissolve gelatin in 2 cups water according to directions on package. Chill until sirupy; fold in orange sections. Whip cream; fold in. Pour into mold which has been rinsed in cold water; chill until firm. Unmold. If desired, garnish with membrane-free orange sections.

Sherry Snow Pudding   Serves 4-6

1 pkg. orange gelatin
1½ cups water
¼ cup sherry flavoring
2 egg whites

¼ cup shredded coconut
Membrane-free orange
  sections
Custard Sauce (p. 322)

Dissolve gelatin in 1½ cups water according to directions on package. Cool; add sherry flavoring. Chill until sirupy. Add egg whites; beat with rotary beater until fluffy. Fold in coconut; pour into mold which has been rinsed in cold water. Chill until firm. Unmold; garnish with orange sections. Serve with sauce.

Cherry Froth   Serves 4-6

Dissolve 1 pkg. cherry gelatin according to directions on pkg. Pour ½ into 8″ x 8″ x 2″ pan which has been dipped in cold water; chill until firm. Chill remaining gelatin until sirupy; beat with rotary beater until fluffy. Pile in individual serving dishes; chill until firm. Cube clear gelatin; pile on whipped gelatin. If desired, serve with whipped cream.

Strawberry Gelatin Trifle   Serves 4-6

⅓ cup sugar
2 cups sliced strawberries
1 pkg. strawberry gelatin

2¼ cups water
Light cream

Sprinkle sugar over berries; let stand 30 min. Dissolve gelatin in 2¼ cups water according to directions on pkg. Chill until sirupy. Fold in berries. Chill until thickened, stirring occasionally. Pile in individual serving dishes. Serve with cream.

Coffee Fluff

Serves 4-6

1 pkg. lemon gelatin
1 cup water
1 cup strong coffee brew
¼ cup whipping cream

3 tbs. powdered sugar
½ cup chopped walnut
meats

Dissolve gelatin in 1 cup water according to directions on package; add coffee. Pour ½ into mold which has been rinsed in cold water; chill until firm. Chill remaining gelatin until sirupy; beat with rotary beater until fluffy. Whip cream; fold in. Add sugar and nut meats; pour over clear gelatin. Chill until firm. Unmold. If desired, garnish with whipped cream.

Spanish Cream

Serves 4-6

1 envelope (1 tbs.)
unflavored gelatine
2 cups milk
⅓ cup sugar

Few grains salt
2 egg yolks
1 tsp. vanilla extract
2 egg whites

Soften gelatine in milk; add sugar and salt. Place over hot water, stirring occasionally, until gelatine is dissolved. Beat egg yolks slightly; add hot milk mixture. Cook over hot water, stirring constantly, until mixture thickens and coats spoon. Cool; add vanilla extract. Beat egg white stiff; fold in. Pour into large or individual molds which have been rinsed in cold water; chill until firm. Unmold.

Chocolate Spanish Cream: Follow recipe for Spanish Cream, adding 1½ squares (1½ oz.) melted unsweetened chocolate to hot milk mixture.

Fruit Spanish Cream: Prepare Spanish Cream. Serve with sliced peaches, apricots, plums, pineapple, raspberries or strawberries.

Jelly Spanish Cream Cake: Spread halved lady fingers or sponge cake strips with raspberry, strawberry or grape jelly; place, jelly side up, in spring-form pan or serving dish.

Follow recipe for Spanish Cream, pouring into lined pan or serving dish. Chill until firm. If desired, garnish with whipped cream.

Macaroon Spanish Cream: Follow recipe for Spanish Cream, folding in ½ cup dried macaroon crumbs with egg whites.

Moorish Cream: Follow recipe for Spanish Cream, blending cooked milk mixture with 1 tbs. peanut butter and folding in ⅓ cup chopped pitted dates with egg whites. Garnish with peanut-butter stuffed pitted dates.

Orange Spanish Cream: Follow recipe for Spanish Cream, omitting ⅓ cup milk and adding ⅓ cup orange juice, 2 tsp. lemon juice and 1 tsp. grated orange rind to cooked milk mixture.

Spanish Cream Refrigerator Cake: Line serving dish with halved lady fingers or sponge cake strips. Follow recipe for Spanish Cream, Chocolate Spanish Cream or Orange Spanish Cream, pouring into serving dish. Chill until firm. If desired, garnish with whipped cream.

Spanish Cream Sponge: Follow recipe for Spanish Cream, folding in 2 cups stale cake cubes with egg whites. Serve with sliced peaches, apricots, plums, pineapple, raspberries or strawberries.

Vanilla Bavarian Cream

Serves 4-6

1 envelope (1 tbs.) unflavored gelatine	¼ tsp. salt
¼ cup cold water	1 cup milk
2 egg yolks	1 tsp. vanilla extract
½ cup sugar	2 egg whites
	1 cup whipping cream

Soften gelatine in water. Beat egg yolks; add ¼ cup sugar and salt. Gradually add milk; cook over hot water, stirring constantly, until slightly thick. Add gelatine, stir until dissolved. Add vanilla extract. Chill until slightly thickened. Beat egg whites stiff; gradually add remaining ¼ cup sugar, beating constantly. Whip cream slightly stiff; fold into gelatine mixture with egg whites. Pour into mold which has been rinsed in cold water. Chill until firm.

Chocolate Bavarian Cream: Follow recipe for Vanilla Bavarian Cream, blending in 1 square (1 oz.) melted unsweetened chocolate to the hot thickened mixture.

Lemon Gelatin
Serves 4-6

1 envelope (1 tbs.)
   unflavored gelatine
¼ cup cold water
1¼ cups hot water

⅓ cup sugar
Few grains salt
¼ cup lemon juice
Cream

Soften gelatine in cold water. Add hot water, sugar, salt and lemon juice; stir until dissolved. Pour into mold which has been rinsed in cold water. Chill until firm. Unmold. Serve with plain or whipped cream.

Fruited Lemon Gelatin: Follow recipe for Lemon Gelatin; chill until sirupy. Add 1 cup membrane-free orange sections and ½ cup sliced bananas. Chill until firm.

Strawberry and Pineapple Gelatin: Follow recipe for Lemon Gelatin; chill until sirupy. Add 1 cup sliced strawberries and ½ cup diced cooked or canned pineapple. Chill until firm.

Coffee Gelatin
Serves 4-6

1 envelope (1 tbs.)
   unflavored gelatine
¼ cup cold water
1½ cups hot coffee brew

⅓ cup sugar
Few grains salt
Cream

Soften gelatine in water. Add coffee, sugar and salt; stir until gelatine is dissolved. Pour into large mold or individual molds which have been rinsed in cold water. Chill until firm. Unmold. Serve with cream.

Molasses Sponge
Serves 4-6

1 envelope (1 tbs.)
   unflavored gelatine
¼ cup cold water
3 eggs
¾ cup light molasses

2 tbs. orange juice
½ tsp. cinnamon
Few grains salt
1½ cups whipping cream

Soften gelatine in water. Beat eggs until light; add molasses. Cook over boiling water, stirring constantly, until thick. Add gelatine, orange juice, cinnamon and salt. Chill until slightly thickened. Whip cream stiff; fold in molasses mixture. Pour into mold which has been rinsed in cold water. Chill until firm. Unmold.

Chocolate Cherry Cream   Serves 4-6

1 cup whipping cream	2 cups coarsely broken
1/3 cup cherry preserves	chocolate wafers

Whip cream slightly stiff; reserve 1/4 cup for garnish. Combine cream and wafers. In each sherbet glass place layer of wafer mixture and 1 tablespoon preserves. Add layer of wafer mixture. Top with remaining cream and preserves.

Gingana Cream   Serves 4-6

1 cup whipping cream	3 bananas
2 tbs. confectioners' sugar	1 tbs. lemon juice
Few grains salt	1 cup ginger snap crumbs

Whip cream slightly stiff. Add sugar and salt. Press bananas through sieve; add lemon juice. Fold into cream. Fold in crumbs. Chill.

Peach Refrigerator Cake   Serves 8

1/2 cup butter or margarine	1 No. 2 1/2 can (3 1/2 cups)
1 cup confectioners' sugar	sliced peaches
2 egg yolks	2 egg whites
1/2 tsp. almond extract	12 lady fingers
	1 cup whipping cream

Cream butter or margarine; add sugar, creaming constantly. Add egg yolks; mix well. Drain peaches; measure 1 cup; chop fine. Add with almond extract. Beat egg whites stiff; fold in. Separate lady fingers. Place 1/2 on bottom of oblong pan. Cover with peach mixture; top with remaining lady fingers. Chill until firm. Unmold. Whip cream; use as garnish with remaining peaches.

Chocolate Almond Refrigerator Cake   Serves 4

1 cup whipping cream
½ cup finely chopped
   chocolate-covered
   almonds

16 graham crackers
8 whole chocolate-covered
   almonds

Whip ½ cup cream stiff; add chopped almonds. Spread on crackers; stack together to make loaf. Wrap in waxed paper; chill overnight. Just before serving, whip remaining cream. Spread on loaf; garnish with whole almonds.

Chocolate Soufflé   Serves 4

2 tbs. butter or margarine
3 tbs. flour
1 cup milk
3 squares (3 oz.)
   unsweetened chocolate
3 tbs. hot water

½ cup sugar
¼ tsp. salt
½ tsp. vanilla extract
3 egg yolks
3 egg whites
Sunshine Sauce (p. 321)

Melt butter or margarine; blend in flour. Gradually add milk. Cook over hot water, stirring constantly, until thick. Melt chocolate over hot water; add 3 tbs. hot water. Mix smooth. Add with sugar, salt and vanilla extract to hot milk mixture; mix well. Beat egg yolks; add milk mixture. Beat egg whites stiff, but not dry; fold in. Pour into greased shallow baking dish. Bake in moderate oven (325°F.) 50-60 min. Serve immediately with sauce.

Fruit Fritters   Serves 4

1 cup flour
1½ tsp. baking powder
¼ tsp. salt
2 cups fruit[1]

3 tbs. confectioners' sugar
⅓ cup milk
1 egg

Sift together flour, baking powder, salt and sugar. Gradually add milk; beat smooth. Beat egg; add. Dip fruit in batter. Fry in shallow fat or salad oil heated to 375°F. until delicate brown. Drain on absorbent paper. Serve hot. If

[1] Use peeled sliced apples, bananas or well-drained peaches or pineapple.

desired, sprinkle with confectioners' sugar and serve with sauce or whipped cream.

Lemon Soufflé   Serves 4

4 egg yolks	2 tsp. lemon rind
1 cup sugar	Few grains salt
3 tbs. lemon juice	4 egg whites

Beat egg yolks until thick and lemon-colored. Gradually add ½ cup sugar, beating constantly. Add lemon juice and rind and salt. Beat egg whites stiff, but not dry; fold into remaining sugar. Fold in egg yolk mixture. Pour into greased shallow baking dish. Bake in moderate oven (325° F.) 50 min. Serve immediately.

Cream Puffs or Eclairs

½ cup water	2 eggs
¼ cup shortening	¼ tsp. salt
½ cup flour	

Bring water to boiling point. Add shortening; stir until melted. Bring to boiling point; quickly add flour and salt. Cook, stirring constantly, about 2 min., or until mixture forms smooth, compact mass. Cool slightly. Add eggs, 1 at a time, beating after each. Beat 5 min., or until mixture is thick and shiny. Using tablespoon or pastry bag, immediately shape 2″ apart on greased baking sheet into mounds 2½″ in diam. or oblongs 1″ x 5″. Bake in very hot oven (450° F.) 10 min., reduce to moderate oven (350°F.); bake 20-25 min. Make slit in side of each; cool. Makes 6 large puffs or éclairs. Fill with Cream Filling (p. 100), whipped cream, ice cream or crushed fruit. If desired, frost with Confectioners' Sugar Frosting I (p. 97), Creamy Fudge Frosting (p. 97) or serve with sauce.

Meringue Layers

2 cups sugar	1 tbs. vinegar
1 tbs. vanilla extract	⅞ cup (6-8) egg whites

Sift sugar; add vanilla extract and vinegar; mix well. Beat

egg whites stiff, but not dry. Add sugar mixture by spoonfuls to egg whites, beating until dissolved. Cover 2 baking sheets with moistened, heavy paper. On each, shape 8″ meringue circle, making swirled pattern with tip of narrow spatula. Bake in slow oven (300°F.) 1-1 hour 15 min. Turn off heat; dry in oven 15 min. Cool; remove from paper.

Meringue Glacé   Serves 8

Spread 1 qt. ice cream between Meringue Layers (see above); garnish with fruit or whipped cream.

Baked Alaska   Serves 8

Sponge cake	5 egg whites
Qt. mold of ice cream	10 tbs. sugar

Cut slice of sponge cake about 1″ thick and about ½″ wider and longer than quart mold of ice cream. Cover small bread board with heavy paper. Place cake on board. Beat egg whites stiff; gradually add sugar, beating constantly. Place ice cream on cake. Entirely cover with meringue. Bake in very hot oven (500°F.) 2-3 min., or until meringue is highly browned. Serve immediately.

Smooth Vanilla Ice Cream   Serves 4-6

⅔ cup sweetened condensed milk	Few grains salt
	1½ tsp. vanilla extract
⅔ cup water	⅔ cup whipping cream

Mix milk, water, salt and vanilla extract; chill. Whip cream slightly; fold in. Pour into freezing tray of automatic refrigerator with cold control set at point recommended by manufacturer for freezing ice cream. Freeze to mush. Place in chilled bowl; beat smooth. Return to tray. Freeze firm. If desired, serve with Snowgold Sauce (p. 324).

Smooth Coffee Ice Cream: Follow recipe for Smooth Vanilla Ice Cream, substituting ⅔ cup strong coffee brew for ⅔ cup water.

Tutti-Frutti Ice Cream: Follow recipe for Smooth Vanilla Ice Cream, increasing 1½ teaspoons vanilla extract to 1 tbs. vanilla extract. After beating, add ¼ cup each chopped candied cherries, pitted dates, citron and walnut meats.

Quick Chocolate Ice Cream   Serves 4-6

1 square (1 oz.) unsweetened chocolate	⅔ cup water
	Few grains salt
⅔ cup sweetened condensed milk	⅔ cup whipping cream
	1 tsp. vanilla extract

Melt chocolate over hot water; add milk. Cook, stirring constantly, 5 min. or until thick. Gradually add water; add salt. Chill. Whip cream slightly; fold in with vanilla extract. Pour into freezing tray of automatic refrigerator with cold control set at point recommended by manufacturer for freezing ice cream. Freeze to mush. Place in chilled bowl; beat smooth. Return to tray. Freeze firm.

Chocolate Cinnamon Ice Cream: Follow recipe for Quick Chocolate Ice Cream adding ½ tsp. cinnamon with water and decreasing 1 tsp. vanilla extract to ¼ tsp. vanilla extract.

Velvet Ice Cream   Serves 4-6

2 egg yolks	2 tbs. light corn sirup
⅔ cup sugar	2 egg whites
Few grains salt	1 tsp. vanilla extract
1½ cups milk	½ cup whipping cream
¼ cup water	

Beat yolks; add ⅓ cup sugar, salt and milk. Cook over hot water, stirring constantly, until mixture thickens and coats spoon. Cool. Pour into freezing tray of automatic refrigerator with cold control set at point recommended by manufacturer for freezing ice cream. Freeze to mush. Boil together water, remaining ⅓ cup sugar and corn sirup to 236°F. (or when small quantity dropped from tip of spoon spins long thread). Beat egg whites stiff; gradually add sirup, beating constantly. Add vanilla extract. Cool. Place first mixture in chilled bowl. Beat smooth; fold in egg white mixture. Whip cream; fold in. Return to tray. Freeze firm. If desired, serve with Quick Chocolate Sauce (pp. 319-20).

Chocolate Velvet Ice Cream: Fellow recipe for Velvet Ice Cream, adding 2 squares (2 oz.) melted unsweetened chocolate to hot cooked egg yolk mixture.

Fruit Velvet Ice Cream: Follow recipe for Velvet Ice Cream, adding 1 cup sweetened puréed fruit to cooled egg yolk mixture.

Butterscotch Coconut Velvet Ice Cream: Follow recipe for Velvet Ice Cream, substituting ⅔ cup firmly packed brown sugar for ⅔ cup sugar. Add ⅓ cup toasted coconut to cooled egg yolk mixture.

Banana Macaroon Velvet Ice Cream: Follow recipe for Velvet Ice Cream, adding 1 sieved banana and ½ cup dried macaroon crumbs to cooled egg yolk mixture.

Chocolate Chip Velvet Ice Cream: Follow recipe for Velvet Ice Cream, adding ½ cup crushed chocolate-covered molasses chip candies to cooled egg yolk mixture.

Basic Custard Ice Cream   Makes 2 qts.

(Freezer Method)

1½ cups milk	½ tsp. salt
3 eggs	1 tbs. vanilla extract
¾ cup sugar	3 cups light cream

Scald milk. Beat eggs; add sugar and salt. Gradually add milk to egg mixture. Cook over hot water, stirring constantly, until mixture thickens and coats spoon. Cool. Add vanilla extract and cream. Place dasher in freezer can; add custard mixture. Cover; adjust crank. Using 8 parts crushed ice to 1 part ice cream salt, pack around freezer can. Turn crank rapidly; freeze to mush. Remove dasher; cover ice cream. Drain off brine. Using 4 parts ice to 1 part salt, pack firmly around freezer can. Cover freezer with burlap or paper; let stand 3-4 hours. If desired, serve with Maple Marshmallow Sauce (p. 320).

Coffee Ice Cream: Follow recipe for Basic Custard Ice Cream, substituting 1 cup strong coffee brew for 1 cup milk.

Mocha Chip Ice Cream: Follow recipe for Coffee Ice Cream, adding ¾ cup chopped semi-sweet chocolate before pouring into freezer can.

Strawberry or Peach Ice Cream: Follow recipe for Basic Custard Ice Cream, adding 2 cups crushed sweetened strawberries or peaches before pouring into freezer can.

Chocolate Ice Cream: Follow recipe for Basic Custard Ice Cream, adding 2 squares (2 oz.) melted unsweetened chocolate to hot custard mixture.

Apricot Ice Cream
Serves 4-6

1½ cups milk
¾ cup sugar
1½ tbs. cornstarch
Few grains salt
1 egg yolk

¾ cup sieved sweetened cooked dried apricots
1 egg white
½ cup whipping cream

Scald milk. Mix sugar, cornstarch and salt; add milk. Cook over hot water, stirring constantly, until thick; cover; cook 15 min. Beat egg yolk; add hot milk mixture. Cool. Add apricots. Beat egg white stiff; fold in. Whip cream; fold in. Pour into tray of automatic refrigerator with cold control set at point recommended by manufacturer for freezing ice cream. Freeze to mush. Place in chilled bowl. Beat smooth. Return to tray. Freeze firm.

Butter Pecan Ice Cream
Serves 4-6

1 cup firmly packed light brown sugar
½ cup water
2 eggs
2 tbs. butter or margarine
Few grains salt

1 cup milk
1 tsp. vanilla extract
1 tsp. sherry flavoring
1 cup whipping cream
½ cup broken pecan nut meats

Combine sugar and water; boil 2 min. Beat eggs; add sirup; cook over hot water, stirring constantly, until slightly thick. Add butter or margarine and salt; cool. Add milk, vanilla extract and sherry flavoring. Whip cream slightly stiff; fold in. Toast nut meats; add. Pour into freezing tray of automatic refrigerator with cold control set at point recommended by manufacturer for freezing ice cream. Freeze to mush. Place in chilled bowl. Beat smooth. Return to tray. Freeze firm.

Lemon Ice Cream
Serves 4-6

2 eggs
½ cup sugar
½ cup light corn sirup
1½ cups milk

¼ cup lemon juice
1 tsp. grated lemon rind
½ cup whipping cream

Beat eggs; gradually add sugar, beating constantly. Add corn sirup, milk, cream, lemon juice and rind. Pour into freezing tray of automatic refrigerator with cold control set at point recommended by manufacturer for freezing ice cream. Freeze to mush. Place in chilled bowl. Beat smooth. Return to tray. Freeze firm.

Lime Ice Cream: Follow recipe for Lemon Ice Cream, substituting ¼ cup lime juice for ¼ cup lemon juice and 1 tsp. grated lime rind for 1 tsp. grated lemon rind.

Pineapple Crunch Ice Cream
Serves 4-6

2 eggs
¼ cup sugar
½ cup light corn sirup
1½ cups milk
½ cup whipping cream
¼ cup pineapple sirup

¾ tsp. vanilla extract
¼ tsp. almond extract
½ cup well-drained crushed pineapple
½ cup toasted coconut

Beat eggs; gradually add sugar, beating until thickened. Add corn sirup, milk, cream and pineapple sirup; mix well. Pour into freezing tray of automatic refrigerator with cold control set at point recommended by manufacturer for freezing ice cream. Freeze to mush. Place in chilled bowl. Beat with rotary beater until light. Add extracts, pineapple and coconut. Return to tray. Freeze firm.

Pumpkin Pecan Ice Cream   Serves 4-6

2 egg yolks
1 cup milk
¾ cup sugar
1 tbs. cornstarch
½ tsp. cinnamon
¼ tsp. ginger
¼ tsp. salt

¾ cup sieved cooked or canned pumpkin
½ cup whipping cream
2 egg whites
⅓ cup broken pecan nut meats

Beat egg yolks; add milk. Mix sugar, cornstarch, cinnamon, ginger and salt; add milk mixture. Cook over hot water, stirring constantly, until thick. Add pumpkin; cool. Whip cream slightly stiff. Beat egg whites stiff. Combine pumpkin mixture, cream and egg whites. Pour into freezing tray of automatic refrigerator with cold control set at point recommended by manufacturer for freezing ice cream. Freeze to mush. Place in chilled bowl. Beat smooth. Add nut meats. Return to tray. Freeze firm. If desired, serve in Baked Tart Shells (p. 257).

Raspberry Ice Cream   Serves 4-6

2 eggs
⅓ cup light corn sirup
1 cup milk
½ tbs. cornstarch

1 cup crushed sweetened raspberries
1½ tbs. lemon juice
Few grains salt
½ cup whipping cream

Beat eggs; add corn sirup. Combine milk and cornstarch; add. Cook over hot water, stirring constantly, until thick. Chill. Combine raspberries, lemon juice and salt. Chill; press through sieve. Combine with egg mixture. Whip cream; fold in. Pour into freezing tray of automatic refrigerator with cold control set at point recommended by manufacturer for freezing ice cream. Freeze to mush. Place in chilled bowl. Beat smooth. Return to tray. Freeze firm.

Vanilla Marlow   Serves 4

¼ lb. marshmallows
1 cup milk
1 cup whipping cream

1 tbs. vanilla extract
Few grains salt

Combine marshmallows and milk; cook over hot water, stirring occasionally, until melted. Cool until slightly thickened. Whip cream slightly stiff; add vanilla extract and salt. Fold into milk mixture. Pour into freezing tray of automatic refrigerator with cold control set at point recommended by manufacturer for freezing ice cream. Freeze firm. If desired, serve with Plombière Sauce (p. 324).

Chocolate Marlow: Follow recipe for Vanilla Marlow, adding 1 square (1 oz.) unsweetened chocolate to hot milk and marshmallow mixture. Heat over hot water, stirring constantly, until chocolate is well blended. Increase 1 tbs. vanilla extract to 1½ tbs.

Strawberry Marlow
Serves 4

1 cup crushed sweetened strawberries
1 tbs. orange juice
¼ lb. marshmallows

¼ cup water
1 cup whipping cream
½ tsp. vanilla extract
Few grains salt

Combine strawberries and orange juice. Combine marshmallows and water; cook over hot water, stirring occasionally, until melted. Fold into strawberry mixture. Cool. Whip cream slightly stiff; add vanilla extract and salt. Fold into strawberry mixture. Pour into freezing tray of automatic refrigerator with cold control set at point recommended by manufacturer for freezing ice cream. Freeze firm.

Plum Marlow
Serves 8

1 No. 2½ can (3½ cups) plums
¼ lb. marshmallows
1 cup milk

¾ cup whipping cream
Few grains salt
1 tbs. lemon juice

Remove plum pits; remove skins. Mash pulp. Combine marshmallows and milk; cook over hot water, stirring occasionally, until melted. Whip cream slightly stiff. Combine cream, marshmallow mixture, plum pulp, salt and lemon juice. Pour into freezing tray of automatic refrigerator with cold control set at point recommended by manufacturer for freezing ice cream. Freeze to mush. Place in chilled bowl. Beat smooth. Return to tray. Freeze firm.

Chocolate Mousse   Serves 8

    2 squares (2 oz.)   ½ cup powdered sugar
      unsweetened chocolate   Few grains salt
    2 cups whipping cream   1 tsp. vanilla extract

Add chocolate to ½ cup cream; heat over hot water until chocolate is melted. Add sugar and salt; mix well. Whip remaining cream slightly; add chocolate mixture and vanilla extract. Pour into freezing tray of automatic refrigerator with cold control set at point recommended by manufacturer for freezing ice cream. Freeze firm.

Coffee Mousse   Serves 8

    2 cups whipping cream   Few grains salt
    ¼ cup ground coffee   1 tsp. vanilla extract
    ½ cup powdered sugar

Combine ½ cup cream and coffee; place over hot water. Cover; heat 5 min. Strain through cheese cloth or fine sieve. Whip remaining cream slightly; add sugar, salt, vanilla extract and coffee mixture. Pour into freezing tray of automatic refrigerator with cold control set at point recommended by manufacturer for freezing ice cream. Freeze firm.

Raspberry Mousse   Serves 8

    1 qt. raspberries   Few grains salt
    1⅓ cups confectioners'   2 cups whipping cream
      sugar

Mix raspberries, sugar and salt. Let stand 1 hour. Press through sieve. Whip cream slightly stiff; fold in sieved berries. Pour into freezing tray of automatic refrigerator with cold control set at point recommended by manufacturer for freezing ice cream. Freeze firm. Or pour into mold; cover. Pack in equal parts crushed ice and ice cream salt. Freeze 4 hours.

Pistachio Parfait   Serves 4-6

1 cup sugar
¼ cup water
2 egg whites
Green vegetable coloring

½ cup chopped pistachio
  nut meats
1 tsp. almond extract
Few grains salt
2 cups whipping cream

Combine sugar and water; boil to 238°F. (or when small amount dropped from tip of spoon spins long thread). Beat egg whites stiff; gradually add sirup, beating constantly. Tint light green. Cool. Add nut meats, almond extract and salt. Whip cream; fold in. Pour into freezing tray of automatic refrigerator with cold control set at point recommended by manufacturer for freezing ice cream. Freeze firm.

Biscuit Tortoni   Serves 4

⅔ cup whipping cream
5 tbs. powdered sugar
2 tsp. sherry flavoring

1 egg white
⅓ cup dried macaroon
  crumbs

Whip cream slightly stiff; add sugar and sherry flavoring. Beat egg white; fold in. Pour into 4 paper cups; sprinkle with crumbs. Set cups in freezing tray of automatic refrigerator with cold control set at point recommended by manufacturer for freezing ice cream. Freeze firm.

Maple Parfait   Serves 4-6

1 tsp. unflavored gelatine
1 cup milk
1 cup whipping cream

¾ cup maple sirup
3 egg whites
Few grains salt

Soften gelatine in milk; heat until gelatine dissolves. Cool. Add cream. Pour into freezing tray of automatic refrigerator with cold control set at point recommended by manufacturer for freezing ice cream. Freeze to mush. Boil sirup to 236°F. (or when small quantity dropped from tip of spoon spins long thread). Beat egg whites stiff; gradually add sirup, beating constantly. Add salt; cool. Beat first mixture with rotary beater until light; fold in egg white mixture. Freeze to mush. Place in chilled bowl. Beat smooth. Return to tray. Freeze firm.

Frozen Virginia Syllabub   Serves 4

½ cup milk
½ cup sweet cider
½ tsp. vanilla extract
½ cup sugar

1 tbs. sherry flavoring
1 cup whipping cream
Few grains nutmeg

Combine milk, cider, vanilla extract, sugar and sherry flavoring. Whip cream slightly stiff; add. Beat with rotary beater until light. Pour into freezing tray of automatic refrigerator with cold control set at point recommended by manufacturer for freezing ice cream. Sprinkle with nutmeg. Freeze firm.

Lemon Ice   Serves 4

1 tsp. unflavored gelatine
2 tbs. cold water
2 cups water
1 cup sugar

1½ tsp. grated lemon rind
⅓ cup lemon juice
Few grains salt

Soften gelatine in cold water. Combine remaining water and sugar; boil 2 min. Add lemon rind and gelatine; stir until gelatine is dissolved. Cool; combine with lemon juice and salt. Strain. Pour into freezing tray of automatic refrigerator with cold control set at point recommended by manufacturer for freezing ice cream. Freeze to mush. Place in chilled bowl. Beat with rotary beater until smooth. Return to tray. Freeze firm, stirring several times.

Frozen Fruit Cake   Serves 8

2 cups milk
½ cup sugar
¼ cup flour
¼ tsp. salt
2 eggs
1 tsp. vanilla extract
1 cup white raisins

1 cup broken pecan nut
   meats
2 cups crumbled macaroons
½ cup chopped candied
   cherries
1 cup whipping cream

Scald milk. Mix sugar, flour and salt; gradually add milk.

Cook over hot water, stirring constantly, until thick. Cover; cook 10 min. Beat eggs; slowly add milk mixture; cook 2 min. Cool. Add vanilla extract, raisins, nut meats, macaroons and cherries. Whip cream slightly stiff; fold in. Pour into freezing tray of automatic refrigerator with cold control set at point recommended by manufacturer for freezing ice cream. Freeze to mush. Place in chilled bowl. Beat smooth. Return to tray. Freeze firm.

Orange Ice
(Freezer Method)

Makes 3 pints

2 cups water
2 cups sugar
2½ cups orange juice

1 tbs. grated orange rind
¼ cup lemon juice
Few grains salt

Combine water and sugar; boil 5 min. Add orange juice and rind, lemon juice and salt. Cool; strain. Follow directions for freezing Lemon Ice.

Lemon Ice
(Freezer Method)

Makes 3 pints

4 cups water
2 cups sugar
⅔ cup lemon juice

1 tbs. grated lemon rind
Few grains salt

Combine water and sugar. Boil 5 min. Add lemon juice and rind and salt. Cool; strain. Place dasher in freezer can; add lemon mixture. Cover; adjust crank. Using 8 parts crushed ice to 1 part ice cream salt, pack around freezer can. Turn crank rapidly; freeze to mush. Remove dasher; cover lemon ice. Drain off brine. Using 4 parts ice and 1 part ice cream salt, pack firmly around freezer can. Cover freezer with burlap or paper; let stand 1 hour 30 min.-2 hours.

Orange Ice

Serves 4

1 tsp. unflavored gelatine
2 tbs. cold water
½ cup water
½ cup sugar

1 tbs. grated orange rind
1½ cups orange juice
1 tbs. lemon juice
Few grains salt

Soften gelatine in cold water. Combine remaining water and sugar; boil 2 min. Add orange rind and gelatine; stir until gelatine is dissolved. Cool; combine with orange and lemon juices and salt. Strain. Pour into freezing tray of automatic refrigerator with cold control set at point recommended by manufacturer for freezing ice cream. Freeze to mush. Place in chilled bowl. Beat with rotary beater until smooth. Return to tray. Freeze firm, stirring several times.

Lemon Sherbet   Serves 4

1 cup water
1¼ cups sugar
1 egg white

½ cup lemon juice
Few grains salt

Combine ½ cup water and sugar; boil 5 min. Beat egg white stiff; slowly add sugar sirup, beating constantly. Combine lemon juice, remaining water and salt. Add slowly to egg white mixture. Cool. Pour into freezing tray of automatic refrigerator with cold control set at point recommended by manufacturer for freezing ice cream. Freeze to mush. Place in chilled bowl. Beat with rotary beater until smooth. Return to tray. Freeze firm, stirring several times.

Orange Lemon Sherbet   Makes 3 pints

(Freezer Method)

2 cups water
1½ cups sugar
1¼ cups orange juice
¼ cup lemon juice

Few grains salt
2 tsp. grated orange rind
2 tsp. grated lemon rind
2 egg whites

Combine water and sugar; boil 2 min. Add orange and lemon juices and salt; cool. Add orange and lemon rinds; strain. Place dasher in freezer can; add orange mixture. Cover; adjust crank. Using 8 parts crushed ice to 1 part ice cream salt, pack around freezer can. Turn crank rapidly; freeze to mush. Beat egg whites stiff; fold into mixture. Freeze firm. Remove dasher; cover sherbet. Drain off brine. Using 4 parts ice to 1 part salt, pack firmly around freezer can. Cover freezer with burlap or paper; let stand 1 hour 30 min.-2 hours.

Orange Sherbet   Serves 4

2 tsp. unflavored gelatine
¾ cup cold water
¾ cup sugar
1½ cups orange juice

3 tbs. lemon juice
1 tbs. grated orange rind
Few grains salt

Soften gelatine in ¼ cup water. Combine remaining water and sugar; boil 1 min. Add gelatine; stir until dissolved. Add orange and lemon juices, orange rind and salt; strain. Cool. Pour into freezing tray of automatic refrigerator with cold control set at point recommended by manufacturer for freezing ice cream. Freeze to mush. Place in chilled bowl. Beat with rotary beater until smooth. Return to tray. Freeze firm, stirring several times.

Lime Sherbet   Serves 4

1½ tsp. unflavored gelatine
2 tbs. cold water
1½ cups water
¾ cup sugar
¼ cup lime juice

⅓ cup orange juice
2 tbs. lemon juice
Few grains salt
Green vegetable coloring
2 egg whites

Soften gelatine in cold water. Combine remaining water and sugar; boil 2 min. Add gelatine; stir until dissolved. Add lime, orange and lemon juices and salt; cool. Tint light green. Pour into freezing tray of automatic refrigerator with cold control set at point recommended by manufacturer for freezing ice cream. Freeze to mush. Place in chilled bowl. Beat with rotary beater until smooth. Beat egg whites stiff; fold in. Return to tray. Freeze firm, stirring several times.

Cranberry Sherbet   Serves 4

1½ cups water
¼ cup sugar
2 tsp. lemon juice

1½ cups canned strained
  cranberry sauce
Few grains salt
1 egg white

Combine water and sugar; boil 1 min. Mash cranberry sauce; gradually add sugar sirup. Press through sieve. Add lemon juice and salt. Cool. Pour into freezing tray of automatic refrigerator with cold control set at point recommended by manufacturer for freezing ice cream. Freeze to mush. Place in chilled bowl. Beat with rotary beater until smooth. Beat egg white stiff; fold in. Return to tray. Freeze firm, stirring several times.

Pineapple Milk Sherbet
Serves 4-6

1 No. 2 can (2½ cups) crushed pineapple
¼ cup orange juice
1 tsp. grated orange rind
½ cup powdered sugar
1 14½-oz. can (1⅔ cups) evaporated milk
Few grains salt

Mix pineapple, orange juice and rind and sugar, stirring until sugar is dissolved. Add evaporated milk and salt. Pour into freezing tray of automatic refrigerator with cold control set at point recommended by manufacturer for freezing ice cream. Freeze to mush. Place in chilled bowl. Beat with rotary beater until smooth. Return to tray. Freeze firm, stirring several times.

Raspberry Sherbet
Serves 4

2 tsp. unflavored gelatine
2 tbs. cold water
½ cup water
⅓ cup sugar
2 cups sieved cooked or canned raspberries
3 tbs. lemon juice
Few grains salt

Soften gelatine in cold water. Combine remaining water and sugar; boil 1 min. Add gelatine; stir until dissolved. Add raspberries, lemon juice and salt; cool. Pour into freezing tray of automatic refrigerator with cold control set at point recommended by manufacturer for freezing ice cream. Freeze to mush. Place in chilled bowl. Beat with rotary beater until smooth. Return to tray. Freeze firm, stirring several times.

Strawberry Sherbet   Serves 4

1 cup crushed sweetened   1 tsp. unflavored gelatine
  strawberries   2 cups milk
1 tbs. orange juice   Few grains salt
1 tbs. lemon juice   1 egg white

Combine strawberries, orange and lemon juices; let stand
30 min. Press through sieve. Soften gelatine in 1 cup
milk; heat until gelatine is dissolved. Combine with remaining milk and salt. Chill. Beat egg white stiff; fold into
strawberry mixture. Combine with milk mixture. Pour into
freezing tray of automatic refrigerator with cold control set
at point recommended by manufacturer for freezing ice
cream. Freeze to mush. Place in chilled bowl. Beat with
rotary beater until smooth. Return to tray. Freeze firm, stirring several times.

22.   EGGS

Soft-Cooked (Coddled) Eggs

Place rack in saucepan, arrange eggs on rack. Cover with
cold water at least 2″ above eggs. Place over low heat.
Slowly bring to boiling point. Reduce heat; simmer 3-5 min.

Hard-Cooked Eggs

Place rack in saucepan, arrange eggs on rack. Cover with
cold water at least 2″ above eggs. Place over low heat.
Slowly bring to boiling point. Reduce heat; simmer 10-15
min. Remove eggs; place immediately under cold running
water.

Poached Eggs

Pour water to depth of 3⁄4″ in shallow pan; bring to boiling point. Break egg into small dish; sprinkle with salt and pepper. Slip into water; cover. Reduce heat; let stand 3-5 min., or until set.

Scrambled Eggs   Serves 4

    6 eggs   1⁄3 cup milk
    3⁄4 tsp. salt   2 tbs. butter or margarine
    Few grains pepper

Beat eggs slightly; add salt and pepper. Add milk; mix well. Melt butter or margarine; add egg mixture. Cook over low heat or boiling water, stirring gently, to loosen eggs from bottom and sides of pan during cooking.

Scrambled Eggs in Popover Shells: Follow recipe for Scrambled Eggs, adding 1⁄3 cup cooked, diced bacon to egg mixture. Split 4 hot Popovers (p. 60); fill with eggs. Serve with crisp bacon strips.

Eggs in Bologna Cups   Serves 4

    1 egg   2 tbs. butter or margarine
    1⁄2 cup milk   4 slices bologna
    4 slices rusk   Scrambled eggs (above)

Beat eggs slightly; add milk. Soak rusk in egg mixture 2 min.; brown on both sides in butter or margarine. Place bologna 2″ below broiler unit or tip of flame; broil until edges curl. Fill with eggs. Place on rusk slices.

Cream Cheese Eggs   Serves 4

    3 tbs. cream cheese   1⁄2 tsp. salt
    2 tbs. milk   1⁄8 tsp. pepper
    6 eggs   2 tbs. butter or margarine

Mash cheese; blend in milk. Beat until fluffy. Beat eggs slightly; add. Add salt and pepper. Melt butter or margarine; add egg mixture. Cook over low heat or boiling water, stirring gently, to loosen eggs from bottom and sides of pan during cooking.

Fried Eggs   Serves 4

Heat 2 tbs. fat or salad oil in skillet. Break 4-8 eggs, 1 at a time, into small dish; slip into skillet. Cook slowly until set.

Eggs-in-a-Frame   Serves 4

    4 bread slices   Salt and pepper
    ¼ cup butter or margarine   Crisp bacon strips
    4 eggs

Using cutter 2½" in diameter, remove centers from bread slices. Brown bread "frames" on one side in butter or margarine. Turn slices; break egg in center of each. Cook slowly until eggs are set. Sprinkle with salt and pepper. Garnish with bacon.

Baked (Shirred) Eggs   Serves 4

    4 eggs   Salt and pepper
    ¼ cup cream

Break each egg into greased individual baking dishes; pour equal amount cream over each. Sprinkle with salt and pepper. Bake in moderate oven (350°F.) 15-20 min.

Baked Eggs Au Gratin   Serves 4

    5 tbs. milk   ½ cup grated American
    2½ cups bread cubes   cheese
    ½ tsp. salt   4 eggs
    Few grains pepper

Combine milk, bread, salt and pepper. Line 4 greased individual baking dishes with bread mixture; sprinkle with cheese. Break egg into each. Bake in moderate oven (350°F.) 15-20 min.

French Omelet   Serves 4

    6 eggs   ⅓ cup milk
    ¾ tsp. salt   2 tbs. butter or margarine
    Few grains pepper

Beat eggs slightly; add salt and pepper. Add milk; mix
well. Melt butter or margarine in skillet. Add egg mixture.
Cook over low heat, lifting edges and tipping skillet so uncooked mixture flows under cooked mixture. When mixture
is set, fold over.

Cheese Omelet: Follow recipe for French Omelet, sprinkling
with grated American cheese before folding.

Fluffy Omelet   Serves 4

    4 egg whites   ¼ cup water
    4 egg yolks   1 tbs. butter or margarine
    ½ tsp. salt   Few grains pepper

Beat egg whites stiff. Beat egg yolks until thick and lemon-
colored; add salt, pepper and water. Fold into whites. Melt
butter or margarine in hot greased skillet; pour in egg
mixture. Cook over low heat 3-5 min., or until omelet is
fluffy and browned on underside. Bake in moderate oven
(350°F.) 10-15 min. Make 1″ cuts on 2 opposite sides of
omelet; indent lightly through center between cuts. Using
spatula, carefully fold over. Serve immediately.

Jelly Omelet: Follow recipe for Fluffy Omelet, spreading
mashed jelly on omelet before folding.

Fluffy Ham Omelet: Follow recipe for Fluffy Omelet, adding
½ cup minced cooked or canned ham to egg yolk mixture.

Fruit Basket Omelet   Serves 4

    1 cup pitted sour red   2 cups sliced peaches
       cherries   1 tbs. butter or margarine
    ½ cup cherry sirup   Fluffy Omelet (see above)
    ½ cup sugar

Combine cherries, sirup and sugar. Cook 5 min., stirring

occasionally. Add peaches and butter or margarine; heat thoroughly. Spread ¾ hot fruit mixture on ½ omelet. Fold omelet; garnish top with remaining fruit.

Fluffy Eggs   Serves 4

8 link sausages	4 eggs
¼ cup chili sauce	Salt and pepper

Fry sausages (p. 238); split lengthwise. Arrange 4 halves in each of 4 individual baking dishes; place 1 tbs. chili sauce in bottom of each. Separate eggs, keeping yolks whole and separate; beat whites stiff. Add salt and pepper; pile in baking dishes. Make well in center of each; drop in yolks. Bake in moderate oven (325°F.) 15 min.

Creamed Eggs   Serves 4

2 tbs. butter or margarine	Few grains pepper
3 tbs. flour	1½ cups milk
¼ tsp. salt	4 hard-cooked eggs

Melt butter or margarine; blend in flour, salt and pepper. Gradually add milk. Cook over hot water, stirring constantly, until thick. Quarter eggs; add. Heat. If desired, serve on toast.

Creamed Eggs California: Follow recipe for Creamed Eggs, adding 1 cup chopped ripe olives with eggs. Serve on toast.

Creamed Bacon and Eggs: Follow recipe for Creamed Eggs, adding ¼ cup chopped crisp bacon with eggs. Serve on squares of hot Corn Bread (p. 59).

Devilled Eggs   Serves 4

4 hard-cooked eggs	½ tsp. Worcestershire
2 tsp. mayonnaise or salad dressing	sauce
1 tsp. lemon juice	½ tsp. salt
¼ tsp. grated onion	⅛ tsp. pepper
½ tsp. dry mustard	Paprika

Halve eggs lengthwise. Remove yolks; mash. Add mayonnaise or salad dressing, lemon juice, onion, mustard, Worcestershire sauce, salt and pepper. Beat until fluffy. Refill egg whites. Garnish with parsley or paprika.

Picnic Eggs
Serves 4

4 hard-cooked eggs
⅓ cup grated Parmesan-style cheese

1 tsp. prepared mustard
Few grains pepper
Milk

Halve eggs lengthwise. Remove yolks; mash. Add cheese, mustard, pepper and enough milk to moisten well. Beat until fluffy. Refill egg whites.

Onion-Stuffed Eggs
Serves 4

4 hard-cooked eggs
1 tbs. minced pickled onion

Mayonnaise or salad dressing
Paprika

Halve eggs lengthwise. Remove yolks; mash. Add onion and enough mayonnaise or salad dressing to moisten well. Beat until fluffy. Refill egg whites. Sprinkle generously with paprika.

Luncheon Casserole
Serves 4

6 hard-cooked eggs
¼ cup softened butter or margarine
¾ tsp. grated onion
3 tsp. minced parsley

1½ tsp. prepared mustard
Salt and pepper
¾ cup sour cream
⅓ cup dry crumbs

Halve eggs lengthwise. Remove yolks; mash. Add 3 tbs. butter or margarine, onion, parsley, mustard, salt and pepper; refill egg whites. Place, cut side up, in shallow baking dish; cover with sour cream. Sprinkle with crumbs; dot with remaining butter or margarine. Bake in hot oven (400°F.) 20 min.

23. FISH AND SHELLFISH

Baked Stuffed Fish   Serves 4-6

Use whole fish weighing 3-5 lbs. If desired, have head and tail removed. Have fish slit and cleaned. Rub inside with salt; stuff with Bread Stuffing (p. 341), Cracker Stuffing (pp. 343-44) or Mushroom Onion Stuffing (pp. 342-43). Fasten edges; place on greased heavy paper in shallow baking pan. Brush with melted fat or salad oil; sprinkle with salt. Bake in hot oven (400°F.) allowing 10 min. per lb. for fish weighing up to 4 lbs. Add 5 min. to total baking time for each lb. in addition. If desired, serve with Caper Sauce (p. 325) or Lemon Chive Butter (p. 330).

Baked Fish Fillets or Steaks   Serves 4

Use fish fillets or steaks about ½″ thick. Cut 1½ lbs. in uniform serving size pieces. Combine ⅓ cup milk and 1 tsp. salt; dip fish in milk mixture. Coat with dry crumbs or finely crushed cereal flakes. Arrange in greased shallow baking pan; dot with butter or margarine. Bake in very hot oven (500°F.) 10 min.

Shrimp-Stuffed Fillets   Serves 4

1 cup cooked or canned shrimp	½ tsp. salt
1 cup cooked wild rice	¼ cup melted butter or margarine
½ tsp. curry powder	2 1-lb. fish fillets

Combine shrimp, rice, curry powder, salt and butter or margarine; spread between fillets. Fasten together. Dot with butter or margarine. Bake in moderate oven (350°F.) 30-40 min.

Broiled Fish   Serves 4

Use whole fish weighing 2 lbs. Have head and tail removed and fish split and cleaned. Place, skin side down, on greased broiler rack with top of food 2″ below broiler unit or tip of flame. Sprinkle with salt and pepper; brush with melted fat or salad oil. Broil 10 min. or until brown. Carefully turn; sprinkle with salt and pepper; brush with melted fat or salad oil. Broil 5 min. or until skin is crisp and brown. If desired, serve with Lemon Butter (p. 330).

Broiled Fish Fillets or Steaks Mayonnaise   Serves 4

Use fish fillets or steaks about ½″ thick. Cut 1½ lbs. in uniform serving size pieces. Place on greased broiler rack with top of food 2″ below broiler unit or tip of flame. Sprinkle with salt and pepper; brush with melted fat or salad oil. Broil 5 min. or until brown; carefully turn. Spread with 2½ tbs. mayonnaise or salad dressing. Sprinkle with flour, salt and pepper. Broil 10 min. or until tender and brown.

Fried Fish   Serves 4

Use 1½ lbs. small lean fish or fillets ½″ thick, cutting fillets in uniform serving size pieces. Roll in seasoned flour, corn meal or dry crumbs. Fry in shallow fat or salad oil heated to 370°F. about 5 min. or until brown. Drain on absorbent paper.

Sautéed Fish   Serves 4

Use 1½ lbs. small lean fish or fillets ½″ thick, cutting fillets in uniform serving size pieces. Roll in seasoned flour, corn meal or dry crumbs. Sauté in fat or salad oil about 10 min., carefully turning once to brown on both sides.

Boiled Fish

Use lean whole fish, fish fillets or steaks, allowing ½ lb. whole fish or ⅓ lb. fillet or steak per person. Wrap fish in cheesecloth; cover with hot water. Add ½ tsp. salt and ½ tbs. vinegar for each quart water. If desired, add 1 bay leaf,

few peppercorns, 1 celery stalk and parsley sprig. Bring to
boiling point; cover. Simmer, allowing 6-10 min. per lb. for
whole fish, 10-20 min. for fillets or steaks. Drain; remove
cheesecloth. Serve with Egg Sauce (p. 325) or Hollandaise
Sauce (p. 331).

Fried Fish Pies

Makes 10

1 cup flaked cooked or
canned fish
5 tbs. mayonnaise or salad
dressing
2 tsp. grated onion

Pastry II (p. 258)
Parsley
Lemon wedges
Tomato Sauce (p. 329)

Combine fish, mayonnaise or salad dressing and onion. Roll
out pastry ⅛″ thick on lightly floured board; cut fish shapes
using cardboard pattern 5″ long or cut with round cutter
3″ in diam. Place fish mixture in center of ½ cutouts; moisten edges with water. Top with remaining cutouts; seal
edges with tines of fork. Fry in deep fat or salad oil heated
to 375°F. about 5 min. or until brown. Drain on absorbent
paper. Garnish with parsley and lemon. Serve with sauce.

Creamed Fish

Serves 4

1½ cups Medium White
Sauce (p. 325)
Salt and pepper

1½ cups flaked cooked or
canned fish
Corn Bread (p. 59)

Combine sauce and fish; heat over hot water. Season with
salt and pepper. Cut hot corn bread in squares. Serve
creamed fish on corn bread.

Creamed Mushrooms and Flaked Fish

Serves 4

⅔ cup sliced mushrooms
2 tbs. butter or margarine
4 tbs. flour
½ tsp. salt
Few grains pepper

2 cups milk
2 cups cooked or canned
flaked fish
1 tbs. chopped parsley
Toast slices

Sauté mushrooms in butter or margarine; blend in flour,

salt and pepper. Gradually add milk. Cook over hot water, stirring constantly, until thick. Add fish and parsley; heat. Serve on toast or, if desired, in Noodle Cheese Ring (p. 137).

Epicurean Halibut
Serves 4

1 can condensed tomato soup
⅓ lb. grated Cheddar cheese

1 lb. cooked halibut (Boiled Fish, pp. 210-11)
Salt and pepper
Toast triangles

Heat soup; add cheese. Heat, stirring occasionally, until cheese is melted. Flake halibut into large pieces; add to tomato mixture. Season with salt and pepper. Serve on toast. If desired, garnish with sautéed mushroom caps.

Sea Food Mélange
Serves 8

2 tbs. butter or margarine
2 tbs. flour
¼ cup cream
1 cup milk
1 cup cooked or canned haddock
¼ tsp. Worcestershire sauce

Few grains cayenne
¼ tsp. paprika
Salt and pepper
1 5¾-oz. can (1 cup) shrimp
Toast points

Melt butter or margarine; blend in flour. Gradually add cream and milk. Cook over hot water, stirring constantly, until thick. Flake haddock; add with Worcestershire sauce, cayenne, paprika. Season with salt and pepper. Add shrimp; heat. Serve on toast. (Lobster or crab meat may be substituted for haddock or shrimp.)

Gloucester Fish Balls
Serves 4

1 cup salt codfish
3½ cups cubed potatoes
2 eggs

1 tbs. melted butter or margarine

Soak codfish in cold water 15 min. Drain; shred. Combine

fish and potatoes; cover with boiling water. Cover; boil 15 min. Drain; mash. Beat eggs; add with butter or margarine. Shape into small balls. Fry in shallow fat or salad oil heated to 385°F. 3-5 min., or until brown. Drain on absorbent paper. If desired, serve with Mustard Sauce (p. 326), Horseradish Sauce (p. 325) or ketchup.

Boiled Lobster

Put 1½ lb. lobster into boiling salted water head first; cover; boil 20-25 min. Remove; cool enough to handle; break off claws. Crack claws. Place lobster on back; make deep cut from head to end of tail. Force open; remove sac just back of head and vein which runs to end of tail. Discard spongy tissue which is found between meat and shell. The green part is edible as well as the coral. Serve in shell with melted butter or margarine or remove meat; cut in pieces. Serves 2 or yields about 1 cup meat.

Broiled Lobster   Serves 1

Insert sharp knife between body and tail of ¾-1 lb. lobster to sever spinal cord. Place on back; make deep cut from head to end of tail. Force open; remove sac just back of head and vein which runs to end of tail. The green part is edible as well as the coral. Crack large claws; place lobster, cut side up, on greased broiler rack with top of food 2" from broiler unit or tip of flame. Brush meat with melted butter or margarine; sprinkle with salt and pepper. Broil 15-20 min., or until browned, turn; broil 5-10 min. Serve with melted butter or margarine.

Lobster Newburg   Serves 4

2 cups cooked or canned lobster
2 tbs. butter or margarine
¼ cup sherry flavoring
2 egg yolks
¾ cup light cream
Salt and pepper
Toast triangles

Heat lobster in butter or margarine 2 min.; add sherry flavoring. Beat egg yolks; add cream. Gradually add to lobster. Cook slowly, stirring constantly, until slightly thickened. Remove from heat; season with salt and pepper. Serve on toast.

Boiled Hard-Shell Crabs

Wash hard-shell crabs in cold running water until all sand is removed. Put into boiling salted water head first; cover; boil 20-25 min. Remove; plunge into cold water. Cool enough to handle; break off claws and apron or tail end. Using knife, force shells open at tail end. Remove spongy substance between halves of body and between sides of shell and body. Remove meat, carefully removing bits of shell and membrane. Crack claws; remove meat. A ½ lb. crab yields ½ cup meat.

Fried Soft-Shell Crabs   Serves 4

Wash 4-6 soft-shell crabs in cold running water until all sand is removed. Using knife, force shells open at tail end. Remove spongy substance between halves of body and between sides of shell and body. Wash crabs in cold running water. Roll in fine crumbs; dip in beaten egg; roll in crumbs. Fry in deep fat or salad oil heated to 375°F. 3-4 min., or until brown. Drain on absorbent paper. Serve with lemon wedges and Tartar Sauce (p. 332).

Crab and Cheese Fondue   Serves 4

1 6½-oz. can (1 cup) crab meat
1 cup diced celery
3 tbs. mayonnaise or salad dressing
1 tbs. prepared mustard
¼ tsp. salt
8 thin bread slices
¾ lb. sliced American cheese
2 eggs
1 cup milk
1 tsp. Worcestershire sauce

Combine crab meat and celery. Combine mayonnaise or salad dressing, mustard and salt; add. Spread between bread slices; halve sandwiches. Alternate layers of sandwiches and cheese in greased baking dish. Beat eggs; add milk and Worcestershire sauce. Pour into baking dish; cover. Bake in moderate oven (325°F.) 45 min.

Crab Meat Canoes

Serves 6

6 medium potatoes	Few grains pepper
2 tbs. butter or margarine	1 6½-oz. can (1 cup) crab
¼ cup milk	meat
1 tbs. grated onion	½ cup grated American
½ tsp. salt	cheese

Bake potatoes (pp. 369-70); slit lengthwise. Carefully scoop out; mash potatoes. Add butter or margarine, milk, onion, salt and pepper; whip until creamy. Add crab meat; refill potato shells, mounding slightly. Sprinkle with cheese. Bake in moderate oven (325°F.) 20 min.

Baked Sea Food Salad

Serves 4-6

1 large green pepper	1 cup mayonnaise or salad
1 small onion	dressing
1 6½-oz. can (1 cup) crab	Few grains pepper
meat	½ tsp. salt
1 cup diced celery	Soft bread crumbs
1 5¾-oz. can (1 cup)	Butter or margarine
shrimp	Paprika
1 tsp. Worcestershire sauce	Lemon wedges

Chop green pepper and onion. Flake crab meat, removing bits of membrane. Combine green pepper, onion, celery, crab meat, shrimp and mayonnaise or salad dressing. Add salt, pepper and Worcestershire sauce. Place in individual shells or in shallow baking dish. Top with crumbs; dot with butter or margarine. Bake in moderate oven (350°F.) 30 min. Sprinkle with paprika; serve with lemon.

Boiled Shrimp

Yields 2 cups

Wash 1 lb. shrimp in cold running water. Put into boiling salted water; cover; boil 15-20 min. Drain. Cool enough to handle; remove shells.

Whole Shrimp in Batter   Serves 4

    1½ cups flour   1 cup milk
    1½ tsp. baking powder   2 5¾-oz. cans (2 cups)
    ¼ tsp. salt   shrimp
    1 egg   Tartar Sauce (p. 332)

Sift together flour, baking powder and salt. Beat egg; add
milk. Add to dry ingredients; beat smooth. Dip shrimp sin-
gly in batter. Fry in shallow fat or salad oil heated to 375°F.
2-3 min., or until brown. Drain on absorbent paper. Serve
with sauce.

Shrimp Medley   Serves 4

    2 5¾-oz. cans (2 cups)   1 No. 2 can (or 2½ cups
      shrimp   cooked) tomatoes
    1 No. 2 can (or 2½ cups   ½ tsp. sugar
      cooked) whole kernel corn 1 cup soft bread crumbs
    1 tsp. salt   Pastry I (p. 257)

Alternate layers shrimp and corn in baking dish. Combine
tomatoes, salt, sugar and crumbs; add. Roll out dough ⅛"
thick on lightly floured board in shape to fit over baking
dish. Prick design in center to allow steam to escape while
baking. Place on shrimp mixture; trim edge; press with
tines of fork. Bake in very hot oven (450°F.) 30 min.

Shrimp and Vegetable Ramekins   Serves 4

    1½ cups Medium White   1½ cups cooked or canned
      Sauce (p. 325)   whole kernel corn
    ⅛ tsp. dry mustard   2 cups cooked or canned
    ¼ tsp. Worcestershire   peas
      sauce   Soft bread crumbs
    2 drops tabasco   Butter or margarine
    1 5¾-oz. can (1 cup)
      shrimp

Combine sauce, mustard, Worcestershire sauce, and tabasco. Add corn and peas. Place in individual shells or rame-
kins. Top with shrimp. Sprinkle with crumbs; dot with butter or margarine. Bake in hot oven (400°F.) 20 min.

Baked Oysters in Shell

Scrub oysters in shell: rinse in cold running water until all sand is removed. Place in baking pan; bake in very hot oven (450°F.) 10 min., or until shells open. Season with salt and pepper. Serve with melted butter or margarine.

Scalloped Oysters

Serves 4

1½ pts. oysters
¾ tsp. salt
Few grains pepper
¾ cup milk

⅓ cup melted butter or margarine
3 cups coarse soda cracker crumbs

Remove any bits of shell from oysters. Strain oyster liquid through cheesecloth. Add salt and pepper to oysters. Mix butter or margarine and crackers. Alternate layers oysters and cracker mixture in greased baking dish. Combine milk and oyster liquid; pour into baking dish. Bake in moderate oven (350°F.) 30 min.

Fried Oysters

Serves 4

1 pt. oysters
1 egg
Dry crumbs

Lemon wedges
Tartar Sauce (p. 332)

Drain oysters; remove any bits of shell. Beat egg. Roll oysters in crumbs; dip in egg; roll in crumbs. Fry in shallow fat or salad oil heated to 375°F. 2-3 min. or until brown. Drain on absorbent paper. Serve with lemon and sauce.

Oyster Fritters

Serves 4

1 pt. oysters
2 eggs
⅓ cup milk
1⅓ cups flour

2 tsp. baking powder
½ tsp. salt
Few grains pepper

Drain oysters; remove any bits of shell. Chop oysters. Beat eggs, add milk. Sift together flour, baking powder, salt and pepper; add milk mixture. Add oysters; mix well. Drop by spoonfuls into shallow fat or salad oil heated to 375°F. Fry 3 min., or until brown. Drain on absorbent paper.

Steamed Clams
Serves 4

4 doz. soft-shelled clams in shell
Salt and pepper

Melted butter or margarine
½ cup hot water

Scrub clams; rinse in cold running water until all sand is removed. Place in large saucepan; add water. Cover; cook slowly 20 min. or until shells open. Place clams on hot platter. Season broth with salt and pepper; serve in cups. Serve individual dishes of butter or margarine with clams.

Seaman's Pie
Serves 4

1 large onion
2 tbs. fat or salad oil
2 cups cooked or canned minced clams

2 cups cubed cooked potatoes
½ tsp. salt
Few grains pepper
Pastry I (p. 257)

Slice onion; cook in fat or salad oil until soft but not brown. Add clams, potatoes, salt and pepper. Heat. Pour into baking dish. Roll out dough ⅛" thick on lightly floured board in shape to fit over baking dish. Prick design in center to allow steam to escape while baking. Place on clam mixture; trim edges; press with tines of fork. Bake in hot oven (400°F.) 20 min. or until brown.

Clamburgers
Serves 4

2 eggs
2 cups drained cooked or canned minced clams
⅔ cup dry crumbs
2 tbs. lemon juice
1 tbs. onion juice
2 tbs. minced parsley

½ tsp. salt
Few grains pepper
Fat or salad oil
4 large soft round buns
Butter or margarine
Ketchup

Beat eggs; add clams, crumbs, lemon and onion juices, parsley, salt and pepper. Mix well. Shape in 4 flat cakes; sauté in fat or salad oil, turning to brown on both sides. Split buns; toast. Spread with butter or margarine. Place clam cakes between halves. Serve with ketchup.

Fried Scallops

Wash 1 pt. (1 lb.) scallops in cold running water; drain on absorbent paper. Follow recipe for Fried Oysters (p. 217) substituting scallops for oysters.

Scalloped Scallops   Serves 4

1 pt. (1 lb.) scallops	¾ cup melted butter or
2 cups coarse soda cracker	margarine
crumbs	½ tsp. salt
1 cup soft bread crumbs	Few grains pepper
	1 cup light cream

Wash scallops in cold running water; drain. Cut in half crosswise. Combine crumbs, butter or margarine, salt and pepper. Alternate layers of scallops and crumb mixture in greased baking dish, ending with crumbs. Pour cream into baking dish. Bake in moderate oven (350°F.) 25 min.

Salmon Noodle Loaf   Serves 4-6

2 eggs	½ tsp. salt
1 cup milk	¼ tsp. ground sage
1 1-lb. can (2 cups) salmon	2 cups cooked fine noodles

Beat eggs; add milk. Add salmon, salt and sage. Add noodles; mix well. Pour into greased loaf pan. Bake in moderate oven (350°F.) 1 hour 15 min.

Salmon and Rice Ring   Serves 4-6

1 tbs. chopped parsley	2 eggs
1 tsp. grated onion	1 1-lb. can (2 cups) salmon
1 tbs. lemon juice	Salt and pepper
¼ cup milk	3 cups cooked rice

Combine parsley, onion, lemon juice and milk. Beat eggs; add. Add salmon. Season with salt and pepper. Place layer of rice in greased ring mold; cover with ½ salmon mixture. Repeat. Place in pan of hot water; bake in moderate oven (325°F.) 1 hour.

Salmon à la King Croquettes

1 1-lb. can (2 cups) salmon
1 cup Thick White Sauce (p. 326)
2 eggs
½ cup chopped cooked or canned mushrooms
2 tbs. water
Dry crumbs

Combine salmon, sauce and mushrooms. Pack into greased pan 8" x 8" x 2"; chill thoroughly. Cut in diamonds. Beat eggs; add water. Roll croquettes in crumbs; dip in egg; roll in crumbs. Fry in shallow fat or salad oil heated to 375°F. about 5 min. or until brown. Drain on absorbent paper.

Salmon Timbales   Serves 4

2 tbs. chopped green pepper
¼ cup chopped onion
2 tbs. fat or salad oil
1 1-lb. can (2 cups) salmon
2 eggs
2 cups soft bread crumbs
Salt and pepper

Sauté green pepper and onion in fat or salad oil; add to salmon. Beat eggs; add with crumbs. Season with salt and pepper. Pack into greased muffin pans; bake in moderate oven (350°F.) 30 min.

Salmon Pinwheels   Serves 4

1 1-lb. can (2 cups) salmon
¼ cup soft bread crumbs
1 tbs. chopped onion
3 tbs. melted butter or margarine
¼ cup chopped olives
2 tsp. Worcestershire sauce
2 tbs. chili sauce
Baking Powder Biscuit dough (p. 52)
2 eggs

Combine salmon, crumbs, onion, butter or margarine, olives, Worcestershire sauce and chili sauce. Beat eggs; add. Roll biscuit dough into oblong ¼" thick on lightly floured board; spread with salmon mixture. Roll up; slice. Bake in hot oven (400°F.) 30 min.

Creamed Salmon and Corn   Serves 4

2 tbs. butter or margarine
4 tbs. flour
¾ tsp. salt
Few grains pepper
1 tsp. sugar
2 cups milk

¾ cup cooked or canned salmon
1½ cups cooked or canned whole kernel corn
1 tbs. chopped pimiento
Toast slices

Melt butter or margarine; blend in flour, salt, pepper and sugar. Gradually add milk. Cook over hot water, stirring constantly, until thick. Add salmon, corn and pimiento. Serve on toast or, if desired, in Spinach Ring (p. 372).

Tuna Loaf   Serves 4-6

1 13-oz. can (2 cups) tuna
½ cup milk
2 cups soft bread crumbs
2 eggs
1 tbs. grated onion

2 tbs. minced parsley
1 tbs. lemon juice
¼ tsp. salt
Few grains pepper

Mix tuna, milk and crumbs. Beat eggs; add. Add onion, parsley, lemon juice, salt and pepper; pack in greased loaf pan. Bake in moderately hot oven (375°F.) 40 min.

Tuna Scallop   Serves 4-6

1 6-oz. pkg. noodles
1 13-oz. can (2 cups) tuna
1½ cups Medium White Sauce (p. 325)

1 cup grated American cheese

Boil noodles (p. 137); drain. Alternate layers of noodles, tuna, sauce and cheese in greased baking dish, ending with cheese. Bake in hot oven (400°F.) 20 min.

Baked Tuna Molds   Serves 4

3 tbs. butter or margarine
⅓ cup soft bread crumbs
1 cup milk
1 7-oz. can (1 cup) tuna

2 tbs. chopped pimiento
2 eggs
1 tsp. salt
Few grains pepper

Melt butter or margarine; add crumbs, milk, tuna and pimiento. Beat eggs slightly; add with salt and pepper. Pour into greased individual molds. Bake in moderate oven (325°F.) 45 min.

Tuna Rarebit   Serves 4

1 tbs. butter or margarine	¼ lb. grated Cheddar
1 tbs. flour	cheese
½ tsp. dry mustard	½ tsp. salt
1 cup milk	1 tsp. Worcestershire
1 egg	sauce
	1½ cups tuna

Melt butter or margarine; blend in flour and mustard. Gradually add milk. Beat egg; add with cheese. Cook over hot water, stirring constantly, until thick. Add salt, Worcestershire sauce and tuna; heat.

24. MEATS

Standing Rib Roast of Beef

Use 2-3 rib roast of beef, allowing ½ lb. per person. Sprinkle with salt and pepper. Place, fat side up, in roasting pan. Insert meat thermometer into center of thickest part of meat, being sure bulb does not rest on bone. Roast in moderate oven (325°F.). If desired, serve with Pan Gravy (p. 328).

For 4-6 lb. roast:
   Rare: Allow 26 min. per lb. or until meat thermometer registers 140°F.
   Medium: Allow 30 min. per lb. or until meat thermometer registers 160°F.

Well-Done: Allow 35 min. per lb. or until meat thermometer registers 170°F.

For 6-8 lb. roast:
Rare: Allow 22 min. per lb. or until meat thermometer registers 140°F.
Medium: Allow 26 min. per lb. or until meat thermometer registers 160°F.
Well-Done: Allow 33 min. per lb. or until meat thermometer registers 170°F.

Rolled Rib Roast of Beef

Use rolled rib roast of beef, allowing ¼ lb. per person. Sprinkle with salt and pepper. Place on rack, fat side up, in roasting pan. Insert meat thermometer into center of thickest part of meat. Roast in moderate oven (325°F.). If desired, serve with Pan Gravy (p. 328).

For 4-6 lb. roast:
Rare: Allow 31-36 min. per lb. or until meat thermometer registers 140°F.
Medium: Allow 35-40 min. per lb. or until meat thermometer registers 160°F.
Well-Done: Allow 40-45 min. per lb. or until meat thermometer registers 170°F.

For 6-8 lb. roast:
Rare: Allow 27-32 min. per lb. or until meat thermometer registers 140°F.
Medium: Allow 31-36 min. per lb. or until meat thermometer registers 160°F.
Well-Done: Allow 38-43 min. per lb. or until meat thermometer registers 170°F.

Broiled Beef Steak

Use sirloin, porterhouse or club steak at least 1″ thick, allowing ½ lb. per person. Place steak on broiler rack with top of food 2″ below unit or tip of flame for steak 1-1¾″ thick, and 3″ below unit or tip of flame for steak 2″ thick. If distance must be less, reduce heat accordingly. Broil, sprinkling with salt and pepper and turning when ½ total cooking time is completed.

For 1" steaks:
  Rare: Allow 12-15 min.
  Medium: Allow 15-18 min.
  Well-Done: Allow 18-22 min.

For 1½" steaks:
  Rare: Allow 20-25 min.
  Medium: Allow 25-30 min.
  Well-Done: Allow 30-35 min.

For 2" steaks:
  Rare: Allow 25-35 min.
  Medium: Allow 35-40 min.
  Well-Done: Allow 40-45 min.

Planked Beef Steak

Follow recipe for Broiled Beef Steak. Heat plank; place steak on plank. Put hot seasoned mashed potatoes through rose tip of pastry bag around edge of plank and around steak. Arrange halved tomatoes seasoned with salt and pepper and sautéed mushrooms on plank. Place under unit or tip of flame until vegetables are browned. Place hot seasoned cooked or canned asparagus on plank just before serving. Spread steak with butter or margarine. Garnish with parsley.

Pan-Broiled Beef Steak

Use sirloin, porterhouse or club steak ¾-1½" thick, allowing ½ lb. per person. Place steak in heavy skillet; quickly brown on both sides. Cook slowly until done, pouring off fat as it accumulates. To test for doneness, cut gash near bone. Sprinkle with salt and pepper.

Pan-Broiled Cube Steaks

Use cube steaks, allowing ¼ lb. per person. Heat small amount fat or salad oil in heavy skillet; quickly brown meat on both sides. Cook slowly 2 min., or until done. Sprinkle with salt and pepper.

Broiled Ground Beef Patties

Use ground beef chuck, allowing ¼ lb. per person. Season with salt and pepper; shape into patties 1″ thick and 3″ in diam. Place on broiler rack with top of food 2″ below unit or tip of flame. Broil, turning when ½ total cooking time is completed. For rare patties, allow 15 min.; for medium patties, allow 25 min.; for well-done patties, allow 35 min.

Pan-Broiled Ground Beef Patties

Use ground beef chuck, allowing ¼ lb. per person. Season with salt and pepper; shape into patties 1″ thick and 3″ in diameter. Rub heavy skillet with small amount fat or salad oil; brown patties on both sides. Cook slowly, turning frequently, about 10-12 min. or until done, pouring off fat as it accumulates.

Braised Beef Steak

Use arm, blade, rump, bottom or top round of beef cut 1″ thick, allowing ¼ lb. per person. To 1 lb. beef, pound in ¼ cup flour with mallet. Brown beef on both sides in small amount fat or salad oil, adding 1 chopped onion before meat is completely browned. Season with salt and pepper; add hot water to cover bottom of pan. Cover; simmer 1-1½ hours, or until tender, adding water if necessary.

Swiss Steak: Follow recipe for Braised Steak, using bottom round of beef and substituting tomato juice for water.

Beef Pot Roast

Use 3-5 lb. beef chuck, rump or heel of round, allowing ½ lb. per person. Brown meat in deep pan on all sides in small amount fat or salad oil. Season with salt and pepper. Add 1 cup hot water. Place rack under meat; cover. Simmer 3-4 hours or until tender, adding water if necessary. If desired, chopped onion may be browned with meat. Serve with Pan Gravy (p. 328).

Beef Pot Roast with Vegetables: Follow recipe for Beef Pot Roast, adding whole carrots, onions and potatoes 1 hour before total cooking time is completed.

Spiced Pot Roast   Serves 8

2 onions
¼ cup fat or salad oil
4 lb. beef chuck, rump or heel of round
¼ cup flour
1 tsp. salt

1 No. 2 can (or 2½ cups cooked) tomatoes
¼ tsp. pepper
1 bay leaf
¼ tsp. whole cloves
¼ cup vinegar
2 tbs. brown sugar

Chop onion; brown in fat or salad oil. Dredge beef in flour; brown on all sides with onion. Place rack under meat. Combine tomatoes, salt, pepper, bay leaf, cloves, vinegar and brown sugar. Pour over beef; cover. Simmer about 3 hours.

"Boiled" Beef

Use 3-6 lb. beef brisket, plate, shank or heel of round, allowing ½ lb. per person. Cover with water; bring to boiling point. If desired, add 1 carrot, 1 stalk celery, 1 bay leaf and a few peppercorns. Cover; simmer 2-4 hours, or until tender. Serve with Horse-radish Cream (p. 331).

Braised Short Ribs   Serves 4

3 lbs. short ribs
Flour
Fat or salad oil
3 tbs. flour
1½ cups water
¼ cup chopped carrot

½ cup cooked or canned tomatoes
¼ cup chopped onion
¼ cup chopped celery tops
½ garlic clove
Salt and pepper

Have short ribs cut in individual portions. Dredge in flour; brown on both sides in fat or salad oil. Place short ribs in baking dish. Blend flour into pan drippings; gradually add water. Add tomatoes, carrot, onion, celery tops, garlic, salt and pepper; pour over short ribs. Cover; simmer 1½ hours, or until tender.

English Beef Stew
Serves 4

2 lb. flank steak
2 tbs. fat or salad oil
4 medium carrots
4 medium onions
4 medium potatoes
1½ cups boiling water

¾ tsp. Worcestershire
sauce
½ tsp. salt
Few grains pepper
8 whole cloves
Flour

Cut steak in cubes; brown in fat or salad oil. Add carrots, onions, potatoes, water, Worcestershire sauce, salt and pepper. Tie cloves in cheesecloth; add. Cover; simmer 1½ hours. Drain off liquid; measure. Mix 1 tbs. flour and water for each cup liquid; blend into liquid. Cook slowly, stirring constantly, until thickened. Add to meat and vegetable mixture.

Rolled Stuffed Flank Steak
Serves 4

1½ lb. flank steak
⅓ cup vinegar
2 tbs. sugar
2 tsp. salt
½ tsp. pepper
½ tsp. whole cloves
¾ tsp. cinnamon
1 bay leaf

1 cup cooked rice
1 tsp. chopped parsley
Few grains salt
2 tbs. melted butter or
margarine
1 small onion
2 tbs. fat or salad oil

Put steak into deep bowl. Combine vinegar, sugar, salt, pepper, cloves and cinnamon; crush bay leaf; add. Bring to boiling point. Cool; pour over steak. Cover; let stand 8 hours in refrigerator, turning several times. Drain steak. Combine rice, parsley, salt and butter or margarine; spread on steak. Roll up; tie firmly. Slice onion; brown with steak in fat or salad oil. Add hot water to almost cover steak; cover. Simmer 1½ hours, or until tender.

Irish Stew
Serves 4-6

1½ lbs. beef
3 tbs. fat or salad oil
¼ cup diced carrots
¼ cup diced turnips
¼ cup sliced onions

1½ cups diced potatoes
1 tsp. salt
Few grains pepper
Flour
1½ cups boiling water

Cut beef in cubes; dredge with flour and ½ salt; brown in fat or salad oil. Add carrots, onions, turnips, potatoes, water, ½ salt and pepper. Cover; simmer 1½ hours. Drain off liquid; measure. Mix 1 tbs. each flour and water for each cup liquid. Blend into liquid. Cook slowly, stirring constantly, until thickened. Add to meat and vegetable mixture. Serve with dumplings (p. 345).

Beef Stroganoff
Serves 8

3 lbs. onions
⅓ cup fat or salad oil
2 lb. beef round steak
1 lb. mushrooms
1 can condensed tomato soup

1 6-oz. can (¾ cup) tomato paste
1 cup sour cream
1 tsp. salt
Few grains pepper
1 tsp. Worcestershire sauce
Hot cooked rice

Using coarse blade, put onions through food chopper. Drain, reserving juice. (There should be 5 cups onions.) Cook onions slowly 20 min. in fat or salad oil. Cut round steak in very thin slices; slice mushrooms. Add steak and mushrooms to onions; cook until brown. Combine tomato soup, tomato paste, onion juice, cream, salt, pepper and Worcestershire sauce; pour over steak mixture. Cover; simmer 1 hour. Serve on rice.

Chicago Casserole
Serves 4

1 lb. dried lima beans
½ lb. beef round steak
¼ cup chopped onion
2 tbs. fat or salad oil

1 can tomato soup
1 tbs. sugar
1 tbs. salt
Salt pork strips

Wash beans; discard imperfect ones. Cover with cold water; soak overnight. Or, cover with large amount boiling water; soak 4-5 hours. Drain; cover with large amount boiling salted water. Cover; boil slowly 2 hours; drain. Cut beef in ½" cubes. Brown with onion in fat or salad oil. Combine with beans. Add tomato soup (to condensed soup, add equal amount of water using soup can to measure). Add sugar and salt. Pour mixture into bean pot; top with salt pork. Bake in moderately hot oven (375°F.) 1 hour.

Beef Loaf
Serves 4-6

1 onion	1 tsp. sage
2 tbs. fat or salad oil	2 tsp. Worcestershire sauce
1½ lbs. ground beef chuck	1 cup soft bread crumbs
1 tsp. salt	½ cup milk

Mince onion; sauté in fat or salad oil. Combine with beef, salt, sage, Worcestershire sauce, crumbs and milk; mix well. Pack into greased loaf pan. Bake in moderate oven (325°F.) 1½ hours.

Two-Crust Patty Pie
Serves 4

Pastry II (p. 258)	2 large onions
¾ lb. ground beef chuck	3 tbs. flour
¼ lb. ground pork shoulder	1 No. 2 can (2½ cups)
¾ tsp. salt	mixed carrots and peas
Pepper	Water
2 tbs. fat or salad oil	1 tsp. Worcestershire sauce

Make pastry, following directions for Two-Crust Pie. Combine beef, pork, ½ tsp. salt and few grains pepper. Form into balls 1" in diam. Sauté in fat or salad oil until brown; remove from pan. Slice onions thin; brown in fat left in pan. Blend in flour. Drain liquor from carrots and peas; measure; add water to make 1 cup. Add to onion mixture; cook, stirring constantly, until thick. Add carrots, peas and meat balls. Add Worcestershire sauce, ¼ tsp. salt and few grains pepper. Pour into pastry shell. Cover with pastry. Bake in very hot oven (450°F.) 25 min.

Pinwheel Meat Roll

Serves 4

½ cup minced onion
2 tbs. fat or salad oil
1½ cups chopped cooked
    or canned carrots
2 tsp. salt
1 egg

6 tbs. dry bread crumbs
2 tbs. milk
¼ tsp. sage
¾ lb. ground beef chuck
¼ lb. ground pork shoulder

Brown ¼ cup minced onion in fat or salad oil; add carrots and ½ tsp. salt; mix well. Beat egg; add crumbs, milk, sage, remaining salt and onion, beef and pork; mix well. Place meat mixture between waxed paper on bread board. Roll in oblong ¼″ thick; remove top paper. Spread with carrot mixture; roll jelly-roll fashion. Place in shallow baking pan. Bake in moderate oven (350°F.) 1 hour.

Mock Drumsticks

Serves 4

½ lb. ground beef chuck
½ lb. ground veal shoulder
¾ tsp. salt
⅛ tsp. pepper

½ tsp. sage
2 tsp. chopped onion
Dry crumbs

Combine beef, veal, salt, pepper, sage and onion; mix well. Shape like drumsticks. Roll in crumbs. Fry in shallow fat or salad oil 10 min. Drain on absorbent paper. Insert wooden skewers. Place paper frills on skewers.

Potato-Topped Meat Loaf

Serves 8

1 lb. ground beef chuck
½ lb. ground veal shoulder
½ lb. ground pork shoulder
2½ cups crushed corn
    flakes
2 eggs

Few grains pepper
½ tsp. salt
½ tsp. sage
½ cup evaporated milk
Hot seasoned mashed
    potatoes

Combine beef, veal, pork and corn flakes. Beat eggs; add to meat mixture with pepper, salt, sage and milk. Pack into greased loaf pan. Bake in moderate oven (350°F.) 1 hour. Unmold; frost with potatoes. Bake in moderate oven (350°F.) until potatoes are browned.

King Cole Pie
Serves 4

2 cups cubed cooked beef
1 can condensed vegetable soup
1 can condensed mock turtle soup

1½ cups biscuit dough (p. 52)
2 tbs. melted butter or margarine

Combine beef with vegetable and mock turtle soups; pour into baking dish. Roll out biscuit dough ½" thick in shape to fit over baking dish. Cut in strips ½" wide; place on filling in open woven design. Trim edges; press with tines of fork. Brush strips with butter or margarine. Bake in very hot oven (450°F.) 25 min.

Baked Curry of Beef
Serves 4

1½ cups Medium White Sauce (p. 325)
1½ tsp. curry powder
2 cups chopped cooked beef
1½ cups cooked or canned peas

1½ cups cooked or canned carrots
3 tbs. minced onion
Salt and pepper
2 cups cooked rice
Chutney
Hard-cooked egg slices

Combine sauce and curry powder; mix well. Add beef, peas, carrots and onion. Season with salt and pepper. Pour into baking dish; top with rice. Bake in hot oven (400°F.) 20 min. Garnish with chutney and egg.

Roast Beef or Corned Beef Hash
Serves 4

2 cups chopped cooked or canned roast beef or corned beef
3 tbs. minced onion

3 cups chopped cooked potatoes
½ cup milk
Salt and pepper
Fat or salad oil

Combine beef, potatoes, onion and milk. Season with salt and pepper. Cook slowly in a little fat or salad oil until browned, turning frequently. If desired, form mixture into patties; roll in flour. Cook in a little fat or salad oil turning to brown on both sides.

Corned Beef Casserole
Serves 4

4 cups cooked rice
2 cups cubed cooked or
    canned corned beef
¼ cup chopped onion

1 No. 2 can (or 2½ cups
    cooked) tomatoes
1 tsp. salt
Few grains pepper
1 tsp. Worcestershire sauce

Alternate layers of rice and corned beef in greased casserole. Combine tomatoes, onion, salt, pepper and Worcestershire sauce. Pour over beef mixture; cover. Bake in moderate oven (350°F.) 30 min.

Corned Beef

Use 4-9 lb. corned beef brisket, allowing ¼ lb. per person. Cover with water; bring to boiling point. Cover; simmer 3-5 hours, or until tender.

"Boiled" Beef Tongue

Use 2-4 lb. beef tongue, allowing ⅓-½ lb. per person. Cover with water; bring to boiling point. Cover; simmer 2-4 hours, or until tender. Remove skin and small bones at base of tongue. If desired, cool in stock.

Braised Tongue with Vegetable Sauce: Follow recipe for "Boiled" Beef Tongue, reserving 1 cup stock. Heat ¼ cup fat or salad oil; blend in ¼ cup flour. Add 1 cup stock and 1 can tomato soup (to condensed soup add equal amount water, using soup can to measure). Cook, stirring constantly, until thick. Add 2 tsp. Worcestershire sauce, few grains salt, 12 small carrots, 3 cups potato balls and 1 cup diced celery. Simmer 30 min. Place tongue in baking pan; add vegetable mixture. Cover; bake in hot oven (400°F.) 1 hour.

Creamed Dried Beef
Serves 4

4 oz. dried beef
Few grains pepper

1½ cups Medium White
    Sauce (p. 325)
Toast triangles

Shred beef; cover with hot water; drain. Combine with sauce; add pepper. Heat. Serve on toast.

Creamed Cabbage and Dried Beef   Serves 4

    4 oz. dried beef   1½ cups Medium White
    3 cups cooked chopped   Sauce (p. 325)
       cabbage   1 cup soft bread crumbs
                                    Butter or margarine

Shred beef; cover with hot water; drain. Combine beef, cabbage and sauce; pour into greased baking dish. Top with crumbs; dot with butter or margarine. Bake in moderate oven (350°F.) 20 min.

Dried Beef Roulades   Serves 4

    1 cup well-seasoned   1 egg
       mashed potatoes   1 cup grated American
    8 slices dried beef   cheese

Place 2 tbs. potatoes on each slice beef. Roll up; fasten with pick. Beat egg. Dip each beef roll in egg; roll in cheese. Place on broiler rack with top of food 3″ below unit or tip of flame. Broil until cheese is melted and slightly browned.

Baked Smoked Whole or Half Ham

Use 10-14 lb. whole smoked ham or 6-8 lb. half ham, allowing ½ lb. per person. Place, fat side up, on rack in roasting pan. Insert meat thermometer into center of thickest part of meat, being sure bulb does not rest on bone. For tender (not cooked) ham, follow manufacturer's directions, if given, to wrap ham loosely in paper wrappings. Bake in slow oven (300°F.). One hour before total baking time is completed, remove paper, if necessary. Remove rind; score fat in diamond pattern. Insert whole cloves; sprinkle with brown sugar. If desired, baste several times with pineapple juice.

For whole ham: Allow 25 min. per lb. or until meat thermometer registers 170°F.

For whole tender (not cooked) ham: Allow 15-18 min. per lb. or until meat thermometer registers 160°F.

For half ham: Allow 30 min. per lb. or until meat thermometer registers 170°F.

For half tender (not cooked) ham: Allow 20-25 min. per lb. or until meat thermometer registers 160°F.

Glazes For Baked Ham

Follow recipe for Baked Smoked Whole or Half Ham, substituting one of the following glazes for brown sugar.

Honey Glaze: Spread with 1 cup liquid honey.

Orange Glaze: Combine 1 cup firmly packed brown sugar, ⅓ cup orange juice and 1 tsp. grated orange rind.

Cider Glaze: Combine 1 cup brown sugar and 1 tsp. dry mustard. Baste ham with cider every 15 min. during last hour of baking.

"Boiled" Smoked Whole or Half Ham

Use 10-14 lb. whole smoked ham or 6-8 lb. half ham, allowing ½ lb. per person. Cover with water; bring to boiling point. Cover; simmer until tender.

For whole ham: Allow 18-25 min. per lb.

For whole tender (not cooked) ham: Allow 15-20 min. per lb.

For half ham: Allow 30 min. per lb.

For half tender (not cooked) ham: Allow 20-25 min. per lb.

Baked Smoked Picnic Shoulder

Use 5-8 lb. smoked picnic shoulder, allowing ½ lb. per person. Place, fat side up, on rack in roasting pan. Insert meat thermometer into center of thickest part of meat, being sure bulb does not rest on bone. Roast in slow oven (300°F.) 30-35 min. per lb. or until meat thermometer registers 170°F.

"Boiled" Smoked Picnic Shoulder

Use 5-8 lb. smoked picnic shoulder, allowing ½ lb. per person. Cover with water; bring to boiling point. Cover; simmer until tender, allowing 45 min. per lb.

Broiled Smoked Ham Slice

Use smoked ham slice cut ½"-1" thick, allowing ¼ lb. per person. Slash edge of fat in several places. Place ham on broiler rack with top of food 3" below unit or tip of flame. Broil, turning when ½ total cooking time is completed. For ham slice ½" thick, allow 15-20 min.; for 1" thick, allow 20-25 min. For tender (not cooked) ham slice ½" thick, allow 10-12 min., for 1" thick allow 16-20 min. If desired, serve with Raisin Nut Sauce (p. 330).

Baked Smoked Ham Slice

Use slice of smoked ham cut ½"-1" thick, allowing ¼-⅓ lb. per person. Slash edge of fat in several places; stud with cloves. Place in baking dish; sprinkle with brown sugar. Add pineapple juice to cover bottom of pan. Bake in moderate oven (350°F.) 25-30 min. per lb. basting occasionally. For tender (not cooked) ham slice, bake 20 min. per lb.

"Boiled" Smoked Cottage Roll

Use 1½-3 lb. smoked cottage roll, allowing ⅓-½ lb. per person. Cover with water; bring to boiling point. Cover; simmer until tender, allowing 40-45 min. per lb.

Baked Cottage Roll With Grapefruit   Serves 4-6

2 lb. smoked cottage roll	½ cup grapefruit juice
Whole cloves	1 grapefruit
Cinnamon	Brown sugar

Cover cottage roll with water; cover. Simmer 1 hour; drain. Place in baking pan; insert cloves. Add grapefruit juice. Bake in moderate oven (350°F.) 1 hour, basting every 15 min. Cut grapefruit in eighths; dip in brown sugar and cinnamon. Brown under broiler unit or burner. Use to garnish cottage roll.

Baked Crown of Ham   Serves 8

3 eggs	2 lbs. ground smoked ham
¾ cup milk	shoulder
3 cups soft bread crumbs	2 lbs. ground veal shoulder
1 cup ketchup	½ cup currant jelly
4 tsp. Worcestershire sauce	2 tbs. fat or salad oil
⅓ cup minced onion	Parsley
⅛ tsp. pepper	Apple wedges
	Fat or salad oil

Beat eggs; add milk and crumbs; let stand 10 min. Add ketchup, Worcestershire sauce, onion and pepper. Add ham and veal; mix well. Pack in greased tube pan 10″ in diam. Bake in moderate oven (350°F.) 2 hours. Unmold in shallow pan; spread top and sides with jelly. Bake in moderate oven (350°F.) 30 min. Sauté apple wedges in fat or salad oil. Use to garnish ham.

Dixie Casserole   Serves 4

6 hard-cooked eggs	2 cups Medium White Sauce
½ lb. sliced boiled ham	(p. 325)
1½ cups cooked or canned	1 cup soft bread crumbs
whole kernel corn	Butter or margarine

Slice eggs; place ½ eggs and ham in bottom of casserole. Add corn; cover with 1 cup sauce. Add remaining eggs, ham, corn, and sauce. Top with crumbs; dot with butter or margarine. Bake in hot oven (400°F.) 15 min.

Creamed Ham Carolina   Serves 4

1 can condensed mushroom	1 cup cubed cooked or
soup	canned ham
¼ cup milk	Salt and pepper
2 hard-cooked eggs	Hot corn bread squares

Heat soup over hot water; gradually add milk. Add ham. Slice eggs; add. Season with salt and pepper; heat thoroughly. Split corn bread; cover with ham mixture.

Ham Cutlets

Serves 4

2 cups ground cooked or canned ham
1 cup Thick White Sauce (p. 326)

1 tbs. chopped parsley
1 tbs. ketchup
1 egg
2 tbs. water
Dry crumbs

Combine ham, sauce, parsley and ketchup. Chill. Shape in small cutlets. Beat egg; add water. Roll cutlets in crumbs; dip in egg mixture; roll in crumbs. Fry in deep fat or salad oil heated to 375°F. 2-3 min. Drain on absorbent paper. If desired, serve with Spanish Sauce (p. 329).

Thrift Special

Serves 4

3 cups well seasoned mashed potatoes
2 cups Medium White Sauce (p. 325)
⅔ cup grated American cheese

1 cup cubed cooked or canned ham
1 cup cooked or canned cubed carrots
1 cup cooked or canned peas

Shape potatoes into 4" nests on greased baking sheet. Bake in very hot oven (450° F.) until browned. Combine sauce, cheese, ham, carrots and peas; heat thoroughly. Pour into potato nests.

Bacon Strips

To fry: Place bacon slices in cold skillet. Cook over low heat, turning to cook evenly, until lightly browned. Drain on absorbent paper. For crisp bacon, drain fat as it accumulates in pan.

To broil: Place bacon slices on broiler rack 3" below unit or tip of flame. Broil 5 min., turning once, until lightly browned. Drain on absorbent paper.

To bake: Place bacon slices on rack in shallow pan. Bake in moderately hot oven (375°F.) 12 min., or until lightly browned. Drain on absorbent paper.

Bacon, Banana and Orange Grill   Serves 4

½ cup firmly packed brown sugar
½ tsp. cinnamon
4 bananas
Lemon juice
4 bacon strips
3 oranges

Mix sugar and cinnamon. Peel bananas; roll in juice, then in sugar mixture. Wrap bacon strip around each banana; fasten with picks. Peel oranges; slice, sprinkle with remaining sugar mixture. Place fruit on broiler rack with top of food 3″ below unit or tip of flame. Broil 8 minutes, turning bananas once.

Sausage Links

Place sausage links in skillet; add small amount water. Cover; cook slowly 5 min. Drain; cook slowly, turning to cook evenly, until center has lost pink color.

Sausage Patties

Shape bulk sausage into thin patties; place in cold skillet. Cook slowly, turning to cook evenly, until center has lost pink color, draining off fat as it accumulates.

Curried Pineapple and Sausage   Serves 4

1 lb. tiny pork sausages
8 canned pineapple slices
½ tsp. curry powder
1 cup pineapple sirup
Hot cooked rice
1 tsp. cornstarch

Fry sausages according to directions (above). Brown pineapple slices in ¼ cup sausage fat; drain on absorbent paper. Halve pineapple. Mix cornstarch and curry powder; add pineapple sirup. Add to fat in pan; cook, stirring constantly, until thickened. Place rice in center of serving platter; arrange pineapple and sausages around rice. Pour sauce over rice.

Sausage Stockade   Serves 4

4 pineapple slices	Few grains pepper
2 tbs. fat or salad oil	5 tbs. milk
2 cups mashed cooked or canned sweet potatoes	4 tbs. melted butter or margarine
¾ tsp. salt	1 lb. cocktail sausages
2 tsp. sugar	

Brown pineapple slices in fat or salad oil. Combine potatoes, salt, sugar, pepper, milk and 3 tbs. butter or margarine. Mound on pineapple; brush with remaining butter or margarine. Place on broiler rack with top of food 3″ below unit or tip of flame; broil until browned. Fry sausage until done; arrange upright around sweet potato mounds.

Frankfurters

Allow 1-2 frankfurters per person. Cover frankfurters with boiling water. Cover; let stand 6-10 min.

Broiled Frankfurters

Heat frankfurters (see above); split lengthwise. Brush with fat or salad oil. Place, skin side down, on broiler rack with top of food 2″ below unit or tip of flame. Broil until brown.

Sautéed Frankfurters

Heat frankfurters (see above); split lengthwise. Sauté in small amount fat or salad oil, turning to brown on both sides.

Spicy Frankfurters   Serves 4

½ lb. frankfurters	2 tbs. vinegar
1 tbs. flour	2 tsp. sugar
¾ cup water	1 tsp. prepared mustard
½ cup ketchup	

Have frankfurters lengthwise; place in skillet. Blend flour with 2 tbs. water; add remaining water, ketchup, vinegar, sugar and mustard. Cook, stirring constantly, until thickened. Pour over frankfurters. Cover; simmer 30 min.

Vienna Sausage Shortcake   Serves 4

  1 9-oz. can Vienna sausage   2 cups Medium White Sauce
  1½ cups cooked or canned   (p. 325)
      whole kernel corn   Hot biscuits (p. 52)

Cut sausage in 1″ pieces; combine with corn and sauce. Heat thoroughly. Split biscuits; cover with sausage mixture.

Roast Fresh Ham

Use 10-12 lb. fresh ham, allowing ½ lb. per person. Sprinkle with salt and pepper. Place on rack in roasting pan. Insert meat thermometer into center of thickest part of meat, being sure bulb does not rest on bone. Roast in moderate oven (350°F.) 30-35 min. per lb. or until meat thermometer registers 185°F. If desired, serve with Pan Gravy (p. 328).

Roast Fresh Loin of Pork

Use 3-4 lb. fresh loin of pork, allowing ½ lb. per person. Sprinkle with salt and pepper. Place, fat side up, in roasting pan. Insert meat thermometer into center of thickest part of meat, being sure bulb does not rest on bone. Roast in moderate oven (350°F.) 35-40 min. per lb. for center cut loin, and 45-50 min. per lb. for end cut loin, or until meat thermometer registers 185°F. If desired, serve with Pan Gravy (p. 328).

Roast Boned Fresh Pork Shoulder

Use 4-6 lb. rolled or cushion-style fresh pork shoulder, allowing ¼ lb. per person. If desired, have pocket cut in cushion-style roast; stuff with Apple Stuffing (p. 343). Sprinkle with salt and pepper. Insert meat thermometer into center of thickest part of meat. Roast in moderate oven (350°F.) 40-45 min. per lb. for rolled shoulder and 35-40 min. per lb. for cushion-style shoulder, or until meat thermometer registers 185°F. If desired, serve with Pan Gravy (p. 328).

Roast Fresh Pork Butt

Use 4-6 lb. fresh pork butt allowing ½ lb. per person. Sprinkle with salt and pepper. Place on rack in roasting pan. Insert meat thermometer into center of thickest part of meat, being sure bulb does not rest on bone. Roast in moderate oven (350°F.) 45-50 min. per lb. or until meat thermometer registers 185°F. If desired, serve with Pan Gravy (p. 328).

Braised Pork Chops

Use rib or loin pork chops ½-1″ thick. If desired, dredge with flour. Sprinkle with salt and pepper. Brown well on fat edge; brown on both sides. Cover tightly; cook slowly 45-60 min. or until tender, turning occasionally.

Stuffed Pork Chops   Serves 4

4 loin pork chops	¼ cup chopped seedless
1 small onion	raisins
2 tbs. butter or margarine	½ tsp. poultry seasoning
2 cups soft bread crumbs	½ tsp. salt
	1½ tbs. water

Have chops cut 2″ thick with pocket in each. Mince onion; brown in butter or margarine. Combine with crumbs, raisins, poultry seasoning, salt and water; mix well. Stuff chops; place in baking dish. Bake in moderate oven (350°F.) 2 hours.

Barbecued Spare Ribs   Serves 4

2 lbs. spare ribs	1 tbs. Worcestershire sauce
1 medium onion	2 tbs. brown sugar
2 tbs. fat or salad oil	½ cup water
¼ cup lemon juice	1 cup chili sauce
2 tbs. vinegar	Salt and pepper

Have spare ribs cut into serving portions. Place in baking pan; bake in moderate oven (350°F.) 30 min. Chop onion; brown in fat or salad oil. Add juice, vinegar, Worcestershire sauce, brown sugar, water, chili sauce, salt and pepper.

Cook slowly 20 min. Pour over spare ribs; continue baking 1 hour.

Mock Squab Stew   Serves 8

2 lb. pork shoulder	Few grains cinnamon
3 large onions	2 cans condensed
2 tbs. fat or salad oil	consommé
4 tart apples	3 cups hot seasoned
½ tsp. salt	mashed potatoes
Few grains pepper	½ cup flour

Cut pork in 1½" cubes. Slice onions; brown with pork in fat or salad oil. Place in baking dish. Dice apples; add. Sprinkle with salt, pepper and cinnamon. Blend consommé with flour; cook slowly, stirring constantly, until thickened. Pour over pork mixture. Cover; bake in moderate oven (350°F.) 1½-2 hours. Top with mashed potatoes; place in oven until brown.

Roast Leg of Veal

Use 7-8 lb. leg of veal, allowing ½ lb. per person. Sprinkle with salt and pepper. Place on rack in roasting pan. Insert meat thermometer into center of thickest part of meat, being sure bulb does not rest on bone. Roast in slow oven (300°F.) 30-35 min. per lb. or until meat thermometer registers 170°F.-180°F. If desired, serve with Pan Gravy (p. 328).

Roast Loin of Veal

Use 4½-5 lb. loin of veal, allowing ½ lb. per person. Sprinkle with salt and pepper. Place in roasting pan. Insert meat thermometer into center of thickest part of meat, being sure bulb does not rest on bone. Roast in slow oven (300°F.) 30-35 min. per lb. or until meat thermometer registers 170°F.-180°F. If desired, serve with Pan Gravy (p. 328).

Roast Veal Shoulder

Use 6-8 lb. shoulder of veal, allowing ½ lb. per person. Sprinkle with salt and pepper. Place on rack in roasting pan. Insert meat thermometer into center of thickest part of meat, being sure bulb does not rest on bone. Roast in slow oven (300°F.) 25-30 min. per lb. or until meat thermometer registers 170°F.-180°F. If desired, serve with Pan Gravy (p. 328).

Roast Boned Veal Shoulder

Use 4-6 lb. boned veal shoulder, allowing ¼-⅓ lb. per person. If desired, have meat prepared at market for stuffing; fill cavity with Savory Stuffing (p. 342); fasten edges. Or, have meat rolled at market. Place on rack in roasting pan. Insert meat thermometer into center of thickest part of meat. Roast in slow oven (300°F.) 40-45 min. per lb. or until meat thermometer registers 170°F.-180°F. If desired, serve with Pan Gravy (p. 328).

Roast Veal Rump

Use 5½-6 lb. rump of veal, allowing ½ lb. per person. If desired, have meat boned and rolled at market. Sprinkle with salt and pepper. Place on rack in roasting pan. Insert meat thermometer into center of thickest part of meat. Roast in slow oven (300°F.) 40-45 min. per lb. or until meat thermometer registers 170°F.-180°F. If desired, serve with Pan Gravy (p. 328).

Veal Pot Roast

Use 4-6 lb. veal rump or heel of round, allowing ½ lb. per person. Brown meat on all sides in fat or salad oil. Sprinkle with salt and pepper, place rack under meat. Add ¾ cup water; cover. Cook slowly 3-4 hours, or until tender. If desired, serve with Pan Gravy (p. 328).

Breast of Veal

Use 6 lb. breast of veal, allowing ½ lb. per person. If desired, have meat boned at market for stuffing; fill cavity with Bread Stuffing (pp. 341-42); fasten edges. Or, have meat boned and rolled at market. Brown meat on all sides in fat or salad oil. Sprinkle with salt and pepper. Add ½ cup water; cover. Cook slowly 2-3 hours, or until tender. If desired, serve with Pan Gravy (p. 328).

Veal Chops or Cutlets

Use veal loin or rib chops, allowing 1 chop per person or leg or round steak ½"-¾" thick, allowing ¼-⅓ lb. per person. Roll in dry crumbs; dip in beaten egg; roll in crumbs. Brown on both sides in fat or salad oil; add ½ cup water, salt and pepper. Cover; cook slowly 45-60 min., turning frequently. If desired, substitute tomato juice for water.

Creole Cutlet   Serves 4-6

1 egg	⅓ cup chopped onion
2 lb. slice veal steak	2 tbs. chopped green
Dry crumbs	pepper
1 No. 2 can (or 2½ cups	1 tsp. salt
cooked) tomatoes	1 tsp. Worcestershire sauce
Fat or salad oil	

Beat egg. Roll veal in crumbs; dip in egg, roll in crumbs. Brown on both sides in fat or salad oil. Add tomatoes, onion, green pepper, salt and Worcestershire sauce. Cover; simmer 1½ hours.

Veal Cutlets With Scallion Stuffing   Serves 8

1 cup chopped scallions	¼ cup flour
½ cup butter or margarine	2 ¾"-thick slices (2¾ lbs.)
5 cups soft bread crumbs	veal steak
2 tsp. salt	3 tbs. fat or salad oil
Few grains pepper	½ cup hot water

Brown scallions in butter or margarine; combine with crumbs, 1 tsp. salt and pepper. Mix flour with remaining salt; dredge veal. Brown in fat or salad oil. Place 1 veal slice in shallow baking pan; spread with stuffing. Top with remaining slice. Fasten with skewers. Pour water into pan in which veal slices were browned; bring to boil. Pour over veal. Cover; bake in moderate oven (350°F.) 50 min. Uncover; bake 30 min. Remove skewers. If desired, serve with Pan Gravy (p. 328).

Veal Shortcake   Serves 4-6

2 lb. veal shoulder or rump
¼ cup chopped onion
2 tbs. fat or salad oil
2 tsp. salt
3 peppercorns
1 bay leaf

2 cups boiling water
1⅓ cups biscuit dough
   (p. 52)
Flour
Sautéed mushrooms

Cut veal in 1″ cubes; brown with onion in fat or salad oil; add salt, peppercorns, bay leaf and boiling water. Cover; simmer 1 hour 45 min., or until veal is tender. Divide biscuit dough in ½; roll each ½ into 6″ round. Place on baking sheet. Bake in hot oven (425°F.) 15 min. Mix a little flour to smooth paste with cold water; blend into veal mixture. Cook, stirring constantly, until thick. Place veal mixture between and on top biscuit layers. Top with mushrooms.

Savory Sour Cream Loaf   Serves 8

3 tbs. chopped onion
⅓ cup ground green pepper
2 cups ground carrot
½ cup sour cream

1 tsp. salt
Few grains pepper
2 lbs. ground veal shoulder
   or rump

Combine onion, green pepper, carrot, cream, salt and pepper. Add veal; mix well. Shape into loaf; place on greased rack in baking pan. Bake in moderate oven (350°F.) 1 hour 45 min.

Veal and Pork Pie   Serves 4

½ lb. veal shoulder or
   rump
½ lb. pork shoulder
2 tbs. fat or salad oil
1½ cups boiling water
½ tsp. salt
Few grains pepper

1 bay leaf
Flour
1 cup cooked carrot balls
1 cup cooked potato balls
1 cup cooked tiny onions
Pastry I (p. 257)

Cut veal and pork in 2″ cubes; brown in fat or salad oil. Add boiling water, salt, pepper and bay leaf; cover. Simmer 1 hour or until meat is tender. Remove bay leaf. Mix a little flour to smooth paste with cold water; blend into meat mixture. Cook, stirring constantly, until thick. Add carrot and potato balls and onions. Pour into shallow baking dish. Roll out pastry ⅛″ thick on lightly floured board; cut into strips ½″ wide. Place on baking dish in open woven pattern. Trim edges; press with tines of fork. Bake in very hot oven (450°F.) 15 min.

Southern Hash   Serves 4

2 large onions
1 lb. ground veal shoulder or rump
1 No. 2 can (or 2½ cups cooked) tomatoes
3 tbs. fat or salad oil
½ cup uncooked rice
1 tsp. chili powder
1 tsp. salt
Few grains pepper

Slice onions; brown in fat or salad oil. Add veal; brown. Add tomatoes, rice, chili powder, salt and pepper. Cover; cook slowly 30 min., or until rice is tender, stirring occasionally.

Veal Tarts   Serves 4

2 cups Medium White Sauce (p. 325)
2 cups cubed cooked veal
1 cup cooked or canned peas
1 cup cooked or canned carrots
2 tbs. chopped parsley
Baked Tart Shells (p. 257)

Combine sauce, veal, peas, carrots and parsley. Heat thoroughly. Fill tart shells.

Roast Leg of Lamb

Use 6½-7 lb. leg of lamb, allowing ½ lb. per person. Do not have outer skin or "fell" removed. Sprinkle with salt and pepper. Place, skin side down, on rack in roasting pan. Insert meat thermometer into center of thickest part of meat, being sure bulb does not rest on bone. Roast in slow oven (300°F.) 30 min. per lb. for medium roast and 35 min. for well-done roast, or until meat thermometer registers 175°F.-180°F. If desired, serve with Pan Gravy (p. 328).

Loin Lamb Roast

Use 2½-3 lb. loin, allowing ½ lb. per person. Have chine bone loosened and ribs cut short at market. Sprinkle with salt and pepper. Place, skin side up, in roasting pan. Insert thermometer into center of thickest part of meat. Roast in slow oven (300°F.) allowing 30 min. per lb. for medium roast and 35 min. per lb. for well-done roast, or until meat thermometer registers 175°F.-180°F. If desired, serve with Pan Gravy (p. 328).

Crown Lamb Roast

Use 6-8 lb. crown roast, allowing ½-¾ lb. per person. Have roast prepared at market. Cover rib ends with salt pork or bread cubes to prevent charring. Fill crown with Pineapple Stuffing (p. 343). Place roast on rack in roasting pan. Insert meat thermometer into center of thickest part of meat, being sure bulb does not rest on bone. Roast in slow oven (300°F.) 30 min. per lb. for medium roast or 35 min. per lb. for well-done roast or until meat thermometer registers 175°F.-180°F. Remove salt pork or bread cubes; replace with paper frills. If desired, serve with Pan Gravy (p. 328).

Roast Cushion Lamb Shoulder

Use 3-4 lb. square-cut lamb shoulder, allowing ½ lb. per person. Have lamb boned and sewed at market, leaving 1 side open for stuffing. Fill cavity with Rice Stuffing (p. 344); fasten edges together. Place, fat side up, on rack in roasting pan. Insert meat thermometer into center of thickest part of meat. Roast in slow oven (300°F.) 40 min. per lb. or until meat thermometer registers 180°F. If desired, serve with Pan Gravy (p. 328).

Roast Rolled Lamb Shoulder

Use 3-4 lb. lamb shoulder, allowing ½ lb. per person. Have lamb boned and rolled at market. Place on rack in roasting pan. Insert meat thermometer into center of thickest part of meat. Roast in slow oven (300°F.) 45 min. per lb. or until meat thermometer registers 180°F. If desired, serve with Pan Gravy (p. 328).

Stuffed Breast of Lamb

Use 2-4 lb. lamb breast, allowing ½ lb. per person. Have pocket cut in wide end of lamb at market. Fill cavity with Rice Stuffing (p. 344); fasten edges together. Brown meat on all sides in fat or salad oil. Sprinkle with salt and pepper. Add ½ cup water; cover. Cook slowly 1½-2 hours or until tender. If desired, serve with Pan Gravy (p. 328).

Broiled Lamb Chops

Use rib, loin or shoulder chops at least 1"-2" thick, allowing 1 chop per person. Place chops on broiler rack with top of food 2" below unit or tip of flame for meat 1"-1¾" thick; 3" below unit or tip of flame for meat 2" thick. If distance must be less, reduce heat accordingly. Broil, sprinkling with salt and pepper and turning when ½ total cooking time is completed.

For 1" chops:
   Medium: Allow 12 min.
   Well-Done: Allow 14-16 min.

For 1½" chops:
   Medium: Allow 18 min.
   Well-Done: Allow 20-24 min.

For 2" chops:
   Medium: Allow 22 min.
   Well-Done: Allow 30-36 min.

Pan-Broiled Lamb Chops

Use rib, loin or shoulder chops ¾"-1½" thick, allowing 1

chop per person. Place chops in heavy skillet; quickly brown on both sides. Cook slowly, turning frequently, until done, pouring off fat as it accumulates. To test for doneness, cut gash near bone. Sprinkle with salt and pepper.

Broiled Lamb Patties

Use ground lamb shoulder or breast, allowing ¼ lb. per person. Season with salt and pepper; shape into patties 1″ thick and 3″ in diameter. If desired, wrap bacon strip around each patty; fasten with pick. Place on broiler rack with top of food 2″ below unit or tip of flame. Broil, turning when ½ total cooking time is completed. For medium patties, allow 18 min.; for well-done, allow 20-24 min.

Lamb Patty Grill
Serves 4

- 1 lb. ground lamb shoulder or breast
- 2 cups cooked or canned green beans
- 4 cooked green pepper halves
- 4 slices Cheddar cheese
- 4 boiled potatoes
- 1 cup Cheese Sauce (p. 325)
- 2 strips bacon

Shape lamb into patties 1″ thick and 3″ in diam. Place patties on broiler rack with top of food 2″ below unit or tip of flame. Broil 7-9 min. on each side. Pile green beans in pepper halves; top with cheese. Slice potatoes; combine with cheese sauce. Arrange patties, pepper halves and potatoes on sizzling platter. Top patties with bacon. Broil until bacon is crisp.

Pan-Broiled Lamb Patties

Use ground lamb shoulder or breast, allowing ¼ lb. per person. Season with salt and pepper; shape into patties 1″ thick and 3″ in diam. If desired, wrap bacon strip around each patty; fasten with pick. Rub heavy skillet with small amount of fat or salad oil; brown patties on both sides. Cook slowly, turning frequently, about 10-12 min., or until done, pouring off any fat which accumulates.

Baked Lamb Shanks   Serves 4

4 lamb shanks	2 tsp. Worcestershire
4 tbs. flour	sauce
1 tbs. fat or salad oil	2 tsp. vinegar
1 cup water	½ tsp. salt
2 tsp. prepared horseradish	Few grains pepper

Dredge shanks in 3 tbs. flour; brown in fat or salad oil in skillet. Place in baking dish. Blend remaining flour into fat or salad oil in skillet; add water. Cook, stirring constantly, until thickened. Add horseradish, Worcestershire sauce, vinegar, salt and pepper. Pour gravy over shanks; cover. Bake in slow oven (300°F.) 2 hours.

Lamb Stew

Use shoulder, flank, breast, shank or neck of lamb, allowing ¼-½ lb. per person. Cut meat in small uniform pieces. Brown lamb in small amount fat or salad oil. Cover with hot water; bring to boiling point. Cover; simmer 1½-2 hours. Thicken stock with a little flour mixed to smooth paste in water. If desired, whole small onions, carrots and potatoes may be added 1 hour before total cooking time is completed.

Lamb Curry   Serves 4

1½ lb. lamb shoulder or	1 small onion
breast	3 tbs. fat or salad oil
2 tbs. flour	1 cup boiling water
¾ tsp. curry powder	¾ tsp. vinegar
¾ tsp. salt	Hot cooked rice

Cut lamb in 1″ cubes. Mix flour, curry powder and salt; roll lamb in flour mixture. Slice onion; lightly brown in fat or salad oil. Add lamb; brown. Add water and vinegar; cover. Simmer 1½ hours, or until meat is tender. Arrange ring of rice on chop plate; fill center with lamb mixture.

Kebabs   Serves 4

2 lb. boned lamb shoulder   1 tsp. salt
½ cup salad oil   ¼ tsp. pepper
⅓ cup vinegar   Green pepper
1 medium onion

Cut meat in 1″ cubes. Combine salad oil and vinegar. Grate
onion; add with salt and pepper. Add meat; cover. Let stand
4 hours; drain. Cut green pepper in squares. On 8 skewers
string meat cubes alternately with green pepper. Place on
broiler rack with top of food 3″ below unit or tip of flame;
broil 15 min., turning several times.

Ragout of Lamb and Lima Beans   Serves 6

1 cup dried lima beans   1 No. 2 can (or 2½ cups
3 lb. lamb shoulder   cooked) tomatoes
Salt   2 tbs. minced parsley
Paprika   2 tbs. flour
2 tbs. fat or salad oil   2 tbs. water
18 small white onions   1 cup sour cream

Wash beans; discard imperfect ones. Cover with cold water;
soak overnight. Or, cover with large amount of boiling water; soak 4-5 hours. Drain. Cut meat from bones in 1½″
cubes. Sprinkle with salt and paprika. Brown meat in fat
or salad oil. Add beans, onions, tomatoes and parsley. Cover;
cook slowly 2 hours. Cover bones with water; simmer 1 hour.
Measure stock. (There should be about 1½ cups.) Blend
flour and water; add with sour cream to stock. Cook 5 min.,
stirring constantly. Add to meat mixture.

Stuffed Cabbage   Serves 4

1 medium head cabbage   Few grains pepper
1 onion   3 tbs. ketchup
6 strips bacon   ¼ tsp. Worcestershire
1 lb. ground lamb shoulder   sauce
1 tsp. salt

Cover cabbage with large amount boiling salted water; boil
30 min. Drain; cool. Carefully remove center. Mince onion;

dice 2 strips bacon; cook together until brown. Add lamb; cook 5 min. Add salt, pepper, ketchup and Worcestershire sauce; stuff cabbage. Place in greased baking dish. Cover; bake in moderate oven (350°F.) 35 min. Fry remaining bacon; use to garnish cabbage.

Lamb Croquettes   Serves 4

2 cups ground cooked lamb	½ tsp. grated onion
1 cup Thick White Sauce (p. 326)	1 egg
	2 tbs. water
1 tsp. chopped parsley	Dry crumbs

Combine lamb, sauce, onion and parsley; chill. Shape in cylinders, pyramids or balls. Beat egg; add water. Roll croquettes in crumbs; dip in egg mixture; roll in crumbs. Fry in deep fat or salad oil heated to 375°F. 2-3 min. Drain on absorbent paper. If desired, serve with Pimiento Pepper Sauce (p. 326).

Chop Stewy   Serves 4

2 cups cubed cooked lamb	1 cup sliced carrots
2 tbs. fat or salad oil	1 cup cooked or canned peas
3½ cups water	
2 tsp. salt	Flour
1 tsp. Worcestershire sauce	Hot canned Chinese noodles
8 small white onions	Hot cooked rice

Brown lamb in fat or salad oil. Add water, salt and Worcestershire sauce; simmer 5 min. Add onions and carrots; cook 20 min. Add peas; heat. Drain off liquid in pan. Blend a little flour to smooth paste with water; add to liquid. Cook slowly, stirring constantly, until thickened. Add to lamb and vegetable mixture. Arrange lamb mixture on platter with noodles and rice.

Broiled Calves Liver

Use calves liver cut ½"-¾" thick, allowing ¼" lb. per person. Brush with melted fat or salad oil. Place liver on broiler rack with top of food 2" below unit or tip of flame. Broil 5-10 min., sprinkling with salt and pepper and turning when ½ total cooking time is completed.

Sautéed Liver

Use calf, beef, pork or lamb liver cut ½" thick, allowing ¼ lb. per person. Dip slices in seasoned flour. Sauté in small amount fat or salad oil, turning to brown well on both sides.

Braised Sliced Liver

Use beef, calf, pork or lamb liver cut ½" thick, allowing ¼ lb. per person. Dip liver in seasoned flour. Brown on both sides in fat or salad oil. Cover; cook slowly 20 min.

Stuffed Liver Rolls   Serves 4

2 cups soft bread crumbs	Few grains pepper
2 tbs. melted butter or margarine	Few grains thyme
1 tsp. grated onion	1 lb. thinly sliced liver
2 tbs. chopped parsley	Flour
½ tsp. salt	Fat or salad oil
	1 cup water

Combine crumbs, butter or margarine, onion, parsley, salt, pepper and thyme; spread on liver slices. Roll up: skewer with picks. Dredge in flour; brown in fat or salad oil. Add water; cover. Cook slowly 20 min., or until tender.

Liver Lyonnaise   Serves 4

1 lb. sliced liver	1½ cups Medium White Sauce (p. 325)
Seasoned flour	1 cup thinly sliced onion
3 tbs. fat or salad oil	
3½ cups thinly sliced potatoes	

Dip liver in flour; brown in 2 tbs. fat or salad oil. Cut liver in 1½" cubes. Sauté potatoes and onion in remaining fat or salad oil until brown and tender. Alternate layers liver, potatoes and onion in baking dish. Add white sauce. Bake in moderate oven (350°F.) 20 min.

Spanish Casserole

Serves 8

2 lb. beef liver, unsliced
½ cup chopped carrots
½ cup chopped celery
½ cup sliced onion

1 No. 2 can (or 2½ cups cooked) tomatoes
1 tsp. salt
Few grains pepper
½ bay leaf

Have upper side of liver larded at market. Place liver in baking dish. Combine carrot, celery, onion, tomatoes, salt, pepper and bay leaf; pour over liver. Cover. Bake in moderate oven (350°F.) 1 hour. Remove cover; bake 30 min. If desired, garnish with crisp bacon.

Broiled Kidneys

Use beef, calf, pork or lamb kidneys, allowing ¼ lb. per person. Wash; remove outer membrane and fatty tissue. Cut kidneys in halves; remove white tubes. Cover with salted water; let stand 1 hour. Drain; cover with boiling water; simmer 5 min.; drain. Dip in melted fat or salad oil; sprinkle with salt and pepper. Place on broiler rack with top of food 3″ below unit or tip of flame. Broil 5-10 min., depending on size of kidneys, turning frequently and brushing with melted fat or salad oil.

Braised Beef Kidney

Use beef kidney, allowing ¼ lb. per person. Wash; remove outer membrane and fatty tissue. Cut in 1″ pieces; remove white tubes. Cover with salted water; let stand 1 hour. Drain. Dip kidney in seasoned flour; slowly brown in small amount fat or salad oil. Add small amount hot water. Cover; simmer 20 min., or until tender. If desired, 1 small chopped onion may be browned with kidney.

Kidney Stew

Serves 4

1 lb. kidneys
2 tbs. fat or salad oil
2 medium onions
1 tsp. dry mustard

1 tsp. salt
⅛ tsp. pepper
3 cups water
2 tbs. flour

Wash kidneys; remove outer membrane and fatty tissue. Cut kidneys in halves; remove white tubes. Cube kidneys. Cover with salted water; let stand 1 hour. Drain; cover with cold water; bring to boiling point. Drain; sauté kidneys in fat or salad oil, turning to brown on both sides; add 3 cups water. Bring to boiling point; skim. Slice onions; add with mustard, salt and pepper. Simmer 30 min., or until kidneys are tender. Mix flour to smooth paste with a little water; blend into kidney mixture. Cook, stirring constantly, until thickened.

Braised Heart

Use calf, lamb, pork or beef heart, allowing ¼-⅓ lb. per person. Wash thoroughly in warm water. Remove some of the membrane. Brown heart on all sides in a little fat or salad oil; season with salt and pepper. Add boiling water to cover bottom of pan; cover. Simmer until tender. If necessary, add boiling water during cooking. If desired, serve with Pan Gravy (p. 328).

For Calf, Lamb or Pork Heart: Allow 1½-2½ hours total cooking time.

For Beef Heart: Allow 2½-3½ hours total cooking time.

Pre-Cooked Sweetbreads

Use calf or lamb sweetbreads, allowing ½-1 pair per person. Cover with cold water; let stand 30 min.; drain. Cover with boiling water, adding 1 tsp. salt and 1 tbs. vinegar for each quart of water. Cover; simmer 15-20 min. Drain; cover with cold water. Cool enough to handle; remove membrane.

Broiled Sweetbreads

Follow directions for Pre-Cooked Sweetbreads (see above). Halve crosswise; sprinkle with salt and pepper. Brush with melted butter or margarine. Place on broiler rack with top of food 3″ below unit or tip of flame. Broil about 10 min., turning once. Serve on toast. If desired, serve with Lemon Chive Butter Sauce (p. 330).

Braised Sweetbreads

Use calf or lamb sweetbreads, allowing ½-1 pair per person. Cover with cold water; let stand 30 min.; drain. Remove membrane. Dip sweetbreads in seasoned flour; sauté in small amount fat or salad oil, turning to brown on all sides. Cover; cook slowly 20 min. If desired, blend together a little flour and water; add to drippings in pan. Cook, stirring constantly, until thickened. Serve on sweetbreads.

Pre-Cooked Brains

Use lamb, pork, veal or beef brains, allowing ½-1 pair per person. Follow directions for Pre-Cooked Sweetbreads (p. 255).

Fried Brains

Follow directions for Pre-Cooked Brains (above). Sprinkle with salt and pepper. Roll in dry crumbs; dip in beaten egg diluted with 1 tbs. water; roll in crumbs. Fry in shallow fat or salad oil until brown. Drain on absorbent paper. Serve on toast. If desired, serve with Mushroom Sauce (p. 325).

"Boiled" Tripe

Use cleaned fresh or pickled tripe, allowing ¼ lb. per person. Cover with cold water. Bring to boil; drain. Cover with boiling water; cover. Simmer 3-4 hours, or until tender, adding ½ tsp. salt per lb. to fresh tripe when ½ total cooking time is completed. Serve with Tomato Sauce (p. 329).

Broiled Tripe

Use cleaned fresh or pickled tripe, allowing ¼ lb. per person. Brush with melted butter or margarine. Place smooth side down on broiler rack with top of food 2" below unit or tip of flame. Broil 10 min., turning once. Serve with crisp bacon and Parsley Sauce (p. 326).

25. PIES AND PASTRIES

Plain Pastry — I

1½ cups flour	½ cup shortening
½ tsp. salt	3 tbs. cold water (about)

Sift together flour and salt. Cut in shortening with 2 knives or pastry blender. Add enough water to hold ingredients together, sprinkling evenly and mixing with fork to form ball. Makes enough for 8″ or 9″ pastry shell or 6 medium tart shells.

Unbaked Pastry Shell: Roll out dough in circular piece ⅛″ thick on lightly floured board. Fit into 8″ or 9″ pie pan or plate. Trim pastry to 1″ of edge of pie pan or plate; fold under. Pinch pastry edge to make even fluted standing rim. Fill.

Baked Pastry Shell: Follow directions for Unbaked Pastry Shell; prick through bottom and sides of pastry with tines of fork. Bake in very hot oven (450°F.) 15 min.

Unbaked Tart Shells: Roll out dough ⅛″ thick on lightly floured board. Cut in rounds about 1½″ wider than diam. of tart pans. Fit each round into tart pan; trim edges. Makes 6 medium shells.

Baked Tart Shells: Follow directions for Unbaked Tart Shells, fitting each round over inverted tart pan; trim edges. Prick through bottom and sides of pastry with tines of folk. Bake in very hot oven (450°F.) 10-15 min.

Patty Shell Rings: Roll out dough ⅛″ thick on lightly floured board. Cut in 16 3½″ rounds. Remove centers from 12 rounds with small cutter. Moisten edges. Place 3 rings on each round. Chill. Place on baking sheet. Bake in very hot oven (450°F.) 10-15 min. Makes 4.

Plain Pastry — II

2½ cups flour	¾ cup shortening
1 tsp. salt	⅓ cup cold water (about)

Sift together flour and salt. Cut in shortening with 2 knives or pastry blender. Add enough water to hold ingredients together, sprinkling evenly and mixing with fork to form ball. Makes enough for 2 crust 8″ or 9″ pie.

Two Crust Pie: Roll out ½ dough in circular piece ⅛″ thick on lightly floured board. Fit into 8″ or 9″ pie pan or plate; fill. Roll out remaining dough in circular piece ⅛″ thick on lightly floured board. Cut slits or design in center to allow steam to escape while baking. Moisten edge of pastry in pie pan or plate with water; place remaining pastry on filling. Press edges together lightly. For plain edge, press edges firmly with tines of fork; trim to edge of pie pan or plate. For rolled edge, trim pastry to 1″ of edge of pie pan or plate; fold under. Pinch pastry edge to make even fluted standing rim.

Lattice Two Crust Pie: Roll out ½ dough in circular piece ⅛″ thick on lightly floured board. Fit into 8″ or 9″ pie pan or plate; fill. Roll out remaining dough ⅛″ thick on lightly floured board; cut in strips ½″ wide. Moisten edge of pastry in pie pan or plate with water; place pastry strips on filling in open woven pattern. Press edges together lightly. Finish edge as above in Two Crust Pie.

Flaky Pastry Shells

1½ cups flour	⅔ cup shortening
¾ tsp. salt	3 tbs. cold water (about)

Sift together flour and salt. Cut in ⅓ cup shortening with 2 knives or pastry blender. Add enough water to hold ingredients together, sprinkling evenly and mixing with fork to form ball. Wrap in waxed paper; chill slightly. Roll ¼″

thick in oblong on lightly floured board. Spread with ⅓ remaining shortening; fold to make 3 layers. Turn ¼ way around. Repeat 2 times rolling, spreading with shortening and folding. Wrap in waxed paper; chill. Roll out ¼" thick on lightly floured board. Cut in rounds about 1½" wider than diameter of tart pans. Fit each round over inverted tart pan; trim edges. Prick through bottom and sides of pastry with tines of fork. Bake in very hot oven (450°F.) 10-15 min. Makes 6 medium tart shells.

Cheese Pastry

1½ cups flour	½ cup grated American
¼ tsp. salt	cheese
½ cup shortening	3 tbs. cold water (about)

Sift together flour and salt. Cut in shortening with 2 knives or pastry blender. Add cheese; mix well. Add enough water to hold ingredients together, sprinkling evenly and mixing with fork to form ball. Roll according to directions for Unbaked Pastry Shell or Unbaked Tart Shells (p. 257) or roll and bake according to directions for Baked Pastry Shell or Baked Tart Shells (p. 257). Makes enough for 8" or 9" pastry shell or 6 medium tart shells.

Cream Cheese Pastry

2 cups flour	½ cup shortening
½ tsp. salt	Cold water
2 cakes (6 oz.) cream cheese	

Sift together flour and salt; cut in cream cheese and shortening with 2 knives or pastry blender. Add enough water to hold ingredients together, sprinkling evenly and mixing with fork to form ball. Wrap in waxed paper; chill slightly. Roll according to directions for Two Crust Pie (p. 258), Unbaked Pastry Shell or Unbaked Tart Shells (p. 257) or roll and bake according to directions for Baked Pastry Shell or Baked Tart Shells (p. 257). Makes enough for 2 crust 8" or 9" pie, 2 8" or 9" pastry shells or 10 medium tart shells.

Crumb Pie Shell

1 cup sweet cracker
crumbs[1]

¼ cup sugar

⅓ cup melted butter or
margarine

1 teaspoon cinnamon

Mix crumbs, sugar and cinnamon. Blend in butter or margarine. Press into 9″ pie pan or plate. Chill.

[1] Use graham crackers, zwieback, rusks, vanilla, chocolate or lemon wafers, or ginger snaps. Omit cinnamon with chocolate or lemon wafers and ginger snaps. (Halved wafers make an attractive border.)

Corn Flake Pie Shell

1 cup finely crushed corn
flakes

⅓ cup melted butter or
margarine

¼ cup sugar

Mix sugar and corn flakes. Blend in butter or margarine. Press into 9″ pie pan or plate. Chill.

Apple Pie

Pastry II (p. 258)
6 tart apples
2 tsp. flour
1¼ cups sugar

1 tsp. lemon juice
½ tsp. cinnamon
¼ tsp. nutmeg
2 tbs. butter or margarine

Make pastry, following directions for Two Crust Pie. Pare apples; core; slice. Rub flour into bottom of pastry shell; sprinkle with ¼ cup sugar. Arrange apples in pastry shell; sprinkle with lemon juice. Mix 1 cup sugar, cinnamon and nutmeg; sprinkle over apples. Dot with butter or margarine. Cover with pastry. Bake in hot oven (425°F.) 40-50 min. If desired, brush pastry with Brown Sugar Pastry Glaze (p. 275).

Buttercrust Apple Cherry Pie

Pastry II (p. 258)
4 tart apples
6 tbs. butter or margarine
1 cup sugar

1 No. 2 can (2½ cups)
pitted sour red cherries
2 tbs. flour
1 tsp. cinnamon
½ tsp. nutmeg

Make pastry, following directions for Two Crust Pie, using 9" pie pan or plate. Pare apples; core; slice. Melt 2 tbs. butter or margarine; brush on bottom of pastry shell. Arrange apples in pastry shell. Drain cherries; place on apples. Mix sugar, flour, cinnamon and nutmeg; sprinkle on fruit. Dot with 2 tbs. butter or margarine. Cover with pastry. Bake in hot oven (425°F.) 30-40 min. Melt remaining butter or margarine; brush on top crust. Bake 10 min.

Orange Apple Pie

Pastry II (p. 258)
6 tart apples
2 tbs. grated orange rind
1 cup firmly packed brown sugar
¼ cup orange juice
2 tbs. butter or margarine

Make pastry, following directions for Two Crust Pie. Pare apples; core; slice. Arrange in pastry shell. Sprinkle with sugar, orange rind and juice. Dot with butter or margarine. Cover with pastry. Bake in hot oven (425°F.) 40-50 min.

Applesauce Mincemeat Pie

1 No. 2 can (2½ cups) applesauce
1-lb. can or jar (1½ cups) prepared mincemeat
½ cup firmly packed brown sugar
2 tbs. melted butter or margarine
Pastry II (p. 258)

Make pastry following directions for Two Crust Pie, using 9" pie pan or plate. Combine applesauce, mincemeat, sugar and butter or margarine; pour into pastry shell. Cover with pastry. Bake in hot oven (425°F.) 35 min.

Deep Dish Apple Pie With Cheese Pastry   Serves 4-6

Cheese Pastry (p. 259)
6 tart apples
1 cup sugar
½ tsp. cinnamon
¼ tsp. nutmeg
2 tbs. butter or margarine

Make ½ recipe for pastry. Pare apples; core; slice. Put into baking dish. Mix sugar, cinnamon and nutmeg; sprinkle over apples. Dot with butter or margarine. Roll out pastry

⅛" thick on lightly floured board in shape to fit over baking dish; prick design in center to allow steam to escape while baking. Place on apples; trim edge; press with tines of fork. Bake in hot oven (425°F.) 30-40 min.

Blueberry Pie

Plain Pastry II (p. 258)
1 qt. blueberries
1 cup sugar
2 tbs. flour

Few grains salt
1 tsp. lemon juice
2 tbs. butter or margarine

Make pastry, following directions for Two Crust Pie. Wash berries; pour into pastry shell. Mix sugar, flour, salt and lemon juice; sprinkle over berries. Dot with butter or margarine. Cover with pastry. Bake in hot oven (425°F.) 40-50 min.

Cranberry Apricot Pie

1½ cups dried apricots
Pastry II (p. 258)
4 cups cranberries

1 cup sugar
2 tbs. butter or margarine

Quarter apricots; cover with cold water. Let stand 1 hour. Make pastry, following directions for Two Crust Pie. Wash cranberries. Drain apricots; combine with cranberries and sugar. Pour into pastry shell; dot with butter or margarine. Cover with pastry. Bake in hot oven (425°F.) 30-40 min.

Cinnamon Cherry Pie

1 No. 2 can (2½ cups)
   pitted sour red cherries
½ cup sugar
½ tsp. cinnamon
⅛ tsp. salt
2½ tbs. quick-cooking
   tapioca

2 tbs. butter or margarine
8" Baked Pastry Shell
   (p. 258)
Marshmallow Meringue
   (pp. 274-75)

Drain cherries, reserving sirup. Mix sugar, cinnamon, salt and tapioca; add sirup. Bring to boiling point over direct heat, stirring constantly. Remove from heat; add butter or margarine. (Mixture will be thin.) Cool, stirring occasionally. (Mixture thickens as it cools.) Add cherries; pour into pastry shell. Swirl meringue on filling. Place top of food 3″ below broiler unit or tip of flame; broil 30 seconds, or until delicate brown.

Horn O' Plenty Pie

1½ cups sugar	Few grains salt
¾ cup water	9″ Baked Pastry Shell
3 cups cranberries	(p. 257)
¾ cup seedless raisins	3 egg whites
½ cup broken walnut meats	6 tbs. brown sugar
2 tbs. butter or margarine	

Combine sugar and water; bring to boiling point. Wash cranberries; add with raisins and nut meats. Cover; cook slowly until berries stop popping. Add butter or margarine and salt. Cool without stirring. Pour into pastry shell. Beat egg whites stiff, but not dry. Gradually add brown sugar, beating constantly. Swirl on filling. Bake in moderate oven (325°F.) 20 min.

Peach Pie

Plain Pastry II (p. 258)	1 tsp. lemon juice
1 cup sugar	4 cups sliced peaches
2 tbs. quick-cooking tapioca	2 tbs. butter or margarine
Few grains salt	

Make pastry, following directions for Lattice Two Crust Pie. Mix sugar, tapioca, salt and lemon juice; combine with peaches. Let stand 15 min. Place peach mixture in pastry shell. Dot with butter or margarine. Cover with pastry strips. Bake in hot oven (425°F.) 40-50 min.

Peach and Blackberry Pie

Cream Cheese Pastry (p. 259)	Few grains salt
	1 tsp. grated orange rind
1½ tbs. quick-cooking tapioca	2 cups sliced peaches
⅔ cup sugar	2 cups blackberries

Make pastry, following directions for Lattice Two Crust Pie. Mix tapioca, sugar, salt and orange rind. Sprinkle 2 tbs. tapioca mixture in bottom of pastry shell. Combine peaches and berries; place in pastry shell. Sprinkle with remaining tapioca mixture. Cover with pastry strips. Bake in hot oven (425°F.) 35-40 min.

Hawaiian Prune Pie

1½ cups pineapple juice	½ cup firmly packed brown
1 lb. dried prunes	sugar
1 tbs. melted butter or	½ tsp. nutmeg
margarine	¼ tsp. salt
1 tsp. cinnamon	1 tsp. grated orange rind
	Pastry II (p. 258)

Add pineapple juice to prunes; let stand overnight. Simmer until prunes are tender; remove prune pits. Add butter or margarine, sugar, cinnamon, nutmeg, salt and orange rind. Make pastry, following directions for Lattice Two Crust Pie. Bake in hot oven (425°F.) 35-40 min.

Deep Dish Fruit Pie

Serves 4-6

Pastry I (p. 257)	1 cup sugar
1 qt. cherries or berries[2]	2 tbs. flour

Make ½ recipe for pastry. Wash fruit, pitting cherries if used; put in baking dish. Mix sugar and flour; sprinkle over fruit. Roll out pastry ⅛″ thick on lightly floured board in shape to fit over baking dish; prick design in center to allow steam to escape while baking. Place on fruit; trim edge; press with tines of fork. Bake in hot oven (425°F.) 30 min.

Danish Apricot Tarts

½ lb. dried apricots	½ cup shortening
¾ cup sugar	1 egg
1 cup flour	½ cup whipping cream
½ tsp. salt	

[2] Use strawberries, blackberries, raspberries, loganberries or blueberries.

Cover apricots with water; bring to boiling point. Boil 30 min., or until tender. Drain, reserving liquid; add enough water, if necessary, to make 1 cup. Add sugar; cook until slightly thickened. Add apricots; cool. Sift together flour and salt. Cut in shortening with 2 knives or pastry blender. Beat egg slightly; add enough to hold ingredients together, mixing with fork to form ball. Roll out dough ⅛″ thick on lightly floured board. Cut in rounds about 1½″ wider than diameter of tart pans. Fit each round over inverted tart pan; trim edges; prick through bottom and sides of pastry with tines of fork. Bake in hot oven (425°F.) 10 min; cool. Fill with apricot mixture. Whip cream; use as garnish.

Cherry Tarts

1 No. 2 can (2½ cups) pitted sour red cherries
½ cup sugar
2½ tbs. cornstarch
¼ tsp. cinnamon
6-8 Baked Tart Shells (p. 257)
½ cup whipping cream

Drain cherries, reserving sirup. Mix sugar, cornstarch and cinnamon; add sirup. Cook, stirring constantly, until thick. Add cherries; cool. Pour into tart shells. Whip cream; use as garnish.

Peach Tarts

Arrange peach halves, cut side down, in Baked Tart Shells (p. 257). Beat jelly with fork; spread over peaches. Chill. Garnish with whipped cream.

Grandmother's Tarts

Makes 18

1¼ cups sliced pitted dates or cooked sweetened dried prunes
¼ cup orange juice
¼ cup chopped walnut meats
Pastry I (p. 257)

Combine fruit, orange juice and walnut meats. Roll out dough ⅛″ thick on lightly floured board; cut with 3½″

cutter. Place spoonful fruit mixture on each round; moisten edges with water. Fold over; press edges together with tines of fork. Place on baking sheet; bake in very hot oven (450°F.) 15 min.

Fried Apple Pies   Makes 12

1 cup cooked or canned applesauce
¼ cup firmly packed brown sugar
¼ cup seedless raisins
½ tsp. allspice
1½ tsp. lemon juice
1 tbs. melted butter or margarine
Pastry I (p. 257)

Combine applesauce, brown sugar, raisins, allspice, lemon juice and butter or margarine. Roll out pastry ⅛″ thick on lightly floured board; cut with 3½″ cutter. Place applesauce mixture in center of ½ rounds; moisten edges with water. Top with remaining rounds; press edges together with tines of fork. Fry in deep fat or salad oil heated to 375°F. until brown. Drain on absorbent paper.

Fluffy Pumpkin Pie

½ cup sugar
1 tsp. cinnamon
½ tsp. nutmeg
¼ tsp. cloves
¼ tsp. ginger
¼ tsp. salt
1 cup strained cooked or canned pumpkin
1 cup milk
2 eggs
1 egg yolk
1 egg white
9″ Unbaked Pastry Shell (p. 257)

Mix sugar, cinnamon, nutmeg, cloves, ginger and salt. Combine with pumpkin; add milk. Beat 2 eggs and 1 egg yolk well; add. Beat 1 egg white stiff; fold in. Pour into pastry shell. Bake in hot oven (425°F.) 45 min.

Tutti-Frutti Pumpkin Pie: Follow recipe for Fluffy Pumpkin Pie, adding ¼ cup finely chopped citron, ½ cup finely chopped pitted dates and ¼ cup finely chopped walnut meats to filling before folding in egg white. Serve with wedges of American cheese.

Mince Pie

2 1-lb. cans or jars (3 cups) prepared mincemeat
1½ cups chopped peeled apple
1 tbs. sherry flavoring
Pastry II (p. 258)

Make pastry, following directions for Two Crust Pie. Mix mincemeat, apple and flavoring; pour into pastry shell. Cover with pastry. Bake in hot oven (425°F.) 40-50 min. For a change, omit sherry flavoring, and serve sherry-flavored Hard Sauce (p. 321) as an accompaniment to the pie.

Mincemeat Pumpkin Pie

1 lb. can or jar (1½ cups) prepared mincemeat
½ tsp. cinnamon
¼ tsp. cloves
¼ tsp. nutmeg
¼ tsp. salt
½ cup sugar
1 cup strained cooked or canned pumpkin
2 eggs
9″ Unbaked Pastry Shell (p. 257)

Combine mincemeat, cinnamon, cloves, nutmeg and salt. Combine sugar and pumpkin; add to mincemeat mixture. Beat eggs; add. Pour into pastry shell. Bake in hot oven (425°F.) 20 min.; reduce to moderately hot (375°F.); bake 35 min.

Plantation Pie

1½ cups cooked or canned sweet potatoes
½ cup firmly packed brown sugar
1 tsp. cinnamon
½ tsp. salt
3 egg yolks
1 cup milk
2 tbs. melted butter or margarine
½ cup chopped walnut meats
9″ Unbaked Pastry Shell (p. 257)
3 egg whites
9 tbs. brown sugar

Mash sweet potatoes until free of lumps. Add ½ cup brown sugar, cinnamon and salt. Beat egg yolks; add. Add milk, butter or margarine and nut meats; mix well. Pour into pastry shell. Bake in hot oven (425°F.) 10 min.; reduce to moderate (350°F.); bake 30 min. Beat egg whites stiff, but not dry; gradually add remaining sugar, beating constantly. Swirl on filling. Bake in moderate oven (325°F.) 20 min.

Cream Pie

⅔ cup sugar
½ cup flour
⅛ tsp. salt
2 cups milk
2 eggs

1½ tsp. vanilla extract
9″ Baked Pastry Shell (p. 257)
⅔ cup whipping cream

Mix sugar, flour and salt. Scald milk; add. Cook over hot water, stirring constantly, until thick. Cover; cook 10 min. Beat eggs slightly; add milk mixture; mix well. Cook over hot water, stirring constantly, 3 min. Cool; add vanilla extract. Pour into pastry shell. Whip cream; swirl on pie.

Coconut Cream Pie: Follow recipe for Cream Pie, sprinkling with plain or toasted shredded coconut before serving.

Chocolate Topped Cream Pie: Follow recipe for Cream Pie, sprinkling with chopped semi-sweet chocolate before serving.

Chocolate Pie

¾ cup sugar
6 tbs. flour
¼ tsp. salt
3 squares (3 oz.) unsweetened chocolate
1½ cups milk

2 egg yolks
1 tsp. vanilla extract
9″ Baked Pastry Shell (p. 257)
½ cup whipping cream

Mix sugar, flour and salt. Chop chocolate; add. Add milk; cook over hot water, stirring constantly, until thick. Cover; cook 10 min. Beat egg yolks; add chocolate mixture. Mix well. Cook over hot water, stirring constantly, 3 min. Cool slightly; add vanilla extract. Pour into pastry shell; chill. Whip cream; if desired, sweeten and flavor. Swirl around edge of filling.

Chocolate Mint Pie: Follow directions for Chocolate Pie, substituting ½ tsp. peppermint extract for 1 tsp. vanilla extract.

Butterscotch Pie

1 cup firmly packed brown sugar	2 tbs. butter or margarine
5 tbs. flour	9″ Baked Pastry Shell (p. 257)
1½ cups milk	Meringue I (p. 274)
2 egg yolks	Few grains salt

Mix brown sugar, flour and salt. Gradually add milk; mix well. Beat egg yolks; add. Cook over hot water, stirring constantly, until thick. Add butter or margarine. Pour into pastry shell. Swirl meringue on filling. Bake in moderate oven (325°F.) 20 min. If desired, omit meringue and garnish with whipped cream.

Lemon Meringue Pie

1 cup sugar	¼ cup lemon juice
¼ cup flour	2 tsp. grated lemon rind
Few grains salt	9″ Baked Pastry Shell (p. 257)
1 cup water	Meringue II (p. 274)
3 egg yolks	
2 tbs. butter or margarine	

Mix sugar, flour, salt and ¼ cup water until smooth. Beat egg yolks, add with ¾ cup water. Cook over hot water, stirring constantly, until thick. Cover; cook 10 min. Add butter or margarine, lemon juice and rind. Pour into pastry shell. Swirl meringue on filling. If desired, sprinkle with nutmeg. Bake in moderate oven (325°F.) 20 min.

Banana Lemon Meringue Pie: Follow recipe for Lemon

Meringue Pie, covering bottom of pastry shell with sliced bananas before filling.

Lime Meringue Pie

1¾ cups sugar
6 tbs. flour
Few grains salt
¾ cup water
¾ cup lime juice
Green vegetable coloring

3 egg yolks
3 tbs. butter or margarine
2 tsp. grated lime rind
9″ Baked Pastry Shell
   (p. 257)
Meringue II (p. 274)

Mix sugar, flour and salt; add water and lime juice. Tint with coloring. Cook over hot water, stirring constantly, until thick. Beat egg yolks; add lime mixture. Cover; cook over hot water 10 min. Add butter or margarine and lime rind. Pour into pastry shell. Swirl meringue on filling. Bake in moderate oven (325°F.) 20 min.

Custard Pie

3 eggs
¼ cup sugar
¼ tsp. salt
2¼ cups milk

2 tsp. vanilla extract
9″ Unbaked Pastry Shell
   (p. 257)
Nutmeg

Beat eggs slightly; add sugar, salt, milk and vanilla extract. Pour into pastry shell; sprinkle with nutmeg. Bake in hot oven (425°F.) 40 min., or until inserted knife comes out clean.

Pecan Pie

1¾ cups sugar
¼ cup dark corn sirup
¼ cup butter or margarine
3 eggs
1 cup chopped pecan nut
   meats

Few grains salt
1 tsp. vanilla extract
9″ Unbaked Pastry Shell
   (p. 229)
   (p. 257)

Mix sugar, corn sirup and butter or margarine; bring to

PIES AND PASTRIES 271

boiling point. Beat eggs; gradually add sirup mixture. Add nut meats, salt and vanilla extract. Pour into pastry shell. Bake in moderately hot oven (375°F.) 35-40 min.

Toasted Coconut Mousse Pie

1 cup whipping cream
3 tbs. confectioners' sugar
½ tsp. vanilla extract
1 egg white

½ cup toasted coconut
9" chocolate wafer Crumb Pie Shell (p. 260)
Sliced peaches

Whip cream; add sugar and vanilla extract. Beat egg white stiff; fold in. Add coconut. Pour into freezing tray of automatic refrigerator with cold control set at point recommended by manufacturer for freezing ice cream. Freeze firm. Pack into pie shell. Garnish with peaches. Serve immediately.

Orange Marshmallow Pie

½ lb. marshmallows
1 cup strained orange juice
1 tbs. lemon juice
½ cup whipping cream

9" lemon wafer Crumb Pie Shell (p. 260)
Membrane-free orange sections
Toasted marshmallow halves

Heat ½ lb. marshmallows over hot water until almost melted. Remove from heat; add orange and lemon juices; cool. Whip cream; fold in. Chill until slightly thickened. Pour into pie shell. Chill overnight. Garnish with orange sections and toasted marshmallow halves.

Raspberry Marshmallow Pie

1 pkg. raspberry gelatin
2 cups water
22 marshmallows

2 tbs. milk
1½ cups raspberries
8" Crumb Pie Shell (p. 260)

Dissolve gelatin in 2 cups of water, according to directions on pkg.; chill until sirupy. Melt 16 marshmallows in milk;

fold into gelatin. Fold in 1 cup raspberries; pour into pie shell. Chill until firm. Toast remaining marshmallows; use as garnish with remaining raspberries.

Ambrosia Chiffon Pie

1 pkg. orange gelatin
½ cup water
1 cup orange juice
1 egg white
½ cup whipping cream
½ cup powdered sugar

1½ cups halved seeded red grapes
9″ Baked Pastry Shell (p. 257)
½ cup shredded coconut
Membrane-free orange sections

Dissolve gelatin in ½ cup water according to directions on pkg.; add orange juice. Chill until sirupy; beat until light. Beat egg white; whip cream. Fold egg white, cream and sugar into gelatin; chill until almost firm. Add 1 cup grapes; pour into pastry shell. Sprinkle with coconut. Garnish with orange sections and remaining grapes. Chill until firm.

Eggnog Pie

1 envelope (1 tbs.) unflavored gelatine
2 cups milk
1 tbs. cornstarch
¼ tsp. salt
6 tbs. sugar

2 egg yolks
2 egg whites
2 tsp. brandy flavoring
9″ Baked Pastry Shell (p. 257)
Nutmeg

Soften gelatine in ¼ cup milk. Mix cornstarch, salt and 3 tbs. sugar; add remaining milk. Cook over hot water, stirring constantly, until slightly thickened. Cover; cook 10 min. Add gelatine; stir until dissolved. Beat egg yolks; slowly add milk mixture; cook over hot water 3 min. Chill until slightly thickened. Beat egg whites stiff. Gradually add remaining sugar, beating constantly; fold into gelatine mixture. Add flavoring. Pour into pastry shell; sprinkle with nutmeg. Chill until firm.

Lemon Chiffon Pie

1 envelope (1 tbs.)
  unflavored gelatine
¼ cup cold water
4 egg yolks
1 cup sugar
⅓ cup lemon juice

½ tsp. salt
1½ tsp. grated lemon rind
4 egg whites
9" Baked Pastry Shell
  (p. 257)
½ cup whipping cream

Soften gelatine in water. Beat egg yolks; add ½ cup sugar, lemon juice and salt. Cook over hot water, stirring constantly, until thickened. Add lemon rind and gelatine; stir until gelatine is dissolved. Cool. Beat egg whites stiff; gradually add remaining sugar, beating constantly. Fold into lemon mixture. Pour into pastry shell; chill until firm. Whip cream; swirl on pie.

Chocolate Chiffon Pie

1 envelope (1 tbs.)
  unflavored gelatine
¼ cup cold water
½ cup boiling water
2 squares (2 oz.)
  unsweetened chocolate
1 cup sugar

¼ tsp. salt
3 egg yolks
1 tsp. vanilla extract
3 egg whites
9" Baked Pastry Shell
  (p. 257)
½ cup whipping cream

Soften gelatine in cold water; add boiling water; stir until gelatine is dissolved. Melt chocolate over hot water. Add gelatine mixture; mix well. Add ½ cup sugar and salt; cook 2 min. Beat egg yolks; add chocolate mixture; cook over hot water 2 min. Cool. Add vanilla extract. Beat egg whites stiff; gradually add remaining sugar, beating constantly. Fold into chocolate mixture. Pour into pastry shell; chill until firm. Whip cream; swirl on pie.

Strawberry Coconut Pie

1 envelope (1 tbs.) unflavored gelatine	½ tsp. salt
¼ cup cold water	4 egg whites
4 egg yolks	½ cup moist-pack shredded coconut
1 cup sugar	Corn Flake Pie Shell (p. 260)
½ cup orange juice	1 cup halved strawberries
1 tsp. grated orange rind	

Soften gelatine in cold water. Beat egg yolks; add ½ cup sugar and orange juice. Cook over hot water, stirring constantly, until thickened. Add orange rind, salt and gelatine; stir until gelatine is dissolved. Cool. Beat egg whites stiff; gradually add remaining sugar, beating constantly. Fold with coconut into gelatine mixture. Pour into pie shell; chill until firm. Garnish with berries.

Meringue — I

2 egg whites	6 tbs. sugar
¼ tsp. salt	

Beat egg whites stiff but not dry. Add salt. Gradually add sugar, beating constantly. Swirl on pie, pudding, etc. Bake in moderate oven (325°F.) 20 min. Cool slowly. Makes enough to cover 8" or 9" pie.

Meringue — II

3 egg whites	9 tbs. sugar
½ tsp. salt	

Beat egg whites stiff but not dry. Add salt. Gradually add sugar, beating constantly. Swirl on pie, pudding, etc. Bake in moderate oven (325°F.) 20 min. Cool slowly. Makes enough to cover 9" or 10" pie.

Marshmallow Meringue

¼ lb. marshmallows	2 egg whites
1 tbs. milk	¼ tsp. salt
¼ tsp. vanilla extract	¼ cup sugar

Combine marshmallows and milk; heat slowly, folding over and over until marshmallows are ½ original size. Remove from heat; add vanilla extract. Continue folding until mixture is smooth, yet light and spongy. Beat egg whites stiff. Add salt. Gradually add sugar, beating constantly. Carefully fold in slightly warm marshmallow mixture. Pile on pie, pudding, etc. Place top of food 3″ below broiler unit or tip of flame; broil 30 seconds or until delicate brown. Makes enough to cover 9″ or 10″ pie.

Brown Sugar Pastry Glaze

Mix 1 tbs. milk and tsp. light brown sugar. Brush on pastry before baking.

26. POULTRY

Directions For Stuffing and Trussing Poultry

If necessary, singe bird over low heat, turning slowly. Remove all pinfeathers with tweezers. Wash outside of bird; dry. Wipe inside with damp cloth; rub lightly with salt. Lightly stuff neck cavity; fold skin over back; fasten. Lightly stuff body cavity. Close cavity by fastening with skewers and lacing with string or by sewing. Fold wing tips under back of bird. Tie together ends of legs with string; bring string around tail piece. Turn bird on breast; cross string on back, bringing up around wings. Tie securely in center of back. Before serving, remove any skewers and string.

Cooked Giblets

Clean gizzard, heart and liver. Cover gizzard and heart with boiling water. Add ½ tsp. salt. If desired, neck may be cooked with giblets. Cover; simmer 1-2 hours, adding liver ½ hour before cooking is completed. Drain giblets, reserving stock for gravy, etc. Chop giblets for use in gravy, stuffing, etc.

Roast Chicken

Use 3½-6 lb. chicken allowing ½-¾ lb. per person. Stuff; truss. (See Directions for Stuffing and Trussing Poultry, p. 275.) Place on side on rack in roasting pan. Brush with melted fat or salad oil; cover with cloth dipped in melted fat or salad oil. Roast in moderate oven (325°F.), turning chicken after ½ total roasting time. If cloth becomes dry, baste with pan drippings. For crisp skin, remove cloth 30 min. before roasting is completed.

For 3½ lb. chicken: Allow 40-45 min. per lb.

For 4-5 lb. chicken: Allow 35-40 min. per lb.

For 6 lb. chicken: Allow 30-35 min. per lb.

Baked Chicken With Oysters   Serves 4

3 lb. chicken	¼ cup fat or salad oil
¼ cup flour	¼ cup hot water
1½ tsp. salt	12 oysters
Few grains pepper	¾ cup cream

Wash chicken; dry; quarter. Mix flour, 1 tsp. salt and pepper; use to dredge chicken. Brown chicken in fat or salad oil; add water. Cover; cook slowly 30 min. Place chicken in shallow baking dish; add oysters. Mix cream and remaining salt; pour into baking dish. Bake in moderate oven (350° F.) 30 min.

Spring Chicken Casserole   Serves 4

2½ lbs. spring chicken	½ cup mushrooms
Corn Stuffing (p. 342)	2 tbs. fat or salad oil
10 white onions	¼ cup hot water

Stuff chicken with corn stuffing; truss. (See Directions for Stuffing and Trussing Poultry, p. 275.) Brown onions and mushrooms in fat or salad oil. Add water. Place chicken in casserole; add onions and mushrooms. Cover; bake in moderate oven (350°F.) 30 min.; uncover; bake 45 min.

Fried Chicken
Serves 4

Use 3-3½ lb. chicken. Wash; dry; disjoint. Dredge in seasoned flour. Fry in fat or salad oil ¾"-1" deep, turning to brown; cover. Cook slowly about 45 min.

Broiled Chicken
Serves 2-4

Use 1½-2½ lb. chicken; wash; dry. Halve lengthwise or quarter. Brush with melted fat or salad oil. Place skin side down on greased broiler rack with top of food 4" below broiler unit or tip of flame. Broil 45-60 min., turning to brown on both sides, basting with melted fat or salad oil. Season with salt and pepper.

Planked Chicken
Serves 4

Follow recipe for Broiled Chicken (see above) using 2½ lb. chicken. Heat plank; arrange chicken on plank. Put hot seasoned mashed potatoes through rose tip of pastry bag around edge of plank and around chicken. Arrange seasoned sliced cooked or canned carrots and cooked small onions on plank. Place under broiler unit or burner until vegetables are browned. If desired, substitute seasoned hot green peas, green beans or asparagus for onions, placing on plank just before serving. Garnish with parsley.

Chicken Fricassee

Use 2½-6 lb. chicken or fowl, allowing ¼-½ lb. per person. If necessary, singe bird over low heat, turning slowly. Remove all pinfeathers with tweezers. Wash; dry; disjoint. Cover with boiling water; add 1½ tsp. salt. Cover. Simmer 2-4 hours, depending on size and age of bird. If desired, add 1 small onion, 1 small carrot and 1 stalk celery, after bird has cooked ½ total time. Remove bird and vegetables from stock. Blend a little flour with water; gradually add stock.

Cook slowly, stirring constantly, until thickened. Season, if necessary. Pour gravy over chicken.

Brown Chicken Fricassee: Follow recipe for Chicken Fricassee, dredging bird with seasoned flour and browning in fat or salad oil before covering with boiling water.

Chicken With Almond Cream Gravy   Serves 4

2½ lbs. chicken
½ cup flour
Salt and pepper
3 tbs. fat or salad oil
¾ cup hot water
½ cup cream
¼ cup chopped salted
　almond nut meats
2 tsp. prepared horse-radish
Salt and pepper
Hot cooked rice

Wash chicken; dry; disjoint. Mix ¼ cup flour, 1 tsp. salt and few grains pepper; use to dredge chicken. Brown chicken in fat or salad oil. Add hot water; cover. Cook slowly 40 min. Add water to stock in pan to make 2 cups; add cream. Blend remaining flour to smooth paste with water. Add to stock in pan; cook slowly, stirring constantly, until thick. Add nut meats and horse-radish; season with salt and pepper. Serve on rice.

Chicken Hawaiian   Serves 4-6

4 lb. chicken
1 No. 2½ can (3½ cups)
　sliced pineapple
1 medium onion
4 tbs. fat or salad oil
⅓ cup flour
Few grains pepper
2 thin slices sautéed ham
4 cups hot cooked rice
1 avocado
1 tsp. salt

Wash chicken; dry; disjoint. Drain pineapple, reserving sirup. Mince onion; cook in 3 tbs. fat or salad oil until tender. Mix flour, salt and pepper; use to dredge chicken. Brown chicken with onion. Measure pineapple sirup; add water to make 2 cups. Pour over chicken; cover. Cook slowly 1½ hours. Dice ham; toss with rice. Sauté pineapple slices in remaining fat or salad oil. Halve avocado lengthwise; remove seed. Slice avocado crosswise. Place rice in center of chop plate; arrange avocado, pineapple and chicken around rice. If desired, thicken gravy; serve with chicken.

Sumter Chicken Stew

Serves 8

5 lb. fowl
¼ cup fat or salad oil
½ cup flour
¾ cup ketchup
4 cups boiling water

3 tbs. lemon juice
1 tsp. salt
1 tsp. Worcestershire sauce
½ tsp. pepper
Sautéed Mush (p. 133)

Singe fowl over low heat, turning slowly. Remove all pinfeathers with tweezers. Wash; dry; disjoint. Heat fat or salad oil; blend in flour. Gradually add ketchup, boiling water, lemon juice, salt, Worcestershire sauce and pepper. Add chicken; cover. Simmer 3 hours or until tender. Serve with mush.

Barbecued Chicken

Serves 4

2 lb. chicken
6 tbs. fat or salad oil
3 tbs. Worcestershire sauce
2 tbs. vinegar
2 tbs. sugar

½ cup ketchup
Few drops tabasco
1 garlic clove
1 medium onion

Wash chicken; dry; halve. Brown in fat or salad oil. Mix Worcestershire sauce, vinegar, sugar, ketchup and tabasco; add. Mash garlic; chop onion; tie in cheesecloth. Add to sauce. Cover; cook 1 hour. Remove cheesecloth.

Chicken Mexicana

Serves 4

3 lb. chicken
3 tbs. fat or salad oil
1 tsp. flour
1 medium onion
1 tsp. salt

1 No. 2 can (or 2½ cups cooked) tomatoes
Few grains pepper
1 tsp. chili powder
Hot cooked rice

Wash chicken; dry; split. Brown in fat or salad oil. Remove chicken. Blend flour with fat or salad oil in pan. Slice onion; add with tomatoes, salt, pepper and chili powder;

heat. Add chicken. Cover; simmer 1 hour 15 min. Serve
on rice.

Creamed Chicken   Serves 4

1½ cups Medium White Sauce (p. 325)	1½ cups diced cooked or canned chicken
Salt and pepper	Toast triangles
	2 tbs. chopped parsley

If desired, substitute ¾ cup chicken stock for equal quantity milk in preparing sauce. Combine sauce and chicken;
heat over hot water. Season with salt and pepper. Serve on
toast; sprinkle with chopped parsley. If desired, add ½
cup sliced sautéed mushrooms.

Chicken à la King   Serves 4

½ cup sliced mushrooms	1½ cups diced cooked or canned chicken
¼ chopped green pepper	
2 tbs. butter or margarine	Salt and pepper
1½ cups Medium White Sauce (p. 325)	1 egg yolk
½ cup cream	Flaky Pastry Shells (pp. 258-59)
2 tbs. chopped pimiento	

Brown mushrooms and green pepper in butter or margarine; combine with sauce, cream, pimiento and chicken.
Season with salt and pepper. Heat over hot water. Beat egg
yolk; add sauce mixture. Heat, stirring constantly, 1 min.
Serve in pastry shells.

Chicken Croquettes   Serves 4

2 cups chopped cooked or canned chicken	Salt and pepper
	2 eggs
1 cup Thick White Sauce (p. 326)	2 tbs. water
	Dry crumbs
2 tsp. chopped parsley	

Combine chicken, sauce and parsley; season with salt and
pepper. Pack into greased pan 8″ x 8″ x 2″; chill thoroughly. Form into croquettes. Beat eggs; add water. Roll
croquettes in crumbs; dip in egg; roll in crumbs. Fry in

shallow fat or salad oil heated to 375°F. 5 min. or until brown. Drain on absorbent paper.

Chicken or Turkey Hash
Serves 4

2 cups chopped cooked chicken or turkey
3 cups chopped cooked potato
3 tbs. minced onion

½ cup milk
2 tbs. minced parsley
Salt and pepper
Fat or salad oil

Combine chicken or turkey, potato, onion, milk and parsley. Season with salt and pepper. Cook slowly in a little fat or salad oil until browned, turning frequently. If desired, form mixture into patties; roll in flour. Cook in a little fat or salad oil, turning to brown on both sides.

Curried Chicken Casserole
Serves 4

3 cups cooked rice
2 cups chopped cooked or canned chicken

½ cup sliced mushrooms
2 cups India Curry Sauce (p. 325)

Combine rice, chicken, mushrooms and sauce. Pour into greased casserole. Bake in moderate oven (350°F.) 20 min.

Quick Casserole
Serves 4

1 can condensed mushroom soup
¼ cup milk
1 tsp. Worcestershire sauce

1 cup chopped cooked or canned chicken
1 cup cooked or canned sliced okra
Potato chips

Combine soup, milk and Worcestershire sauce. Add chicken and okra. Pour into greased casserole. Bake in moderate oven (350°F.) 20 min. Top with potato chips. Bake 5 min.

Curried Chicken Livers in Noodle Cheese Ring
Serves 4

4 tbs. butter or margarine
10 chicken livers
4 tbs. flour
½ tsp. salt

½ tsp. curry powder
2 cups milk
Noodle Cheese Ring (p. 137)

Melt butter or margarine; add chicken livers; brown. Blend in flour, salt and curry powder. Gradually add milk; cook over hot water, stirring constantly, until thick. Unmold ring; fill with chicken liver mixture.

Roast Turkey

Use 8-20 lb. turkey, allowing ¾ lb. per person. Stuff; truss. (See Directions for Stuffing and Trussing Poultry, p. 275.) Place on side on rack in roasting pan. Brush with melted fat or salad oil. Cover with cloth dipped in melted fat or salad oil. Roast in moderate oven (325°F.) for 8-14 lb. turkey; roast in slow oven (300°F.) for 14-20 lb. turkey. Turn turkey to other side after ¼ total roasting time; turn breast side up after ½ total roasting time. If cloth becomes dry, baste with pan drippings. Cut trussing string 1 hour before total cooking time is completed. For crisp skin, remove cloth 30 min. before roasting is completed.

For 8-10 lb. turkey: Allow 20-25 min. per lb.

For 10-14 lb. turkey: Allow 18-20 min. per lb.

For 14-18 lb. turkey: Allow 15-18 min. per lb.

For 18-20 lb. turkey: Allow 13-15 min. per lb.

Turkey in Many Forms: Nowadays turkeys come in forms to meet many demands—large or small, halves or quarters, disjointed and cut up, or by-the-piece. More and more markets are carrying broiler-fryer turkeys—pocket edition birds ranging in size from 4 to approximately 8 pounds, ready-to-cook weight. The broiler-fryers should be roasted at 325°F. for 3 to 4 hours.

Devilled Mock Drumsticks   Serves 4

2 eggs	½ tsp. salt
1 cup Thick White Sauce (p. 326)	Few drops tabasco
1 tsp. Worcestershire sauce	1½ cups ground leftover turkey
2 tbs. chopped parsley	2 tbs. water
2 tbs. minced onion	Dry crumbs

Beat 1 egg; add to sauce. Add Worcestershire sauce, parsley, onion, salt, tabasco and turkey; mix well. Chill. Shape like drumsticks. Beat remaining egg; add water. Roll drumsticks in crumbs; dip in egg; roll in crumbs. Fry in deep fat or salad oil heated to 375°F. 5-7 min. or until brown. Drain on absorbent paper. Insert wooden skewers; place paper frills on skewers.

Hot Turkey Mousse   Serves 4

3 tbs. butter or margarine
3 tbs. flour
1 cup milk
Salt and pepper
1½ cups minced leftover turkey
½ cup minced cooked or canned ham
½ cup soft bread crumbs
2 eggs

Melt butter or margarine; blend in flour. Gradually add milk; cook over hot water, stirring constantly, until thick. Season with salt and pepper. Cool slightly; add turkey, ham and crumbs. Beat eggs; add. Pour into individual greased molds. Place in pan of warm water. Bake in moderate oven (350°F.) 45 min., or until inserted knife comes out clean.

Roast Capon

Use 7-10 lb. capon, allowing ½-¾ lb. per person. Stuff; truss. (See Directions for Stuffing and Trussing Poultry, p. 275.) Place on side on rack in roasting pan. Brush with melted fat or salad oil; cover with cloth dipped in melted fat or salad oil. Roast in moderate oven (325°F.) 25 min. per lb., turning capon after ½ total roasting time. If cloth becomes dry, baste with drippings. For crisp skin, remove cloth 30 min. before roasting is completed.

Roast Duck

Use 3-5 lb. duck, allowing 1 lb. per person; stuff; truss. (See Directions for Stuffing and Trussing Poultry, p. 275.)

Place on back in roasting pan. Roast in moderate oven (325°F.) 25-30 min. per lb.

Roast Goose

Use 8-10 lb. goose, allowing 1-1¼ lb. per person. Stuff; truss. (See Directions for Stuffing and Trussing Poultry, p. 275.) Place on back in roasting pan. Prick skin several times. Roast in moderate oven (325°F.) 20-25 min. per lb.

27.   SALADS AND SALAD DRESSINGS

Waldorf Surprise Salad   Serves 4

2 cups cubed unpeeled red apple
½ cup chopped pitted dates
½ cup chopped celery
¼ cup Horse-radish Mayonnaise or Salad Dressing (p. 311)
Lettuce

Combine apple, dates and celery. Combine with mayonnaise or salad dressing. Serve on lettuce.

Flower Basket Salad   Serves 4

2 large red apples
¼ cup orange juice
½ cup chopped celery
2 tbs. chopped walnut meats
2 tbs. mayonnaise or salad dressing
4 walnut meat halves
1 cup white grapes
1 cup red grapes
¼ cup Fruit Salad Dressing (p. 312)
Romaine
Onion rings

Wash apples; core; halve crosswise. Partially scoop out centers; flute edges with sharp pointed knife. Dip cut surfaces in orange juice. Chop apple centers; measure ¼ cup; combine with celery, chopped nut meats and mayonnaise or salad dressing. Fill apple halves with celery mixture; top with nut meat halves. Halve grapes; remove seeds. Combine with dressing. Arrange romaine on serving dish; place apples on romaine. Place grapes in center of dish; garnish with onion rings.

Tutti-Frutti Salad

Serves 4

- 1 large banana
- 2 cups diced plum
- 1 cup cubed peeled apple
- ½ cup minced maraschino cherries
- ½ cup chopped celery
- ¼ cup whipping cream
- ⅓ cup mayonnaise or salad dressing
- Lettuce

Peel banana; slice. Combine immediately with plum, apple, celery and cherries. Whip cream slightly; add mayonnaise or salad dressing. Combine with fruit. Serve on lettuce.

Royal Slaw

Serves 4

- ¼ cup French Dressing (p. 309)
- ½ cup sliced peeled apple
- 1 banana
- 2 cups shredded red cabbage
- ½ cup diced celery

Combine dressing and apple slices. Slice banana; add. Combine with cabbage and celery.

Western Salad

Serves 4

- 2 cups diced unpeeled red apple
- 1 cup chopped celery
- 6 slices bacon
- ½ cup Chive Mayonnaise or Salad Dressing (p. 311)
- Lettuce

Combine apple and celery. Dice bacon; fry until crisp. Drain; add to apple mixture. Add mayonnaise or salad dressing. Serve on lettuce.

Summer Sunset Salad   Serves 4

1 small head lettuce
2 oranges
1 cup cottage cheese

1 cup blueberries
Honey Fruit Salad Dressing
(p. 310)

Wash lettuce; drain. Arrange leaves on salad plates. Peel oranges; slice thin; halve slices. Mound cottage cheese in center of each salad plate; surround with circle of blueberries; edge with half slices of orange. Serve with dressing.

California Salad Cups   Serves 4

1 cup diced membrane-free
    grapefruit sections
1 cup diced pineapple
1 cup diced membrane-free
    orange sections
1 cup sliced banana
½ cup broken walnut meats

Lettuce
1 pkg. (3 oz.) cream cheese
1 tbs. liquid honey
1 tbs. lemon juice
½ cup whipping cream
4 walnut meat halves

Combine grapefruit, pineapple, orange and banana; drain. Add broken nut meats. Arrange lettuce on salad plates; fill with fruit mixture. Mash cream cheese; add honey and lemon juice. Whip cream slightly; add to cream cheese mixture. Mask fruit with cheese mixture. Garnish with nut meat halves.

Grapefruit Carrot Slaw   Serves 4

¾ cup membrane-free
    grapefruit sections
1½ cups grated carrot
1½ cups shredded cabbage

½ cup French Dressing
    (p. 309)
½ cup cottage cheese
Salt and pepper
Lettuce

Drain grapefruit; add carrot and cabbage. Toss with dressing. Season cottage cheese with salt and pepper; form into tiny balls. Add to salad. Serve on lettuce.

Orange Raisin Slaw

Toss shredded cabbage, membrane-free orange sections and seedless raisins with Fruit Salad Dressing (p. 312).

California Salad   Serves 4

1 avocado
1 cup membrane-free
    grapefruit sections
6 ripe olives

Lemon Lime Dressing
    (p. 312)
Lettuce

Peel avocado; halve lengthwise. Remove seed; cut avocado in crosswise slices. Chop olives; combine with avocado and grapefruit. Moisten with dressing. Serve on lettuce.

Rainbow Salad   Serves 4

1 avocado
2 red apples
Lemon juice
2 oranges
½ grapefruit

Red grapes
½ honeydew melon
Lettuce
French Dressing (p. 309)

Peel avocado; halve lengthwise. Remove seed; cut avocado in crosswise slices. Core apples; cut in wedges. Dip avocado and apple in lemon juice. Separate orange and grapefruit into membrane-free sections. Halve grapes; remove seeds. Scoop out melon into balls. Arrange lettuce in bowl or on serving plate. Arrange ring of overlapping avocado and apple wedges at outside edge. Arrange ring of melon balls, of orange and of grapefruit sections toward center. Garnish with grapes. Serve with dressing.

Avocado Circle Salad   Serves 4

1 avocado
2 tbs. lemon juice
Few grains salt
½ cup cottage cheese
1 tsp. grated onion

¼ tsp. paprika
Lettuce
Tangy French Dressing
    (p. 310)

Peel avocado; halve lengthwise. Remove seed. Sprinkle

avocado with lemon juice and salt. Combine cheese, onion and paprika; pack into cavities of avocado. Place avocado halves together; chill. Slice; serve on lettuce with dressing.

Fruit Salad Chantilly
Serves 4

2 bananas
2 cups strawberries
2 tbs. maraschino sirup

1 cup diced pineapple
Orange Cream Mayonnaise
   or Salad Dressing (p. 311)
Lettuce

Peel bananas; slice. Wash strawberries; hull. Combine bananas, 1½ cups berries, pineapple and sirup. Combine with mayonnaise or salad dressing. Serve on lettuce; garnish with remaining berries.

Strawberry Patch Salad
Serves 4

1½ cups cottage cheese
3 tbs. mayonnaise or salad
   dressing
⅓ cup chopped salted
   almond nut meats
¾ cup strawberry halves

Lettuce
Whole strawberries
Mint leaves
Green-tinted citron strips
Lemon Lime Dressing
   (p. 312)

Combine cottage cheese and mayonnaise or salad dressing. Add nut meats and strawberry halves. Arrange lettuce in salad bowl or on serving plate; pile cheese mixture on lettuce. Arrange whole berries, mint leaves and citron on cheese mixture in wreath design. Serve with dressing.

Dessert Salad
Serves 4

2 bananas
2 tbs. orange juice
Fruit Salad Dressing (p. 312)

1 No. 2 can (2½ cups)
   pitted sour red cherries
3 oranges
Watercress

Peel bananas; sprinkle with orange juice. Drain cherries. Peel oranges; slice thin; halve slices. Arrange watercress on serving plates; arrange fruits on watercress. Serve with dressing.

Spiced Peach Dessert Salad   Serves 4

1 No. 2 can (2½ cups)   6-8 large prunes
   peach halves   American cheese
½ tsp. cinnamon   Lettuce
½ tsp. nutmeg   Mayonnaise or salad
12 whole cloves   dressing

Drain peach halves, reserving sirup. To sirup add cinnamon, nutmeg and cloves; bring to boiling point. Boil 3 min. Pour over peach halves; chill several hours, or overnight. Drain. Steam prunes 15 min.; cool; remove pits. Grate cheese; stuff prunes. Arrange lettuce on salad plates; place peaches on lettuce. Place prune in cavity of each peach half. Serve with mayonnaise or salad dressing.

Melon Ball and Grape Salad   Serves 4

2 cups honeydew melon   ¼ cup mayonnaise or salad
   balls   dressing
1½ cups seedless grapes   Lettuce
1 pkg. (3 oz.) cream cheese

Combine melon balls and grapes; chill. Mash cream cheese; blend in mayonnaise or salad dressing. Combine with fruit. Serve on lettuce.

Fruit Salad in Melon Ring

Cut cantaloupe in ¾" thick crosswise slices; remove rind and seeds. Arrange lettuce on salad plates; place melon rings on lettuce. Combine pitted halved grapes, diced bananas and pineapple. Pile inside melon rings. Serve with Maraschino Dressing (p. 312).

Winter Fruit Salad

Sprinkle sliced bananas with pineapple juice; combine with equal quantities diced, unpeeled red apples and tangerine sections. Add a few tablespoons chopped peanut meats. Toss with shredded lettuce and Fruit French Dressing (p. 309).

Ring O'Gold Salad

Place lettuce on serving plate; arrange ring of overlapping halved orange slices at outside edge. Arrange pear halves, sliced bananas and strawberries in center. Serve with Fruit Salad Mayonnaise or Salad Dressing (p. 311).

Coleslaw
Serves 4

3 cups shredded cabbage
Paprika

½ cup Cooked Salad
Dressing (pp. 311-12)

Combine cabbage and dressing; mix well. Sprinkle with paprika. Serve immediately.

Pimiento Cup Salad

Fill canned whole pimientos with Coleslaw (above); garnish with chopped green pepper. Serve on lettuce.

Winter Slaw
Serves 4

⅓ cup French Dressing
(p. 309)
3 cups shredded cabbage

½ cup chopped peanut
meats
¼ tsp. salt

Heat dressing; add cabbage, nut meats and salt. Heat.

Jackstraw Salad
Serves 4

½ lb. Swiss-style cheese
2 tart apples
⅔ cup Cooked Salad
Dressing (pp. 311-12)

3 cups shredded cabbage
1 tsp. salt
Few grains pepper
Lettuce

Shred cheese. Pare apples; cube. Combine cheese, apple, cabbage, dressing, salt and pepper; chill. Serve on lettuce.

Pineapple Slaw
Serves 4

3 cups shredded cabbage
½ cup cubed pineapple

⅓ cup mayonnaise or salad
dressing

Combine cabbage, pineapple and mayonnaise or salad dressing.

Turnip and Carrot Slaw
Serves 4

3 cups grated turnip
1½ cups grated carrot
¼ cup mayonnaise or salad dressing
¼ cup sour cream

½ tsp. salt
Few grains pepper
¼ tsp. prepared mustard
Lettuce
Sliced pickles

Mix turnip and carrot; chill. Combine mayonnaise or salad dressing, cream, salt, pepper and mustard; add to vegetables. Toss together lightly. Serve on lettuce; garnish with pickles.

Raw Cauliflower Salad
Serves 4

2 cups thinly sliced cauliflower
½ cup chopped celery
⅓ cup chopped stuffed olives

Tarragon French Dressing (p. 310)
Lettuce
Paprika

Combine cauliflower, celery and olives. Moisten with dressing; chill. Serve on lettuce; sprinkle with paprika.

Bermuda Salad Bowl
Serves 4-6

1 small head cauliflower
½ large Bermuda onion
½ cup stuffed olives
⅔ cup French Dressing (p. 309)

½ cup crumbled Roquefort-style cheese
1 head lettuce

Wash cauliflower. Separate into flowerets; cut in thin crosswise slices. Cut onion in crosswise slices; separate in rings. Slice olives. Combine cauliflower, onion, olives and dressing; chill. Wash lettuce; drain; shred. Toss with cheese and cauliflower mixture in salad bowl.

Tossed Spring Salad
Serves 4

⅔ cup grated carrot
⅔ cup shredded cabbage
⅔ cup chopped celery

½ cucumber
½ bunch radishes
Russian Dressing (p. 311)

Combine carrot, cabbage and celery. Dice cucumber; slice radishes; add to first mixture. Mix with dressing.

Stuffed Tomatoes New-Style   Serves 4

4 medium tomatoes
Few grains salt
1 cup cubed cooked potato
½ cup chopped celery
½ tsp. grated onion

2 tbs. chopped anchovies
½ cup mayonnaise or salad dressing
Lettuce

Scoop out tomatoes; sprinkle with salt. Invert on plate; chill. Combine potato, celery, onion, anchovies and mayonnaise or salad dressing. Fill tomatoes. Serve on lettuce.

Hot Potato Salad   Serves 4

4 large potatoes
4 slices bacon
2 tsp. minced onion
½ cup vinegar
¼ cup water

¼ cup sugar
2 tsp. salt
¼ tsp. pepper
½ tsp. dry mustard
¼ cup chopped parsley

Cook potatoes according to directions for Boiled Potatoes (p. 368). Drain; peel; slice. Mince bacon; fry until crisp; drain. Combine onion, vinegar, water, sugar, salt, pepper and mustard; heat. Add to potatoes. Add bacon and parsley, mixing carefully with fork so potato slices are not broken. Heat slowly.

Potato Salad   Serves 4

2 hard-cooked eggs
3 cups cubed cooked potato
1 tbs. chopped chives
1 cup diced celery

¾ cup Cooked Salad Dressing (pp. 311-12)
Salt and pepper
Lettuce

Chop eggs; combine with potato, chives, celery and dressing. Season with salt and pepper. Chill. Serve on lettuce.

Through-The-Garden Salad   Serves 4

½ tsp. grated onion
½ tsp. vinegar
¼ tsp. paprika
½ tsp. salt
½ cup mayonnaise or salad dressing
2 cups cubed cooked potato

½ cup diced celery
½ cup diced cucumber
¼ cup sliced radishes
¼ cup chopped green pepper
Lettuce
Watercress

Mix onion, vinegar, paprika, salt and mayonnaise or salad dressing. Combine with potato, celery, cucumber, radishes and green pepper. Chill. Serve on lettuce and watercress.

Macedoine of Vegetable Salad   Serves 4

1½ cups cooked or canned lima beans
1½ cups diced cooked or canned carrot
1½ cups diced celery

French Dressing (p. 309)
Lettuce
2 hard-cooked eggs
Mayonnaise (p. 311)

Combine beans, carrots and celery. Moisten with dressing; chill. Line salad bowl with lettuce; fill with vegetable mixture. Slice eggs; use as garnish. Serve with mayonnaise.

Mixed Vegetable Salad Bowl

In separate bowls of French Dressing (p. 309) marinate cooked or canned asparagus tips, narrow strips of cooked or canned tongue, cooked or canned green beans, diced cooked or canned beets. Arrange on romaine in individual salad bowls. Garnish with watercress; serve with Russian Dressing (p. 311).

Mixed Green Salad

Wash lettuce, chicory and romaine; separate leaves. Drain; coarsely chop. Wash tomatoes and leeks; slice. Combine lettuce, chicory, romaine, tomatoes and leeks; toss lightly with Roquefort Onion French Dressing (p. 310) or Chiffonade French Dressing (p. 309).

Spring Salad Bowl
Serves 4

1 bunch radishes
1 bunch scallions
1 large cucumber

1 bunch watercress
Diet Dressing (p. 310)

Trim radishes; wash. Cut into roses. Drop into water; chill. Trim scallions; wash; chill. Pare cucumber; score with tines of fork; slice thin. Wash watercress; drain. Arrange watercress, radishes, scallions and cucumber in salad bowl. Serve with dressing.

Salad Bowl
Serves 4

1 small head lettuce
3 tomatoes
1 medium onion

2 hard-cooked eggs
Roquefort French Dressing
   (p. 310)

Wash lettuce; separate leaves; drain. Wash tomatoes; slice thin. Slice onion; separate into rings. Slice eggs. Line salad bowl with lettuce. Combine tomatoes, onion and eggs; place in salad bowl. Toss with dressing.

Savory Salad Bowl
Serves 4

1 head lettuce
1 head romaine
1 hard-cooked egg

8 anchovies
⅓ cup Caper French
   Dressing (p. 309)

Wash lettuce and romaine; separate leaves. Drain. Chop egg and anchovies very fine; add to dressing. Toss greens with dressing.

Chef's Salad Bowl
Serves 4

½ Bermuda onion
2 tomatoes
1 small head chicory
⅔ cup slivered cooked or
   canned tongue

Chef's French Dressing
   (p. 309)
Lettuce

Cut onion in thin crosswise slices; separate into rings. Wash tomatoes; cut in thin wedges. Wash chicory; separate leaves. Drain; coarsely chop. Combine onion, tomato, chicory and tongue. Toss with dressing. Serve on lettuce in salad bowl.

Summer Salad Bowl
Serves 4

1 cucumber
12 large stuffed olives
1 bunch watercress

¼ cup cubed Swiss-style cheese
Tarragon French Dressing (p. 310)

Peel cucumber; score. Slice very thin. Slice olives. Wash watercress. Combine cucumber, olives and cheese. Toss with watercress and dressing in salad bowl.

Stuffed Tomatoes Florentine
Serves 4

4 tomatoes
Salt
2¾ cups shredded raw spinach

½ cup sour cream
Few grains pepper
Lettuce

Scoop out tomatoes; sprinkle with salt. Invert on plate; chill. Combine spinach and cream; season with salt and pepper. Stuff tomatoes. Serve on lettuce.

Basic Meat Salad
Serves 4

2 cups cubed cooked or canned meat
1 cup diced celery
1 tsp. Worcestershire sauce

⅓ cup mayonnaise or salad dressing
Salt and pepper
Lettuce

Combine meat, celery, Worcestershire sauce and mayonnaise or salad dressing. Season with salt and pepper. Serve on lettuce. If desired, garnish with tomato wedges and mayonnaise or salad dressing.

Devilled Potato Salad

Cube cooked potatoes; mix with equal amount diced cooked frankfurters and diced celery. Moisten with Caper French

Dressing (p. 309). Serve on lettuce; garnish with hard-cooked egg slices and mayonnaise or salad dressing.

Sunday Supper Ring   Serves 4

Pack Potato Salad (p. 292) into 7½" ring mold. Chill. Unmold on chicory. Garnish with assorted sliced cold meats and radish roses. Fill center with chicory.

Corned Beef Slaw   Serves 4

1 12-oz. can (or 2 cups cooked) corned beef	¼ cup Garlic French Dressing (p. 309)
1½ cups grated carrot	⅓ cup mayonnaise or salad dressing
2 cups shredded cabbage	Lettuce
¼ cup sliced sweet pickle	

Cube corned beef; add carrot, cabbage, pickle and dressing. Chill. Add 3 tbs. mayonnaise or salad dressing. Serve on lettuce; garnish with remaining mayonnaise or salad dressing.

Square Meal Salad   Serves 4

1½ cups cubed spiced pork	Cooked or canned asparagus tips
1 cup chopped celery	Cooked or canned sliced carrots
Snappy Salad Dressing (p. 312)	
Lettuce	

Combine pork and celery; moisten with dressing. Serve on lettuce; garnish with asparagus tips and overlapping carrot slices.

Ham Roll-Ups   Serves 4

½ cup diced cooked or canned carrot	Mayonnaise or salad dressing
1 cup cubed cooked potato	Salt and pepper
½ cup cooked or canned peas	12 thin slices boiled ham
½ cup diced celery	Vinaigrette French Dressing (p. 310)
2 tbs. chopped onion	Shredded lettuce
2 tbs. chopped pickle	

SALADS AND SALAD DRESSINGS 297

Combine carrot, potato, peas, celery, onion and pickle. Moisten with mayonnaise or salad dressing; season with salt and pepper. Put spoonful of salad mixture on each slice of ham; roll up. Fasten with picks; chill. Arrange lettuce on individual salad plates; place 3 ham roll-ups on each. Serve with dressing.

Favorite Sunday Supper Salad

Serves 4

½ lb. cooked or canned ham
½ lb. American cheese
1 small head cabbage
1 green pepper
1 Bermuda onion
Olive French Dressing (p. 309)

Cut ham and cheese into thin strips. Shred cabbage. Slice green pepper and onion thin. Combine ham, cheese, cabbage, green pepper and onion. Chill. Toss lightly with dressing.

Veal and Bacon Salad

Serves 4

2 cups cubed cooked veal
⅓ cup diced crisp bacon
¾ cup diced celery
¼ tsp. salt
⅓ cup mayonnaise or salad dressing
Few grains pepper
Lettuce

Combine veal and bacon; add celery, mayonnaise or salad dressing, salt and pepper. Chill. Serve on lettuce.

Luncheon Salad

Serves 4

2 cups cooked potato balls
2 cups cooked carrot balls
1 cup sliced cooked frankfurters
1 tbs. chopped parsley
2 tbs. French Dressing (p. 309)
¼ cup mayonnaise or salad dressing
Chicory

Combine potato, carrot, frankfurters and parsley. Add dressing and mayonnaise or salad dressing; chill. Serve on chicory.

Tomato Salad Ritz
Serves 4

1 cup cubed cooked or
    canned ham
1 cup cubed cooked potato
½ tbs. chopped parsley
½ tbs. chopped chives
½ tsp. salt
¼ cup French Dressing
    (p. 309)

4 large firm tomatoes
Salt
4 green pepper rings
Watercress
Lettuce
Stuffed celery
Cucumber slices
Carrot slices

Combine ham, potato, parsley, chives, salt and dressing;
chill. Peel tomatoes; cut slice from tops, reserving tops.
Scoop out tomatoes; sprinkle with salt. Invert on plate; chill.
Fill tomatoes with ham mixture. Top with pepper rings; replace tomato tops. Place on platter. Garnish with watercress, lettuce, celery, cucumber and carrot.

Substantial Salad
Serves 4

1 cup cottage cheese
4 tsp. chopped chives
12 thin slices dried beef
Lettuce

Coleslaw (p. 290)
Curry French Dressing
    (p. 309)

Combine cheese and chives; spread on beef. Roll up; fasten
with picks. Chill. Arrange lettuce on individual salad plates;
pile slaw on lettuce. Place 3 rolls on each plate. Serve with
dressing.

Chicken Salad
Serves 4

1 12-oz. can (or 2 cups
    cooked) chicken
1 cup diced celery

½ cup mayonnaise or salad
    dressing
Salt and pepper
Lettuce

Combine chicken, celery and mayonnaise or salad dressing;
mix well. Season with salt and pepper. Serve on lettuce. If
desired, garnish with asparagus tips and chopped pimiento.

Celebration Salad

Serves 8

- 1 12-oz. can (or 2 cups cooked) chicken
- 2 cups cubed cooked or canned ham
- 2 cups diced celery
- 1 cup salted almond nut meats
- ½ cup mayonnaise or salad dressing
- Lettuce
- 2 hard-cooked eggs
- Pimientos

Combine chicken, ham, celery, nut meats and mayonnaise or salad dressing. Arrange on lettuce. Cut eggs lengthwise; cut pimientos in strips. Garnish salad with egg and pimiento.

Fish Salad

Serves 4

- 2 cups cooked or canned fish
- 1 cup diced celery
- Lettuce
- ½ cup mayonnaise or salad dressing
- Salt and pepper

Flake fish, removing bits of membrane, if necessary; combine with celery and mayonnaise or salad dressing. Season with salt and pepper. Serve on lettuce. If desired, garnish with hard-cooked eggs and capers.

Fish Salad Supreme

Serves 4

- 1 7¾-oz. can (1 cup) salmon
- 1 cup cooked or canned peas
- 2 cups shredded cabbage
- 2 tbs. chopped pimiento
- Herb French Dressing (p. 309)
- Lettuce
- Thousand Island Dressing (p. 311)
- Tomato wedges

Drain salmon; combine with peas, cabbage and pimiento; moisten with French dressing. Arrange on lettuce; garnish with tomatoes. Serve with dressing.

Crab and Olive Salad   Serves 4

1 13-oz. can (2 cups) crab
meat
⅔ cup chopped ripe olives
Romaine

1⅔ cups diced celery
¼ cup mayonnaise or salad
dressing
Salt and pepper

Flake crab meat, removing bits of membrane; combine with olives, celery and mayonnaise or salad dressing. Season with salt and pepper. Serve on romaine.

Fish Salad in Avocado Shells   Serves 8

1 7-oz. can (1 cup) tuna
1 7¾-oz. can (1 cup)
salmon
1 3¾-oz. can (½ cup)
sardines
1 2-oz. can (⅓ cup)
anchovies
1 cup diced celery
3 tbs. chopped olives

6 tbs. mayonnaise or salad
dressing
2 tbs. chili sauce
⅛ tsp. dry mustard
1 tsp. Worcestershire sauce
1 tsp. tarragon vinegar
4 avocados
Lemon juice
Watercress
Lettuce

Drain tuna, salmon, sardines and anchovies; flake. Combine with celery and olives. Mix mayonnaise or salad dressing, chili sauce, mustard, Worcestershire sauce and vinegar; add. Cut avocados in half lengthwise; remove seeds; sprinkle avocados with lemon juice. Fill with fish mixture. Garnish with watercress and lettuce.

Sea Salad Supreme   Serves 8

1 13-oz. can (2 cups) tuna
1 6-oz. can (1 cup) lobster
2 5¾-oz. cans (2 cups)
shrimp
2 cups diced celery

¾ cup mayonnaise or salad
dressing
Watercress
Lemon wedges

Drain tuna, lobster and shrimp; flake tuna and lobster, removing bits of membrane from lobster. Reserve 12 whole shrimp for garnish. Combine remaining shrimp, tuna, lobster, celery and mayonnaise or salad dressing. Serve on watercress; garnish with whole shrimp and lemon.

Bar Harbor Salad
Serves 4

4 firm tomatoes
1 7½-oz. can (1 cup) fish flakes
2 tbs. capers
½ cup minced celery
2 tsp. prepared horse-radish
½ cup chili sauce
Watercress

Quarter tomatoes without cutting through bottoms; scoop out. Combine fish flakes, capers, celery, horse-radish and chili sauce; chill. Fill tomatoes with fish mixture. Serve on watercress. If desired, garnish with pickled onions.

Lenten Salad
Serves 4

6 hard-cooked eggs
8 anchovies
¼ cup mayonnaise or salad dressing
1 cup diced celery
¼ tsp. salt
Few grains pepper
Lettuce

Slice eggs; chop anchovies. Combine with celery, mayonnaise or salad dressing, salt and pepper. Serve on lettuce.

Sardine Salad Bowl
Serves 8

1 No. 2 can (or 2½ cups cooked) green beans
1 No. 2 can (or 2½ cups cooked) shredded carrot
2 cups cubed cooked potato
1 cup diced celery
2 cups shredded romaine
1 7-oz. can sardines
1 cup French Dressing (p. 309)

Drain beans and carrot, reserving liquor for use in soups, sauces, etc. Combine with potato, celery and romaine. Drain sardines; chop, reserving 4 for garnish. Combine beans, carrots, potato, celery, romaine and chopped sardines; chill. Toss with dressing. Garnish with remaining sardines.

Sunset Salad
Serves 4-6

1 pkg. lemon gelatin
1½ cups water
1 cup canned cranberry
　sauce
2 bananas

¼ cup chopped walnut
　meats
Lettuce
Mayonnaise or salad
　dressing

Dissolve gelatin in 1½ cups water according to directions
on pkg.; press cranberry sauce through fine sieve; gradually
add gelatin. Chill until sirupy. Peel bananas; dice. Fold in
with nut meats. Pour into mold which has been rinsed in
cold water. Chill until firm. Unmold on lettuce. Serve with
mayonnaise or salad dressing.

Autumn Salad
Serves 4-6

1 pkg. lemon gelatin
1 cup water
½ cup grape juice
2 tbs. lemon juice
¼ tsp. salt
1 cup diced celery
1 cup cubed unpeeled red
　apple

½ cup seedless raisins
½ cup cubed American
　cheese
Watercress
Mayonnaise or salad
　dressing

Dissolve gelatin in 1 cup water according to directions on
pkg.; add grape juice, lemon juice and salt. Chill until
sirupy. Fold in celery, apple, raisins and cheese. Pour into
individual molds which have been rinsed in cold water; chill
until firm. Unmold on watercress. Serve with mayonnaise or
salad dressing.

Wedding Ring Salad

2 pkg. orange gelatin
1½ cups water
2 cups pineapple juice
12 canned apricot halves

1 cup cottage cheese
Watercress
Mayonnaise or salad
　dressing

Dissolve gelatin in 1½ cups water according to directions
on package; add pineapple juice. Chill until sirupy. Pour 1
cup into 9″ ring mold which has been rinsed in cold water;

chill until firm. Fill apricot halves with ¼ cup cottage cheese; place each 2 halves together. Arrange on gelatin in mold. Pour clear gelatin into mold, reserving ½ cup. Chill until firm. Combine remaining cheese and gelatin; pour into mold. Chill until firm. Unmold. Garnish with watercress. Serve with mayonnaise or salad dressing.

Golden Winter Salad   Serves 4-6

1 pkg. orange gelatin
2 cups water
1 apple
2 tbs. lemon juice
Few grains salt
1½ cups diced membrane-free grapefruit sections

¼ cup chopped walnut meats
Lettuce
Mayonnaise or salad dressing

Dissolve gelatin in 2 cups water according to directions on package; chill until sirupy. Core apple; pare; cube; sprinkle with lemon juice and salt. Combine with grapefruit and nut meats; fold into gelatin. Pour into individual molds which have been rinsed in cold water. Chill until firm. Unmold on lettuce; serve with mayonnaise or salad dressing.

Ginger Fruit Salad   Serves 4-6

1 pkg. lime gelatin
1 cup water
1 cup membrane-free grapefruit sections
1 cup ginger ale

1½ cups pitted black cherries
Lettuce
Mayonnaise or salad dressing

Dissolve gelatin in 1 cup water according to directions on package; cool. Add ginger ale. Chill until sirupy; fold in grapefruit and 1 cup cherries. Pour into mold which has been rinsed in cold water; chill until firm. Unmold on lettuce; garnish with remaining cherries and mayonnaise or salad dressing.

Emerald Salad

Serves 4-6

1 pkg. lime gelatin
2 cups water
2 pkg. (6-oz.) cream cheese
Few grains salt
Watercress
2 pineapple slices

4 membane-free grapefruit
sections
4 membrane-free orange
sections
Fruit Salad Mayonnaise or
Salad Dressing (p. 311)

Dissolve gelatin in 2 cups water according to directions on package; chill until sirupy. Mash cream cheese; gradually add gelatin and salt. Beat with rotary beater until well mixed. Pour into mold which has been rinsed in cold water. Chill until firm. Unmold; garnish with watercress, pineapple, grapefruit and orange. Serve with mayonnaise or salad dressing.

Grapefruit Perfection Salad

Serves 4-6

1 envelope (1 tbs.)
unflavored gelatine
1/4 cup cold water
1 No. 2 can (2½ cups)
grapefruit sections
1/4 cup vinegar
1/4 cup sugar

½ tsp. salt
1 pimiento
2/3 cup finely shredded
cabbage
Lettuce
French Dressing (p. 309)

Soften gelatin in cold water. Drain grapefruit, reserving sirup. Heat sirup; add to gelatine with vinegar, sugar and salt. Stir until dissolved; chill until sirupy. Chop pimiento; fold in with grapefruit and cabbage. Pour into mold which has been rinsed in cold water; chill until firm. Unmold on lettuce; serve with dressing.

Jellied Spring Salad

Serves 4-6

1 envelope (1 tbs.)
unflavored gelatine
½ cup cold water
1 cup hot water
2 tbs. sugar
½ tsp. salt
1/4 cup lemon juice

1 cup diced cucumber
1 cup sliced radishes
½ cup sliced scallions
Watercress
Mayonnaise or salad
dressing

Soften gelatine in cold water; add hot water. Add sugar, salt and lemon juice; stir until dissolved. Chill until sirupy. Fold in cucumber, radishes and scallions. Pour into mold which has been rinsed in cold water; chill until firm. Unmold on watercress; serve with mayonnaise or salad dressing.

Tomato Aspic Ring   Serves 8

1 bay leaf
Few drops tabasco
4 onion slices
½ tsp. salt
3¾ cups tomato juice

2 envelopes (2 tbs.) unflavored gelatine
⅔ cup cold water
2 tbs. vinegar
Lettuce

Add bay leaf, tabasco, onion and salt to tomato juice; simmer 10 min. Soften gelatine in cold water; dissolve in tomato juice mixture. Add vinegar; strain. Pour into 7″ ring mold which has been rinsed in cold water; chill until firm. Unmold on lettuce. If desired, serve with Tarragon French Dressing (p. 310).

Tomato Aspic Ring with Potato Salad: Follow recipe for Tomato Aspic Ring. Follow recipe for Potato Salad (p. 292). Fill center of aspic with salad.

Egg and Asparagus Mousse   Serves 4-6

4 hard-cooked eggs
2 envelopes (2 tbs.) unflavored gelatine
¼ cup cold water
½ cup whipping cream
⅔ cup sieved cooked asparagus

½ tsp. salt
Few grains pepper
1 tbs. ketchup
¼ cup mayonnaise or salad dressing
Lettuce

Chop eggs. Soften gelatin in cold water; dissolve over hot water. Whip cream; add gelatin. Fold in asparagus, eggs, salt, pepper, ketchup and mayonnaise or salad dressing. Pour into individual molds which have been rinsed in cold water. Chill until firm; unmold on lettuce.

Salmon Aspic Ring   Serves 4-6

1 envelope (1 tbs.)
   unflavored gelatine
¼ cup cold water
1 cup hot water
¼ cup sugar
¼ tsp. salt
¼ cup vinegar

1 tbs. lemon juice
½ cup chopped celery
1 cup chopped cucumber
2 tbs. chopped green pepper
Salmon Mixture (below)
Watercress

Soften gelatine in cold water; dissolve in hot water. Add sugar, salt, vinegar and lemon juice; chill until sirupy. Add celery, cucumber and green pepper. Pour into mold, which has been rinsed in cold water. Chill until firm. Add salmon mixture. Chill until firm. Unmold; garnish with watercress.

Salmon Mixture

1 envelope (1 tbs.)
   unflavored gelatine
½ cup mayonnaise or salad
   dressing

2 tbs. cold water
1 lb. can (2 cups) salmon
¼ cup diced green pepper
½ cup diced celery

Soften gelatin in cold water; dissolve over hot water. Add to mayonnaise or salad dressing. Flake salmon; add with green pepper and celery.

Tuna Tomato Aspic   Serves 4-6

2 cups tomato juice
1 envelope (1 tbs.)
   unflavored gelatine
¼ cup cold water
1 tsp. Worcestershire sauce
¼ tsp. salt

2 tsp. lemon juice
1 7-oz. can (1 cup) tuna
¾ cup diced celery
½ tsp. capers
Lettuce
French Dressing (p. 309)

Heat tomato juice. Soften gelatine in cold water; dissolve in tomato juice. Add Worcestershire sauce, salt and lemon juice; chill until sirupy. Flake tuna; add with celery and capers. Pour into individual molds which have been rinsed in cold water; chill until firm. Unmold on lettuce; serve with dressing.

Veal and Ham Mousse
Serves 4-6

1 envelope (1 tbs.) unflavored gelatine
2 tbs. cold water
1 cup chopped cooked veal
1 cup chopped cooked or canned ham
¼ cup chopped celery
⅛ tsp. paprika
2 tbs. minced parsley
¾ cup whipping cream
Lettuce
Relish French Dressing (p. 309)
Stuffed olives

Soften gelatin in cold water; dissolve over hot water. Combine veal, ham, celery, paprika and parsley. Whip cream; add gelatine. Fold into meat mixture. Pour into individual molds or one large mold, which has been rinsed in cold water. Chill until firm. Unmold on lettuce; serve with dressing. Garnish with olives.

Sunday Night Supper Salad
Serves 8

1 pkg. gelatin aspic
2 cups water
1 bunch watercress
3 cups cubed cooked or canned corned beef
4 hard-cooked eggs
6 tbs. mayonnaise or salad dressing
½ tsp. Worcestershire sauce
2 cups shredded cabbage
1 cup grated carrot
Tangy French Dressing (p. 310)

Dissolve gelatin in 2 cups water according to directions on pkg.; chill until sirupy. Wash watercress; drain. Using medium blade, put watercress and corned beef through food chopper. Add mayonnaise or salad dressing and Worcestershire sauce. Chop eggs; add. Fold meat mixture into gelatin. Pour into ring mold which has been rinsed in cold water. Chill until firm. Combine cabbage and carrot; moisten with dressing. Unmold gelatin salad; fill center with cabbage mixture.

Luncheon Salad Mousse

Serves 4-6

- 1 envelope (1 tbs.) unflavored gelatine
- 6 tbs. cold water
- 6 tbs. whipping cream
- ¼ cup mayonnaise or salad dressing
- 1½ cups minced cooked or canned ham
- 1½ cups minced cooked lamb
- 6 tbs. minced sweet pickle
- 1½ tbs. minced parsley
- ¼ tsp. salt
- ⅛ tsp. paprika
- 1 tbs. Worcestershire sauce
- Lettuce
- Caper French Dressing (p. 309)

Soften gelatin in cold water; dissolve over hot water. Whip cream; combine with mayonnaise or salad dressing. Add gelatine. Fold in lamb, ham, pickle, parsley, salt, paprika and Worcestershire sauce. Pour into mold which has been rinsed in cold water. Chill until firm. Unmold on lettuce. Serve with dressing.

Cottage Salad

Serves 4

- ½ cup cottage cheese
- ½ cup grated Cheddar cheese
- 1 tsp. grated onion
- Lettuce
- Tangy French Dressing (p. 310)

Combine cottage cheese, Cheddar cheese and onion; shape into balls. Serve on lettuce with dressing.

Macaroni Salad

Serves 4

- 3 cups cooked elbow macaroni
- 2 tbs. chopped onion
- 1 cup cubed American cheese
- Mayonnaise or salad dressing
- Lettuce or watercress

Combine macaroni, onion and cheese. Moisten with mayonnaise or salad dressing. Serve on lettuce or watercress.

French Dressing   Makes 1½ cups

- 1 cup salad oil
- ⅓ cup vinegar
- 1½ tsp. salt
- 2 tsp. sugar

- 1½ tsp. dry mustard
- 1 tsp. paprika
- Few grains pepper

Combine salad oil, vinegar, salt, sugar, mustard, paprika and pepper. Beat with rotary beater until well mixed. Chill in tightly covered jar. Mix well before serving.

Caper French Dressing: Follow recipe for French Dressing, adding 2 tbs. minced capers and 2 tbs. minced onion before serving.

Chef's French Dressing: Follow recipe for French Dressing, adding ¼ tsp. celery salt, 1 tbs. minced onion and ½ cup ketchup before beating.

Chiffonade French Dressing: Follow recipe for French Dressing, adding 1 tsp. minced capers, 1 minced hard-cooked egg and ½ cup minced cooked beets before serving.

Curry French Dressing: Follow recipe for French Dressing, adding ¾ tsp. curry powder before beating.

Fruit French Dressing: Follow recipe for French Dressing, substituting ⅓ cup orange juice for ⅓ cup vinegar and adding 1 tbs. lemon juice. If desired sweeten slightly with liquid honey.

Garlic French Dressing: Follow recipe for French Dressing, adding 1 crushed clove garlic before beating. Before storing, remove garlic.

Herb French Dressing: Follow recipe for French Dressing, adding 1 tbs. each minced parsley, watercress and chives before serving.

Olive French Dressing: Follow recipe for French Dressing, adding ¼ cup chopped olives before serving.

Relish French Dressing: Follow recipe for French Dressing, adding ¼ cup sweet pickle relish before serving.

Roquefort French Dressing: Follow recipe for French Dressing, adding ½ cup crumbled Roquefort-style cheese before serving.

Roquefort Onion French Dressing: Follow recipe for Roquefort French Dressing, adding 2 tbs. minced onion before serving.

Tangy French Dressing: Follow recipe for French Dressing, adding 1 tsp. Worcestershire sauce, 2 drops tabasco and 2 tbs. prepared horse-radish before beating.

Tarragon French Dressing: Follow recipe for French Dressing, substituting ⅓ cup tarragon vinegar for ⅓ cup vinegar.

Vinaigrette French Dressing: Follow recipe for French Dressing, adding 2 tsp. minced pickle, 2 tsp. minced capers, 1 tsp. minced parsley, 1 tsp. minced onion and 1 tsp. prepared mustard before beating.

Diet Dressing   Makes 1¼ cups

½ cup salad oil
¼ cup lemon juice
¼ cup water
½ tsp. salt
¼ cup ketchup

1 tsp. dry mustard
¼ tsp. paprika
½ tsp. Worcestershire sauce

Combine salad oil, lemon juice, water, salt, ketchup, mustard, paprika and Worcestershire sauce. Beat with rotary beater until well mixed. Chill in tightly covered jar. Mix well before serving.

Honey Fruit Salad Dressing   Makes ¾ cup

⅓ cup salad oil
3 tbs. lemon juice

½ tsp. salt
⅓ cup liquid honey

Combine salad oil, lemon juice and salt. Slowly add honey, beating constantly. Chill in tightly covered jar. Mix well before serving.

Mayonnaise   Makes 2 cups

1 egg

1 tsp. salt

1 tsp. sugar

¾ tsp. dry mustard

Few grains pepper

Few grains paprika

Few grains cayenne

2 tbs. vinegar

1½ cups salad oil

2 tbs. lemon juice

Combine egg, salt, sugar, mustard, pepper, paprika and cayenne. Add 1 tbs. vinegar. Add ½ cup salad oil, 1 tbs. at a time, beating constantly with rotary beater. Slowly add remaining oil, alternately with remaining vinegar and lemon juice, beating constantly until thick.

Mayonnaise or Salad Dressing Variations

Chive Mayonnaise or Salad Dressing: To 1 cup mayonnaise or salad dressing add 2 tbs. minced chives.

Fruit Salad Mayonnaise or Salad Dressing: To 1 cup mayonnaise or salad dressing add ½ cup whipped cream.

Horse-radish Mayonnaise or Salad Dressing: To 1 cup mayonnaise or salad dressing add 2 tbs. prepared horse-radish.

Orange Cream Mayonnaise or Salad Dressing: Follow recipe for Fruit Salad Mayonnaise or Salad Dressing, adding 2 tbs. grated orange rind.

Russian Dressing: To 1 cup mayonnaise or salad dressing add ¼ cup drained chili sauce.

Thousand Island Dressing: To 1 cup mayonnaise or salad dressing add 1½ tbs. chopped green pepper, 2 tsp. capers, 2 tsp. chopped stuffed olives and ½ tsp. minced parsley.

Cooked Salad Dressing   Makes 1⅔ cups

2 tbs. flour

1½ tsp. salt

¾ tsp. dry mustard

1 tbs. sugar

Few grains pepper

Few grains paprika

1 egg

1 cup milk

¼ cup vinegar

2 tbs. butter or margarine

Mix flour, salt, mustard, sugar, pepper and paprika. Beat

egg; add. Gradually add milk; cook over boiling water, stirring constantly, until thick. Add vinegar and butter or margarine; cover. Cool.

Snappy Salad Dressing   Makes 1½ cups

1 tsp. dry mustard   Few grains cayenne
½ tsp. salt   2 egg yolks
2 tsp. flour   ⅓ cup vinegar
3 tbs. sugar   ½ cup whipping cream

Mix mustard, salt, flour, sugar and cayenne. Beat egg yolks; add. Slowly add vinegar; cook over boiling water, stirring constantly, until thick; cool. Whip cream stiff; fold in.

Fruit Salad Dressing   Makes ¾ cup

1 pkg. (3 oz.) cream cheese   1 tbs. mayonnaise or salad
3 tbs. cream   dressing
Few grains salt   2 tbs. orange juice
                                    ½ tsp. grated orange rind

Mash cheese; add cream. Beat until fluffy. Add mayonnaise or salad dressing, salt, orange juice and rind.

Lemon Lime Dressing   Makes 1¾ cups

4 tsp. lemon juice   ½ cup whipping cream
2 tsp. lime juice   ½ cup mayonnaise or salad
2 tbs. sugar   dressing

Combine lemon and lime juices, mayonnaise or salad dressing and sugar. Whip cream slightly; fold in.

Maraschino Dressing   Makes 1¼ cups

¼ cup whipping cream   2 tsp. sugar
½ cup mayonnaise or salad   ¼ cup chopped maraschino
    dressing   cherries

Whip cream stiff; fold into mayonnaise or salad dressing with sugar. Add cherries.

28. SANDWICHES

Sandwich Fillings

Use these fillings to spread between thin slices of bread. Crisp lettuce or watercress is good with any of these fillings, if they are to be served immediately.

Meat and Poultry

Savory Meat: Combine chopped cooked or canned meat with chopped celery. Moisten with mayonnaise or salad dressing. Season with Worcestershire sauce.

Ham and Coleslaw: Combine chopped cooked or canned ham and chopped cabbage. Moisten with mayonnaise or salad dressing. Season with prepared mustard.

Ham and Chutney: Combine ground cooked or canned ham and chopped chutney. Moisten with mayonnaise or salad dressing.

Spiced Pork and Egg: Combine chopped canned spiced pork, chopped hard-cooked egg and sweet pickle relish. Moisten with mayonnaise or salad dressing.

Meat Loaf: Combine chopped cooked meat loaf with chili sauce.

Corned Beef: Combine chopped cooked or canned corned beef with a little prepared mustard. Moisten with mayonnaise or salad dressing.

Chopped Tongue and Olive: Combine chopped cooked or canned tongue with chopped stuffed olives. Moisten with mayonnaise or salad dressing.

Dried Beef and Horse-radish: Moisten shredded dried beef

with mayonnaise or salad dressing. Season with prepared horse-radish.

Liver and Egg: Combine minced cooked liver and chopped hard-cooked egg. Moisten with mayonnaise or salad dressing. Season with prepared horse-radish, salt and pepper.

Mock Paté: Blend liverwurst with cream cheese. Season with grated onion.

Chicken or Turkey: Moisten chopped cooked chicken or turkey with mayonnaise or salad dressing. Season with salt and pepper. If desired, add a few finely chopped almond nut meats.

Chicken and Ripe Olive: Combine chopped cooked or canned chicken, chopped celery and chopped ripe olives. Moisten with mayonnaise or salad dressing.

Fish

Fish Salad: Combine tuna, salmon, shrimp, lobster or crab meat with chopped celery. Moisten with mayonnaise or salad dressing.

Tuna and Egg: Combine flaked tuna and chopped hard-cooked egg. Moisten with mayonnaise or salad dressing. If desired, add chopped chives.

Salmon and Cucumber: Combine flaked salmon and chopped cucumber. Moisten with mayonnaise or salad dressing. Season with salt and pepper.

Sardine: Moisten mashed sardines with mayonnaise or salad dressing. Season with lemon juice.

Cheese

Assorted Cream Cheese: Blend cream cheese with cream or top milk. Combine with any one of the following: finely chopped olives, pickles, nut meats, raisins, pitted dates, crystallized ginger, maraschino cherries, preserved figs, crushed drained pineapple, chives or watercress.

Creamy Roquefort: Blend Roquefort-style cheese with cream cheese. Moisten with cream or top milk.

Cheese and Peanut Butter: Blend grated American cheese and peanut butter. Moisten with mayonnaise or salad dressing.

Miscellaneous

Vegetable Relish: Combine finely chopped celery, radishes and olives. Moisten with mayonnaise or salad dressing.

Chopped Egg and Watercress: Combine chopped hard-cooked egg and chopped watercress. Moisten with mayonnaise or salad dressing. Season with salt and pepper. If desired, add chopped chives.

Peanut Butter and Relish: Blend peanut butter with mayonnaise or salad dressing. Add sweet pickle relish.

Baked Bean: Combine mashed baked beans and ketchup.

Cornucopias

Cut fresh bread in thin slices. Spread with Mock Paté Filling (p. 314) or Creamy Roquefort Filling (above). Roll cone shape, having one end closed and opposite end open. When ready to serve, garnish open end with watercress.

Pinwheels

Remove crusts from loaf unsliced bread; cut in thin lengthwise slices. Soften cream cheese; tint pink, green or yellow with vegetable coloring. Spread on bread slices; roll up jellyroll fashion. Wrap in waxed paper; cover with damp towel. Chill thoroughly. Cut in thin slices.

Ribbon Sandwiches

Spread softened butter or margarine or cream cheese between white and whole-wheat bread slices. Spread softened butter or margarine or cream cheese between each two sandwiches, alternating white and whole-wheat bread. Press firmly together. Wrap in waxed paper; cover with damp towel. Chill thoroughly. Cut in thin slices.

Asparagus Tip Rolls

Cut fresh bread in thin slices; remove crusts. Spread slices with prepared mustard; wrap each around well-drained cooked or canned asparagus tip. Fasten with pick. Wrap in waxed paper; cover with damp cloth. Chill thoroughly. When ready to serve, remove picks.

Egg Relish Rolls   Serves 4

3 hard-cooked eggs
½ cup grated carrot
¼ cup minced celery
Few grains salt
Few grains pepper
2 tbs. sweet pickle relish

3 tbs. mayonnaise or salad dressing
4 large soft rolls
Butter or margarine
Lettuce

Chop eggs; add carrot, celery, salt, pepper and relish. Add mayonnaise or salad dressing. Slit rolls in center. Soften butter or margarine; spread on rolls. Line rolls with lettuce; fill with egg mixture.

Salad Roll

Slit long, soft rolls in center. Spread with softened butter or margarine. Line rolls with lettuce; fill with meat, fish or vegetable salad. If desired, garnish with pimiento strips and olives.

Club Sandwich

For each sandwich toast 3 bread slices; spread with softened butter or margarine. Arrange lettuce and chicken slices on one toast slice; sprinkle with salt and pepper. Spread second toast slice with mayonnaise or salad dressing; place on filling, cover with tomato slices and crisp bacon strips. Top with third toast slice; cut in triangles. Garnish with stuffed olives or pickles.

Sandwich Loaf

Remove crusts from loaf unsliced bread. Cut in four thin lengthwise slices. Spread bottom slice with softened butter or margarine and Chicken or Turkey Filling (p. 314). Cover with second slice; spread with mayonnaise or salad dressing and Vegetable Relish Filling (p. 315). Cover with third slice; spread with Russian Dressing (p. 311) and Chopped Egg and Watercress Filling (p. 315). Cover with fourth slice; press together. Blend cream cheese with cream or top milk; spread on top and sides of loaf. Garnish with sliced stuffed olives. Chill thoroughly. Slice.

Broiled Cheese, Tomato, and Bacon Sandwiches

On each bread slice place cheese slice; if desired, sprinkle with curry powder. Place tomato slices on cheese; top with bacon strips. Place under broiler unit or burner until bacon Sauce (p. 329).

Broiled Sardine Sandwiches: Follow recipe for Broiled Cheese, Tomato, and Bacon Sandwiches, placing layer of sardines on cheese before topping with tomato slices.

Broiled Crab Meat Sandwiches   Makes 6

1 6½-oz. can (1 cup) crab meat
¼ cup mayonnaise or salad dressing
6 bread slices
½ lb. sliced American cheese

Combine crab meat and mayonnaise or salad dressing. Toast bread slices on one side; spread untoasted side with crab meat mixture. Top with cheese. Place under broiler unit or burner until cheese is melted.

Toasted Corned Beef Sandwiches

Spread bread slices with softened butter or margarine and prepared mustard. Place corned beef slice between bread slices; toast. Serve hot. If desired, serve with Quick Tomato Sauce (p. 329).

Toasted Tongue and Cheese Sandwiches

Chop tongue; add chopped celery. Moisten with mayonnaise or salad dressing. Spread between bread slices. Dip sandwiches in melted butter or margarine; sprinkle with grated American cheese. Place in moderate oven (350°F.) 10 min. or until browned. Serve hot.

Toasted Turkey Rolls   Serves 4

4 round soft rolls

1½ tbs. minced onion

3 tbs. butter or margarine

1 cup minced leftover turkey

½ tsp. salt

Few grains pepper

4 eggs

Cut thin slices from tops of rolls. Scoop out centers; shred into fine crumbs. (There should be 1 cup.) Brown onion in 2 tbs. butter or margarine; add crumbs. Add turkey, salt and pepper; heat. Melt remaining butter or margarine; brush on rolls. Heat rolls in hot oven (400°F.) 10 min.; fill with turkey mixture. Poach eggs (p. 204); place 1 on each roll.

Hot Salmon Sandwiches   Makes 4

1 cup flaked cooked or canned salmon

⅓ cup chopped celery

¼ cup mayonnaise or salad dressing

Few grains pepper

3 tbs. sweet pickle relish

8 bread slices

1 egg

⅔ cup milk

2 tbs. butter or margarine

Combine salmon, celery, pepper, mayonnaise or salad dressing and relish. Spread on 4 bread slices; cover with remaining slices. Beat egg; add milk. Dip sandwiches in egg and milk mixture. Brown on both sides in butter or margarine. Serve hot.

Hot Sandwich Loaf   Serves 4-6

1 small loaf bread

4 hard-cooked eggs

⅓ cup chopped stuffed olives

1 can condensed mushroom soup

1 7-oz. can (1 cup) tuna

1½ tsp. minced onion

2 tsp. mayonnaise or salad dressing

Melted butter or margarine

⅓ cup top milk

Remove crusts from bread; cut in three lengthwise slices.

Chop eggs; add olives and ¼ cup soup. Combine tuna, onion and mayonnaise or salad dressing. Spread egg mixture between first and second bread slices; spread tuna mixture between second and third slices. Brush top and sides of loaf with butter or margarine. Bake in hot oven (400°F.) 20 min. To remaining soup add milk; heat. Slice sandwich loaf; serve hot with hot soup mixture.

Golden Ham Sandwiches

Makes 4

- 1 cup ground cooked or canned ham
- ¼ cup sweet pickle relish
- 3 tbs. ketchup
- 8 bread slices
- 1 egg
- ½ cup milk
- 2 tbs. butter or margarine

Combine ham, relish and ketchup. Spread between bread slices. Beat egg; add milk. Dip sandwiches in egg mixture. Brown on both sides in butter or margarine. Serve hot.

Creamed Dried Beef Sandwiches

Toast 4 bread slices; top with Creamed Dried Beef (pp. 232-33). Garnish with sliced hard-cooked egg and watercress. Serve hot.

Hot Roast Beef Sandwiches

Toast bread slices; top with hot roast beef slices. Cover with hot roast beef gravy. Garnish with Broiled Mushrooms (p. 364).

29. SAUCES (DESSERT, MEAT, FISH AND VEGETABLE)

Quick Chocolate Sauce

Makes 1⅓ cups

- 3 squares (3 oz.) unsweetened chocolate
- ½ cup water
- ¾ cup sugar
- Few grains salt
- ¼ tsp. almond extract

Combine chocolate and water. Heat, stirring constantly, until chocolate is melted. Add sugar; stir until dissolved. Remove from heat; add salt and almond extract. Serve hot.

Quick Chocolate Cinnamon Sauce: Follow recipe for Quick Chocolate Sauce, adding ½ tsp. cinnamon to sugar and omitting ¼ tsp. almond extract. Before serving, add 2 tbs. butter or margarine.

Hot Fudge Sauce
Makes 1 cup

1 cup light corn sirup
1 tsp. vanilla extract

2 squares (2 oz.)
unsweetened chocolate

Combine corn sirup and chocolate. Cook over hot water, stirring constantly, until chocolate is melted. Remove from heat; beat with rotary beater until smooth. Add vanilla extract. Serve hot. (Can be stored in refrigerator. Reheat over hot water.)

Butterscotch Sauce
Makes 2 cups

⅔ cup firmly packed brown sugar
⅔ cup light corn sirup

3 tbs. butter or margarine
⅔ cup light cream

Combine sugar, corn sirup and butter or margarine; boil 5 min., stirring until sugar is dissolved. Gradually add sirup mixture to cream, stirring constantly. Quickly bring to boiling point. Serve hot or cold. (Sauce thickens as it stands. May be stored several days in covered container in refrigerator.)

Maple Marshmallow Sauce
Makes 1½ cups

¾ cup maple sirup

8 marshmallows

Heat maple sirup to boiling point. Quarter marshmallows; add. Stir until marshmallows are partially melted. Serve hot. Serve with ice cream.

Hard Sauce

Makes 1 cup

⅓ cup butter or margarine   1 tsp. vanilla extract
1 cup confectioners' sugar

Cream butter or margarine; add confectioners' sugar, creaming until fluffy. Add vanilla extract; mix well.

Sherry Fluff Sauce

Makes 2⅓ cups

2 tsp. cornstarch   3 egg yolks
¼ cup sugar   3 egg whites
¼ tsp. salt   1 tbs. sherry flavoring
2 cups milk   Few grains nutmeg

Combine cornstarch, sugar and salt; gradually add milk. Cook over hot water, stirring constantly, until slightly thickened. Beat egg yolks; slowly add milk mixture. Cook over hot water, stirring constantly, until mixture thickens and coats spoon. Beat egg whites stiff; fold in milk mixture. Cool. Add flavoring and nutmeg. Serve with hot fruit puddings.

Sunshine Sauce

Makes 1 cup

½ cup butter or margarine   ½ tsp. vanilla extract
1 egg   1 cup confectioners' sugar

Cream butter or margarine; add sugar, creaming well. Add egg and vanilla extract. Place over hot water; beat constantly with rotary beater until fluffy. Serve hot.

Almond Sunshine Sauce: Follow recipe for Sunshine Sauce, substituting ½ tsp. almond extract for ½ tsp. vanilla extract.

Satiny Dessert Sauce

Makes 1½ cups

1 egg white   ½ cup whipping cream
½ cup powdered sugar   1 tsp. vanilla extract
1 egg yolk   Few grains salt

Beat egg white stiff. Gradually add sugar, beating constantly. Beat egg yolk; fold in. Whip cream; fold in with vanilla extract and salt.

Custard Sauce
Makes 2 cups

3 tbs. flour	2 eggs
½ cup sugar	2 cups milk
Few grains salt	1 tsp. vanilla extract

Mix flour, sugar and salt. Beat eggs slightly; add. Scald milk; gradually add. Cook over hot water, stirring constantly, until mixture thickens and coats spoon. Add vanilla extract; chill.

Chocolate Custard Sauce: Follow recipe for Custard Sauce, adding 1 square (1 oz.) melted unsweetened chocolate and 3 tbs. sugar to flour mixture.

Orange Tang Custard Sauce: Follow recipe for Custard Sauce, adding thin outside peel of 1 orange to milk before scalding; remove peel after scalding.

Winter Fruit Sauce
Makes 1 cup

1 tbs. flour	1 egg yolk
1½ tbs. sugar	½ cup orange juice
Few grains salt	¼ cup whipping cream

Mix flour, sugar and salt. Beat egg yolk; add. Add orange juice. Cook over hot water, stirring constantly, until thick. Cover; cook 10 min. Chill. Whip cream; fold in. Serve with fruit.

Lemon Sauce
Makes 1½ cups

1 tbs. cornstarch	1 cup water
½ cup sugar	2 tbs. lemon juice
1 tbs. grated lemon rind	2 tbs. butter or margarine
Few grains salt	

Mix cornstarch, sugar, lemon rind and salt; gradually add water. Cook over low heat, stirring constantly, until thickened. Cook over hot water, stirring occasionally, 5 min. Add lemon juice and butter or margarine.

Orange Sauce
Makes 1¼ cups

½ cup sugar
2 tbs. flour
⅛ tsp. salt
½ cup water

½ cup orange juice
2 tbs. lemon juice
2 tbs. grated orange rind
1 tbs. butter or margarine

Mix sugar, flour and salt; gradually add water. Boil, stirring constantly, until thickened. Add orange and lemon juices, orange rind and butter or margarine. Serve hot. Serve with puddings.

Lemon Peach Sauce
Makes 2 cups

½ cup sugar
1 tbs. cornstarch
Few grains salt
1 cup canned peach sirup

¼ cup seedless raisins
1 egg yolk
3 tbs. lemon juice
2 tbs. butter or margarine

Mix sugar, cornstarch and salt; gradually add sirup. Bring to boiling point, stirring constantly; add raisins. Cook over boiling water, stirring occasionally. Beat egg yolk slightly; add peach mixture. Add lemon juice and butter or margarine; stir until butter or margarine is melted. Serve hot. Serve with puddings or fritters.

Hot Spiced Blueberry Sauce
Makes 1¼ cups

1 cup blueberries
¼ cup sugar

½ tsp. cinnamon
¼ tsp. nutmeg

Combine blueberries, sugar, cinnamon and nutmeg. Bring to boiling point; boil 5 min., stirring occasionally. Serve hot. Serve on ice cream.

Spiced Cherry Sauce
Serves 4

1 No. 2 can (2½ cups)
    pitted sour red cherries
½ cup sugar

2 2″ sticks cinnamon
15 whole cloves
2 tsp. cornstarch

Drain cherries, reserving sirup. Measure sirup, adding enough water to make 1 cup. Add sugar, cinnamon and cloves. Bring to boiling point; cook 10 min. Remove spices.

Add a little hot sirup to cornstarch; add to hot sirup mixture. Cook 10 min., or until slightly thickened. Add cherries; heat. Serve on Creamy Rice (p. 167).

Spiced Pineapple Sauce
Makes 1⅓ cups

⅔ cup pineapple sirup
⅛ tsp. cinnamon
⅛ tsp. nutmeg

⅛ tsp. cloves
⅔ cup drained crushed pineapple

Combine pineapple sirup, cinnamon, nutmeg and cloves; bring to boiling point. Add pineapple; heat. Chill. Serve on puddings.

Snowgold Sauce
Makes 1½ cups

½ cup sugar
¾ cup water

½ cup finely chopped dried apricots
6 tbs. shredded coconut

Combine sugar and water; bring to boiling point. Add apricots; simmer 15 min. Cool; add coconut. Serve with ice cream or puddings.

Thin White Sauce
Makes 1 cup

1 tbs. butter or margarine
1 tbs. flour
1 cup milk

½ tsp. salt
Few grains pepper

Melt butter or margarine; blend in flour; gradually add milk. Cook over hot water, stirring constantly, until thick. Add salt and pepper. Cook 5 min., stirring occasionally.

Plombiére Sauce
Makes ¾ cup

½ cup orange marmalade
2 tbs. water

¼ cup toasted coconut

Combine marmalade and water; add coconut. Serve with ice cream.

Medium White Sauce   Makes 1 cup

2 tbs. butter or margarine   ½ tsp. salt
2 tbs. flour   Few grains pepper
1 cup milk

Melt butter or margarine; blend in flour; gradually add milk. Cook over hot water, stirring constantly, until thick. Add salt and pepper. Cook 5 min., stirring occasionally.

Caper Sauce: Follow recipe for Medium White Sauce, adding 3 tbs. chopped capers and 1 tsp. lemon juice when thickened. Serve with fish.

Carrot Sauce: Follow recipe for Medium White Sauce, adding 1½ cups cubed cooked or canned carrots and few grains thyme when thickened. Serve with rice or noodles.

Cheese Olive Sauce: Follow recipe for Medium White Sauce, omitting ½ tsp. salt and adding ¾ cup grated American cheese and ½ cup sliced stuffed olives when thickened. Serve with vegetables, rice, noodles or macaroni.

Cheese Sauce: Follow recipe for Medium White Sauce, adding ½ cup grated American cheese and few grains paprika when thickened. Cook, stirring constantly, until cheese is melted. Serve with vegetables, rice, noodles or macaroni.

Egg Sauce: Follow recipe for Medium White Sauce, adding 2 chopped hard-cooked eggs and few grains paprika when thickened. Serve with fish.

Horse-radish Sauce: Follow recipe for Medium White Sauce, adding 1 tbs. prepared horse-radish and ½ tsp. prepared mustard when thickened. Serve with boiled beef.

India Curry Sauce: Follow recipe for Medium White Sauce, adding 1 tsp. curry powder with flour. Serve with rice or fish.

Mushroom Sauce: Follow recipe for Medium White Sauce, adding ½ cup sliced cooked or canned mushrooms when thickened. Serve with vegetables or chicken.

Mustard Sauce: Follow recipe for Medium White Sauce, adding 1 tbs. prepared mustard when thickened. Serve with tongue.

Parsley Sauce: Follow recipe for Medium White Sauce, adding 3 tbs. chopped parsley when thickened. Serve with vegetables or fish.

Pimiento Pepper Sauce: Follow recipe for Medium White Sauce, adding ¼ cup each diced pimiento and green pepper when thickened. Serve with vegetables.

Sea Food Sauce: Follow recipe for Medium White Sauce, substituting ½ cup cream for ½ cup milk and adding ½ cup cooked or canned chopped shrimp, lobster or crab meat and ¼ teaspoon paprika when thickened. Serve with baked or broiled fish.

Yellow Sauce: Follow recipe for Medium White Sauce. Beat one egg slightly; add 2 tbs. milk. Add white sauce; cook over hot water 3 min. Serve with vegetables.

Thick White Sauce   Makes 1 cup

    4 tbs. butter or margarine   ½ tsp. salt
    4 tbs. flour   Few grains pepper
    1 cup milk

Melt butter or margarine; blend in flour; gradually add milk. Cook over hot water, stirring constantly, until thick. Add salt and pepper. Cook 5 min., stirring occasionally.

Mock Hollandaise: Follow recipe for Thick White Sauce. Beat one egg; add sauce. Cook over hot water 3 min. Just before serving, remove from heat; add 2½ tbs. lemon juice and few grains cayenne. Serve with vegetables or fish.

Mineral-Rich White Sauce   Makes 1 cup

    2 tbs. butter or margarine   ½ cup evaporated milk
    2 tbs. flour   ¼ tsp. salt
    ½ cup vegetable liquor   Few grains pepper

Melt butter or margarine; blend in flour. Gradually add
vegetable liquor and milk. Cook over hot water, stirring
constantly, until thick. Add salt and pepper. Cook 5 min.
Serve with vegetables.

Velvet Sauce

Makes 1 cup

2 tbs. butter or margarine   ¼ tsp. salt
2 tbs. flour   Few grains pepper
1 cup chicken or veal stock

Melt butter or margarine; blend in flour. Gradually add
stock. Cook, stirring constantly, until thick and boiling.
Add salt and pepper; boil 2 min. Serve with vegetables,
veal or poultry.

Béchamel Sauce

Makes 1 cup

1 tbs. sliced onion   2 tbs. flour
1 tbs. sliced carrot   2 tbs. butter or margarine
½ bay leaf   ½ cup light cream or top
5 peppercorns   milk
Small sprig parsley   ½ tsp. salt
1 cup chicken or veal stock   ¼ tsp. pepper

Combine onion, carrot, bay leaf, peppercorns and parsley.
Add stock; cover. Simmer 20 min.; strain. (There should be
½ cup liquid; if not, add water or stock.) Melt butter or
margarine; blend in flour. Gradually add stock mixture and
cream. Cook, stirring constantly, until thick; add salt and
pepper. Serve with vegetables, veal or poultry.

Sour Cream Sauce

Makes 1 cup

2 tbs. minced onion   Few grains paprika
1 tbs. butter or margarine   1 tsp. sugar
1 tbs. flour   ¾ tsp. salt
1 tsp. vinegar   ¾ cup sour cream

Brown onion in butter or margarine; add flour, paprika,
sugar and salt. Add cream; cook over hot water, stirring

constantly, until thick. Add vinegar. Serve hot. Serve with vegetables.

Brown Sauce
Makes 2 cups

4 tbs. fat or salad oil
6 tbs. flour
2 cups meat or poultry
stock

1 tsp. salt
Few grains pepper

Heat fat or salad oil; blend in flour. Cook, stirring constantly, until browned. Gradually add stock; cook, stirring constantly, until thick. Add salt and pepper; boil 2 min. Serve with meat or poultry.

Pan Gravy: Follow recipe for Brown Sauce, substituting pan drippings for fat or salad oil and using water for stock if desired.

Giblet Gravy: Follow recipe for Pan Gravy, adding chopped cooked chicken or turkey giblets.

Mushroom Brown Sauce: Follow recipe for Brown Sauce, sautéeing 1 tbs. chopped onion and 1 cup sliced mushrooms in fat or salad oil before adding flour.

Creole Sauce: Follow recipe for Brown Sauce, sautéeing ¼ cup chopped onion and ½ cup chopped green pepper in fat or salad oil before adding flour.

Meat and Tomato Sauce
Serves 4

½ garlic clove
¼ cup chopped onion
½ cup chopped mushrooms
3 tbs. fat or salad oil
¼ lb. ground beef chuck
1 tsp. salt

½ tsp. sugar
Few grains pepper
1 No. 2 can (or 2½ cups
cooked) tomatoes
2 tbs. flour

Chop garlic; combine with onion and mushrooms. Brown in fat or salad oil. Add beef, salt, sugar and pepper; simmer 15 min., stirring occasionally. Blend in flour. Add tomatoes; cover; simmer 20 min.

Tomato Sauce
Makes 1½ cups

- 1 stalk celery
- ¼ cup chopped onion
- 1 No. 2 can (or 2½ cups cooked) tomatoes
- ½ tsp. salt
- Few grains pepper
- 2 tsp. Worcestershire sauce
- 2 tbs. fat or salad oil
- 2 tbs. flour

Chop celery; combine with onion, tomatoes, salt, pepper, and Worcestershire sauce. Cover; simmer 10 min.; press through sieve. Heat fat or salad oil; blend in flour. Gradually add tomato mixture. Cook, stirring constantly, until thick. Cook, stirring occasionally, 2 min. Serve with spaghetti, macaroni, noodles, rice, meat or vegetables.

Quick Tomato Sauce
Makes 1⅔ cups

Combine 1 can condensed tomato soup with ⅓ cup water, 1 tbs. sautéed minced onion and 2 tsp. Worcestershire sauce. Heat, stirring occasionally, to boiling point.

Tomato Cheese Sauce: Follow recipe for Quick Tomato Sauce, adding 1 cup grated American cheese before heating.

Spanish Sauce
Makes 1¾ cups

- 2 tbs. fat or salad oil
- 2 tbs. chopped onion
- 2 tbs. chopped celery
- 1 tbs. chopped green pepper
- 1½ tbs. flour
- 1 cup meat stock
- ½ cup thick tomato purée

Heat fat or salad oil; add onion, celery and green pepper; sauté. Blend in flour. Gradually add stock and tomato purée. Cook about 10 min., stirring occasionally. Serve with spaghetti or meat.

Orange Sauce For Duck
Makes 2 cups

- 3 tbs. butter or margarine
- ¼ cup flour
- 1⅓ cups water
- ¼ tsp. salt
- Few grains pepper
- ⅔ cup orange juice
- 2 tbs. grated orange rind
- 1 tbs. sherry flavoring

Melt butter or margarine; blend in flour. Cook until browned. Gradually add water. Cook, stirring constantly, until thick. Add salt and pepper. Just before serving, add orange juice, rind and sherry flavoring.

Raisin Nut Sauce
Makes 2 cups

¼ cup firmly packed brown sugar
1 tbs. flour
1 cup water
¼ tsp. salt

3 tbs. lemon juice
½ cup seedless raisins
¼ cup chopped nut meats
1 tbs. butter or margarine

Mix sugar and flour; add water. Bring to boiling point; add salt, lemon juice and raisins. Simmer 5 min. Add nut meats and butter or margarine. Cook until butter or margarine melts. Serve with ham or tongue.

Barbecue Sauce
Makes ½ cup

¼ cup ketchup
3 tbs. vinegar
1½ tbs. fat or salad oil

2 tbs. water
2 tsp. Worcestershire sauce
¼ tsp. salt

Combine ketchup, vinegar, fat or salad oil, water, Worcestershire sauce and salt. Bring to boiling point, stirring occasionally; cook 3 min. Serve with meat or poultry.

Lemon Butter Sauce
Makes ½ cup

½ cup butter or margarine
2 tbs. lemon juice

Melt butter or margarine; remove from heat; add lemon juice. Serve with vegetables or fish.

Lemon Chive Butter Sauce: Follow recipe for Lemon Butter Sauce, adding 1 tbs. minced chives with lemon juice.

Worcestershire Butter Sauce
Makes ½ cup

½ cup butter or margarine
½ tsp. Worcestershire sauce

Brown butter or margarine; add Worcestershire sauce. Serve with vegetables or fish.

Indienne Sauce
Makes ⅔ cup

½ cup butter or margarine
Few grains paprika

2 hard-cooked eggs
½ tsp. curry powder

Melt butter or margarine; chop eggs. Add with curry powder; sprinkle with paprika. Serve with vegetables or fish.

Hollandaise Sauce
Makes 1 cup

½ cup butter or margarine
2 egg yolks
Few grains cayenne

1½ tbs. lemon juice
½ cup boiling water
½ tsp. salt

Divide butter or margarine into 3 pieces. Beat egg yolks slightly, add lemon juice and ⅓ butter or margarine. Cook over boiling water, stirring constantly, until butter or margarine is melted. Add ⅓ butter or margarine; cook, stirring constantly, until mixture begins to thicken. Add remaining ⅓ butter or margarine; cook, stirring constantly, until mixture thickens. Slowly add water, stirring constantly; add salt and cayenne. (If mixture curdles, add 2 tbs. boiling water very slowly, beating constantly.) Serve immediately.

Horse-Radish Cream
Makes 1¼ cups

½ cup whipping cream
¼ cup prepared
   horse-radish

1 tbs. vinegar
½ tsp. salt

Whip cream stiff. Mix horse-radish, vinegar and salt; fold into cream. Serve with beef.

Red Cocktail Sauce
Makes 1¾ cups

1 cup ketchup
¼ cup lemon juice
1 tsp. salt

1 tsp. Worcestershire sauce
Dash tabasco
4 tsp. prepared horse-radish

Combine ketchup, lemon juice, salt, Worcestershire sauce, tabasco and horse-radish; chill. Serve with fish cocktails.

Yellow Cocktail Sauce
Makes ¾ cup

½ cup mayonnaise or salad dressing

¼ cup chopped pickled onions

1 tbs. lemon juice

Combine mayonnaise or salad dressing, onion and lemon juice; chill. Serve with fish cocktails.

Tartar Sauce
Makes 1⅓ cups

1 cup mayonnaise or salad dressing

1 tbs. chopped parsley

1 tbs. chopped pickle

1 tbs. chopped capers

1 tbs. chopped stuffed olives

1 tsp. onion juice

Combine mayonnaise or salad dressing, parsley, pickle, capers, olives and onion juice. Chill. Serve with fish.

Vinaigrette Sauce
Makes 1 cup

¼ cup sweet pickle relish

2 tbs. chopped parsley

1 tsp. sugar

1 tsp. salt

Few grains pepper

¼ cup vinegar

½ cup salad oil

Combine relish, parsley, sugar, salt, pepper, vinegar and salad oil. Mix well. If desired, heat. Serve with vegetables.

Mint Sauce
Makes ⅔ cup

¼ cup lemon juice

½ cup water

2 tbs. sugar

¼ tsp. salt

1 tsp. dried or chopped fresh mint

¼ tsp. mint extract

Combine lemon juice, water, sugar and salt; heat. Add mint extract and mint. Serve with lamb.

Applesauce
Serves 4

4 tart apples

½ cup water

¼ cup sugar

⅛ tsp. nutmeg

1/16 tsp. grated lemon rind

1 tsp. lemon juice

Pare apples; quarter; core. Cut apples in eighths; add water. Cover; cook 20 min., or until tender. Add sugar, nutmeg, lemon rind and juice; cook until sugar dissolves. Serve hot or cold.

Cranberry Sauce   Serves 6

    1 lb. cranberries   1 cup water
    2 cups sugar

Wash cranberries; drain. Combine with sugar and water; bring to boiling point; cover. Boil slowly 10 min., or until skins are broken. Skim; chill.

30. SOUPS

Soup Garnishes

For variety, garnish clear soups with chopped chives, parsley, hard-cooked eggs, popcorn or croutons (p. 63), etc. Garnish cream soups with salted whipped cream, grated cheese, slivered toasted almonds, etc.

Cream of Tomato Soup   Serves 4-6

    1 No. 2½ can (or 3½ cups   1 bay leaf
       cooked) tomatoes   6 whole cloves
    2 tbs. grated onion   4 tbs. butter or margarine
    1½ tsp. salt   4 tbs. flour
    Few grains pepper   2 cups milk
    2 tsp. sugar   ⅛ tsp. baking soda

Combine tomatoes, onion, salt, pepper, sugar, bay leaf and cloves; cover; simmer 10 min. Strain; reheat. Melt butter or margarine; blend in flour. Gradually add milk; cook over

hot water, stirring constantly, until thick. Add soda to tomato mixture; gradually add to milk mixture. Serve immediately.

Vegetable Soup
Serves 4-6

1 lb. beef chuck
Veal bones
2 qts. water
3 large carrots
1 leek
1 cup diced white turnip
1 cup peas

1 cup chopped celery
1 cup diced potato
1 No. 2 can (or 2½ cups
   cooked) tomatoes
Salt and pepper
2 tbs. chopped parsley

Cut beef in 1" cubes; place in kettle with bones and water.
Cover; simmer 1 hour. Scrape carrots; dice carrots and
leek. Add with turnip, peas, celery, potato and tomatoes;
simmer 1 hour. Remove bones. Season with salt and pepper;
add parsley.

New England Vegetable Chowder
Serves 4-6

¼ cup butter or margarine
1 cup diced celery
1 cup diced carrot
2 tbs. grated onion
1½ cups cooked or canned
   whole kernel corn
½ cup water
1 tsp. salt

Few grains pepper
1 tsp. sugar
4 cups milk
1 cup cooked or canned
   peas
2 tbs. chopped parsley
Grated American cheese

Melt butter or margarine; add celery, carrot, onion, corn,
water, salt, pepper and sugar. Cover; cook 1 hour. Add milk
and peas; heat. Add parsley. Sprinkle with cheese.

Potato Soup
Serves 4-6

2 potatoes
4 onion slices
2 cups boiling water
2 tbs. butter or margarine
2 tbs. flour

3 cups milk
1½ tsp. salt
Few grains pepper
2 tsp. chopped parsley
¼ tsp. celery salt

Pare potatoes; slice. Combine with onion and water. Cook until tender. Drain; reserving 1 cup liquor. Press potato and onion through fine sieve. (There should be about 1 cup.) Melt butter or margarine; blend in flour. Gradually add potato liquor and milk. Cook over hot water, stirring constantly, until thick. Add potato and onion purée, salt, pepper, parsley and celery salt; heat thoroughly.

Mushroom Bisque   Serves 4-6

¾ lb. mushrooms	¼ cup flour
3 cups water	2 cups milk
1 onion slice	Salt, pepper and paprika
½ tsp. salt	1 egg yolk
3 tbs. butter or margarine	⅓ cup whipping cream

Scrub mushrooms; chop. Add water, onion and ½ teaspoon salt; simmer 30 min. Press through medium sieve. (There should be about 2 cups.) Melt butter or margarine; blend in flour. Gradually add milk. Cook over hot water, stirring constantly, until thick. Add mushroom purée. Season with salt, pepper and paprika. Beat egg yolk; add mushroom mixture. Whip cream; use as garnish on soup with paprika.

Corn Chowder   Serves 4-6

3 medium potatoes	1½ cups cooked or canned
1 small onion	whole kernel corn
1 cup water	4 cups milk
¼ cup butter or margarine	Salt and pepper

Pare potato; dice. Grate onion. Add water and butter or margarine; simmer until tender. Add corn and milk; simmer 15 min. Season with salt and pepper. If desired, garnish with chopped chives.

Split Pea Soup   Serves 4-6

1 carrot	5 cups water
1 small onion	1 bay leaf
1 cup split peas	Salt and pepper
Cooked ham bone	

Scrub carrot; slice. Slice onion. Wash peas; drain. Combine carrot, onion, peas, ham bone, water and bay leaf. Cover; simmer 2 hours or until peas are tender. Remove bone. Press mixture through sieve; season with salt and pepper. If desired, thin with milk; heat.

Chicken Soup
Serves 4-9

4 lb. fowl	2 stalks celery
6 cups water	1 bay leaf
1 carrot	1½ tsp. salt
1 small onion	Few grains pepper

Disjoint fowl; wipe with damp cloth. Put in kettle with water. Scrape carrot; slice carrot and onion. Chop celery. Add carrot, onion, celery and bay leaf. Cover; simmer 2½-3 hours. Add salt and pepper; strain.

Turkey Mushroom Soup
Serves 4-6

1 carrot	¼ cup rice
1 celery stalk	2 cans cream of mushroom
Roast turkey bones	soup
6 cups water	Sliced Brazil nut meats
2 onion slices	

Scrub carrot; slice. Chop celery. Combine carrot, celery, turkey bones, water and onion. Cover; simmer 2 hours. Strain. (There should be 4 cups stock.) Wash rice, add to stock; simmer until tender. Combine stock and mushroom soup (to condensed soup add equal amount milk or water, using soup can to measure). Heat. Garnish with nut meats.

Oyster Stew
Serves 4

1 pt. oysters	2 cups milk
Parsley sprig	2½ tbs. butter or margarine
½ bay leaf	1½ tbs. flour
1 onion slice	Salt and cayenne

Remove any bits of shell from oysters. Strain oyster liquor through cheesecloth. Halve oysters; cook in oyster liquor 3-5 min., or until edges curl. Add parsley, bay leaf and onion to milk; scald; strain. Melt butter or margarine; blend in flour.

Gradually add milk. Cook until slightly thickened, stirring constantly; add oysters. Season with salt and cayenne. Serve immediately.

Clam Chowder   Serves 4-6

¼ cup minced onion
2 tbs. minced green pepper
2 tbs. butter or margarine
1 cup diced potato
¼ cup chopped celery
2 cups boiling water

1 cup strained cooked or
  canned tomatoes
1 tsp. salt
Few grains pepper
¼ tsp. thyme
1 cup chopped clams
1 cup clam liquor

Brown onion and green pepper in butter or margarine. Add potato, celery and water; cover; cook 10 min. or until potato is tender. Add tomatoes, salt, pepper, thyme, clams and clam liquor. Cover; simmer 20 min.

Manhattan Fish Chowder   Serves 4-6

1 onion
2 tbs. fat or salad oil
1 potato
1 cup diced celery
1¼ cups cooked or canned
  tomatoes
Salt and pepper

1½ cups cooked or canned
  whole kernel corn
1 cup cooked or canned
  flaked codfish
Hard roll
Grated Parmesan-style
  cheese

Mince onion; sauté in fat or salad oil. Pare potato; cube; add with celery, tomatoes, salt and pepper. Simmer 15 min. Add corn and fish; heat. Slice roll. Toast. Place slice on each serving; sprinkle with cheese.

Fish Chowder Gaspé   Serves 4-6

2 leeks
1 carrot
1 garlic clove
¼ cup fat or salad oil
¾ lb. haddock
1 cup cooked or canned
  tomatoes

1¼ cups water
½ bay leaf
Salt and pepper
1 tbs. lemon juice
⅔ cup cooked or canned
  shrimp
1½ tbs. chopped parsley

Clean leeks; trim. Scrub carrot. Chop leeks, carrot and garlic. Brown in fat or salad oil. Cut haddock in medium uniform pieces; add to first mixture with tomatoes, water, bay leaf, salt and pepper. Simmer 30 min. Add lemon juice and shrimp; heat 5 min. Add parsley.

Cheese and Crab Meat Soup
Serves 4-6

2 tbs. butter or margarine
2 tbs. flour
¼ tsp. salt
Few grains pepper
4 cups milk

½ lb. Cheddar cheese
Dash tabasco
1 6½-oz. can (1 cup) crab meat
1 tbs. minced chives

Melt butter or margarine; blend in flour, salt and pepper. Gradually add milk. Cook over hot water, stirring constantly, until thickened. Add cheese; stir until cheese melts. Add tabasco. Flake crab meat, removing bits of shell; add. Heat. Garnish with chives.

Tomato Soup Savarin
Serves 4

1 can tomato soup
⅓ cup whipping cream

1 tbs. chopped chives

Heat soup (to condensed soup add equal amount milk, using soup can to measure). Whip cream; add chives. Pour soup into oven-proof cups; place spoonful cream in each cup. Brown under broiler unit or burner.

Tomato Corn Chowder
Serves 4

1 can tomato soup
½ cup canned cream-style corn

¼ tsp. curry powder
1 tsp. sugar
¼ tsp. salt

Heat soup (to condensed soup add equal amount milk using soup can to measure). Add corn, curry powder, sugar and salt. Heat.

Curried Tuna Soup
Serves 4

1 7-oz. can (1 cup) tuna
1 can vegetable soup

¼ tsp. curry powder
Thin lemon slices

Coarsely flake tuna; cook over low heat until lightly browned. Add to soup (to condensed soup add equal amount of water, using soup can to measure). Add curry powder. Heat. Garnish with lemon.

Purée Mongole   Serves 4-6

1 can tomato soup   ½ cup finely sliced leeks
1 can pea soup   2 tbs. butter or margarine

Combine soups (to condensed soups add equal amount milk, using soup can to measure). Heat. Brown leeks in butter or margarine; use as garnish.

Tomato Pepper Pot   Serves 4-6

1 can tomato soup   1 can pepper pot soup

Combine soups (to condensed soups add equal amount water, using soup can to measure). Heat.

Tomato Vegetable Soup   Serves 4-6

1 medium onion   1 can vegetable soup
2 tbs. butter or margarine 1 can tomato soup
½ tsp. thyme

Mince onion; brown in butter or margarine. Add thyme. Add soups (to condensed soups add equal amounts milk or water, using soup can to measure). Heat.

Mock Turtle Vegetable Soup   Serves 4-6

1 can vegetable soup   1 can mock turtle soup

Combine soups (to condensed soups add equal amount water, using soup can to measure). Heat.

Shrimp Minestrone   Serves 4-6

2 cans vegetable soup   3 tbs. butter or margarine
1 can bean soup   4 slices French bread
2 5¾-oz. cans (2 cups)   Grated Parmesan-style
   shrimp   cheese

Combine soups (to condensed soups add equal amount water, using soup can to measure). Heat. Add shrimp and butter or margarine. Heat. Toast bread. Place slice on each serving; sprinkle with cheese.

Mushroom Vegetable Chowder   Serves 4-6

   1 can vegetable soup   1 can mushroom soup

Combine soups (to condensed soups add equal amount water, using soup can to measure). Heat.

Asparagus Mushroom Soup   Serves 4-6

   1 can asparagus soup   Chopped pimiento
   1 can mushroom soup

Combine soups (to condensed soups add equal amount milk or water, using soup can to measure). Heat. Garnish with pimiento.

Company Soup   Serves 4-6

   1 can mushroom soup   1 tsp. prepared horse-radish
   1 can chicken noodle soup Paprika
   1/3 cup whipping cream

Combine soups (to condensed soups add equal amount water, using soup can to measure). Whip cream; add horseradish. Place spoonful on each serving. Sprinkle with paprika.

Chicken Celery Soup   Serves 4-6

   1 can chicken noodle soup   1 can celery soup

Combine soups (to condensed soups add equal amount water, using soup can to measure). Heat.

Chicken Clam Chowder   Serves 4-6

   1 can chicken noodle soup   1 can clam chowder

Combine soups (to condensed soups add equal amount water, using soup can to measure). Heat.

Pea Soup Gratinée

Serves 4

1 can pea soup
Sherry flavoring
⅓ cup whipping cream

Grated Parmesan-style
cheese

Heat soup (to condensed soup add equal amount milk or water, using soup can to measure); add flavoring. Whip cream. Pour soup into oven-proof cups; place spoonful of cream in each cup. Sprinkle with cheese. Brown under broiler unit or burner.

Baltimore Pea Soup

Serves 4-6

1 can pea soup

1 can mock turtle soup

Combine soups (to condensed soups add equal amount milk or water, using soup can to measure). Heat.

Boston Bisque

Serves 4-6

1 can bean soup

1 can pea soup

Combine soups (to condensed soups add equal amount milk or water, using soup can to measure). Heat.

31. STUFFINGS AND DUMPLINGS

Bread Stuffing

¼ cup chopped onion
¼ cup butter or margarine
6 cups soft bread crumbs
1 tsp. salt

1½ tsp. poultry seasoning
Few grains pepper
¼ cup water

Brown onion in butter or margarine; mix with crumbs, salt, poultry seasoning and pepper. Add water; mix well. Makes enough to stuff 5 lb. chicken or fish. For 7 lb. duck, increase recipe by ½. For 12 lb. turkey or 10 lb. goose, double recipe.

Corn Stuffing: Follow recipe for Bread Stuffing, adding 1 cup chopped cooked or canned whole kernel corn.

Chestnut Stuffing: Follow recipe for Bread Stuffing, adding 1 cup chopped cooked chestnuts.

Giblet Stuffing: Follow recipe for Bread Stuffing, adding chopped cooked giblets.

Oyster Stuffing: Follow recipe for Bread Stuffing, adding 1 cup chopped oysters.

Sausage Stuffing: Follow recipe for Bread Stuffing, adding ½ cup well-drained fried sausage meat.

Mushroom Stuffing

3 tbs. chopped onion	1½ tsp. salt
¾ cup sliced mushrooms	Few grains pepper
3 tbs. butter or margarine	6 tbs. water
9 cups soft bread crumbs	

Brown onion and mushrooms in butter or margarine; mix with crumbs, salt and pepper. Add water; mix well. Makes enough to stuff 7 lb. duck.

Savory Stuffing

4 cups soft bread crumbs	½ tsp. sage
2 tbs. chopped onion	⅓ cup melted butter or
2 tbs. chopped parsley	margarine
1 egg	Few grains pepper
1 tsp. salt	

Combine crumbs, onion and parsley. Beat egg slightly; add with salt, sage and pepper. Add butter or margarine; mix well. Makes enough to stuff 6 lb. boned veal shoulder.

Mushroom Onion Stuffing

¾ cup chopped mushrooms	¼ cup butter or margarine
3 tbs. minced onions	2½ cups soft bread crumbs

Brown mushrooms and onion in butter or margarine; combine with crumbs. Makes enough to stuff 3-5 lb. fish.

Bacon and Oatmeal Stuffing

- 2 cups chopped onion
- 1 cup butter or margarine
- 6 cups uncooked quick-cooking oats
- 2 cups soft bread crumbs
- 1 cup chopped crisp bacon
- 2½ tsp. salt
- 5 tsp. poultry seasoning
- Few grains pepper
- ½ cup water

Brown onion in butter or margarine; add oats, crumbs, bacon, salt, poultry seasoning and pepper. Add water; mix well. Makes enough to stuff 12 lb. turkey.

Apple Stuffing

- ¼ lb. salt pork
- ¼ cup chopped onion
- 2 cups diced tart apple
- ¼ cup firmly packed brown sugar
- 2 cups soft bread crumbs
- Few grains salt

Fry salt pork until crisp. Add onion; sauté. Add apples and sugar; cook until tender. Add crumbs and salt. Mix well. Makes enough to stuff 6 lb. boned pork shoulder.

Pineapple Stuffing

- 3 cups soft bread crumbs
- 3 cups rye bread crumbs
- ¾ tsp. cinnamon
- ½ cup drained crushed pineapple
- ½ tsp. salt
- ¼ cup melted butter or margarine

Combine crumbs, cinnamon, pineapple and salt. Add butter or margarine; mix well. Makes enough to stuff 14-16 rib lamb crown roast.

Cracker Stuffing

- ⅓ cup chopped onion
- ½ cup butter or margarine
- 4 cups unsalted soda cracker crumbs
- ¾ tsp. salt
- Few grains pepper
- 2 tbs. chopped parsley
- ½ cup water

Brown onion in butter or margarine; mix with crumbs, salt, pepper and parsley. Add water; mix well. Makes enough to stuff 4-5 lb. chicken or fish.

Corn Bread Chestnut Filling

½ cup minced onion	8 cups chopped cooked
¾ cup butter or margarine	chestnuts
8 cups crumbled corn bread	1 tsp. salt
2 tsp. poultry seasoning	⅛ tsp. pepper
	¾ cup hot water

Brown onion in butter or margarine; mix with bread, chestnuts, poultry seasoning, salt and pepper. Add water; mix well. Makes enough to stuff 10-12 lb. turkey.

Rice Stuffing

1½ cups cooked rice	2 tbs. melted butter or
2 tbs. chopped green pepper	margarine
¼ tsp. curry powder	¼ tsp. salt
¼ tsp. paprika	

Combine rice, green pepper, curry powder, paprika and salt. Add butter or margarine; mix well. Makes enough to stuff 3-4 lb. boned lamb shoulder.

Wild Rice and Mushroom Stuffing

¼ cup chopped onion	4 cups cooked wild rice
1 cup sliced mushrooms	1 tsp. salt
⅓ cup butter or margarine	Few grains pepper

Brown onion and mushrooms in butter or margarine; mix with rice, salt and pepper. Makes enough to stuff 8-10 lb. turkey or goose.

Potato Stuffing

⅓ cup minced onion	1 tsp. salt
⅓ cup butter or margarine	1 tsp. poultry seasoning
2 cups hot mashed potatoes	2 eggs
1 cup stale bread crumbs	

Cook onion in butter or margarine until golden brown; add potatoes, crumbs, salt and poultry seasoning. Beat eggs; add. Makes enough to stuff 4-5 lb. duck.

Dumplings   Serves 4-6

2 cups flour	2 tbs. shortening
1 tsp. salt	1 cup milk
3 tsp. baking powder	

Sift together flour, salt and baking powder. Cut in shortening with 2 knives or pastry blender. Gradually add milk; mix smooth. Drop by tablespoons on hot stew or fricassee. Cover tightly; cook 10-12 min. without removing cover.

Corn Dumplings   Serves 4-6

1 cup yellow corn meal	¾ cup cooked or canned
2 tsp. salt	whole kernel corn
2 cups boiling water	1 tsp. finely chopped onion
1 cup flour	2 tbs. melted butter or
2½ tsp. baking powder	margarine
Few grains pepper	1 egg

Slowly add corn meal and salt to water; cook, stirring constantly, 2 min. or until thick. Remove from heat; cool. Sift together ¾ cup flour, baking powder and pepper. Add to corn meal; mix well. Beat egg; add. Chop corn; add with onion and butter or margarine. Shape into balls; roll in remaining flour. Drop on hot fricassee. Cover tightly; cook 12 min. without removing cover.

Cheese Dumplings   Serves 4-6

1 cup flour	1 cup grated American
1½ tsp. baking powder	cheese
½ tsp. salt	½ cup water
1 tbs. shortening	

Sift together flour, baking powder and salt. Cut in shortening with 2 knives or pastry blender. Add cheese. Gradually add water; mix smooth. Drop by tablespoons on hot stew or fricassee. Cover tightly; cook 10 min. without removing cover.

Ham Dumplings   Serves 4-6

1 cup flour
1 tsp. baking powder
¼ tsp. rosemary

1 cup ground cooked or
canned ham
¼ cup milk

Sift together ¾ cup flour, baking powder and rosemary; add ham. Add milk. Shape into small balls; roll in remaining flour. Drop on hot stew or fricassee. Cover tightly; cook 12 min. without removing cover.

Potato Dumplings   Serves 4-6

2 cups mashed potatoes
⅔ cup flour
¾ tsp. salt
Few grains pepper

2 tsp. melted butter or
margarine
1 tsp. minced onion
⅛ tsp. mace
1 egg

Combine potatoes, flour, salt, pepper, butter or margarine, onion and mace. Beat egg; add. Shape into balls; drop on hot stew or fricassee. Cover tightly; cook 8 min. without removing cover.

32. VEGETABLES

The Right Way To Heat Canned Vegetables

Drain liquor into saucepan; boil quickly, uncovered, to reduce amount. Add vegetable; heat quickly.

To Use Vegetable Liquor

Drain all liquor from vegetables; substitute for part or all liquid in soups, sauces and gravies.

Creamed Vegetables   Serves 4

2 cups cooked or canned   2 tbs. melted butter or
   vegetable[1]   margarine
1 cup Medium White Sauce
   (p. 325)

Combine vegetable and sauce; heat. If desired, serve on toast.

Scalloped Vegetables   Serves 4

2 cups cooked or canned   2 tbs. melted butter or
   vegetable[1]   margarine
1 cup Medium White Sauce   1 cup soft bread crumbs
   (p. 325)

Place alternate layers vegetable and sauce in greased baking dish. Mix butter or margarine and crumbs; sprinkle on mixture. Bake in hot oven (400°F.) 20 min.

Vegetables au Gratin: Follow recipe for Scalloped Vegetables, alternating layers grated American cheese with vegetables and sauce.

Vegetable Fritters   Serves 4

1 cup flour   1 cup chopped well-drained
1 tsp. baking powder   cooked or canned
½ tsp. salt   vegetables[2]
1 egg   ½ cup milk
1 tsp. melted fat or salad
   oil

Sift together flour, baking powder and salt. Beat egg; add milk and fat or salad oil. Add to flour mixture; beat smooth. Add vegetable. Drop by tablespoons into shallow fat or salad oil reheated to 375°F.; fry for 4 min. or until brown on all sides. Drain on absorbent paper.

---

[1] (Use asparagus, broccoli, Brussels sprouts, cabbage, carrots, cauliflower, celery, corn, eggplant, green beans, leeks, lima beans, mushrooms, onions, peas, potatoes or spinach.)

[2] (Use asparagus, carrots, cauliflower, corn, green beans, lima beans, mushrooms or peas.)

Boiled Asparagus   Serves 4

Snap off tough ends of 1 lb. asparagus. Remove scales; scrub stalks. Separate stalks into 4 bunches; tie loosely with string. Cover with boiling salted water; boil, uncovered, 15-20 min., or until tender. Drain, reserving liquor for use in soups, sauces and gravies. Remove string. Add to asparagus 2 tbs. melted butter, margarine or salad oil. Season with salt and pepper.

Boiled Cut Asparagus   Serves 4

Snap off tough ends of 1 lb. asparagus. Remove scales; scrub stalks. Cut stalks in 1″ pieces. Cover with boiling salted water; boil, uncovered, 15-20 min., or until tender. Drain, reserving liquor for use in soups, sauces, gravies. Add to asparagus 2 tbs. butter, margarine or salad oil. Season with salt and pepper.

Asparagus Parmesan   Serves 4

1 No. 2 can (or 30 stalks cooked) asparagus	⅓ cup dry crumbs
Salt and pepper	Grated Parmesan-style cheese
2 tbs. melted butter or margarine	

Drain asparagus; place in greased shallow casserole. Sprinkle with salt and pepper. Mix butter or margarine and crumbs; sprinkle over asparagus. Top with cheese. Bake in moderately hot oven (375°F.) 20 min.

Asparagus Peanut Scallop

Cut cooked or canned asparagus in 1″ pieces. Arrange layer in greased baking dish. Dot with butter or margarine; sprinkle with finely ground peanut meats. Repeat until baking dish is almost full. Cover with 1 cup Medium White Sauce p. 325). Top with soft bread crumbs; dot with butter or margarine. Bake in hot oven (400°F.) until brown.

Asparagus Vinaigrette
Serves 4

3 tbs. sweet pickle relish	Few grains pepper
1½ tbs. chopped parsley	3 tbs. vinegar
¾ tsp. sugar	⅓ cup salad oil
¾ tsp. salt	Cooked or canned asparagus

Mix thoroughly relish, parsley, sugar, salt, pepper, vinegar and salad oil. Serve on hot or cold asparagus. (Tarragon vinegar may be substituted for ½ the vinegar.)

Boiled Dried Beans or Peas
Serves 4

Wash 1½-2 cups navy, pea, lima or kidney beans or split peas; discard imperfect beans or peas. Cover with cold water; soak overnight. Or, cover with boiling water; soak 4-5 hours. Drain; cover with large amount of boiling salted water. Cover; boil slowly 2-3 hours, or until tender. Drain; add 2 tbs. butter, margarine or salad oil. Season with salt and pepper.

Boston Baked Beans
Serves 4

2 cups navy or pea beans	½ tsp. dry mustard
1½ tsp. salt	2 tbs. finely chopped onion
2 tbs. brown sugar	1 cup boiling water
¼ cup dark molasses	¼ lb. piece salt pork
1 bay leaf	

Wash beans; discard imperfect beans. Cover with cold water; soak overnight. Or, cover with boiling water; soak 4-5 hours. Drain. Cover with large amount boiling salted water; boil slowly 1 hour; drain. Combine salt, sugar, molasses, bay leaf, mustard, onion and water; add to beans. Pour into bean pot. Score rind of pork; press into beans leaving rind exposed. Cover beans with additional boiling water. Cover; bake in slow oven (300°F.) 4 hours, or until beans are tender, removing cover during last ½ hour.

Baked Kidney Beans

Follow directions for Boston Baked Beans, substituting kidney beans for navy or pea beans.

Baked Lima Beans

Follow directions for Boston Baked Beans, substituting lima beans for navy or pea beans.

Lima Bean and Tomato Casserole   Serves 4

4 cups boiled dried lima
  beans
1 No. 2 can (or 2½ cups
  cooked) tomatoes
¾ tsp. salt

Few grains pepper
½ tsp. sugar
2 bay leaves
6 thin slices cooked ham

Combine beans, tomatoes, salt, pepper, sugar and bay leaves. Pour into greased baking dish; top with ham. Bake in moderate oven (350°F.) 30 min.

Kidney Beans Vinaigrette   Serves 4

2½ cups cooked or canned
      kidney beans
3 tbs. salad oil
3 tbs. vinegar
½ tsp. salt
Few grains pepper

1 tsp. sugar
1½ tsp. minced onion
1 tbs. chopped parsley
2 tbs. sweet pickle relish
½ cup chopped celery

Combine beans, salad oil, vinegar, salt, pepper, sugar, onion, parsley, relish and celery. Chill.

Boiled Beets   Serves 4

Remove tops from 1 lb. beets 2″ from roots. Scrub beets; cover with boiling salted water. Cover; boil 25-60 min. (depending on age and size of beets), or until tender. Drain. Dip in cold water; rub off skins. If desired, slice or cube. Add 2 tbs. melted butter, margarine or salad oil; heat. Season with sugar, salt and pepper.

Boiled Beet Greens   Serves 4

Remove tough stems and wilted leaves from 1½ lbs. beet greens. Wash several times in cold water until all sand is removed. Drain slightly; place in saucepan. Cover; cook 10-20 min. or until tender, turning greens once during cooking. Add 2 tbs. melted butter, margarine or salad oil. Season with salt and pepper.

Harvard Beets   Serves 4

- ¼ cup sugar
- 1 tbs. cornstarch
- ¼ cup water
- ¼ cup vinegar

- 1 No. 2 can (or 2½ cups cooked) beets
- 1 tbs. butter, margarine or salad oil
- Salt and pepper

Mix sugar and cornstarch; add water and vinegar. Boil 5 min. Drain beets; add. Cook slowly, stirring occasionally, until beets are heated. Add butter, margarine or salad oil; season with salt and pepper.

Piccalilli Beets   Serves 4

- 1 No. 2 can (or 2½ cups cooked) diced beets

- 2 tbs. sweet pickle relish

Drain beets; add relish. Heat.

Beet Relish   Serves 4

- ½ cup sugar
- 6 tbs. vinegar
- 1 No. 2 can (or 2½ cups cooked) diced beets

- ¼ cup prepared horse-radish

Dissolve sugar in vinegar. Drain beets; add horse-radish and vinegar mixture. Cover; chill several hours or overnight.

Boiled Broccoli   Serves 4

Remove tough outer leaves and ends of stalks of 1 medium bunch broccoli. Let stand in cold water 15-20 min. Rinse thoroughly in cold running water. Peel and split stalks. Cover with boiling salted water; boil, uncovered, 15-30 min., or until tender. Drain; add 2 tbs. butter, margarine or

salad oil. Season with salt and pepper. Serve with lemon
wedges.

Broccoli with Horse-radish Cream   Serves 4

¾ cup sour cream

½ tsp. prepared
horse-radish

½ tsp. prepared mustard

Few grains salt

Cooked or canned broccoli

Combine cream, horse-radish, mustard and salt; heat. Heat
broccoli; serve with sauce.

Boiled Brussels Sprouts   Serves 4

Remove wilted leaves from 1¼ lbs. Brussels sprouts. Let
stand in cold salted water 10-15 min. Rinse thoroughly in
cold running water. Cover with large amount boiling salted
water; boil, uncovered, 8-12 min., or until tender. Drain;
add 2 tbs. melted butter, margarine or salad oil. Season with
salt and pepper.

Brussels Sprouts Pierre   Serves 4

1 No. 2 can (or 2½ cups
cooked) Brussels sprouts

1 cup diced cooked or
canned celery

1 cup Medium White Sauce
(p. 325)

½ cup grated American
cheese

Salt and pepper

Drain sprouts; combine with celery, sauce and cheese. Heat;
season with salt and pepper.

Brussels Sprouts and Chestnuts à la Creme   Serves 4

1 tbs. flour

¼ cup chicken broth

¼ cup cream

¼ tsp. salt

1 No. 2 can (or 2½ cups
cooked) Brussels sprouts

1 cup cooked chestnuts

Grated American cheese

Blend flour to smooth paste with chicken broth. Add cream
and salt. Cook, stirring constantly, until thick. Drain
sprouts; combine with chestnuts. Place in greased shallow
casserole; add sauce. Sprinkle with cheese. Brown under
broiler unit or burner.

Boiled Cabbage Wedges

Serves 4

Remove wilted leaves from small head cabbage; cut in
eighths. Rinse in cold running water. Cover with large
amount boiling salted water; boil, uncovered, 15-20 min.,
or until tender. Drain; add 2 tbs. melted butter, margarine
or salad oil. Season with salt and pepper.

Boiled Shredded Cabbage

Serves 4

Remove wilted leaves from small head cabbage; shred cabbage. Rinse in cold running water. Cover with boiling salted
water to ⅓ depth of cabbage; cover. Cook 8-12 min., or until tender. Drain, if necessary. Add to cabbage 2 tbs. melted
butter, margarine or salad oil. Season with salt and pepper.

Savory Cabbage

To chopped cooked cabbage, add diced crisp hot bacon and
few celery seeds; heat.

Winter Slaw

Serves 4

⅓ cup French dressing
3 cups shredded cabbage

½ cup chopped peanut
   meats
¼ tsp. salt

Heat dressing; add cabbage, peanut meats and salt. Heat
thoroughly.

Boiled Carrots

Serves 4

Remove tops from 1 bunch carrots; scrub carrots. Slice
thin. Cover with boiling salted water to ⅓ depth of carrots.
Cover; boil 10-15 min., or until tender. Drain, if necessary.
Add to carrots 2 tbs. melted butter, margarine or salad oil.
Season with salt and pepper.

Carrots Lyonnaise

Serves 4

1 bunch carrots
1 medium onion

3 tbs. butter, margarine or
   salad oil
Salt, pepper and sugar

Remove tops from carrots. Scrub carrots; score deeply with tines of fork; slice thin. Mince onion; brown in butter, margarine or salad oil. Add carrots; cover. Cook slowly 15-20 min., or until tender. Season with salt, pepper and sugar.

Mint-Glazed Carrots
Serves 4

1 No. 2 can (or 2½ cups cooked) diced carrots

1 tbs. butter, margarine or salad oil
2 tbs. mint jelly

Drain carrots; add jelly and butter, margarine or salad oil. Heat slowly, stirring constantly, until jelly is melted and carrots are heated.

Carrots and Celery
Serves 4

2 cups sliced carrots
2 cups diced celery
Few grains sugar

1 tbs. chopped parsley
2 tbs. butter, margarine or salad oil

Combine carrots and celery; cover with boiling salted water to ⅓ depth of vegetables. Cover; boil 10-15 min., or until tender. Add sugar, parsley and butter, margarine or salad oil.

Boiled Cauliflower
Serves 4

Remove leaves and stalk from 1 medium head cauliflower. Let stand in cold salted water 10-15 min. Rinse thoroughly in cold running water. Cover with large amount boiling salted water; boil, uncovered, 8 min., or until tender. Drain; add 2 tbs. melted butter, margarine or salad oil. Season with salt and pepper.

Boiled Cauliflower Flowerets
Serves 4

Remove leaves and stalk from 1 medium head cauliflower; separate into flowerets. Rinse thoroughly in cold running water. Cover with large amount boiling salted water; boil, uncovered, 8 to 10 min., or until tender. Drain; add 2 tbs. melted butter, margarine or salad oil. Season with salt and pepper.

Cauliflower Polonaise   Serves 4

1 medium head cauliflower   ½ cup dry crumbs
6 tbs. butter or margarine

Cook cauliflower as directed for Boiled Cauliflower Flowerets (p. 354). Melt butter or margarine; add crumbs; brown
lightly. Serve on cauliflower.

Cauliflower Mexican   Serves 4-6

1 medium head cooked   1 cup grated American
  cauliflower   cheese
1 tsp. salt   Soft bread crumbs
Few grains pepper   Butter or margarine
1 No. 2 can (or 2½ cups
  cooked) tomatoes

Place cauliflower in greased shallow casserole. Add salt and
pepper to tomatoes; cook rapidly until most of liquor has
evaporated. Pour over cauliflower; top with cheese and
crumbs. Dot with butter or margarine. Bake in moderate
oven (325°F.) 15 min.

Cauliflower With Mushroom Sauce   Serves 4

½ lb. mushrooms   1 medium head cooked
¼ cup butter or margarine   cauliflower
¼ cup flour   2 cups milk
                              Salt and pepper

Clean mushrooms; slice. Brown in butter or margarine;
blend in flour. Gradually add milk; cook over hot water,
stirring constantly, until thick. Season with salt and pepper.
Serve on hot cauliflower.

Boiled Celery   Serves 4

Remove roots and leaves of 1 large bunch celery. Scrub
stalks. Scrape outer stalks. Cut celery in 1″ pieces. Cover
with boiling salted water to ⅓ depth of celery. Cover; cook
10-20 min., or until tender. Drain, if necessary. Add to
celery 2 tbs. melted butter, margarine or salad oil. Season
with salt and pepper.

Braised Celery
Serves 4

Remove roots and leaves of 1 large bunch celery. Scrub stalks. Scrape outer stalks. Cut in 4″ pieces. Brown lightly in 2 tbs. butter, margarine or salad oil. Add ¾ cup meat stock or consommé. Cook slowly until tender and stock is reduced to about ¼ cup. Season with salt and pepper.

Mustard Celery
Serves 4

¼ cup butter or margarine
1 tsp. prepared mustard
¼ tsp. salt

Few grains pepper
4 cups boiled 1″ pieces celery

Melt butter or margarine; slowly add to mustard. Add salt and pepper. Add to celery; heat.

Creamed Celery and Almonds
Serves 4

2 cups cubed cooked celery
¼ cup chopped toasted almond nut meats

1 cup Medium White Sauce (p. 325)
1 cup soft bread crumbs
Salt and pepper

Mix celery, nut meats, sauce and ½ cup crumbs; season with salt and pepper. Pour into baking dish; top with remaining crumbs. Bake in moderate oven (350°F.) 15 min.

Boiled Chestnuts

Wash chestnuts; cover with boiling salted water. Cover; boil 15-20 min. Drain; cool. Using sharp knife, remove shells and skins.

Baked Chestnuts

Wash chestnuts; cut small gash on flat side of each nut. Place in heavy shallow pan. Add 1 tsp. salad oil for each cup nuts. Place over heat 5 min., stirring constantly. Bake in very hot oven (450°F.) 20 min. Cool. Using sharp knife, remove shells and skins.

Stewed Corn
Serves 4

8 medium ears corn	2 tbs. butter, margarine or
1 cup milk	salad oil
Few grains pepper	½ tsp. sugar
	¾ tsp. salt

Husk corn; remove silk. Score through kernels with tip of sharp knife; slice from cob. Scrape cob with back of knife to remove remaining pulp. Add milk; cover. Simmer 10 min., or until tender. Add butter, margarine or salad oil. Season with sugar, salt and pepper.

Boiled Corn-on-the-Cob

Husk uniform medium ears of corn; remove silk. Cover corn with boiling salted water; cover. Boil 5-7 min. Drain.

Sautéed Corn
Serves 4

4 medium ears cooked corn	½ tsp. sugar
2 tbs. butter, margarine or	Few grains pepper
salad oil	¼ cup cream
½ tsp. salt	

Score through corn kernels with tip of sharp knife; slice from cob. Scrape cob with back of knife to remove remaining pulp. Brown corn in butter, margarine or salad oil; add salt, sugar, pepper and cream; heat.

Corn-on-the-Cob au Gratin

Brush cooked or canned corn-on-the-cob with melted butter or margarine; roll in grated American cheese. Bake in hot oven (400°F.) 10 min.

Chili Corn à la Crème
Serves 4

1½ cups cooked or canned	⅓ cup light cream
whole kernel corn	¼ tsp. chili powder
¼ tsp. salt	

Combine corn, salt, cream and chili powder. Heat.

Corn Pudding   Serves 4

    2 eggs   1 No. 2 can (2½ cups)
    2 cups milk   cream-style corn
    1 cup soft bread crumbs   Salt and pepper

Beat eggs; add milk, crumbs and corn; season with salt and
pepper. Pour into greased baking dish; bake in moderate
oven (350°F.) 1½ hours.

Corn Soufflé   Serves 4

    2 tbs. butter or margarine   ½ tsp. salt
    2 tbs. flour   Few grains pepper
    1 cup milk   2 egg whites
    2 egg yolks   1½ cups cooked or canned
    ½ cup grated American   whole kernel corn
       cheese

Melt butter or margarine; blend in flour. Gradually add milk.
Cook over hot water, stirring constantly, until thick. Beat
egg yolks. Add corn. Combine sauce, corn mixture, cheese,
salt and pepper. Beat egg whites stiff but not dry; fold in.
Pour into greased baking dish; bake in moderate oven
(350°F.) 45 min. Serve immediately.

Cucumbers in Sour Cream   Serves 4

    3 cucumbers   ¼ cup sour cream
    ⅔ cup sliced radishes   ½ tsp. salt
    3 tbs. butter or margarine   Few grains pepper

Pare cucumbers; slice thin. Melt butter or margarine; add
cucumbers and radishes. Cover; cook rapidly 10 min. Uncover; cook 5 min., or until most of liquor has evaporated.
Add cream, salt and pepper; heat.

Boiled Eggplant   Serves 4-6

Pare 1 medium eggplant; cut in ½" cubes. Cover with boiling salted water to ⅓ depth of eggplant; cover. Cook 10-15
min., or until tender; drain thoroughly. Add 2 tbs. butter,
margarine or salad oil; season with salt and pepper.

Sautéed Eggplant   Serves 4-6

Pare 1 medium eggplant; slice ¼" thick. Sprinkle with salt
and pepper; dredge with flour. Sauté slowly in 3 tbs. fat or
salad oil, turning to brown on both sides.

French Fried Eggplant   Serves 4-6

1 medium eggplant	Few grains pepper
1 cup dried crumbs	1 egg
Salt	1 tbs. water

Pare eggplant; slice ¼" thick. Mix crumbs, ½ tsp. salt and
pepper. Beat egg slightly; add water. Roll eggplant in
crumbs; dip in egg mixture; roll in crumbs. Fry in shallow
fat or salad oil, heated to 375°F., 3-5 min., turning to brown
on both sides. Drain on absorbent paper; sprinkle with salt.

Party Eggplant: Follow recipe for French Fried Eggplant,
spreading eggplant slices with prepared mustard before rolling in crumbs.

Eggplant Sandwiches   Serves 4-6

Prepare French Fried Eggplant (above). Spread ½ slices
with chili sauce; sprinkle with grated American cheese. Top
with remaining slices. Bake in moderately hot oven
(375°F.) 5 min.

Creole Eggplant   Serves 4-6

1 medium eggplant	1 6-oz. can (¾ cup) tomato
Salt and pepper	paste
Flour	⅔ cup water
3 tbs. fat or salad oil	1 cup grated Parmesan-
½ cup chopped onion	style cheese

Pare eggplant; slice ¼" thick. Sprinkle with salt and pepper; dredge with flour. Sauté slowly in fat or salad oil.
Drain on absorbent paper. Sauté onion in fat or salad oil remaining in pan; add tomato paste and water. Heat; season
with salt and pepper. Arrange eggplant, tomato mixture and
cheese in alternate layers in greased baking dish. Bake in
moderate oven (350°F.) 20 min.

Baked Stuffed Eggplant

Serves 4

1 large eggplant
¼ cup chopped onion
3 tbs. butter or margarine
½ cup soft bread crumbs
½ tsp. salt

Few grains pepper
1½ cups cooked or canned
    whole kernel corn
4 strips crisp bacon

Wash eggplant; halve lengthwise; parboil 15 min. Drain. Scoop out center; chop fine. Brown onion in butter or margarine; add crumbs, salt, pepper and chopped eggplant. Drain corn; add. Fill eggplant shells with corn mixture. Place in baking dish; bake in hot oven (400°F.) 20 min. Top with bacon.

Eggplant Columbia

Serves 4-6

1 small eggplant
1¾ cups Medium White
    Sauce (p. 325)

¾ cup chopped ripe olives
½ cup grated American
    cheese

Pare eggplant; quarter; cover with boiling salted water. Cover; boil 15 min. Drain; place in greased baking dish. Combine sauce and olives; pour over eggplant. Top with cheese; bake in moderately hot oven (375°F.) 10 min.

Boiled Green Beans

Serves 4

Break off ends of 1 lb. green beans; rinse in cold running water. If desired, cut in 1″ pieces or in julienne strips. Cover with boiling salted water to ⅓ depth of beans. Cover; boil 20-30 min., or until tender. Drain if necessary, reserving liquor for use in soups, sauces and gravies. Add to beans 2 tbs. melted butter, margarine or salad oil. Season with salt and pepper.

Connecticut Green Beans

Serves 4

2 tbs. butter or margarine
¼ tsp. nutmeg

1 No. 2 can (or 2½ cups
    cooked) green beans
Salt and pepper

Brown butter or margarine; add nutmeg. Drain beans; combine with sauce. Heat. Season with salt and pepper.

Green Bean Succotash

Combine equal quantities cooked or canned green beans and cooked or canned whole kernel corn. Moisten with top milk or cream. Heat; season with salt, pepper and sugar.

Green Bean Casserole   Serves 4

1 No. 2 can (2½ cups   ½ cup grated American
  cooked) green beans   cheese
1 can condensed mushroom
  soup

Drain beans; combine with soup. Place in greased baking dish. Top with cheese. Bake in moderate oven (350°F.) 25 min.

Barbecued Green Beans and Corn   Serves 4-6

1 medium onion   1 No. 2 can (or 2½ cups
2 tbs. fat or salad oil   cooked) green beans
½ tsp. Worcestershire   1½ cups cooked or canned
  sauce   whole kernel corn
¼ cup ketchup

Mince onion; sauté in fat or salad oil. Add Worcestershire sauce and ketchup. Drain beans; combine with corn and sauce. Heat.

Devilled Green Beans   Serves 4

¼ cup butter or margarine   Few grains pepper
1 tsp. prepared mustard   Few grains cayenne
1 tsp. Worcestershire sauce 1 No. 2 can (or 2½ cups
¼ tsp. salt   cooked) green beans

Cream butter or margarine; blend in mustard, Worcestershire sauce, salt, pepper and cayenne. Heat beans; drain. Combine with creamed mixture.

Creole Green Beans   Serves 4-6

1 medium onion
2 tbs. fat or salad oil
1 No. 2 can (or 2½ cups cooked) tomatoes
1 small bay leaf
1 tsp. sugar
1 tsp. salt
Few grains pepper
1 No. 2 can (or 2½ cups cooked) green beans
2 tbs. flour
2 tbs. water

Mince onion; sauté in fat or salad oil. Add tomatoes, bay leaf, sugar, salt and pepper. Cover; simmer 10 min. Remove bay leaf. Drain beans; add. Mix flour and water to smooth paste; add. Cook, stirring constantly, until thick. If desired, serve in center of Noodle Cheese Ring (p. 137).

Browned Butter Hominy   Serves 4-6

1 No. 2½ can (or 3½ cups cooked) hominy
2 tbs. butter or margarine
Salt and pepper

Drain hominy. Brown butter or margarine; add hominy. Cover; cook slowly 15 min. Season with salt and pepper.

Hominy Louisiana   Serves 4-6

1 onion
2 tbs. fat or salad oil
1 No. 2 can (or 2½ cups cooked) tomatoes
1 tsp. salt
Few grains pepper
1 tsp. sugar
1 No. 2½ can (or 3½ cups cooked) hominy
1 cup grated American cheese

Mince onion; sauté in fat or salad oil. Add tomatoes, salt, pepper and sugar. Cook slowly until most of liquor has evaporated. Drain hominy; add with cheese. Heat.

Boiled Kale   Serves 4

Remove roots, tough stems and wilted leaves from 1½ lbs. kale. Wash kale several times in cold water until all sand is removed. Cover with boiling salted water to ⅓ depth of kale. Cover; boil 20 min., or until tender. Drain. Add 2 tbs. melted butter, margarine or salad oil; season with salt and pepper.

Boiled Leeks
Serves 4

Remove roots and wilted leaves from 2 large bunches leeks. Wash leeks. Cover with boiling water to ⅓ depth of leeks. Cover; boil 12 min., or until tender. Drain; add 2 tbs. melted butter, margarine or salad oil; season with salt and pepper.

Poor Man's Asparagus
Serves 4

2 tbs. butter or margarine	Few grains pepper
¼ cup dry crumbs	16 medium boiled leeks
¼ tsp. salt	

Melt butter or margarine, add crumbs, salt and pepper. Place leeks in shallow baking dish; sprinkle with crumb mixture. Brown under broiler unit or burner.

Creamed Leeks and Pimientos
Serves 4

3 tbs. butter or margarine	1½ cups milk
3 tbs. flour	1 pimiento
¼ tsp. salt	4 boiled, sliced leeks
Few grains pepper	

Melt butter or margarine; blend in flour, salt and pepper; gradually add milk. Cook over hot water, stirring constantly, until thick. Chop pimiento; combine with leeks and sauce.

Boiled Green Lima Beans
Serves 4

Shell 2 lbs. lima beans; rinse in cold running water. Cover with boiling salted water to ⅓ depth of beans. Cover; boil 20-40 min. (depending on age and size of beans), or until tender. Drain, if necessary. Add to beans 2 tbs. butter, margarine or salad oil. Season with salt and pepper.

Spicy Lima Beans
Serves 4

¾ cup ketchup	1 No. 2 can (or 2½ cups cooked) lima beans
½ tsp. minced onion	Salt and pepper

Combine ketchup and onion. Drain beans; combine with ketchup mixture. Heat; season with salt and pepper.

Sage Succotash
Serves 4-6

1 No. 2 can (or 2½ cups cooked) lima beans
1½ cups cooked or canned whole kernel corn
¼ tsp. sage
½ tsp. salt
2 tbs. butter, margarine or salad oil
½ cup top milk

Drain beans; combine with corn, sage, salt, milk and butter, margarine or salad oil. Heat.

Sautéed Mushrooms
Serves 4

1 lb. mushrooms
½ tsp. salt
Few grains pepper
1 bay leaf
¼ cup fat or salad oil

Scrub mushrooms; if desired, peel. Slice; add salt, pepper and bay leaf. Sauté in fat 8-10 min., or until tender. Remove bay leaf.

Broiled Mushrooms

Remove stems from large mushrooms; clean caps. Brush-with melted butter, margarine or salad oil; place caps, top sides up, 3″ below broiler unit or tip of flame. Broil 8-10 min.; turn. Place cube Cheddar cheese in each cap. Broil until cheese is melted. Serve on toast.

Stuffed Mushrooms Maryland
Serves 4

8 large mushrooms
1 tbs. minced onion
3½ tbs. butter or margarine
½ tsp. Worcestershire sauce
1 cup chopped cooked or canned oysters
¼ tsp. salt
1½ cups soft bread crumbs
1 tbs. water

Clean mushrooms. Remove stems; chop fine. Combine stems and onion; cook slowly in 2 tbs. butter or margarine 8 min., or until tender. Add oysters, Worcestershire sauce, salt and crumbs. Stuff mushroom caps with oyster mixture; place in shallow baking dish. Add water; dot with remaining butter or margarine. Bake in hot oven (400°F.) 25 min.

Mushroom Soufflé   Serves 4

½ lb. mushrooms	Few grains pepper
¼ cup butter or margarine	1 cup milk
¼ cup flour	3 egg yolks
½ tsp. salt	3 egg whites

Clean mushrooms; chop fine. Brown lightly in butter or margarine. Blend in flour, salt and pepper. Add milk gradually; cook, stirring constantly, until thick. Cool. Beat egg yolks well; add. Beat egg whites stiff, but not dry; fold in. Pour into greased baking dish; bake in moderate oven (325°F.) 50 min. Serve immediately.

Boiled Okra   Serves 4

Wash 1 lb. okra; remove stems. Slice ½" thick. Cover with boiling salted water; boil, uncovered, 15-20 min., or until tender. Drain; add 2 tbs. melted butter, margarine or salad oil. Season with salt and pepper.

Boiled Onions   Serves 4

Peel 8 medium onions. Cover with large amount boiling salted water; boil, uncovered, 20-30 min., or until tender. Drain; add 2 tbs. melted butter, margarine or salad oil. Season with salt and pepper.

Sautéed Onions   Serves 4

8 medium onions	½ tsp. salt
3 tbs. fat or salad oil	Few grains pepper

Peel onions; slice ¼" thick. Sauté in fat or salad oil, stirring frequently, until lightly browned and tender. Add salt and pepper.

French Fried Onions   Serves 4

3 large mild onions	Few grains pepper
⅔ cup flour	¼ cup milk
Salt	

Peel onions; slice ¼" thick; separate into rings. Combine flour, ¼ teaspoon salt and pepper. Dip rings in milk; dredge in flour mixture. Fry in shallow fat or salad oil, heated to 380°F., 4-5 min., or until browned. Drain on absorbent paper; sprinkle with salt.

Glazed Onions   Serves 4

12 small white onions
3 tbs. butter or margarine
¼ tsp. salt

Few grains pepper
2 tbs. sugar

Peel onions; cover with large amount boiling salted water; boil, uncovered, 15 min., or until almost tender. Drain. Brown butter or margarine lightly; add salt, pepper and sugar; stir until dissolved. Add onions; cook slowly 10 min., or until browned, turning to glaze all sides.

Gratinéed Stuffed Onions   Serves 4-6

6 cooked medium onions
⅓ cup grated American
   cheese
3 tbs. butter or margarine

1 cup soft bread crumbs
Salt and pepper
Few grains sage

Cut slice off tops of onions. Remove centers; chop. Brown chopped onion in 2 tbs. butter or margarine; add crumbs and cheese. Season with salt, pepper and sage. Stuff onions; place in baking dish. Dot with remaining butter or margarine; add enough hot water to cover bottom of baking dish. Bake in moderate oven (325°F.) 30 min., basting occasionally.

Boiled Parsnips   Serves 4

Wash 8 medium parsnips; scrape. Cover with boiling salted water. Boil, uncovered, 30-60 min. (depending on age and size), or until tender. Drain; quarter. Add 2 tbs. melted butter, margarine or salad oil; season with salt and pepper.

Sautéed Parsnips   Serves 4

Boil 8 medium parsnips (see above); slice lengthwise. Roll

in seasoned flour. Sauté in 2 tbs. fat or salad oil, turning to brown on both sides.

Boiled Green Peas
Serves 4

Shell 2 lbs. green peas; rinse in cold running water. Cover with boiling salted water to ⅓ depth of peas. Cover; boil 15-20 min., or until tender. Drain, if necessary, reserving liquor for use in soups, sauces and gravies. Add to peas 2 tbs. melted butter, margarine or salad oil. Season with salt and pepper.

Peas à la Crème
Serves 4

2 cups cooked or canned peas
2 slices bacon
½ cup evaporated milk
Few grains pepper

Dice bacon; fry until crisp. Drain off fat. Add peas, milk and pepper; heat.

Pimiento Peas
Serves 4

2 tbs. butter or margarine
1 pimiento
½ tsp. salt
Few grains pepper
2 cups cooked or canned peas

Brown butter or margarine. Chop pimiento; add. Cook 2-3 min. Add salt and pepper. Add peas; heat.

Peas Anglaise
Serves 4

¼ cup chopped scallions
2 tbs. butter, margarine or salad oil
½ tsp. flour
¼ tsp. sugar
¼ cup milk
2 cups cooked or canned peas
Salt and pepper

Cook scallions in butter, margarine or salad oil 3 min. Mix flour and sugar; add to scallions. Add milk and peas. Season with salt and pepper. Cook 5 min.

Peas and Cauliflower   Serves 4

2 tbs. butter or margarine
1 tsp. minced onion
2 cups cooked or canned peas

1 cup cooked cauliflower flowerets
Salt and pepper

Brown butter or margarine; add onion. Cook until tender. Add peas and cauliflower; heat. Season with salt and pepper.

Stuffed Green Peppers   Serves 4

4 green peppers
Salt
3 tbs. chopped onion
1/4 cup butter or margarine

1/2 tsp. poultry seasoning
2 1/2 cups cooked rice
1/4 tsp. salt
Few grains pepper

Wash peppers; cut slice from stem end; remove seeds. Cover with boiling salted water; boil, uncovered, 3-5 min.; drain. Halve lengthwise; sprinkle with salt. Brown onion in butter or margarine; add poultry seasoning, rice, salt and pepper. Fill peppers with rice mixture. Place in baking dish; bake in hot oven (400°F.) 15-20 min.

Boiled Potatoes   Serves 4

Scrub 4 medium potatoes. Cover with boiling salted water. Cover; boil 20-30 min., or until tender. Drain; peel. Add 2 tbs. melted butter or margarine; season with salt and pepper.

Mashed Potatoes   Serves 4

Scrub 4 medium potatoes; pare. Cover with boiling salted water; cover. Boil 20-30 min., or until tender. Drain; force through sieve or ricer, or mash well. Season with 3/4 tsp. salt and few grains pepper; add 1/4 cup hot milk and 2 tbs. melted butter, margarine or salad oil. Beat until light and fluffy.

Pan-Browned Potatoes

Serves 4

Pare 8 small potatoes of uniform size; cover with boiling salted water. Boil 15 min. Place potatoes in pan in which meat is roasting, during last hour. Baste with juice in pan or mixture of equal amounts melted fat or salad oil and water. Turn occasionally.

Hashed Brown Potatoes

Serves 4

¼ cup fat or salad oil	¾ tsp. salt
3¾ cups finely chopped cooked potatoes	Few grains pepper
	1 tbs. chopped parsley

Heat fat or salad oil; add potatoes, salt, pepper and parsley. Cook slowly until underside is brown. Fold over like omelet.

French Fried Potatoes

Serves 4

Wash 4 medium potatoes; pare; cut in lengthwise strips. Soak in cold water 1 hour. Drain; dry thoroughly. Divide into 3 portions. Fry, 1 portion at a time, in shallow fat or salad oil, heated to 370°F., 5-7 min., or until tender but not brown. Drain on absorbent paper. Just before serving, fry each portion again in shallow fat or salad oil, heated to 390°F., 1½ min., or until brown. Drain on absorbent paper; sprinkle with salt.

Scalloped Potatoes

Serves 4

4 medium potatoes	1½ tbs. flour
½ tsp. salt	2 cups milk
Few grains pepper	1 tbs. butter or margarine

Scrub potatoes; pare; slice thin. Place layer potatoes in greased baking dish; sprinkle with salt, pepper and flour. Repeat until potatoes are used. Add milk; dot with butter or margarine. Bake in moderate oven (350°F.) 1½ hours, or until potatoes are tender.

Baked Potatoes

Serves 4

Scrub 4 medium potatoes. For soft, thin skin, rub with

melted fat or salad oil. Bake in hot oven (450°F.) 45-60 min., or until tender.

Bombay Potatoes

Cut cross on top hot baked potatoes; fold back skins. Place 1 tbs. chutney and slice American cheese on each; bake in moderate oven (350°F.) 10 min.

Surprise Potatoes

Serves 4

    4 large baked potatoes
    1 cup Medium White Sauce
      (p. 325)
    ⅓ cup diced cooked or
      canned asparagus
    ⅓ cup cooked or canned
      peas
    Salt and pepper

Cut slice off tops of potatoes. Scoop out centers; mash. Season with salt and pepper. Combine sauce, peas and asparagus. Fill potato shells ⅔ full with creamed mixture; top with mashed potatoes. Bake in very hot oven (450°F.) until brown.

Country-Style Potatoes

Serves 4

    1 tbs. chopped onion
    2 tbs. fat or salad oil
    1 cup cooked or canned
      whole kernel corn
    1 tsp. chopped parsley
    2 cups cubed cooked
      potatoes
    ¼ tsp. salt
    Few grains pepper

Sauté onion in fat or salad oil; combine with corn, parsley and potatoes. Add salt and pepper. Heat, stirring occasionally.

Potatoes and Eggs Au Gratin

Serves 4

    1 tbs. butter or margarine
    1 tbs. flour
    ½ tsp. salt
    ¾ cup milk
    3 hard-cooked eggs
    2 cups sliced cooked
      potatoes
    ⅔ cup grated American
      cheese
    2 tsp. chopped pimiento

Melt butter or margarine; blend in flour and salt. Gradually add milk; cook, stirring constantly, until thick. Slice eggs. Arrange alternate layers potatoes, eggs, pimiento, sauce and cheese in greased baking dish. Bake in moderate oven (325°F.) 25 min.

Boiled Red Cabbage   Serves 4

Remove wilted leaves from small head red cabbage; shred cabbage. Rinse in cold running water. Cover with boiling salted water to ⅓ depth of cabbage. Add 1 tbs. vinegar; cover. Cook 8-12 min., or until tender. Drain, if necessary. Add to red cabbage 2 tbs. melted butter, margarine or salad oil. Season with salt and pepper.

Country Red Cabbage   Serves 4

1 small head red cabbage	2 tbs. butter, margarine or
2 tbs. minced onion	salad oil
1½ cups thinly sliced apple	1 tsp. salt
½ cup water	½ cup grape jelly
2 tbs. vinegar	

Remove wilted leaves from cabbage; shred cabbage. Rinse in cold running water. Combine with onion, apple, water, vinegar, butter, margarine or salad oil, salt and jelly. Cover; cook slowly 1 hour.

Boiled Salsify (Oyster Plant)   Serves 4

Scrub 1½ lbs. salsify; scrape. Halve lengthwise. Place in cold water, adding 1 tbs. vinegar to 1 qt. water to prevent discoloration. Drain; cover with boiling salted water. Cover; boil 20-40 min. (depending on age and size), or until tender. Drain; add 2 tbs. melted butter, margarine or salad oil. Season with salt and pepper.

Sautéed Salsify (Oyster Plant)   Serves 4

Boil salsify (see above); drain. Dredge in seasoned flour. Sauté in fat or salad oil, 8-10 min., or until brown.

Boiled Spinach
Serves 4

Remove roots, tough stems and wilted leaves from 1½ lbs. spinach. Wash spinach several times in cold water until all sand is removed. Drain slightly. Cover; cook 8-10 min., or until tender, turning spinach once during cooking. Drain if necessary, reserving liquor for use in soups, sauces and gravies. Add to spinach 2 tbs. melted butter, margarine or salad oil. Season with salt and pepper.

Spinach Ring

Pack hot cooked or canned seasoned spinach in greased ring mold. Unmold on hot plate. Serve immediately.

Spinach Carinthia
Serves 4

⅓ cup mayonnaise or salad dressing
2 tbs. chopped pickle
1 tbs. chili sauce
1 No. 2 can (or 2½ cups cooked) spinach

Combine mayonnaise or salad dressing, pickle, and chili sauce. Heat spinach; drain. Serve with sauce.

Parker House Spinach
Serves 4

1 No. 2 can (or 2½ cups cooked) spinach
½ cup light cream
Few grains nutmeg
Salt and pepper

Drain spinach; chop. Add cream and nutmeg; heat. Season with salt and pepper.

Spinach Algonquin
Serves 4

1 No. 2 can (or 2½ cups cooked) spinach
1 tsp. grated onion
¼ cup sour cream
2 tbs. prepared horse-radish
¾ tsp. salt
Few grains pepper

Drain spinach; chop. Add onion, cream, horse-radish, salt and pepper; heat.

Spinach Timbales   Serves 4

1 No. 2 can (or 2½ cups cooked) spinach
¼ cup melted butter, margarine or salad oil
½ tsp. salt
Few grains pepper
Few grains nutmeg
1 tbs. prepared horse-radish
1 cup milk
2 eggs

Drain spinach; chop. Add butter, margarine or salad oil, salt, pepper, nutmeg and horse-radish. Beat eggs; add milk. Combine with spinach mixture. Pack in greased timbale molds or custard cups. Place in pan of hot water; bake in moderate oven (350°F.) 45 min.

Boiled Summer Squash   Serves 4

Scrub 1½ lbs. summer squash; slice ¼″ thick. Remove seeds and stringy portion. Cover with boiling salted water to ⅓ depth of squash. Cover; boil 10-20 min., or until tender. Drain; mash. Add 2 tbs. melted butter, margarine or salad oil; season with salt and pepper.

Golden Squash Circles

Pare summer squash; slice ½″ thick. Roll in seasoned flour or corn meal. Sauté in fat or salad oil 5 min., or until tender.

Baked Acorn Squash   Serves 4

Scrub 2 acorn squash; halve lengthwise; remove seeds and stringy portion. Brush with melted butter, margarine or salad oil. Sprinkle with salt, pepper and sugar. Place in baking dish; add hot water to cover bottom of baking dish. Cover; bake in hot oven (400°F.) 45-60 min., or until tender, removing cover after 20-30 min.

Mashed Acorn Squash: Prepare Baked Acorn Squash. Remove pulp; mash well.

Boiled Winter Squash   Serves 4

Scrub 2 lbs. winter squash. Halve lengthwise; remove seeds and stringy portion. Pare; cut in 1″ cubes. Cover with boiling salted water to ⅓ depth of squash. Cover; boil 20-30 min., or until tender. Drain; mash. Add 2 tbs. melted margarine or salad oil; season with salt, pepper and sugar.

Baked Winter Squash
Serves 4

Scrub 2 lbs. winter squash. Halve lengthwise; remove seeds and stringy portion. Pare; cut in uniform serving pieces. Place in shallow baking dish; sprinkle with salt, pepper and sugar; brush with melted butter, margarine or salad oil; cover. Bake in moderately hot oven (375°F.) 45-60 min., or until tender.

Brazilian Squash
Serves 4

2 cups mashed cooked Hubbard squash	1 tbs. butter or margarine
½ tsp. salt	2½ tbs. brown sugar
Few grains pepper	⅓ cup chopped Brazil nut meats
1 tbs. sugar	⅛ tsp. cinnamon
1 tbs. heavy cream	

Combine squash, salt, pepper, sugar and cream. Place in greased baking dish. Melt together butter or margarine and brown sugar; add cinnamon and nut meats. Cook 3 min., or until nut meats are coated, stirring constantly; sprinkle on squash. Bake in moderate oven (350°F.) 15 min.

Stewed Tomatoes
Serves 4

Dip 4-5 ripe tomatoes in boiling water 1 min.; peel. Remove stem ends. Quarter; place in saucepan. Cover; cook 5-15 min., or until tender. Add 2 tbs. butter, margarine or salad oil. Season with salt, pepper and sugar. If desired, brown 2 tbs. chopped onion in butter, margarine or salad oil before adding to tomatoes.

Broiled Tomato Halves
Serves 4

4 medium tomatoes	2 tbs. melted butter, margarine or salad oil
Salt and pepper	

Wash tomatoes; halve. Sprinkle with salt and pepper. Brush with butter, margarine or salad oil. Place top of food 3″ below broiler unit or tip of flame; broil 3-5 min. or until browned.

Sautéed Tomato Slices
Serves 4

4 medium tomatoes
½ cup flour
½ tsp. salt

Few grains pepper
3 tbs. fat or salad oil

Wash tomatoes; remove stem ends. Slice ½" thick. Mix flour, salt, and pepper. Dredge tomatoes in flour mixture. Sauté in fat or salad oil until browned, turning once.

Stuffed Baked Tomatoes
Serves 4

4 medium tomatoes
1 small onion
2 tsp. fat or salad oil

⅔ cup soft bread crumbs
Few grains allspice
Salt and pepper

Scoop out tomatoes. Mince onion; sauté in fat or salad oil. Add tomato pulp, crumbs and allspice. Season with salt and pepper. Stuff tomatoes. Place in greased baking dish; add hot water to cover bottom of baking dish. Bake in moderate oven (350°F.) 30 min.

Two-in-One Tomatoes
Serves 4

4 large tomatoes
1 medium onion
¼ cup butter, margarine or salad oil

1½ cups cooked summer squash
½ cup soft bread crumbs

Scoop out tomatoes. Mince onion; cook in butter, margarine or salad oil until tender. Combine with squash and crumbs; stuff tomatoes. Place in baking dish; add hot water to cover bottom of baking dish. Bake in moderate oven (350°F.) 30 min.

Scalloped Tomatoes
Serves 4

1 No. 2 can (or 2½ cups cooked) tomatoes
2 tbs. chopped onion
1 tsp. salt

½ tsp. sugar
Few grains pepper
1 cup soft bread crumbs
3 tbs. butter or margarine

Combine tomatoes, onion, salt, sugar and pepper; pour into greased baking dish. Top with crumbs; dot with butter or margarine. Bake in hot oven (400°F.) 25 min., or until brown.

Scalloped Tomatoes and Leeks   Serves 4

1 cup sliced leeks	1 tsp. salt
2 tbs. fat or salad oil	Few grains pepper
1 No. 2 can (or 2½ cups cooked) tomatoes	1 cup soft bread crumbs
1 tsp. sugar	2 tbs. butter or margarine

Sauté leeks in fat or salad oil; combine with tomatoes, sugar, salt and pepper. Pour into greased baking dish. Top with crumbs; dot with butter or margarine. Bake in hot oven (400°F.) 25 min., or until brown.

Scalloped Tomatoes and Cucumbers   Serves 4-6

1 No. 2 can (or 2½ cups cooked) tomatoes	1 medium onion
½ tsp. salt	1 large cucumber
1½ tsp. Worcestershire sauce	2 cups soft bread crumbs
	¾ cup grated American cheese

Combine tomatoes, salt and Worcestershire sauce; chop onion; add. Slice cucumber. Arrange layers of tomato mixture, cucumber and crumbs in greased baking dish. Sprinkle with cheese. Bake in moderately hot oven (375°F.) 40 min.

Boiled Sweet Potatoes   Serves 4

Scrub 4 medium sweet potatoes. Cover with boiling salted water. Cover; boil 20-25 min., or until tender. Drain; peel. Add 2 tbs. melted butter, margarine or salad oil; season with salt and pepper.

Mashed Sweet Potatoes   Serves 4

Boil 4 medium sweet potatoes; peel. Force through sieve or ricer, or mash well. Add 2 tbs. melted butter, margarine or salad oil, ½ tsp. salt, few grains pepper and nutmeg and about ⅓ cup milk; beat until light and fluffy.

Baked Sweet Potatoes
Serves 4

Scrub 4 medium sweet potatoes. For soft, thin skin, rub with melted fat or salad oil. Bake in hot oven (400°F.) 35-40 min., or until tender.

Candied Sweet Potatoes
Serves 4

4 medium cooked or canned sweet potatoes
½ cup sugar

½ cup firmly packed brown sugar
¼ cup water
¼ cup butter or margarine

Halve potatoes lengthwise. Place in greased shallow baking dish. Combine sugar, brown sugar, water, butter or margarine; bring to boiling point. Pour over potatoes; bake in hot oven (400°F.) 20 min., basting several times with sirup in baking dish.

Sweet Potato Puff
Serves 4

2 tbs. melted butter, margarine or salad oil
¼ cup milk

2 cups mashed cooked or canned sweet potatoes
1 egg
Salt and pepper

Combine butter, margarine or salad oil, milk and potatoes. Beat egg; add. Beat until light and fluffy. Season with salt and pepper. Pile lightly by large spoonfuls on greased baking sheet. Bake in moderately hot oven (375°F.) until brown.

Boiled Swiss Chard
Serves 4

Remove tough stems and wilted leaves from 1½ lbs. young Swiss chard. Wash chard several times in cold water until all sand is removed. Drain slightly. Cover; cook 10-15 min. or until tender, turning once during cooking. Add 2 tbs. melted butter, margarine or salad oil. Season with salt and pepper. If older chard is used, cut off white stalks; cook stalks like Boiled Asparagus (p. 348). Cook leaves as above.

Boiled White Turnips   Serves 4

Remove tops from 1 large bunch white turnips; scrub; pare. Halve; cover with large amount boiling salted water; boil, uncovered, 20-35 min., or until tender. Drain; mash. Add 2 tbs. melted butter, margarine or salad oil; season with salt and pepper.

Boiled Yellow Turnip   Serves 4

Scrub 1 medium yellow turnip; cut in eighths; pare. Cover with large amount boiling salted water; boil, uncovered, 25-45 min. (depending on age and size of turnip). Drain; mash. Add 2 tbs. melted butter, margarine or salad oil; season with salt and pepper.

Turnip Potato Fluff   Serves 4

1 small yellow turnip	2 tbs. melted butter,
3 medium potatoes	margarine or salad oil
1 tsp. salt	Paprika
Few grains pepper	

Scrub turnip; pare; cut in 1" cubes. Scrub potatoes; pare; cut in thirds. Cover with boiling salted water; boil together, uncovered, 25-35 min., or until tender. Drain; mash. Add salt, pepper, and butter, margarine or salad oil. Sprinkle with paprika.

Boiled Turnip Greens   Serves 4

Remove tough stems and wilted leaves from 1½ lbs. turnip greens. Wash greens several times in cold water until all sand is removed. Drain slightly. Cover; cook 20-30 min., or until tender, turning greens once during cooking. Add 2 tbs. melted butter, margarine or salad oil; season with salt and pepper.

33. HELPS FOR REDUCERS

A LOT of good reducing resolutions go glimmering because of simple boredom. We get so deadly tired of the same old dishes day after day!

Here's help—a listing of recipes given in this book which are especially suitable for reducing diets. As the length of the list shows, the safe reducing diet includes a wide variety of foods. Naturally, the amounts you eat of certain essential foods (such as breads, cereals, sweets and fats) should be regulated carefully in order not to increase your calorie intake beyond the daily total you have set.

[1] Use small amount of dressing, preferably one of those listed on pp. 309–12.

[1] Use small amount of dressing, preferably one of those listed on pp. 309–12.

[1] Use small amount of dressing, preferably one of those listed on pp. 309–12.

[1] Use small amount of dressing, preferably one of those listed on pp. 309–12.

INDEX

A

387

O

Oases (cookies), 147
Oatmeal (cereal)
    Quick-Cooking Oats, 132
    Rolled Oats, 132
Oatmeal Bars (cakes), 151-52
    Bread (Rolled Oats), 65
Oatmeal Cookies, 154
    Chocolate, 154
    Sugarplum, 154
    Tropical, 154
Oatmeal Muffins, 55
    Stuffing, Bacon and, 343
Okra, Boiled, 365
Old-fashioned Foldovers (rolls), 68
    Strawberry Shortcake, 176
Olive French Dressing, 309
    Salad, Crab and, 300
Olive Sandwiches, Chicken and Ripe, 314
    Chopped Tongue and, 313
Olive Sauce, Cheese, 325
Olives, Garlic, 43
Omelet, Cheese, 206
    Fluffy, 206
    French, 206
    Fruit Basket, 206-07
    Ham, Fluffy, 206
    Jelly, 206
Onion French Dressing, Roquefort, 310
    Stuffed Eggs, 208
    Stuffing, Mushroom and, 342-43
Onions, Boiled, 365
    French Fried, 365-66
    Glazed, 366
    Sautéed, 365
    Stuffed Gratinéed, 366
Orange, Bacon and Banana Grill, 238
    Bavarian Cream, 182
Orange Cake, Banana, 72
    Chocolate, 73-74
    Sponge, 90
    Square Loaf, 78
    Walnut, 71
Orange Coffee Cake, 60
    Crescents (cookies), 146
    Cup, Strawberry, 160
    Divinity Fudge, 106
    Filling, 101

Orange Frosting, 98
    Lemon, 98
    Seven Minute, 95-96
Orange Gingerbread Dessert, **177**
    Glaze (for ham), 234
    Julep, 50
    Milk, Spiced, 50
Orange Marmalade, Walnut, 129-30
    Muffins, 55
    Sauce (Plombière), 324
Orange Pie, Apple, 261
    Marshmallow, 271
Orange Pocket Book Rolls, **70**
    Salad Dressing, 311
Orange Sauce, for Duck, 329-30
    Tang Custard, 322
Orange Sherbet, 201
    Lemon, 200-01
Orange Slaw, Raisin, 287
    Spanish Cream, 184
    Sugared Walnuts, 114
Oriental Gems (candy), 110
Ornamental Frosting, 99
Oyster Fritters, 217-18
    Stew, 336-37
    Stuffing, 342
Oyster Plant, Boiled, 371
    Sautéed, 371
Oysters, Baked in Shell, 217
    Baked with Chicken, 276
    Fried, 217
    on Half Shell, 44
    Scalloped, 217

P

Pan Gravy, 328
    Rolls, 64
Pan-broil, to, definition, 2
Parboil, to, definition, 2
Pare, to, definition, 2
Parfait, Maple, 197-98
    Pistachio, 197
Parisiennes, Peaches, 158-59
Parker House Rolls, 66-67
    Spinach, 372
Parmesan Asparagus, 348
Parsley Sauce, 326
Parsnips, Boiled, 366
    Sautéed, 366-67
Paste, definition, 2

ABOUT THE AUTHORS

Elizabeth Woody

confesses to a lifelong love of good eating. Years of earning her living by inventing and writing about new dishes of all kinds have, she says, brought about no dimming of the anticipatory glint that lights her eye with unfailing regularity three times each day. Born in Kentucky (*fried chicken, hot biscuits and coffee "creamed to the color of a new saddle"!*) . . . graduated from Wellesley College in Massachusetts . . . four years a resident of England (*roast beef and Yorkshire pudding!*) . . . and of France (*lyrical soufflés and sauces!*) . . . she found her niche in New York's business world as a specialist in the planning and presentation of food copy. Her record of combining successfully the practical and the persuasive led to her appointment as Director of Foods for *McCall's Magazine.* Approximately a decade later she became Director of the General Electric Consumers Institute. For five years she served as Consulting Food Editor for *Holiday* magazine and *Collier's* magazine successively. Travel in Europe and the United States by car, and, most recently, a two-year trip around the world have been her pleasant lot.

Gertrude Lynn

was the kind of cook every man is traditionally supposed to think his mother used to be. Famous in the food world as "America's number-one kitchen artist," she made glamour edible before Hollywood even so much as thought of boasting about making it visible. Her professional experience included work as home economics director for a leading chain-store organization, manager of a coffee shop, and for a little over ten years, Associate Food Editor of *McCall's Magazine*. She left magazine staff work to found her own business as a food consultant specializing in the planning and preparation of foods for color photography. Many of the most mouth-watering food pictures are products of her skill. Married soon after her graduation from Teachers College, Columbia University, Miss Lynn combined a business career with that of mother and homemaker in her native state of New Jersey.

Peg Heffernan

was awarded her Bachelor of Science degree by a college in her home state—Troy, New York's, Russell Sage. Between commencement and the day she joined the staff of *McCall's Magazine* she gathered experience in the teaching field and in the test kitchens of nationally known food companies. As an Associate Food Editor at *McCall's*, she replied to the lion's share of the letters which came from readers of the magazine's food pages. Her other responsibilities included recipe origination and testing, reports on new food products and collaboration with other staff members in background work for photographs and articles. She left the magazine field to enter that of public relations and subsequently became Home Economics Director of the National Biscuit Company. She has since become a full-time homemaker in Connecticut where she and her husband have built the country home of their dreams.

A SUGGESTION FOR THE READER

It is the policy of POCKET BOOKS to endeavor to get the widest distribution for its own publications and at the same time to encourage the reading of good books generally, aside from its own list. In this spirit, the publishers list here a number of other books which they believe will be of special interest to the reader of this book. These are available at bookshops and public libraries.

The Southern Cook Book
    by Marion Brown. (Univ. of N. C. Press). (Pocket Books)

The Best from Midwest Kitchens
    by Ada B. Lothe, Breta L. Griem and Ethel M. Keating. (M. S. Mill)

Helen Brown's West Coast Cook Book
    by Helen Evans Brown. (Little, Brown)

The Settlement Cook Book
    by Lizzie B. Kander. (Simon and Schuster)

The Joy of Cooking
    by Irma S. Rombauer and Marion Rombauer Becker. (Bobbs-Merrill)

The Fireside Cook Book
    by James A. Beard. (Simon and Schuster)

The Art of Fish Cookery
    by Milo Miloradovich. (Doubleday)

Herbs for the Kitchen
    by Irma Mazza. (Little, Brown)

Ann Pillsbury's Baking Book
   by Ann Pillsbury. (Pocket Books)

The Meat and Poultry Cook Book
   by Beth Bailey McLean and Thora H. Campbell. (Pocket Books)

The Art of Italian Cooking
   by Maria Lo Pinto and Milo Miloradovich. (Doubleday)

Perfect Hostess Cook Book
   by Mildred O. Knopf. (Knopf)

Cooking for Two
   by Janet Mackenzie Hill and Sally Larkin. (Little, Brown)

The Art of Fine Baking
   by Paula Peck. (Pocket Books)

The Pleasures of Chinese Cooking
   by Grace Chu. (Pocket Books)

New York Times Cook Book
   by C. Claiborne. (Harper & Row)

Mastering the Art of French Cooking
   by Julia Child. (Knopf)